In Memory

Of

William V. Totman

Cogs,
Caravels
and
Galleons

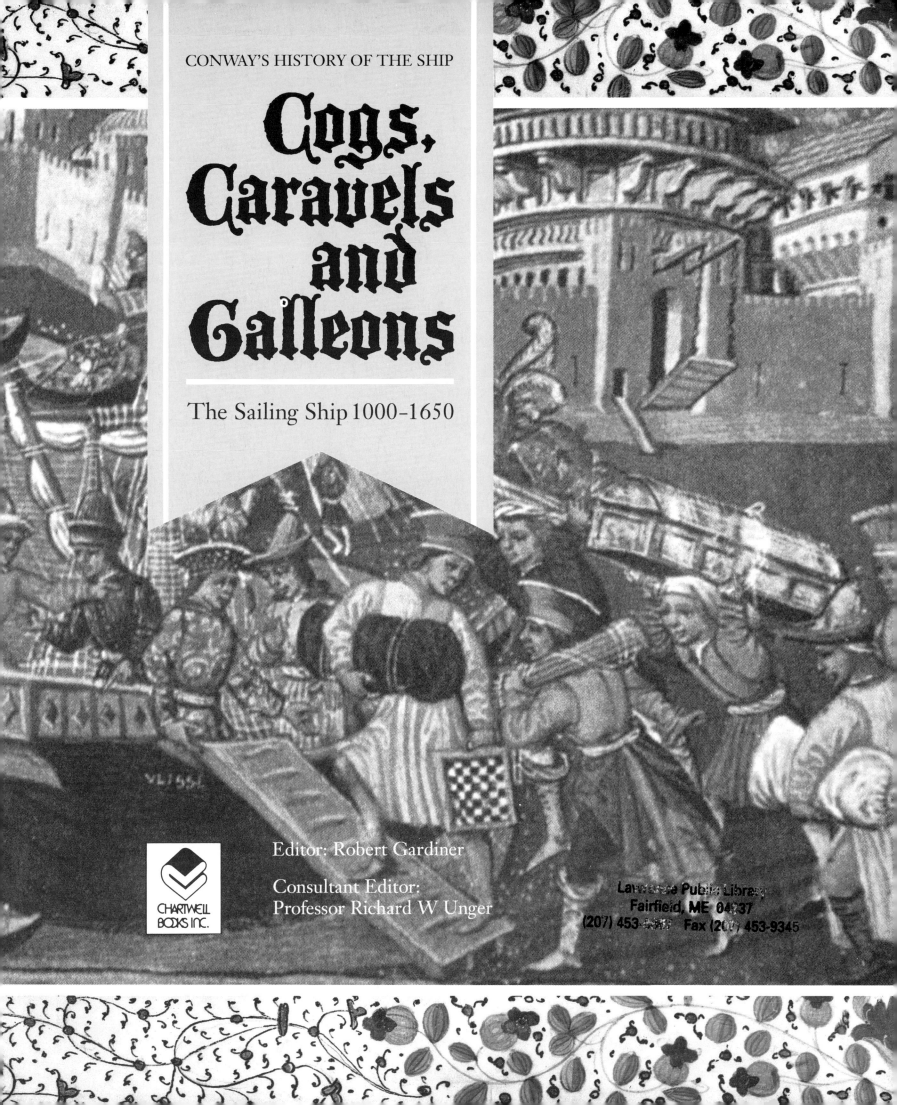

CONWAY'S HISTORY OF THE SHIP

Cogs, Caravels and Galleons

The Sailing Ship 1000–1650

Editor: Robert Gardiner

Consultant Editor:
Professor Richard W Unger

CHARTWELL
BOOKS INC.

Series Consultant   DR BASIL GREENHILL
CB, CMG, FSA, FRHistS

Series Editor   ROBERT GARDINER

Consultant Editor   PROFESSOR RICHARD W UNGER

Contributors   PROFESSOR MICHEL BALARD
JAN BILL
JOHN E DOTSON
MARTIN ELBL
PROFESSOR DR DETLEV ELLMERS
IAN FRIEL
DR JOHN F GUILMARTIN
PROFESSOR CARLA RAHN PHILLIPS
PROFESSOR JOHN H PRYOR
OWAIN T P ROBERTS
PROFESSOR TIMOTHY J RUNYAN
PROFESSOR RICHARD W UNGER
CHRISTIANE VILLAIN-GANDOSSI

Frontispiece: Although in recent years the understanding of medieval ship development has advanced – most notably through underwater archaeology – many of the most important mysteries remain unresolved. Foremost among these is the precise dating of the first three-masted ship. The documentary evidence is too patchy to be specific, while the visual sources, as represented by this manuscript illumination, present problems of accuracy and interpretation. From the Codice Virgiliano *(Biblioteca Riccardiana in Florence), this depiction is usually dated to about 1450 and is particularly interesting for its portraits of Mediterranean round ships at the transitional stage where they have a mizzen but no fore mast. The other principal Mediterranean ship type, the galley, is also represented, along with a number of boats and small craft.* (By courtesy of Christiane Villain-Gandossi)

© Conway Maritime Press 1994

This edition published in North America in 2000 by
CHARTWELL BOOKS INC.
A Division of Book Sales Inc.
114 Northfield Avenue
Edison, New Jersey 08837

ISBN 0-7858-1265-2

First published in Great Britain 1994 by
Conway Maritime Press,
a division of Chrysalis Books Ltd
9 Blenheim Court, Brewery Road
London N7 9NT

Designed by Tony Hart
Typeset by Dorwyn Ltd, Rowlands Castle, Hants

Printed and bound in Spain by Bookprint, S.L, Barcelona

Ships, Medieval

Cogs (Sailing Ships) — Hist.

Caravels — His

Galleons — His

Sailing Ships — His

Shipbuilding — His

(Student)

(girl)

(Boy)

Contents

Preface

This title is the eighth in an ambitious programme of twelve volumes intended to provide the first detailed and comprehensive account of a technology that has shaped human history. It has been conceived as a basic reference work, the essential first stop for anyone seeking information on any aspect of the subject, so it is more concerned to be complete than to be original. However, the series takes full account of all the latest research and in certain areas will be publishing entirely new material. In the matter of interpretation care has been taken to avoid the old myths and to present only the most widely accepted modern viewpoints.

To tell a coherent story, in a more readable form than is usual with encyclopaedias, each volume takes the form of independent chapters, all by recognised authorities in the field. Most chapters are devoted to the ships themselves, but others deal with topics such as 'navigation' that are more generally applicable, giving added depth to the reader's understanding of developments. Some degree of generalisation is inevitable when tackling a subject of this breadth, but wherever possible the specific details of ships and their characteristics have been included. With a few historically unavoidable exceptions, the series is confined to sea-going vessels; to have included boats would have increased the scope of an already massive task.

The history of the ship is not a romanticised story of epic battles and heroic voyages, but equally it is not simply a matter of technological advances. Ships were built to carry out particular tasks and their design was as much influenced by the experience of that employment – the lessons of war, or the conditions of trade, for example – as purely technical innovation. Throughout this series an attempt has been made to keep this clearly in view, to describe the *what* and *when* of developments without losing sight of the *why*.

The series is aimed at those with some knowledge of, and interest in, ships and the sea. It would have been impossible to make a contribution of any value to the subject if it had been pitched at the level of the complete novice, so while there is an extensive glossary, for example, it assumes an understanding of the most basic nautical terms. Similarly, the bibliography avoids general works and concentrates on those which will broaden and deepen the reader's understanding beyond the level of the *History of the Ship*. The intention is not to inform genuine experts in their particular area of expertise, but to provide them with the best available single-volume summaries of less familiar fields.

Each volume is chronological in approach, with the periods covered getting shorter as the march of technology quickens, but organised around a dominant theme – represented by the title of the book – that sums up the period in question. In this way each book is fully self-sufficient, although when completed the twelve titles will link up to form a coherent history, chronicling the progress of ship design from its earliest recorded forms to the present day.

With this volume the series enters some of the most poorly documented areas of ship history. For over a century sparse and fragmented sources have compromised the best efforts of scholars to produce a coherent technical account of the medieval ship. Ships were not a prime concern to medieval historians and much of the evidence that survives is either incidental comment by those who understood little of shipping, or else takes the form of bare data – like inventories and contracts – which need careful interpretation. Much the same is true of contemporary visual depictions, where the artist had little interest in technical accuracy.

Recent archaeological discoveries have thrown considerable light on some aspects of medieval naval architecture, but the seren-dipitous nature of underwater finds puts emphasis on those types which have been excavated, at the expense of those that have not. For example, much is now known about the cog, while the other main northern cargo carrier, the hulk, remains as much a mystery as ever; similarly, the details of Viking ship construction are thoroughly documented, while Mediterranean shipbuilding in the high Middle Ages lacks any significant physical remains. In general, large ships are better understood than small ones.

The nature of both the evidence and its study has implications for this volume. It is a truly international story, so no one country's archives are sufficient, and thus the scholar is required to master a myriad of languages, many of them long dead, and the arcane palæography in which so much was written. Just as archaeology is now in the hands of professionals, so the documentary study of the medieval ship leaves little room for dedicated amateurs of the kind who have contributed so much to the understanding of later periods of ship development. This makes us entirely dependent on a small number of academics, whose interests sometimes overlap, but often do not actually touch, leaving areas which are still uncharted. To fulfil the aim of the series, these territories cannot be left entirely blank, but equally the book cannot answer questions that have defied the best research for decades. As a compromise, we have allowed individual contributors to start and finish their chapters wherever seems most appropriate for the coherence of their story – even if this means some duplication – and to concentrate on what is best documented. What is still unknown, or poorly understood, has been freely admitted, with a summary of existing knowledge and any reasonable theories that pertain.

Robert Gardiner
Series Editor

Introduction

SOMEWHERE in the murky background, obscured from contemporaries as well as from historians, during the era when Europeans engaged in significant voyages of exploration to all parts of the world, something even more important occurred in the technology of transportation. Dramatic developments in the design and construction of sea-going vessels from the fourteenth to the sixteenth centuries not only made possible those voyages but also laid the foundations for extensive changes in virtually all aspects of life, first in Europe and later in the rest of the world. The greatest breakthrough in the evolution of sailing vessels came with the emergence of the three-masted full rigged ship. This achievement was the greatest single improvement in pre-modern ship design, and established the form of the sailing ship down to the great clippers of the nineteenth century. The radical mutation in shipbuilding which was the creation of the full rigged ship, like all mutations in technology, was not instantaneous. It was heavily dependent on what had come before and, for it to be fully effective, relied on many subsequent efforts to work out the implications of the transformation.

The development of the full rigged ship was to a great degree a result of the drawing together of boatbuilding traditions already well-established by the fourteenth century. Shipwrights combined the building techniques and designs of northern Europe with those descended from Roman practice which had continued in southern Europe. A few innovative craftsmen merged these two traditions in the years around 1400 in the first modest efforts to create a new vessel type, one which at first received various names but in the end settled on the generic term 'ship'.[1] Once the principal change had occurred what was left was modification and adjustment to try to find the optimum way to exploit the advantages of the new rig. Fortunately the mutation in shipbuilding came in a period for which surviving sources, and especially visual sources, improve both in number and in accuracy. Traditionally, ships and shipbuilding were not typical subjects of works of art: if sailing vessels appeared at all, it was incidentally. They did appear in mosaics, drawings, paintings, graffitti, on seals and in a number of other different art forms, the form itself effecting to some degree what was shown. The increase over time in the sheer volume of depictions of ships makes it much easier for historians to discern, document and describe the tentative technical advances of the late Middle Ages and the Renaissance; certainly easier than with developments in earlier periods.

By 1000 there was already a rather sophisticated range of different kinds of vessels, some relying on sails, some on oars and some on both for propulsion. The high Middle Ages and the Renaissance was a period of better and improving communications within Europe. The long-term economic and demographic growth beginning certainly by the mid tenth century and going on to the mid fourteenth meant that there was greater exchange of goods among Europeans and so more opportunities for the use of ships of different types. There was a sharp setback in population in the fourteenth and early fifteenth century but that was followed by recovery and renewed economic expansion. As in the high Middle Ages the growth of the Renaissance led to more exchange of goods, of people and, of greater importance for shipbuilding, of ideas among all parts of Europe. The increased contact sharply increased the possibility for shipwrights to gain firsthand experience of different and varied shipbuilding traditions, and to borrow from them. Nevertheless, despite exposure to different designs, artisans typically rejected novelty. Shipbuilders have long enjoyed a justified reputation for being highly conservative, and old ways died very hard. Learning the 'mystery' of medieval craft took a long time and so the craftsmen had a vested interest in continuing as they had in the past. More important, however, in the context of ship design was the unforgiving environment in which the ship operated: failed experiments were very costly to crews and shipowners, so a reluctance to take chances reflected rational calculation as much as, or more than, an unadventurous frame of mind. What did grow up as a consequence of improving contact among different regions of Europe was some diversity and an impetus to experiment, but always with care. In the fourteenth century a sudden drop in population, followed by repeated setbacks in the recovery of numbers, generated an economic crisis and, above all, disrupted established ways of doing things. It was in that atmosphere of much altered and changing circumstances that a number of advances came in the design of ships.

Before that crisis the existing forms came from two broad categories, one common in the North and the other common in the South. The vessels of northern Europe were descended, loosely, from Viking boatbuilding traditions or from Celtic ones. The descendants of the rowing craft used by the Vikings, whether they should be more accurately described as ships or boats, were able to make sea voyages and do so consistently. For mariners in the high Middle Ages the Scandinavian type in its many variants was able to fulfill a number of functions. Typically that class of ship served as coastal vessels and fishing boats. The descendants of coasters used by the Celts at least as early as Roman times had made great strides in the hands of shipwrights from the expanding ports of north Germany. The cog, once it developed a keel and a sternpost rudder and a true square sail, was the principal cargo ship of high medieval northern Europe. The cog proved highly effective in moving bulky goods and played a major role in the development of trading networks among ports of the Baltic and North Sea. The cog also proved highly effective as a warship, and it remained the principal type for fighting at sea well into the fifteenth century. It was also the best military transport available and so governments in wartime made

---

1. For most of the remaining period of sail if otherwise unqualified the word 'ship' carried the technical meaning of a three-masted square rigged vessel.

THE EVOLUTION OF THE SAILING SHIP, AD 1000–1650

(All drawings to the same scale; drawn by Lionel Willis)

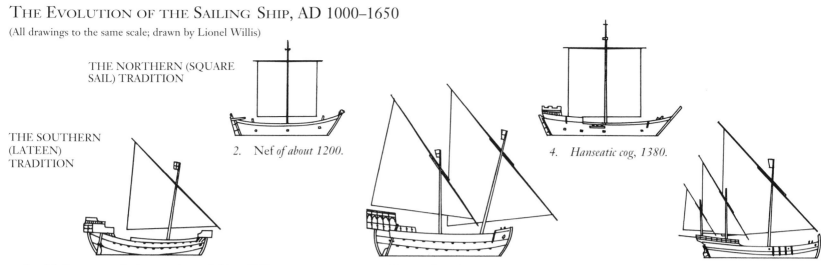

THE NORTHERN (SQUARE SAIL) TRADITION

THE SOUTHERN (LATEEN) TRADITION

2.   Nef of about 1200.

4.   Hanseatic cog, 1380.

1.   Mediterranean single-masted round ship, c1200.

3.   Genoese Crusader transport, 1268.

5.   Portuguese caravel, c1450.

1. From Late Antiquity the standard Mediterranean trading vessel was a lateen rigged vessel, usually referred to as a 'round' ship in contrast to the 'long' ship or galley. This example is based on evidence which is usually dated a century or so later, but the hull form, construction and rig were probably much the same as early as AD 1200. The hull would have been flush-planked over pre-erected frames (carvel construction) and was steered by means of oars over the quarters.

2. The typical northern vessel of AD 1000 was a Viking-type open boat hull, built shell-first of over-lapping strakes (clinker construction). Early medieval developments included towers fore and aft in some craft and from about 1200 there is evidence of the replacement of steering oars with a stern rudder, as in this example. In contemporary sources such ships are sometimes called *nefs*, but the word is not much more specific than 'ship'.

3. A large Genoese vessel reconstructed from data in contracts placed by the French crusading king Louis IX for vessels to transport his army to the Holy Land. This example is two-masted, but three-masted lateen vessels were not uncommon.

4. The most important northern trading vessel of the high Middle Ages was the cog, which was characterised by a capacious, flat-bottomed hull, straight raked stempost and a centreline stern rudder. By the fourteenth century the structures fore and aft were becoming less tower-like and more integrated into the hull shape. This was still essentially built shell first, but internal framing was becoming more important.

5. Although Portugal is an Atlantic country, its most characteristic vessel was very Mediterranean in most of its features, with a lateen rig and frame-first

an effort to enlist, either through bribery or force, cogs for naval purposes.

Vessels in southern Europe were descended from classical or Roman types, although shipbuilders had been forced to modify those late Antique designs. First, they made adjustments because of the changeover to the use of lateen sails as the exclusive form of wind-powered propulsion, which came some time in the early Middle Ages. Second, they made adjustments because of the adoption of a new form of hull construction developed in the same period. Instead of putting together the external skin of the ship first, by AD 1000 shipbuilders put up the internal ribs and then tacked the hull planking to the internal framework. Wherever and whenever it took place, much has been made of their changeover. The different and novel method of building which was gradually accepted as the norm throughout Europe offered some clear advantages. It was possible to build larger vessels, with more flexible hull shapes while employing the same amount of wood and effort. It gave shipbuilders many more options in terms of hull design, but was less demanding of the shipwrights' time and skill. Building the frames first promoted a distinction (which probably already existed in em-

bryo) in the shipyard between the 'designer' in charge of the entire process, both technical and financial, of building, and the men who did the work of forming, shaping and joining wood. Through the course of the high Middle Ages builders in southern Europe explored the new approach to putting up a hull. It was at the end of the Middle Ages that their counterparts to the west and north first tried to see what they could do with the different way of building a hull.

The two design traditions, one in the South and the other in the North, continued to develop through the later Middle Ages. Improvements came in Mediterranean vessels as builders learned how to exploit construction techniques while improvements came in northern vessels as different designs were merged or builders borrowed features from one type to add to another. More important in the long run, however, was the fact that the two traditions were in contact. Already by the early twelfth century northern ships made their way into the Mediterranean, so shipbuilders there knew about the other tradition. It was not until the fourteenth century, though, that clear evidence exists of borrowing from the very different practices of the other part of Europe

and, with that borrowing, the creation of entirely new types of sailing ship. In the fifteenth century builders began to produce a ship which was both northern and southern, which had features from both traditions. The construction of the hull was southern. The guidance system, which was a sternpost rudder, was northern. The rigging, using both square sails and a single lateen sail at the stern, was both northern and southern.

By the late fifteenth century, the result of this cross-fertilisation and combination of practices was the carrack. Known by various names and itself modified to meet specific needs, it was this new type of full rigged ship which served for exploration and for establishing trading relations worldwide. It was also the type of ship which excelled at projecting power, especially now that European vessels carried heavier and ever more reliable guns. The combination of a superior sailing ship and improving guns made possible the dominance of the oceans of the world by Europeans.

The conversion of maritime Europe to the new type of ship was not immediate. This new design only slowly gained a foothold, first in Iberia and along the western coasts of Europe before making its way into the Mediterranean

THE TRADITIONS COMBINED

6. *Catalan* não, *c1450.*

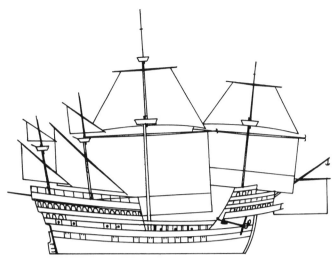

7. *Man-of-war carrack, 1545.*

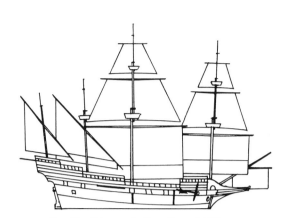

8. *English race-built galleon, 1588.*

construction – indeed the northern term for this type of building, 'carvel', is closely connected to the caravel. While the lateen had advantages when beating to windward, it was less satisfactory before the wind, which led to the development of the *caravela redonda*, or square rigged caravel, which carried square canvas forward and lateen aft.

6. In the fifteenth century – although exactly where and when is still a mystery – there began a process of combining square and lateen canvas that was to lead to the development of the full rigged ship. The details of this process are still disputed,

but a square rigged ship may have first acquired a lateen mizzen to help balance the rig and aid manoeuvrability. This Catalan *não*, based on the famous Mataro model, represents the beginning of this evolution.

7. The development of the full ship rig allowed a rapid expansion in size, and very soon the three-masted rig had acquired a further bonaventure or counter-mizzen. To build ships of this size, however, required a change among northern shipbuilders to embrace frame-first construction techniques (although there are some very large

clinker-built 'transitional' vessels known from both documentary and archaeological sources). Another innovation of the early sixteenth century was the gunport in the hull. This drawing is based on present knowledge of Henry VIII's *Mary Rose*.

8. The lower and finer lined galleon took over some of the roles of the carrack in the sixteenth century, but remained relatively high-charged in some countries. However, the English developed a 'race-built' version, which was lower and more manoeuvrable; these are usually attributed to the experience and ideas of Sir John Hawkins.

---

and the North and Baltic Seas. Builders from the various parts of Europe had to learn how to produce these new types, a skill they developed by experience and experiment. By the sixteenth century it was also possible to learn from books, from treatises on shipbuilding since skilled men started, somewhat belatedly, to write about the technology they practised. The number of manuscript works, almost non-existent before 1500, began to multiply and by the close of the sixteenth century even printed books describing the essential features of ships and how to build them began to appear.

Once known, the full rigged ship found ever greater uses, but that is not to say that established designs disappeared. Old types held on in places and trades where they had specific advantages. Well-known designs were modified and concentrated in certain regions or even specific locations. The caravel, for example, started as a fishing boat but changed in the fifteenth century to a vessel for exploring the coast of Africa and then in the sixteenth changed again to a cargo carrier, used principally for maintaining trade between Iberia and the Atlantic islands. Adjustments in design were part of adjustments in the function of the type and changes in the mercantile niches

found for the caravel. Typically, existing types found themselves reduced in size and in the scope of their uses as the new, superior and more versatile ship supplanted them.

Modifications made over time in the full rigged ship through to 1650 largely related to hull forms, making the specialist types more effective and leading ultimately to their domination of most maritime enterprise in Renaissance Europe. As warships or armed traders the full rigged ship took the form of the galleon. Long relative to its width and low slung, this modified type was expensive to operate but, being well-armed, it proved ideal for war and for dangerous trades. As pure cargo ships, especially for carrying bulk goods, the full rigged ship took the form of the *fluit*. This specialist type, which came from Dutch shipyards originally, was long relative to its width but bluff-bowed, slow, typically lightly armed if armed at all, and so with a small crew it proved very inexpensive to operate. The type was highly efficient and so was ideal for use in bulk trades and in regions that were peaceful. From earliest times the goal of shipbuilders producing sailing ships for commercial purposes had been to create a reliable cargo ship powered by the wind which could move goods

at relatively low cost. Builders finally obtained the result they wanted in the *fluit*, the culmination of a development which started with the addition of a lateen sail to the square sail of the cog. The *fluit* showed what could be done with the full rigged ship to make an efficient cargo vessel.

The design was modified over time, exploiting its advantages, with variants on the basic theme appearing which were even more specialised in their use. The ultimate result in this development of the full rigged ship was a sharp differentiation between warships and cargo carriers. The former protected the latter in convoys. Producing, maintaining, and operating warships became the job of governments, which in turn generated a need for permanent navies and for bureaucracies to administer those navies.

A wide variety of ship types and their variations always existed in Europe. Despite the changes and marked improvements of the fourteenth and fifteenth centuries that generalisation always remained true. The coastal vessels of the Mediterranean are only the most obvious and best documented example. That would remain true even after the development of galleon and *fluit* because for certain needs a

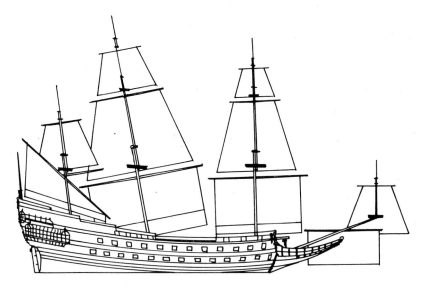

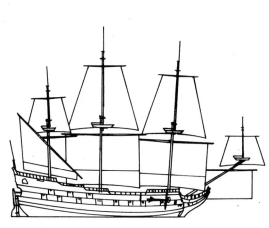

9.   *The Swedish* Wasa, *1627*.

10.   *A Dutch* fluit, *c1650*.

9.   From the galleon developed what the English navy came to call the 'great ship', a dedicated warship with two, and eventually three, complete tiers of guns. Line ahead tactics were not yet common so these ships were not strictly ships of the line, but they were a step in that direction. The best-known of these large prestige ships is the Swedish king's *Wasa*, built and lost in 1627. By this period the

fourth mast had proved superfluous, but there were additions to the standard rig in the form of a mizzen topsail and the sprit topsail at the end of the bowsprit.

10.   The archetypal seventeenth-century merchant ship was the Dutch *fluit*. At its most simple and economic, the *fluit* featured a capacious round-

sterned hull form, with no beak, few guns and a low crew:tonnage ratio. Larger, better armed versions, like the one depicted here, were developed for trades where peace and stability could not be guaranteed. Such vessels could protect themselves against most piratical and privateering craft, but their economic advantage was eroded by the carriage of guns and the larger crews necessary to fight them.

unique design proved best. The variety of ship designs was mirrored in the wide variety of navigational techniques in use. The period of improvements in ships was also one of advances in the accuracy and consistency of the navigator's art. The supplementing of coastal navigation with some reliance on the stars was certainly known by the high Middle Ages but further advances were to come, especially in the Mediterranean. There sailors found an expanding range of instruments and methods made available to them which by the sixteenth century made possible the voyages between continents across the open ocean. Nevertheless, old navigational techniques did not die. Sailors used them side by side with the novel methods of finding the way at sea in both northern and southern Europe. For most voyages, and even for some of those outside of Europe, the old and trusted methods were enough.

The progression in ship technology from cogs through caravels to galleons and all of the steps, stages and variants that fall in between, distinguishes one of the greatest changes in shipbuilding history. For sea-going vessels, by 1600 the clinker-built rowing boat traditions of the North and the shell-first cargo ship traditions of the Greeks and Romans in the Medi-

terranean had been left behind for good. The men who built ships in the Renaissance established an entirely new basis for their trade. Standards for the ships of the era just before the Industrial Revolution were set in the fifteenth and sixteenth centuries. The basis for the greatest achievements of wooden ship construction and for the greatest achievements of voyages under sail were set by the shipwrights who created new types of vessels in the high Middle Ages and through the Renaissance. Shipbuilders expanded their technical capability. Shipbuilders modified what they had discovered, producing consistently more efficient and effective vessels. They accomplished all of that with a limited tool kit and one which changed little in its basic composition from the high Middle Ages. Renaissance shipbuilders established the principal lines of development for the next 400 years. There would be modifications and continued development, of course, but the builders of ships had already confirmed the primary attributes of the 'ship'.

The design of the ship opened new possibilities for the people of Europe and ultimately the people of the rest of the world. The superior type created a potential for the intensification as well as expansion of trade. It also created a greater ability to employ force at

sea, force which could be used both offensively and defensively. The ship of 1600 was the most expensive single item made by man. It was also the most productive and among the most impressive of man's creations. The golden age of the sailing ship falls perhaps from 1650 to 1850, the period of the greatest naval battles fought with sailing ships and the period of the development of worldwide trading networks. That apex in the history of sailing ships was based firmly on the many different experiments and efforts of the builders of ships in the years from 1200 to 1600. The use of and borrowing from existing designs, the mixing together of different features of known types to get new combinations, and the modifying and extension of what had already been found, all served to create ships that were effective, efficient, reliable and which pushed back people's horizons. In their simple efforts to meet the needs of sea captains, shipowners and governments Renaissance shipbuilders produced a unique and special kind of ship, a type which came to define the term and a vessel which proved to be, over time, the vehicle for the maritime history of Europe to the modern era and even beyond.

Richard W Unger

1

Descendants of Viking Boats

THE NAVAL power vacuum left by the departure of the Romans from the seas of northern Europe was quickly filled by the activity of the Saxons and later by those Scandinavians who became known as Vikings. It is remarkable that their development as seafarers owed nothing to the hundreds of years of Roman-influenced boat-building and seamanship, nor to the parallel activities of Celtic seamen.[1]

A totally distinct concept of hull shapes and boat and ship structures had evolved in Scandinavia. Confined to coastal waters, their craft remained as small, many-oared pulling boats until the restraints of a patrolling foreign navy were removed. Eschewing all that might have

---

1. O Crumlin-Pedersen, *From Viking Ships to Hanseatic Cogs*, Third Paul Johnstone Memorial Lecture, National Maritime Museum (Greenwich 1983).

Artist's impression of some of the vessels found near Roskilde. The largest (Skuldelev 5) is a longship of about 59ft (18m) length, but more significant for the development of ships is the shorter cargo vessel (Skuldelev 1) and identified as the famous knaar of the sagas. Unlike the longship, there is no evidence that this heavy craft was regularly beached, and it probably represents the kind of sea-going vessel that allowed the Vikings to explore the northern extremities of the Atlantic. (From History from the Sea *by kind permission of Mitchell Beazley International Ltd)*

been learnt from the Romans, when the Saxons and later the Vikings emigrated and invaded northern Europe they did it, at least initially, in rowing boats such as those found at Sutton Hoo in southern England. These boats, clinker-planked and of the same pointed shape at the bow and the stern, were discovered in burial mounds. Only their imprints in the sand were recovered, but in excellent detail. The largest was over 27m (88½ft) long but none of them showed any form of mast-step structure or other clues which would have indicated the use of sail. Bleak evidence for the use of sail by Scandinavians and Saxons is to be seen scratched on a small stone found on a Jutland beach near Karlby and dated to the seventh century. Its double-ended boat is propelled by a modest square sail set on what has been suggested, based on an interpretation of the mast steps found in Viking boat remains, is a free-standing mast.[2] Steering is by side rudder. Only later, after the departure of the Romans, does it seem that sail was adopted within Saxon and Scandinavian nautical culture. The question is whether they had to look outside their borders for inspiration. For instance, the Celtic users of sail would still be active in their trade along the Channel coast and around those of the British Isles. It is possible, therefore, that pre-Viking sails found on some Gotland grave stones were derived from contact with peoples on the eastern and southern Baltic coasts.

The classical Mediterranean 1500 years earlier had been through this rowing boat phase, adopted its own rig and diversified early into a parallel development of 'long' ships, which were rowed or sailed as required for piracy or war, and of 'round' ships which traded, showing all the advantages of a seaworthy hull and a

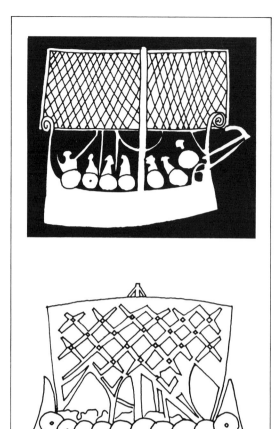

Depiction of Viking boats under sail from Gotland stone carvings. (By courtesy of Basil Greenhill)

minimal dependency on oars. The Romans in northern Europe were at the forefront in the use of this seafaring skill.

Nearer to home waters, Julius Caesar's navy had clashed with a fully sail-dependent fleet operated off the coast of Brittany by the Celtic Veneti.[3] These vessels were well regarded for their seaworthiness in the hazardous conditions found in the western end of the English Channel. Their high freeboard made it difficult for the Roman marines to attack them. Interestingly, this same reason is given to explain the inability of the Viking longships to overcome the Hanseatic cogs about twelve hundred years later. Good freeboard contributes greatly to seaworthiness but adds weight to a hull. This would be reflected in the displacement and hence a useful draught which contributed to the Veneti ships' envied sailing ability, a level not attained by the Vikings for another 1000 years. Though similar craft would have been on view along the Frisian coast and into the Baltic for many centuries and eventually were to grow into the successful cog form, the sailing lesson was learnt only

slowly by the early Saxons and Scandinavians. This apparent disinclination to build on the previous expertise of more advanced technologies and skills, combined with the Viking disruption of commerce and transport for the latter part of the millenium, set back boat and ship development some hundreds of years in the waters of northern Europe. Probably the Viking's major contribution was to infuse the techniques of a particularly successful version of clinker boatbuilding into that which already existed in some of their areas of influence both east and west of Scandinavia.[4]

Continued adherence by the Scandinavians to rowing as well as sailing arose from a maritime culture which rightly saw the need for oars in a homeland coasting environment. This restricted the development of a seaworthy ship – seaworthy, that is, by modern definitions – from the handsome fine-lined Viking hull with its square sail. It remained essentially an open boat until well after the end of the first millenium, capable of being swamped or capsized in bad weather and providing little shelter for the crew. That such boats or undecked ships undertook arduous voyages is a reflection of the physique and hardiness of the excellent seamen manning them rather than an indicator of the suitability of the craft for such work.

Viking boat structure by AD 1000

The five Viking boats dating from the end of the tenth century and recovered from Roskilde Fjord in the 1960s represent some of the different uses given to such boats. The two cargo boats and the smaller longship should be indicators of the direction in which they were developing. Viking boats found before the Skuldelev fleet showed well developed keels tending towards a narrow 'T' in section.[5] Their builders understood that hull stiffness could be improved by using the best girder shape. Some slight contribution would be made to sailing performance too, since when going to windward some keel would be better than nothing for these otherwise shallow hulls whose sailing ability depended on other features to be considered later. These improve-

2. O T P Roberts, 'Shroudless in Scandinavia?', *International Journal of Nautical Archaeology* 19/2 (1990), pp123–127.

3. Julius Caesar, *The Conquest of Gaul*, Penguin Classics 21 (London 1953), pp98–99.

4. B Greenhill and S Manning, *The Evolution of the Wooden Ship* (London 1988), p52.

5. B Greenhill, *Archaeology of the Boat* (London 1976), pp207–233.

Dated to the seventh century, the Karlby stone carving was found on a beach in Denmark's Jutland peninsula in the mid 1980s. It offers perhaps the earliest evidence of the use of a sail in Scandinavian or Saxon culture. (Vikingeskibshallen, Roskilde)

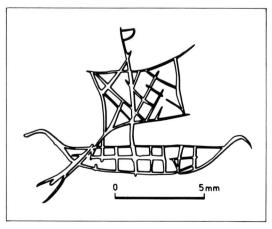

0   5mm

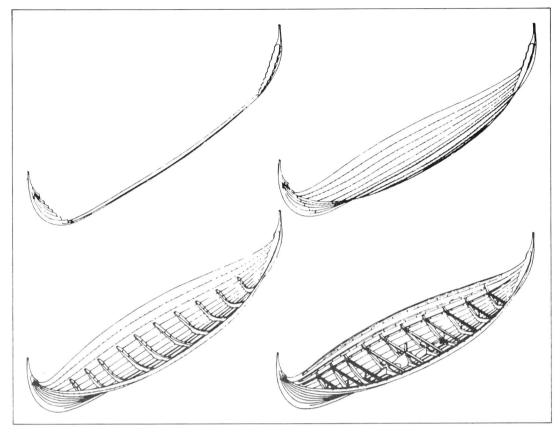

Much of the evidence for the structure of Viking ships around 1000 AD comes from the five wrecks found at Skuldelev in Roskilde Fjord, Denmark. Skuldelev 3, a small coastal cargo-carrier, shows the main elements of clinker construction as practised at the time. From Aspects of the History of Wooden Shipbuilding, *NMM Monograph No 1 (1970)*

is the mast step, which straddles a few of the frames in that area. Ahead of the socket for the mast's heel is an upright timber joining on to the upper beam. It is a part of the mast step and would have been a branch of the tree from which the step was carved.[7] This unique structure may once have been a support for an unstayed mast many centuries before, when the people who eventually became the Vikings were just beginning to use sail.[8] Mast steps are the obvious sign for the use of sail by the Skuldelev and other boats, together with perti-

6. O Crumlin-Pedersen, 'The Skuldelev Ships' *Acta Archaeologica* 38 (1967), pp73–174.

7. E McKee, 'Drawing the Replica', in V Fenwick (ed), *The Graveney Boat*, NMM Archaeological Series No 3, BAR 53, (Oxford 1978), p300.

8. O T P Roberts, 'Shroudless in Scandinavia?', pp123–127.

ments are also to be seen in the Skuldelev boats' keels. As in earlier times, their stem- and sternposts were still carved, hollow pieces of timber, stepped and shaped to accept the strakes in a continuous curve. All five boats are clinker or lap-strake planked, these being fastened with iron nails, the inner ends of which are clenched or riveted over roughly square roves. In such boat construction where strakes are edge-joined, the framing is fitted at a later stage in building. The frames are notched over the plank lands at Skuldelev. They are fastened neither to the keel nor to the garboards, but to the remaining strakes, usually by large dowels called treenails.[6] Bracing within the hull is by beams, fitted at two levels in some situations. The lower level rests on the tops of the frames which stop at the junction of the bottom strakes with the topsides. The upper level rests on the tops of the lower beams' standard knees and are locked in place by lodging knees fastened to the planking. Such an arrangement gives some further control over the hogging and sagging stresses which bedevil all hulls but which are a much greater problem within the shallow, undecked hulls used by the Vikings.

Locked into a pair of beams about midships

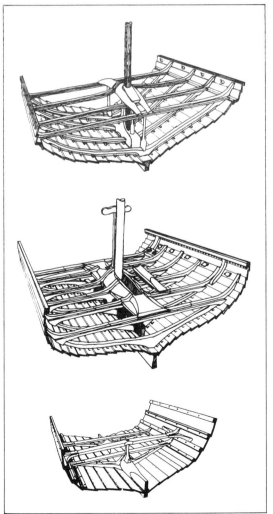

The development of Scandinavian boat structure from about 800 to 1000 AD based on evidence from the Oseberg, Gokstad and Skuldelev ships. (Ole Crumlin-Pedersen, by courtesy of Basil Greenhill)

Sections of Skuldelev 3 showing the transverse strengthening - notched frames, beams and narrow thwarts (rowing benches). (From Basil Greenhill and Sam Manning, The Evolution of the Wooden Ship)

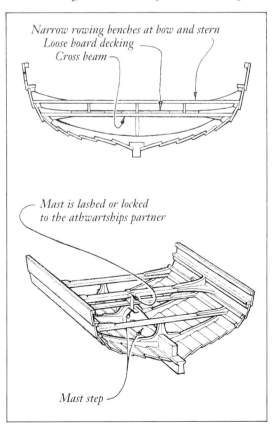

Narrow rowing benches at bow and stern
Loose board decking
Cross beam

Mast is lashed or locked to the athwartships partner

Mast step

A model of Skuldelev 3, originally regarded as a small cargo vessel but now thought to be a farmer's 'great boat' of the kind used in the Baltic archipelagoes until this century. (By courtesy of Basil Greenhill)

nent holes bored in the sheer strake at those places one would expect to see running and standing rigging. For fittings it is necessary to consider the toggles, blocks, cleats and pieces of rope, some including knots and splices, which come from the earlier Norwegian finds such as the Oseberg from AD 800 and the Gokstad from AD 850. There is no known contemporary illustration showing a Viking boat under sail, and no complete masts with yards have survived which would give correct proportions of sails. However, Thomas Gillmer has estimated that the Gokstad ship's sail would have measured 40ft along the yard and 25ft up the luff (12.2m by 7.6m).[9] This was based on a complete yard and a calculation based on the taper of a lower piece of mast buried with the boat. The sailing boats carved on the grave stones from Gotland prior to the emergence of the Vikings are in themselves an enigma which may at last have been interpreted by Dr Erik Mylen of the Visby Museum, Gotland.[10] Perhaps the low, broad square sails and sail controls of the Gotland Stones are much more like the rig used about AD 1000 than those tall, sophisticated versions from the nineteenth century presently applied to reconstructions of the Skudelev boats and others from this period.

Both before and after the Viking period the side rudder, usually hung over the starboard quarter, was the norm. The Roman ships in the North Sea had carried one on each quarter, but perhaps their sterns were broader than the boats which followed them to become those of the Saxons and then the Vikings. Side rudders require two attachments on the side of the hull from which they can swivel. The Viking system consisted of a large timber boss near the waterline, through which a withy rope emerged and gripped the rudder stock, while a leather strap

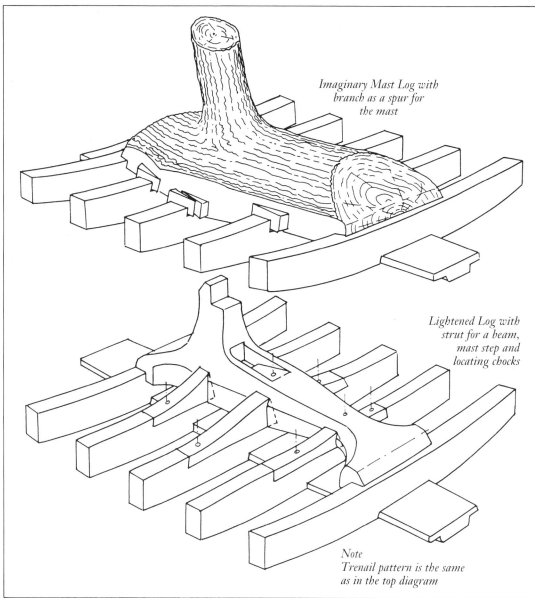

Imaginary Mast Log with branch as a spur for the mast

Lightened Log with strut for a beam, mast step and locating chocks

*Note
Trenail pattern is the same as in the top diagram*

9. T Gillmer, 'The Capability of the Single Square Sail Rig', in S McGrail (ed), *Medieval Ships & Harbours in Northern Europe*, NMM Archaeological Series No 5, BAR International Series 66 (Oxford 1979), p169.

10. O T P Roberts, 'Viking Sailing Performance', in S McGrail (ed), *Aspects of Maritime Archaeology & Ethnography* (Greenwich 1984), pp123–149.

Eric McKee's imaginative reconstruction of the development of a sophisticated mast step arrangement from its primitive origin as a log with a branch extension used as a mast support. From The Graveney Boat, *edited by Valerie Fenwick (Greenwich 1978)*

The stern of the Oseberg Viking boat showing the side rudder and its associated fittings, notably the timber boss on which the rudder was pivoted. The end of the tiller extension can be seen at the top of the oar-like rudder. The fine lines and shallow hull of these Viking boats must have restricted their utility in open-water conditions. (Basil Greenhill)

at the sheer line did a similar job. The stock is slotted to take a tiller at right angles to the blade.

Few rudders belonging to ancient boat discoveries have been found, though numerous isolated ones are recorded. All tend towards a slight rake aft. Some, such as that from South-wold, have an extended stock further slotted at the top to resite the tiller should it be necessary to raise the blade in shallow water by decreasing the angle the rudder makes with the waterline. Those illustrations which are available from before and after the emergence of the Vikings show rudders which protrude well below the shallow hull. It is believed that not only did the rudders steer but they also acted as leeboards, reducing leeway to a useful limit and enabling courses to be sailed closer to the wind.[11] This combination is not unusual, as it is found in cobles from northeast England and in certain Chinese sampans, to cite recent examples, and seems to have been used in Queen Hatsheput's sea-going ships about 1500 BC and later in the classical Mediterranean.

Skuldelev 5, as the longship from Roskilde is known, is a narrow, open pulling boat, 17.5m (57½ft) in length and able to be sailed. Her type was well established and could contribute nothing to the future form of the late medieval sea-going ship.

An even larger boat was Skuldelev 2, which has been identified as the great longship of the sagas. She is almost 30m (98½ft) long and is of a type that continued to be built for the defence of Denmark for some centuries to come.[12] She had equivalents in the contemporary English galleys built during the twelfth and thirteenth centuries, so that much of their structural details preserved in the Treasury Accounts must be similar due to their common ancestry. The freeboard of the opposing Fri-

---

11. O T P Roberts, 'Viking Sailing Performance'.

12. O Crumlin-Pedersen, 'Vikings & the Hanseatic Merchants, 900–1450', in G Bass (ed), *A History of Seafaring* (London 1972), p191.

The bow structure of Skuldelev 1, the so-called 'knaar'. The stem piece was a single, elaborately carved 'V' in plan form, with ends cut to take the ends of the upper strakes of planking. (By courtesy of Basil Greenhill)

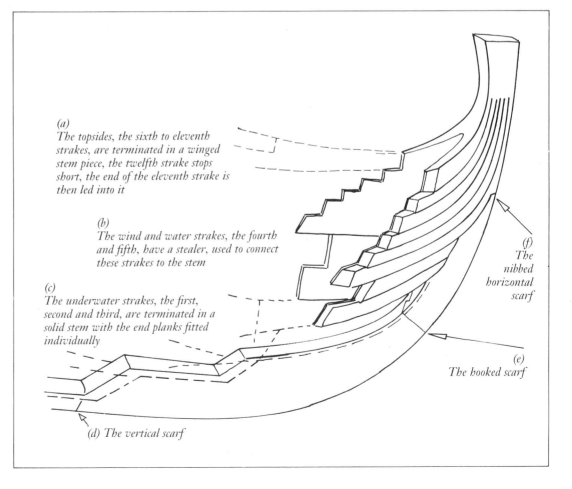

(a) The topsides, the sixth to eleventh strakes, are terminated in a winged stem piece, the twelfth strake stops short, the end of the eleventh strake is then led into it

(b) The wind and water strakes, the fourth and fifth, have a stealer, used to connect these strakes to the stem

(c) The underwater strakes, the first, second and third, are terminated in a solid stem with the end planks fitted individually

(d) The vertical scarf

(e) The hooked scarf

(f) The nibbed horizontal scarf

The cargo-carrying vessel of the Vikings is known from literary sources as the 'knaar', but hard evidence for its characteristics had to await the discovery of the Skuldelev ships, No 1 of which has been identified as a 'knaar'. This shows the imaginative display at the Roskilde museum, where the remains are fitted into a skeletal framework of thin steel which gives an impression of the complete hull, rather like a three-dimensional ship's draught. (Photo by Basil Greenhill)

sian cogs reduced the Danish longships' combat effectiveness so that by 1304 naval defence was transferred to a handful of Danish cogs and the days of the Scandinavian longship were over.

The largest of the cargo vessels from Roskilde, Skuldelev 1, is about 15m (49ft) long, and has been identified as the knaar type mentioned in the sagas. The lines of the knaar were much more full, as might be expected of a cargo carrier. The Roskilde knaar shows early steps towards improving the Viking hull form in terms of sailing qualities and seaworthiness. These are the deepening of the hull, thus allowing an increase in both draught and freeboard, coupled with greater beam. These two changes push the knaar type away from an equal dependence on oars and in the direction of becoming a pure sailing vessel. Such changes indicate a confidence in the sailing ability of the knaar and an opening of minds to the prospect of an entirely capable and independent sailing vessel. *Saga Siglar*, a reconstruction of the Skuldelev 1, has made highly creditable ocean crossings, although the design on which she is based may be thought of as unsuitable for such passages since it still exhibits all the features which now would cause her to be regarded as unseaworthy, yet were typical of the Viking undecked vessel.[13]

During the next few centuries these 'boat' features were eliminated, so paving the way for the development of a seaworthy hull able to transport crew, victuals and cargo with fair comfort and reasonable certainty in spite of the extremes of weather which would be met on long voyages. Evidence exists that the Scandinavians followed this route and built much larger vessels than the Skuldelev knaar. In Bergen the remains of a substantial cargo ship over 28m long by 9m beam (92ft by 29½ft) were found, and from other structures she could be dated before 1248. Vessels of this size are the result of continuous long-term development, so this may be assumed to have been preceded by hundreds of others and indeed succeeded by more and better. Vessels of this round hull form must have been on a

par with the largest cogs for sailing performance and cargo carrying. After all, the cog shape was hydrodynamically crude but had gained a head start in size and in simplicity of construction on the Scandinavian form. Regrettably, hard evidence for the latter is still to come to light, though the remains of the Aber Wrac'h I wreck from about the middle of the fourteenth century may be considered to support the concept of the greatly developed Scandinavian hull form.[14] To understand the likely development of the Scandinavian boat it is necessary to consider that evidence which is more plentiful to the west of Scandinavia.

The influence of the Vikings waned in northern Europe after the first millenium, but there remained a distinctive legacy of boatbuilding methods which lasted to the present. In Scandinavia clinker construction methods reigned supreme for nearly all boats up to the sizes needed for coastal trade, changes being made to proportions, sterns, steering, rig and other details but with the basic construction

methods established in Viking times remaining much the same.

As is already known from the Skuldelev 1 knaar, a move was being made to meet the need for a better-proportioned cargo-carrying boat during the beginning of the eleventh century. It is inconceivable that this development was confined to one area, and this assumption is supported by the two other similar boat remains, from the twelfth century, at Eltang (also in Denmark) and at Galtaback in Sweden, and as noted in Bergen, Norway. The demands for more substantial transport both for goods and people were the same throughout northern Europe, so the direction in which the Viking boat had to be improved would be followed in

13. R Thorseth, 'Operation Viking', in O Crumlin-Pedersen and M Vinner (eds), *Sailing into the Past* (Roskilde 1984), pp78–83.

14. M L'Hour and E Veyrat, 'A mid-15th century clinker boat off the north coast of France, the Aber Wrac'h I wreck: a preliminary report', *International Journal of Nautical Archaeology* 18/4 (1989), pp285–298.

any number of boatbuilding and trading communities throughout the old Viking world. Unfortunately, the evidence for this is sparse in the extreme, and what there is needs careful interpretation. The few archaeological boat discoveries which are dated after the Vikings, even in Scandinavia, make possible an understanding of the hull bottom, but little else. To follow a coherent line of development is almost impossible. Individual improvements may be identified which are seen more frequently in association with others. Our most reliable knowledge leans heavily on those sources which are almost entirely iconographic but are garnered from all areas which enjoyed or endured Viking attention.

Skuldelev 1, the 'knaar': a reconstruction based on a full consideration of all the evidence. The structure and lines are reasonably certain, being based on the extensive remains of the hull excavated at Roskilde Fjord, but the masting and rigging is more conjectural, drawing on evidence from other boat finds collated with an understanding of traditional practices that survived down to recent memory. (Vikingeskibhallen, Roskilde)

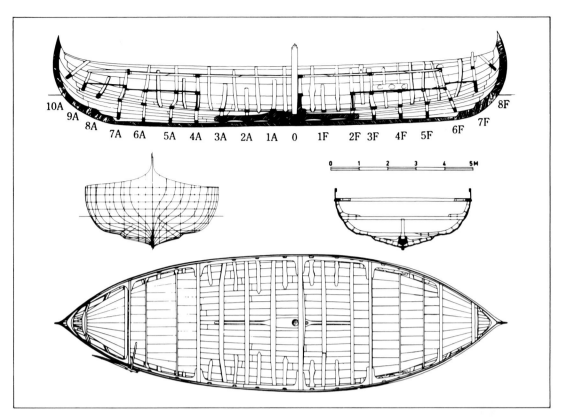

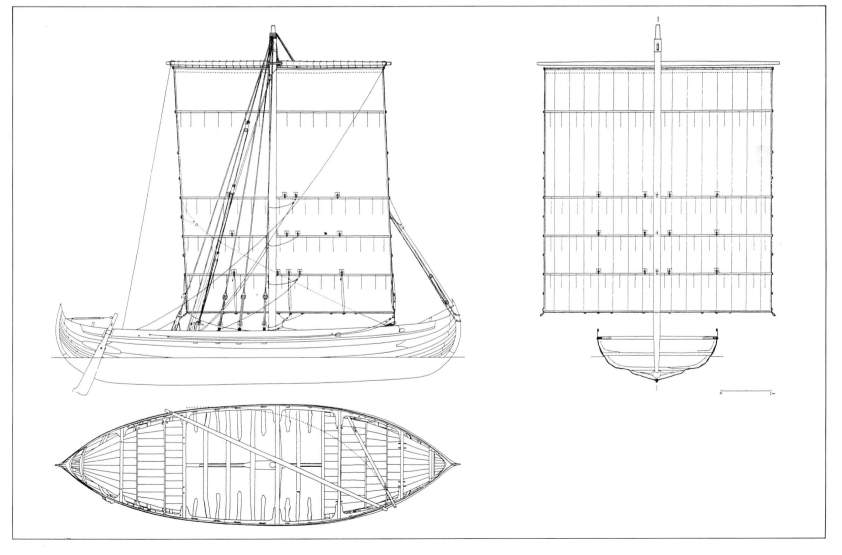

The Bayeux Tapestry as evidence

Following William of Normandy's defeat of King Harold at Hastings there was produced an incredibly informative record of the event whose details were immediately accessible to its viewers, the vast majority of whom were illiterate. Fortunately the Bayeux Tapestry includes an account of the preparation of boats and of the passage of the invasion fleet across the English Channel. These boats do not seem to have advanced at all from that of the Skuldelev 5 type. The construction of the hulls is still of overlapping clinker construction and some interesting details of woodworking tools and boatbuilding techniques are shown in the preamble to the invasion. Long, shallow hulls display rows of holes in the sheerstrake for oars, and suggest the ability to be totally independent of the wind if needs be. Some boats have shields hung over the side which would increase freeboard like a washstrake and reduce the amount of spray blowing aboard. Deep side rudders are allowed to trail more as the fleet approaches the shallows of the landing beach. These rudders show a high aspect ratio – that is, they are long and narrow in proportion. Such rudder shapes tend to have too little 'feel' at low speeds and the extra area shown at the lowest part of the trailing edge may have been a means of overcoming this. Such a shape is often seen in other views of Viking boats.

William's fleet sailed across from Nor-

In the past much reliance has been placed on the evidence of the seals of maritime towns in the study of medieval ships. Obviously the form placed restrictions on the artist, but many of the features once dismissed as 'licence' – such as short strake lengths and protruding beam ends – have been verified by archaeology. They seem to reveal the continuation of the Viking-style hull construction with the gradual addition of castellated structures fore and aft, which are usually free-standing in the earliest examples, but in the Dover (1284) seal they encompass the heads of the stem- and sternposts; some also show a masthead 'castle'. Unlike earlier Viking vessels, the ship depicted seems designed for sailing only. The seals of San Sebastian and Sandwich show bowsprit-like projections which were presumably to give a satisfactory lead to bowlines, to allow the ship to be sailed closer to the wind.

Sandwich

Dover

San Sebastian

Dunwich

mandy. All boats are rigged with a forestay, backstay and shrouds. Not one shows braces from the yards, which might be regarded as an omission. By inference from evidence for the knaar's being used without reliance on oars, it is clear that boats were sailed close to the wind when obliged to do so. Braces are essential when sailing to windward since without them a momentary luff may result in the square sail going aback, possibly leading to a capsize in an open boat.[15] Perhaps William's fleet was never intending to sail close-hauled.

Sail-handling of these boats has caused much discussion due to the triangular form in which the square sails seem to be set. The most likely interpretation is that marrying the tack to the clew – that is, holding together the two bottom corners of the square sail – was a method of sail reduction more than acceptable for sailing with a free wind. Indeed, the method has been tried successfully in practical research.[16] The Bayeux illustration of the square sail shortened this way is not quite unique in medieval iconography; for example, the thirteenth-century seal of Bristol shows a 'triangular' sail, though its function still remains in the arena of interpretation rather than of absolute certainty.

As with the braces, reef points may not have been fitted, with the intention of expediting the building and rigging of an invasion fleet. The need for sail reduction suggests that a fresh breeze drove the fleet, and this is supported by every helmsman, or a seaman standing near him, having the sheet in his hand ready for instant release should a gust of wind threaten stability.

A clue to the internal structure of these vessels is provided by the way the crew stand higher than the military passengers when working forward or aft. Evidently there is a raised deck at each end.

Further evidence from seals and accounts

City and port seals which appeared after the Bayeux Tapestry contain a wealth of information. Because the vessels shown on them are cramped into a circular space, their proportions are the first aspect to suffer. Nevertheless, the details of hull construction, rig, crew activities and armaments are plentiful, and their close examination is essential if development of the original Viking hull is to be traced into the later Middle Ages. The ports and cities named on the borders of the seals are scattered along the Baltic and North Sea coasts, on both sides of the English Channel and down the Bay of Biscay. Their widespread use is an indication of the busy trading links by now re-established throughout northern Europe after the depredations of the Vikings. Not all show Viking derivatives since the cog was in the ascendency during the twelfth century, so those from the more eastern ports tend to favour cog designs.

In England those Scandinavian-derived merchant vessels sometimes were known as *keels*. It is uncertain whether this was due to that part of their structure being prominent or whether it was the general description given to any working craft, as Tinniswood thought in his masterly intepretation of the Treasury Accounts for the building of the English galleys, 1272–1377. Another term for these vessels, in use on both sides of the English Channel, was *nef*, which in the late Middle Ages tended to be applied only to what would be thought of now as naval vessels.

The seals are from the thirteenth and fourteenth centuries, and by the end of the period certain distinct changes are evident. To distinguish between warships and trading vessels is not possible with certainty. Those showing armed men may be warships, but then the vessels may also be recently conscripted from the merchant fleet. This and payment for the addition of castles as part of their conversion to war service is noted in the Treasury records kept in those times. At the same time, warships no longer needed for service were sold off to merchants who put them to work. In 1232 King Henry III of England was happy to charter some of his fleet to private traders to defray their costs.[17] Apart from a number of galleys built in England specifically for the king's fleet, it is unlikely that any differences existed structurally between war and merchant vessels.

15. O T P Roberts, 'Viking Sailing Performance'.

16. O T P Roberts, 'Viking Sailing Performance'.

17. D Loades, 'The King's Ships and the Keeping of the Seas, 1413–1480', *Medieval History* 1/1 (1993), pp93–104.

The seal of Winchelsea appears to depict the vessel of Viking inspiration with light framed castle structures standing free of the hull topsides fore and aft.
(By courtesy of Basil Greenhill)

However, on the seals the proportions of the latter are seen to be much stockier, much deeper in the hull. Since no seals show galleys and are concerned solely with depicting a much more robust type of sailing vessel, one must believe that galleys are unrepresentative of the ambitions and activities of the ports noted on them.

Hints about structure

Whereas the seals provide pictorial evidence of vessels from the thirteenth and fourteenth centuries, knowledge of terms used for all the various parts and fittings come from records maintained between 1272 and 1377, when the English king's galleys were planned and in some cases built. According to the various detailed builders' and Treasury Accounts which exist – unfortunately only for eight of them – these were large boats. How many were built is unknown. The language used is a mixture of Latin with some French, but where neither language can provide the right word the local English one appears, usually with a Scandinavian overtone.[18]

Despite some problems of interpretation, which are still unsolved, the Accounts list the items and jobs which confirm the continuance of the Viking boatbuilding methods. In Southampton there were *clenchatores*; in Newcastle, *repurcussores*; in Ipswich, *clyngkeres*; and in Lyme, *cleyncherers*; their efforts hammered down the thousands of nails over the iron roves. These craftsmen had their mates who 'held up' that is, pressed a large hammer against the head of each nail in turn as its end was clenched, and were known variously as *tenenties contra*, *clenchatores* and *holderes*.

Planking was bought ready-sawn, mostly in lengths of 12ft (3.7m) or less with longer boards of 28ft (8.5m) being reserved for garboards and sheer strakes. This use of short planking is attested by many of the vessels shown on the seals, where the staggered pattern of the plank scarph-joints is a feature of a seal's design.

Squared timber for beams, boards for decking and reference to what would be hatches are clues to the internal structure of these galleys. Shelter for the crews was minimal, being a canvas awning over the only deck on which they worked and slept. The space under it would be for equipment, and in any case would be rather cramped since freeboard had to be kept low to avoid excessive oar angles and lengths.

The two logs bought for the Newcastle galley built in 1295 were intended for her keel, which would have been about 100ft (30m) long after scarphing and fastening with five iron bolts. Long curving stem- and sternposts would have increased her overall length, which, judging from other accounts, was unusually great. Stems are listed as being made from one to five sections depending on their size, each section being identified by a name. The sternposts are treated similarly. Framing is deduced to have been spaced at 3ft (0.9m) and fastened to the planking using treenails. As in their Viking predecessors, the galleys had massive mast steps, some fitted after launching. It is thought that in some galleys, to permit raising the mast, the beams in the way of the heel were cut to leave a gap and no doubt mast partners edged the slot.

Much detail is given of cordage, sail cloth, yards, masts and bowsprits. Calculations, by past interpreters of the accounts for the sail carried by individual galleys, are based on the uncertain unit of an *ell* and an assumed width of cloth. The results would seem to over-canvas and over-spar these galleys drastically in a manner quite unsuited for what are in fact open boats built without the benefit of a weather deck. Proportions of sails shown on the seals are also at variance with the results.

The builders' accounts indicate the problems of hanging a stern rudder on the rounded sternposts of some of the later galleys. Items listed refer to timber to be fitted over felt and iron-fastened to form a deadwood extending aft from the curved sternpost. This created a near-vertical straight edge to which the rudder was fitted. Quantities of iron are listed from which the yard's blacksmith produced gudgeons, pintles and binding straps, probably in the same fashion that they were made for large cathedral doors.

Side rudders had been fitted in the earlier period of the accounts but were not rejected entirely, and for some time it is clear that galleys with stern rudders included two or more side rudders in their inventories. Perhaps the stern rudder fittings were not that reliable in the early stages. On the other hand it has been proposed that such shallow hulls missed the grip given by the old side-rudders, so carried them to be used as leeboards when sailing.[19]

18. J T Tinniswood, 'The English Galleys, 1272–1377', *The Mariner's Mirror* XXXV (1949), pp276–315.

19. O T P Roberts, 'Viking Sailing performance'.

The mural from Skamstrup church in Denmark, dated to the second half of the fourteenth century, showing a race between St Olaf in the Lazy Oxen *(left) and his brother in the* Merry Serpent *(right). Both vessels have stern rudders, but that of the* Merry Serpent *has to conform to a curved sternpost, with a tiller that is also curved to clear the top of the sternpost. The* Lazy Oxen *has an unusually long aftercastle. (Vikingeskibhallen, Roskilde)*

Tillers were fitted probably as is seen in a mural in Skamstrup Church, Denmark. This is of a fourteenth-century boat having all the appearance of a Viking longship and showing the high, curving stem- and sternposts. However, she is different in that she has a stern rudder. The pintles and gudgeons are clearly seen. To avoid striking the sternpost, the tiller is shaped somewhat like an old-style hockey stick. It is fixed to the side of the rudder-head then curves to point forward to where the helmsman would stand, thus clearing the sternpost and also leaving enough room for the tiller to swing the rudder. A similar method is seen in Fide Church, Gotland, in a drawing scratched into the plaster about the end of the thirteenth century.

Oar lists and sizes are given for the various galleys and their attendant barges, as the large tenders were called. Some difficulty is found in fitting in so many oarsmen in some of the large galleys, if the allotted number of oars is correct. In some a space, or room as it was called, of about three feet (0.9m), considered usual for an oarsman, is possible. In others this allowance would imply an unacceptably long galley or a bireme, which would be distinctly unusual for northern waters. A room of two feet has been mooted, but this would be unworkable unless the oarsmen stood to pull their oars, a not unreasonable thought since this would allow an uncluttered deck. As a bonus a steeper oar angle could be managed which would permit an increase in freeboard. The methods by which the galleys arranged their oars is still open to conjecture.

Because the galleys were big, mechanical power in the form of a windlass was fitted aft for raising the yard and sail, whose combined weight would be substantial. The Treasury Accounts also list 'fore-windlasses' for raising anchors and others for working bilge pumps in the manner of a cottage-well windlass but having a continuous chain of buckets.

The Accounts list the costs of building offensive castles, as illustrated on some seals. These were supported on upright posts and followed the outline of the deck in plan. Later versions were built to overhang the hull. Most information comes from the accounts for the Southampton galley. Timber was bought for the fore-, the after- and also the top-castle which was fitted near the masthead, on the fore side to clear the shrouds but apparently with the forestay passing through a slot in its deck.

Externally the galley hulls were payed with mixtures of tar, resin, oil and tallow. It could be that the strake lands, that is the corners created by the overlaps of the lines of planking, were

The ship on the town seal of Haverfordwest suggests with its lowered yard that the width of the square sail probably exceeded its depth. This would make sense of the apparently over-length main yards depicted in many ship portraits on seals. (National Museum of Wales, Cardiff)

picked out in black. However, the mixture already applied would have darkened the hull considerably, so that treatment may have been simply extra protection or a sealant. Lime was prepared in order to whitewash the hold and the inside of the bulwarks. Colours were used on the sheer strake and in plenty on the fore- and aftercastles. On their panels would be painted appropriate coats of arms by which the galleys could be identified. Figureheads do not appear in the Accounts, which suggests that such adornments were not fitted at that time.

Examining the seals

Most of the city and port seals appear during the period of the Accounts for the building of the English galleys, so it is revealing to examine them with the written evidence in mind. Some of the seals are those of the Cinque Ports, which had an obligation to provide ships for the King of England whenever the need arose. The Accounts identify only a few of them as places where the new galleys were built during the twelfth and thirteenth centuries, though no doubt all of the Cinque Ports were involved.

The Treasury Accounts are for large boats dependent on oars as much as sail. The seals on the other hand depict sailing ships capable of going about their trading activities in a manner which was to establish in northern Europe a pattern of coastal and short-sea commercial activity under sail that lasted into the beginnings of the twentieth century.

Sailing problems

For a vessel to depend entirely on sail, two sets of criteria must be satisfied.[20] The sail must be capable of being supported, set and trimmed to gain power from the wind. This is especially important if sailing to windward is regularly undertaken. Even so, if the sail cloth is prone to stretch under the great strain of being trimmed for close-hauled sailing, then courses to windward must be much less than the theoretical optimum.

The other set of conditions for efficient sailing apply to the hull. Its surface should be smooth, which is a relative term when applied to a working craft's planking. The hull should be as fine in its form as is compatible with the business of moving heavy cargoes. Stability is needed to match the sail's heeling force. There should be some means of reducing leeway to an acceptable and useful level. This may be attained by deep rudders, as in the Viking boats and in English cobles, or by increasing draught so that the complete hull is acting as a foil to use the leeway to advantage. Most leeway occurs when sailing to windward so that the vessel with the best-trimmed, best-cut sail and cleanest, deep-draughted hull is going to complete the smartest passages where a mix of headwinds and freewinds are the norm in its trading area.

Few of the seals show vessels under sail, and even then little difference seems to exist between the twelfth and the end of the fourteenth centuries. Perhaps this is not surprising, since the major developments in weaving, sailmaking and ropemaking would have been made centuries before and many of their applications in a single square sail rig would have been long established.

The thirteenth-century Seal of Dublin realistically shows a baggy sail bulging between the seams joining the typical vertical cloths and the horizontal reinforcing bands sewn at the three lines of reef points, which are again a common feature of this period. Baggy sails, one suspects, would be the norm and indicate the inherent quality of the sail cloth. Bonnets are not in evidence during this period.

Standing and running rigging

It is in the hulls of these small cargo ships that clues are to be found to their success in growing away from the limitations of their origins in the Viking boats. With such a rig the fourteenth-century ship still has her mast stepped about the middle of the hull, as it had been by the Vikings. It was the best place for sail balance for this symmetrical hull form. Differing

The exaggeration of the thirteenth-century seal of Dublin emphasises the baggy nature of contemporary sail cloth, which required bands of reinforcement both vertically and horizontally. The seal also indicates three lines of reef points.

from that of the longships of the Bayeux Tapestry, the standing rigging shows no backstay but a forestay and a number of shrouds, often led well aft. Sometimes there is an indication of their fastening at the side of the hull in the form of a row of rings or perhaps holes, as was found in the Bremen cog of 1380.[21]

Unless sail is set, most yards are shown part hoisted with a furled sail. Since neither brails, buntlines nor footropes for the crew are ever illustrated, the conclusion must be that the sail is lowered to be furled from the deck. Seamen are shown straddling the yards in order to let go the gaskets, the ropes used to tie the furled sail, so it must be that sails were set from an already hoisted yard. The manner in which the crew sit astride the yard or crawl along suggests that they sometimes climbed on to a partly raised yard from the forecastle, to be hoisted with the sail. On the other hand some crew are shown climbing the rigging. In the fifteenth century Jacob's ladders and ratlines were in use. The yards were held to their masts by parrels which look similar to that found in the Oseberg Viking grave boat. No halliard is distinguishable from the shrouds, which are generally led well aft of the mast. Lifts to the yardarms, which would have made tensioning the luff of the square sail much more effective for close-hauled sailing, seem never to have been fitted. The seals would seem to show over-long yards, possibly as a result of the restrictions of the circular format. However, the Haverfordwest seal from 1291 shows the yard lowered, complete with furled sail, and it is shown overlapping the fore- and aftercastles,

which is quite unnecessary if the yard were not really of that length. If yards had been that long then the hulls would have been over-canvassed with a sail that was square, which returns one to the possibility, as in the Gokstad Viking boat, of the medieval sail's being rect-angular, the long side to the yard. With stretching sail material it would be more effi-cient to have a shorter, straighter luff when sailing to windward than a long, sagging luff with all the difficulty of being unable to set it properly. This problem was rediscovered in the sixteenth century, when large topsails were invented. The best solution came in the nine-teenth century with the development of finer and hence more weatherly hulls. The topsail was divided to give two shorter-luffed rect-angular sails capable of holding the desired flatter shape when sailing to windward. Such a slightly rectangular medieval single 'square' sail may have been the norm and would set perfectly well on other points of sailing. It is noticeable that the mainsails of the three-masted ships which were to develop in the fif-teenth and sixteenth centuries are all shown to be of this shape.

The control of the fourteenth-century square sail is by the usual sheet and tack and by braces to the yardarms. Bowsprits are in evi-dence on some of the seals, but very few indeed show the use of bowlines to them from the luffs of the sails. Bowlines were ropes fixed at one or two places along the sail's luff or leading edge. These were then led forward to the stem or the bowsprit. When the vessel was sailing close-hauled, the bowlines were tightened to try to reduce the luff's sag to leeward and its spoiling of the set and hence the efficiency of the sail. The use of bowlines was not widespread, it seems, though they are first identifiable in some of the pre-Viking Gotland Stones ship carvings.

Anchors and anchoring problems

Bowsprits may have been used for catting the anchor as in later drawings. Some seals show a hawse hole for the cable which indicates the increasing size of these ships.[22] Anchors are frequently shown swinging from the bows. This is what one might expect, since being ready to let go is prudent seamanship in con-fined coastal waters. They would have been a regular feature of ships seen by the seals' de-signers. The anchors are of the kind now known as a 'fisherman's anchor', looking rather like pick-axes in general outline. In the Bayeux Tapestry a similar anchor with a warp bent on to it is being carried up the beach after the longship has grounded. She has arrived on a

rising tide and is taking the precaution of set-ting the anchor further up so that she will not float away as the flood continues.

Two anchors found from the Viking period, one from the Ladby boat and the other from the Gokstad boat, are similar and both had wooden stocks. Somewhat similarly shaped an-chors continued to be used through to the present century, though wooden anchor stocks virtually disappeared during the last century in northern waters. The Ladby boat used chain next to her anchor, though how widespread this good practice was by the fourteenth cen-tury is not known. It was used by the Celtic Veneti seafarers, since Julius Caesar reported seeing it, but he does not state if its use was as a few fathoms between the anchors and the rope cable. An anchor and its short chain were found at Bulbury Camp, a Veneti hillfort in Dorset.[23] However, this is 1400 years earlier than the seals and it may be that rope was still preferred for its reliability compared with early chains, and the latter never found favour. Chain would be heavy to handle, even with the help of the windlasses with which a number of ships on the seals are seen to be fitted. There is no evidence for the use of chain from later pictures of ships in the following centuries. An-choring using only rope is an unpredictable procedure at best and requires a considerable scope of warp to be effective. The reliability of anchoring in the Middle Ages may have been of a low order. Perhaps this is reflected in the growth in the sizes of anchors following the end of this period, growth which is out of all proportion to the increase in the size of ships. It seems that a part of the technology of an-choring had been forgotten and awaited rediscovery.

Side rudders and stern rudders

The description given of rudders in the Treas-ury Accounts supports what is to be seen in the seals. Predominant is the side rudder, though little detail is given of how it is hung – except in the Winchelsea Seal of 1300, where a short horizontal clamp is fixed to the planking at some distance below the sheer. The rudder crosses it in a way that is not clear, so examina-tion of earlier wreck finds is needed to under-stand the arrangement. The shapes of the blades usually show the sudden widening at the

20. See Bibliography for C A Marchaj's works on this subject.

21. U Baykowski, *Hansekogge* (Kiel 1991), p60.

22. N E Upham, *Anchors*, Shire Album 110 (Aylesbury 1983), p11.

23. N E Upham, *Anchors*, p9.

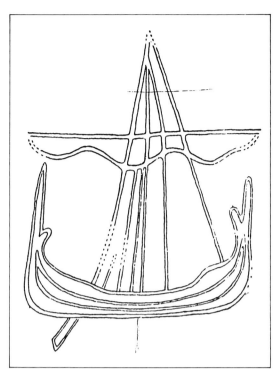

The boat carving on the Hedin Cross, Manghold Churchyard, Isle of Man. The deep side rudder is evident.

bottom seen in past rudder discoveries. Many of these seem to hang below keel level. On the Isle of Man, in Maughold Churchyard, there is an old gravestone on which is carved a full-length cross. To one side of it there is the only Manx representation of a Viking-style boat. Her side rudder is shown to protrude well below the keel. This carving on the Hedin Cross has been dated about 1250, though some think it earlier.[24]

At about that time stern rudders make their appearance on some of the seals, becoming more frequent into the next century. As suggested in the Accounts, the rounded sternposts are seen adapted to take the straight stern rudders by filling in that space between the curve of the sternpost and the near-vertical edge of the rudder with what is known as deadwood. The Accounts deal only with new building, but it is likely that existing vessels would have been converted to stern rudders as advantages be-

A small thirteenth-century Baltic coaster was discovered during harbour works at Kalmar, Sweden, in 1934. This reconstruction by Sam Manning shows the straight sternpost but curved stem that could produce noticeably different waterlines fore and aft. In a more extreme form this might well have caused enough imbalance in the hull to require a second sail – a possible impetus to the later development of multi-masted rigs. From The Evolution of the Wooden Ship *by Basil Greenhill and Sam Manning. (S F Manning)*

came evident. This would happen in the deep-hulled cargo vessels where the vulnerability and frailty of the side-rudder would be a constant anxiety. Having to lengthen the unsupported blade to match the increasing draught would exacerbate constructional problems. The greater draught may also have created a problem when steering, since the deep, swinging hulls would tend to blanket the side-rudders from the flow of water which gives them their power, soon after beginning to turn, whether to port or starboard.[25]

The Kalmar boat dating from the thirteenth century is an example of a medieval boat having a straight raking sternpost. The change to a straight, near-vertical sternpost was of immense importance to the development of large ships in the next century. This is not because of the ease with which a stern rudder could be

24. P M C Kermode, 'The Hedin Cross, Maughold, Isle of Man', in *Saga Book of the Viking Society for Northern Research*, Manx Folk Museum (1925), pp1–10.

25. See Marchaj's works in the Bibliography.

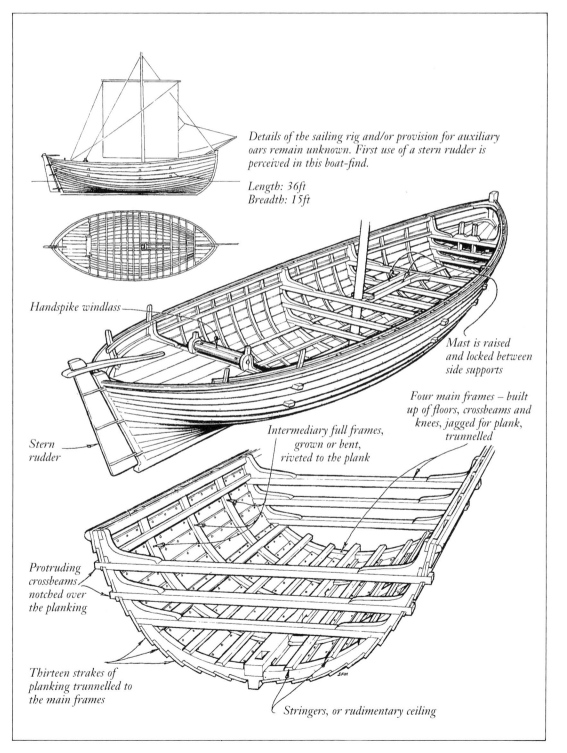

Details of the sailing rig and/or provision for auxiliary oars remain unknown. First use of a stern rudder is perceived in this boat-find.

Length: 36ft
Breadth: 15ft

Handspike windlass

Stern rudder

Mast is raised and locked between side supports

Four main frames – built up of floors, crossbeams and knees, jagged for plank, trunnelled

Intermediary full frames, grown or bent, riveted to the plank

Protruding crossbeams notched over the planking

Thirteen strakes of planking trunnelled to the main frames

Stringers, or rudimentary ceiling

hung, since builders of cogs had discovered that already: it is that the straight sternpost forced the shipwright to rethink the geometry of his strakes, which for over a thousand years had followed with little effort the sweeping curve of both ends of the hull. Cog builders had not faced this problem. The simple shapes, even in an advanced cog like that from Bremen, required little more than the bending of the hull's strakes. Establishing the run of the strakes to a straight sternpost in a round hull, which still retained a stem owing its curve to the Vikings, highlighted and solved the problems for those future shipwrights who would turn to a carvel planking technique.

From the departure of the Romans until the absorption of the straight sternpost into the developed Viking hull, no sea-going craft with different ends had been seen in north European waters. Even the cog was virtually the same at both ends. The adoption of the straight sternpost meant that vessels developed from the knaar tradition would, thanks to the new geometry of the strakes, have comparatively finer lines aft or at least below the waterline but would remain quite full-lined at the bows.

A full waterline forward and a slightly finer form aft, coupled with subtle changes in the distribution of hull volume, especially when heeled, may not have been noticeable in the standard cargo carrier with her mast amidships and a baggy sail. However, the combination would be a design time-bomb ticking away until larger traders were needed towards the end of the fourteenth century. Such unbalanced waterlines and volume distribution often show up as lee-helm when heeled; that is, the bow falls away from the wind, which is detrimental to manoeuvrability.[26] Early in the fifteenth century, for a brief period, ships with two masts, produced by the addition of a mizzen, are noted. If, as has been suggested elsewhere, the mizzen came into being as a balancing sail,[27] then lee helm is what it was countering. It had to be a fore-and-aft sail (*ie* a lateen) in order to be sheeted hard, down the centreline, to hold the bows up to the wind when close-hauled. This would hardly improve windward performance, as is often said, but merely ensure it.

Castles – defence and offence

A distinctive feature of medieval ships is their castles. A drawing in a church at Siljan, in the Telemark district of Norway, shows a ship with a sterncastle but more interesting is that the castle is built on to the sternpost from which swings a stern rudder. The image is dated to the mid 1200s, which is about the same as

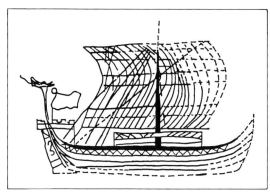

The ship from a mural in Siljan church – dated to the mid thirteenth century – shows a straight sternpost and rudder, with a sterncastle that is built on to the sternpost. The drawing also indicates some form of midships structure. (Vikingeskibshallen, Roskilde)

castles in the seals. The use or fitting of castles seen in the seals ranges from a single castle aft to a castle both forward and aft and also to an occasional castle at the masthead too. Their windage would have reduced windward sailing performance significantly, so they must have been important for defence and offence.

The English Galleys Accounts indicate that these were not necessarily fixed parts of the ship and could be added or removed as the exigencies of naval warfare demanded. The tactics for their use were devised during the thirteenth and fourteenth centuries, as was the concept of building above the sheer strake for whatever advantage. Even late into the fifteenth century the same tactics were employed by larger warships having protruding platforms built out from their high stems, instead of castles.[28]

In offence the aim would be to come from upwind and attack the enemy at right angles amidships. As is suggested by in a fifteenth-century French illustration of a sea battle in *Passages Outre-mer*, such a ramming tactic could split open the enemy's hull, sufficient to sink.[29] Even if this did not structurally damage the enemy ship, the warriors in the attacker's castle would be overlooking the main deck and be able to maim and kill those below them with fair impunity, before swinging their ship alongside to complete their attack. In defence, a ship about to be attacked would turn her stern to the enemy and retain the height advantage of her aftercastle. Defenders would be able to return fire and deter the attackers. Those on the deck would have some shelter to handle the ship and the chance to turn at the last second on to a course which would put them to weather of the attacker with a chance to sail away. With an understanding of such tactics it may be correct to think that those

seals showing ships with two castles and an embryo fighting top were in the king's service, while those with a single aftercastle were merchant vessels.

Clinker planking and other details

Both the Accounts and seals confirm the ubiquity of clinker planking for boat- and ship-building in northern Europe. The seals show the lands of the strakes and their curvature at the stem- and sternposts. Many have an almost brick-wall appearance due to the seals' designers trying to indicate the scarph joints between the many short lengths of planking which made up each strake. They must have been a prominent feature of medieval ships for them to be drawn on the seal. This has been found to be so in the parts of medieval wrecks which have been recovered. It may be recalled that in the Accounts, boards 12ft long were bought for the hull planking and in the seals this is demonstrated. In a vessel, say, 60ft long there might be five to six planks in most of her strakes, and indeed this is what is to be seen in the Seal of Dover and others. The Seal of La Rochelle even shows the pattern of nailing employed to join the scarphs. In just a few of the seals the clinker nailing is indicated, as are the heads of the treenails which fasten the strakes to the frames. All of this structure has been confirmed in recovered boat remains.

Beams and the development of the weather deck

The method used in northern Europe about AD 1000 by which beams were fitted into large boats is well known from wreck discoveries. Due to the boat hulls being shallow, the beams inevitably were sited at or very near the waterline, even in the largest of the wrecks discovered, except for a raised deck forward and aft. As described earlier, natural crooks of timber known as knees made the ends secure and spread the destructive strains. The fact that these techniques continue to be used to the present day, admittedly in a modified form, strongly suggests the continuation and survival of Viking methods of fastening the beams throughout the Middle Ages.

26. A Turner, 'A Law of Hydrostatics and its influence on the shapes of sailing yachts', *Transactions of the Institution of Naval Architects* 79 (1937), pp207–240.

27. A Moore, 'Rig in Northern Europe', *The Mariner's Mirror* 42/1 (1956), pp6–37.

28. F Howard, *Sailing Ships of War, 1400–1860* (London 1979), p14.

29. C Villain-Gandossi, 'Navires du Moyen-age', *Archaeologia* 114 (Jan 1978), p23 and lower illustration.

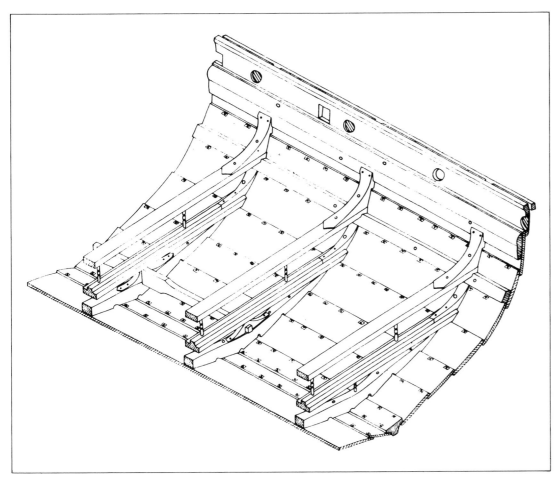

Reconstructed cross section near amidships showing the structure of Skuldelev 5, the 'longship'. (By courtesy of Basil Greenhill)

The through-beam may be seen as an attempt to improve on the Viking type of beam. The latter had to be fastened to the hull planking. Strains which tried to spread out the hull were produced a thousand, thousand times during a rough passage when it was momentarily supported by its ends on two waves. These stresses acted to pull the fastenings, mostly treenails, through the planking. Wear and tear, and the resulting need for repair, would be a recurring problem. When the hull was lifting a similar number of times on a single wave, the beams would be attempting to push through the sides, but the support given by the knees would distribute the load. By hooking the beam end through and over the planking, in conjunction with the usual assembly of knees, much of the stress problem was solved well enough so that no other solution needed to be devised. Neither method led to the invention of a clamp or beam shelf, which would have revolutionised the solid fixing of beams within hulls without localised loading of the planking. Clinker planking, by definition a shell-first hull-building technology, would not encourage its development. The clamp or beam shelf probably had to wait for north European carvel planking techniques, where building would begin by assembling most of the framework of the hull. Beams fitted that way spread their loading via knees to the rest of the framework and only indirectly and slightly into the planking.

From boat to ship

From the eleventh to the fourteenth centuries the original concept of the Viking boat advanced a long way, due mainly to the vast and ever increasing demands of international trade during the high Middle Ages. Merchants required craft of greater volume for their growing quantities of valuable goods. Boatbuilders met this demand by increasing the depth of their hulls, as we have seen depicted in the seals. Increased depth led to greater draught, which saw the gradual demise of the side rudder as it was replaced by the stern rudder. Vertical or raked sternposts replaced the high curving Viking form and gave the boatbuilder

Other methods were developed, as can be seen in the Galtaback wreck from the twelfth century or the Kalmar I wreck. In these there are lower beams fastened in the Viking manner. However, the upper beams, which would be at deck level, protrude through the planking. Slots are cut near the ends of the beams and corresponding slots in the planking locate the beams precisely so that no movement is possible. Knees are also used to spread the beam's load. Such beam-fitting techniques are only to be found in boats which have deep hulls and consequently far more freeboard than any Viking boat ever had. Such beam ends therefore are clear of the water and are only immersed if the hull is well heeled while sailing in a fresh breeze. It is known that moss was used to caulk the joint between the beam slot and the planking.[30]

As early as the twelfth century, beam ends were being drawn on views of boats. In a French miniature painted for a Norman book three beam ends are to be seen in a descendant of the kind of boat William used to invade England. Scarphing details and other features already discussed are well illustrated. Beam ends were to be seen in some of the boats of the two types that dominated northern waters, that is the keel, the nef of Viking ancestry, and the

cog, which had developed on the Frisian coast, from the end of the twelfth century onwards. Many of the medieval seals exhibit from three to five small squares or rectangles on the hull about midway or more up the topsides, equally spaced and parallel to the sheer. Often one beam is placed just ahead of the mast. Some, like the Seal of Rye, have what appear to be truncated triangles instead of squares to show the ends of the through-beams. These are also to be seen on two fourteenth-century cogs shown fighting in a miniature from the Smithfield Decretals.[31] Archaeology solved this puzzle when, in one boat-find with through-beams, it was seen that the beams had smooth deflecting chocks fitted ahead of their protruding ends so that they could not be snagged and damaged in contact with other boats or harbour walls. The through-beam suggests the development within the high-sided hulls of a deck supported by these beams well above the level of the sea. Such a deck can be made watertight, a weather deck, and designed to drain over the side. Its adoption leads on to the concept of total watertight integrity for a hull, which is a profound step in the design of a seaworthy ship. During the late thirteenth century, ships built to such a standard would have been increasingly common.

30. U Baykowski, *Hansekogge* (Kiel 1991), pp34–35.

31. Fighting cogs miniature from Smithfield Decretals, British Library, Royal Ms E 10, IV, fig, reproduced below, page 51.

A close-up of the ship in the Skamstrup Church mural with the curved tiller. Note also that the yard is secured to the mast by a parrel and the sail has two rows of reef points. (By courtesy of Richard Unger)

experience in developing a new run to his strakes. The different ends to the hull may well have caused the first attempts in northern European waters to balance a ship with more sail. Good draught led to better stability in rough weather, which showed the need for more freeboard to improve seakeeping qualities. The main deck was now well above the waterline. Changing it to a proper weather deck was the final step towards producing the seaworthy medieval ship. Now all spray and wave crests breaking aboard would drain to the sea instead of over the cargo and into the bilges to menace the safety of the ship. Piracy and war inspired the construction of castles and paved the way to building up the topsides fore and aft into useful permanent structures by the fifteenth century.

Trade routes

Grain, salt, wool, wine, metals, hides and cloth were the basic bulk cargoes and the backbone of seaborne trade for those cargo boats which were gradually distancing themselves from their Norse Viking origins. It is fortuitous that the estuaries of those major rivers which drain vast European and Baltic hinterlands form identifiable and accessible havens, since the medieval cargo ship depended on both for safe arrival and secure anchorage in the quieter reaches. All movement at sea depended either on pilotage or on dead-reckoning. Until nearly the end of the thirteenth century, after which steering compasses were in use, courses sailed would depend on the skipper's mental chart based on experience.[32]

The shorter of the major inter-estuarine trade routes was that between the River Thames and the Schelde of the Low Countries, where the great Rhine and Maas reach the sea. The principal trading centres were London and Bruges. Throughout the late medieval

32. S McGrail, *Ancient Boats in NW Europe* (London 1987), pp275–285.

A later interpretation of the boat race between St Olaf and his brother, in Høgby Church. The positions of the crew imply a weather deck and the aftercastles of the ships are an integral part of the structure – an anticipation of the later quarterdeck. The ships have a straight sternpost and centreline rudder, but a rounded stem. (Vikingeskibshallen, Roskilde)

period Flanders had an almost insatiable demand for wool, since it was the major cloth producer in northern Europe. England was one of its main sources of wool and an importer of cloth.

The 120 miles or so from the Thames estuary to a Flemish port would often have let the medieval cargo boat enjoy a free wind. After the coast of Flanders had been found in the early morning of the second day at sea it would be followed eastwards on the rising tide and into the mouth of the estuary by the evening. Continuously changing weather patterns would let the return passage for the Thames be a direct course, and a landfall anywhere between North Foreland and Orford Ness would be acceptable.

Coasting would be the method from the Low Countries to Scandinavia and the Baltic Sea. This tended to be (though not exclusively) in the hands of the Frisians, who preferred to use their own craft, from which developed the cog. From the nature of those coasts pilotage would be the technique for reaching destinations. In the Baltic, Visby, the port for Gotland and strategically placed on many of the routes crossing the sea in all directions, had dominated the trade in the area in the days before the formation of the powerful league of north German towns called the Hanse. Visby's multistorey warehouses, now a long way from the harbour and used as museums, date from those heady days, as does the wall enclosing the medieval harbour and town. Early trade in the Baltic involved the movement southwards of skins, furs, amber, wax, and salted and dried fish. Northwards went pottery, glass, salt and cloth. As large centres of population developed in northwest Europe, the hinterlands to the east of the Baltic became very important grain exporters, while the major return cargo was salt. The Germans who had settled along the southern Baltic and established the Hanseatic League sought to control trade, but the eastern Baltic ports were happy to trade using whatever vessels were available. Those returning with salt would have sailed northwards in the Bay of Biscay from the extremely important sea-salt pans on the French Atlantic coast. Whatever the weather, Ushant, with all its outlying dangers, had to be found and rounded to enter the English Channel; then the course was eastwards, working the tides if winds were light, avoiding the many major headlands on both coasts in poor visibility and darkness; then

A very late survivor of the Viking tradition is the Hebridean galley. The carving of the galley in St Clement's Kirk, Rodel, Isle of Harris is dated to 1528.

finding the clearest way through the Straits and out into the North Sea for an offshore passage to the north of Denmark, with a little coasting through the Skagerrak and Kattegat before the final leg across the Baltic to the eastern and southern shores. This was a summer trade because of the winter ice in the Baltic. It is unlikely that any vessel would complete more than a very few round trips per year. Similar sized cargo ships of the nineteenth century only managed at best 35 per cent of their time at sea.[33] In the Middle Ages the figure was surely no higher. Other materials shipped over long distances would include iron from the Basque country in northern Spain to western Europe; tin from Cornwall to the Low Countries to be alloyed with lead to make pewter; and copper from central European mines to England, which did not produce enough for itself until the sixteenth century.

The shipping of wine was important, both from the growing regions of the Rhineland and from the Duchy of Gascony, lost by the English in 1452. It was a major source of wine for England and Wales, the ports of export being Bayonne and Bordeaux on the estuaries of the Adour and the Garonne, which imported wool, cloth and grain from England together with dried herring, coarse woollen cloth and

hides from Wales. Bristol, on the Severn estuary, was a major port for the wine trade, but declined after 1452, the merchants having to turn to Iberian wines.

Voyages along the Atlantic seaboard of Europe and the British Isles were commonplace, as is shown by the English, who, in 1405 while trying to annex Wales, supplied wine by sea to their invading armies and the garrisons of their subjugating castles sited on Welsh estuaries. Similarly, wine was being landed directly in Wales from France for the French soldiers who were helping the Welsh Prince Owain Glyndwr in his war against the English King Henry IV.[34]

Voyages taking many days from near the Spanish border would require the sighting of Ushant, the Isles of Scilly and the Irish coast off Tuskar Rock in order to find the Irish Sea. Alternatively, laying-off a course for the middle of the Irish coast somewhere between the Fastnet Rock and Carnsore Point, making a recognisable landfall and turning east might

---

33. O T P Roberts, 'The Sloop *Darling* of Beaumaris, 1781 to 1893', *Cymru A'r Mor/Maritime Wales* 7 (Caernarfon 1983), pp5–21.

34. K Lloyd Gruffydd, 'Wales' Maritime Trade in Wine during the Late Middle Ages', *Cymru A'r Mor/Maritime Wales* 15 (Caernarfon 1992), pp7–42.

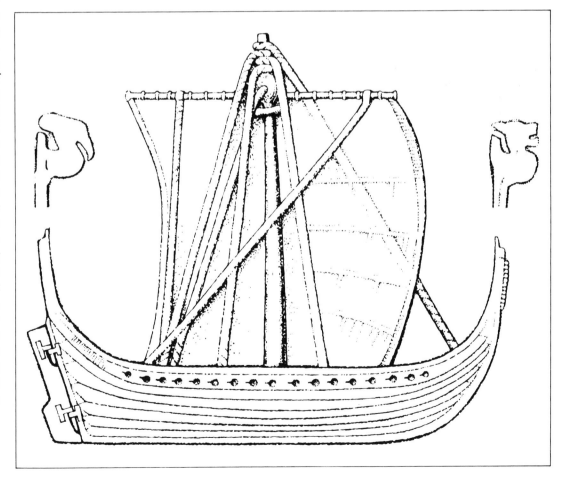

have been thought satisfactory. These methods may seem improbable in the twentieth century as a basis for conducting trade, but skills were being improved steadily. Ships from Chepstow, which carried on an illicit trade with Iceland in the 1430s, traded wine for salted fish. Such a journey is as hazardous as any noted above. It has been estimated that over a thousand ships were involved annually in the wine trade and that nearly a fifth of those hailed from Wales and England.

The long trading routes established by their crews show a determined and successful use of their ships. Not only were there natural hazards to overcome, but piracy and war were permanent additions to the perils of the sea. The wide-ranging medieval trade routes of the north European sailor, including the deep sea voyaging along the eastern fringes of the Atlantic ocean, suggest competence and knowledge the equal of any found south of the Bay of Biscay.

Conclusion

It should not be thought that the application of the two- and three-masted rigs during the fifteenth century saw the immediate disappearance of the widespread fleet of single-masted and square-sail rigged vessels having a common ancestry in the old Norse Viking technology. On the contrary, they were spread like confetti throughout the ports of Europe and along the high seas, going about their business as earnestly as ever. In them were to be found all the improvements of the last four hundred years that had changed the Viking boat into a ship of the Middle Ages and without which the hull and rig developments of the fifteenth century would have been delayed. Perhaps no more vessels of any size would be built with one mast, and in any case carvel planking, with all its advantages for big-ship building, was waiting to take over. In the local coasting scene the demise of the old rig was to take a long time, and it probably dropped out of fashion only as new, small coasters – still clinker-built – adopted the newer rigs, like the spritsail. The single square-sail rig never faded completely in north European waters, continuing to be found in isolated areas. A carving of a sailing galley in St Clement's Kirk, Isle of Harris, shows in effect a Viking longship with a

Perhaps the longest lasting example of the single-masted square rig, appropriately, is in Norwegian waters, where the jekta *operated as a sailing coaster until relatively recently. From* Inshore Craft of Norway, *edited by Arne Emil Christensen.*

stern rudder. It is similar to the Danish Skamstrup Church mural from the fourteenth century, but the Hebridean galley dates from 1528. An engraving from the eighteenth century shows coasters with single square sails beached in a North Wales river. The Humber keels operated successfully into this century on the Yorkshire coast under the same rig. Other examples, by now unique, are to be found from

the Bay of Biscay to the Baltic Sea. One of the longest enduring uses was on the Scandinavian coasts, especially in Norway, where that country's coastal trade was carried on well into living memory in a variety of craft like the single-square-sailed *jekta*, a clinker-planked, transom-sterned coaster some 20m in length.

Owain T P Roberts

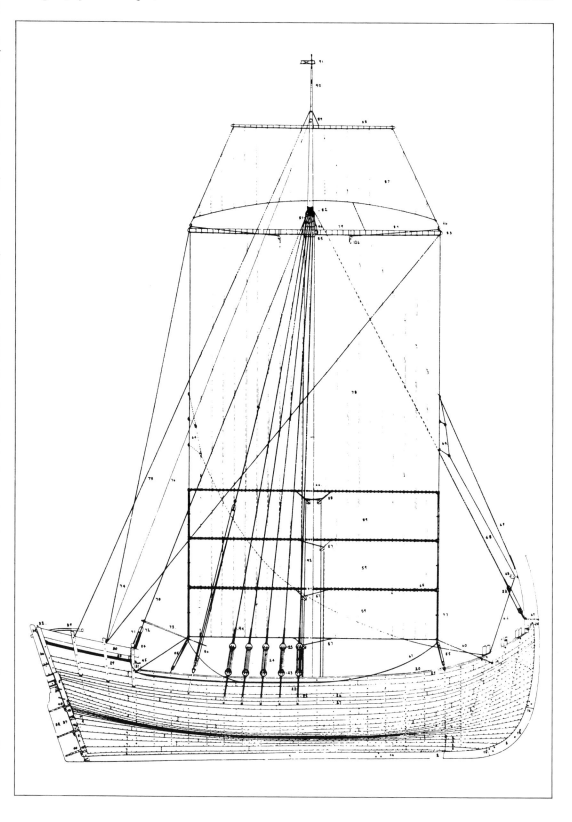

2

The Cog as Cargo Carrier

DURING dredging operations in the river Weser some two kilometres downstream of the medieval city of Bremen in October 1962, the wreck of a 24m long wooden hull emerged from the muddy water at low tide. While other ship finds have just been named after their place of excavation and connected with a general term for the ship, such as the Nydam boat in Denmark, Utrecht ship in the Netherlands or the Gokstad Viking ship in Norway, the Bremen discovery from the very beginning of its excavation was given the name of a very specific type of ship: the cog of Bremen. How could the excavator, Dr Siegfried Fliedner, head of the medieval and maritime departments of the Museum for the History of Bremen, be sure his wreck was that of a cog and not of any other type of ship?

The term 'cog' only appears in written sources for ships of the Hanseatic League from

The wreck of the Hanseatic cog from 1380, as uncovered in the river Weser near Bremen in October 1962. The remains, which had been quickly covered by silt after the ship was lost, were relatively well preserved. (Deutsches Schiffahrtsmuseum)

about AD 1200, but in the course of the fifteenth century this type of ship disappeared so completely from the sea that nobody after the Middle Ages knew precisely what a cog looked like. In Hanseatic towns around 1900 people just knew the term, but used it for any wooden sailing vessel more than a century old. Books of that period dealing with maritime history depicted cogs as three-masted ships like Columbus' *Santa Maria*. In the twentieth century, Hanseatic historians like Walter Vogel and Paul Heinsius (see Bibliography) discovered that a cog had just one mast like the Viking ships, but those historians had difficulty distinguishing cogs from Viking vessels.

For a profile view of a fourteenth-century cog, Siegfried Fliedner was the first to reach firm ground. Just like several other Hanseatic seaports in the Baltic, the town of Stralsund showed a very specific type of ship on its town seal, the last edition of which had been cut in 1329 and used down to the nineteenth century. Fliedner found out that Stralsunders themselves called the seal 'the cog' (*'unser Stad Siegel ghenomed den kogghen'*) in 1483 and also later,

The ship depicted on the Stralsund seal of 1329 is described as a cog in historical sources. It shows the main features of a relatively short hull, straight stem and sternpost, centreline rudder, and light superstructure fore and aft. The rig is a single square sail, but there is also a bowsprit-like spar forward, which may have been used to improve purchase to the bowlines for the square sail. (Uncredited illustrations by courtesy of the author)

the name coming from the type of ship depicted on it. The seal shows the cog with a high, box-like hull, clinker-built with straight and steep stem- and sternposts, a centreline rudder with tiller, fore and aft castles, one mast and one square sail. In a second step, Fliedner compared the ship on the seal with the wreck he was going to excavate and, with the exception of the rigging and the forecastle, which were missing, found all those details exactly as depicted on the seal. In addition to that, Fliedner saw five crossbeams with their heads protruding through the planking of the Bremen hull. This very construction feature can be seen in other cogs of the Stralsund shape depicted on seals of other Hanseatic towns, such as Damme and Harderwijk. There was, and is, no doubt that the Bremen wreck was that of a fourteenth-century cog. As dendrochronologists established later, the oak trees for the crossbeams, planking and other straight parts of the hull had been cut in the autumn of 1378. That discovery was a welcome confirmation of the date Fliedner had developed by comparing the seals with the real ship.

Fliedner really had been very lucky, since 'his' wreck was so very well preserved. When the cog capsized, her starboard side sank into the mud so that it remained nearly complete, including the keel and the stem- and sternposts. The iron gudgeons for the missing stern rudder are nailed to the sternpost. Even the traces of the roof shingles between the castle deck and the upper part of the hull of the Bremen cog were comparable to the roof shingles of the cog on the Stralsund seal. Apparently no one had understood this detail in the seal before the actual remains had been found on the Bremen cog. Fliedner, then, had no methodological problems comparing a nearly complete hull with a complete picture of the same type of ship. He just had to transfer the iconographic definition of the cog from the picture to the real vessel.

The third step in establishing a solid base for the collection of more knowledge of the

cog was taken in the Deutsches Schiffahrtsmuseum, to which the Bremen cog had been handed over as an inaugural gift when the German national maritime museum had been founded at Bremerhaven in 1971. To establish an archaeological definition of the 'cog' type the museum staff examined all constructional details, not just those visible in the pictures on the town seals. The aim was to find those criteria which might enable archaeologists to identify as such even small and decayed fragments of cogs.

Boats and ships are constructed following the principles developed in different boatbuilding traditions. These traditions differ from one another in the shapes of boats and ships as well as in the way of joining their different members. For example, Viking ships with their elegantly curved lines differ significantly in shape from the box-like contours of cogs, but they also differ in the way the planks are joined. Whereas the thin planks of Viking ships are fastened together by iron rivets, the points of which are hammered flat over lozenge-shaped roves, the thick planks of cogs are kept together by iron nails, the points of which are bent twice. With Viking ships, the caulking material is just hammered into long grooves running along the strakes, whereas the caulking of cogs is kept in position by flat iron caulking clamps. As a result of research on the traditions, archaeologists are now able to differentiate the remains of Viking ships from those of cogs even when no timber has been preserved, just by the different iron fastenings used in the clinker seams.

Using the cog nails as a guide, two very interesting facts emerge. First, the Bremen cog

was not the first cog to be excavated; she was only the first one to be identified as a cog. For example, Wreck V from the old harbour of Kalmar in Sweden, excavated in 1933–34, was also a cog. Second, in northern Germany in different coastal and inland waters small fishing boats of cog construction are still in use. This observation fits very well with what is known from Viking ships. The big Viking ships vanished from northern European waters toward the end of the Middle Ages, but small boats constructed using the principal characteristics of Viking ships are still being built and used at many places along the North Sea and Baltic. The same is the case with the cog. The big Hanseatic cog-type cargo vessels did not survive the middle of the fifteenth century, whereas small boats built using the same principles as the cogs in northern Germany are still being used for fishing today. All of these boats have flat, flush-laid bottoms, steep clinker-built sides and straight stem- and sternposts, and in most cases the nails in the clinker seams are re-bent with their points into the timber.

Logboat origins of the cog

Having reached this state of knowledge, the next step was to look for the most primitive cog-like boat among excavated and recent boats. The simplest find was a type of logboat, and it fitted the definition of the cog by shape. This boat had a flat bottom, steep sides (not clinker-built of course, since the vessel was carved in one piece) and pointed ends which appear in side view like straight stem and stern posts. As the root end of the log served as the bow, the boat was wider here than at the stern.

The various shipbuilding traditions can be distinguished by the seams:
A Hulk-shaped boat find from Antwerp
B Barge
C Clinker seams with short, smooth iron nails (ship find from Antwerp)
D Clinker seams with curved iron nails (cog)
E Clinker seams with iron rivets (Viking ship)
F Clinker seams concealed (Chiemsee-Plätte of 1964)
G Flush seams with curved iron nails (Romano-Celtic)
H Flush seams with wooden dowels (from the late Middle Ages)
I Flush seams with dowel plug

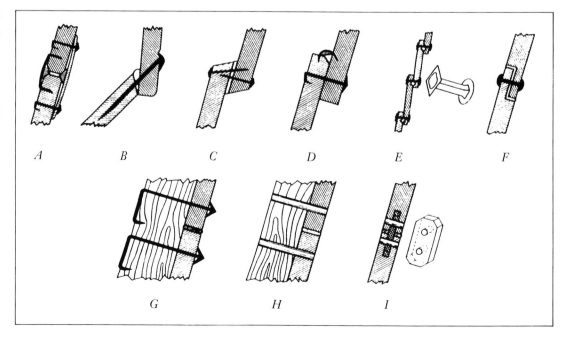

A reconstructed midship section of a cog displayed in the Deutsches Schiffahrtsmuseum, showing both shape and principal structural features – flat floors, clinker external planking and through-beams. The carrying capacity of the type compared with its boat-like predecessors is evident. (By courtesy of Basil Greenhill)

Logboats of this type have been excavated in Schleswig-Holstein, but are not yet dated. In some Danish islands this type had survived until about AD 1900. The interior of most of these boats was divided into three compartments by two bulkheads left there from the solid wood during the process of carving.

When there was a lack of large trees, people tried to build their boats in the shape of the old logboats but out of at least three single planks, one shaped like a lancet with two pointed ends serving as the flat bottom. The two others were nailed alongside the flat bottom at a distinct angle and met at both ends where stem- and sternposts strengthened the construction. Knee-shaped ribs ran across the flat bottom, with one arm supporting one or the other side alternately. This type of construction is represented in the Deutsches Schiffahrtsmuseum by the *Julle* from the Grosses Meer near Aurich, Ostrfriesland, where it had been used for duck hunting up to 1975.

Another unusual member of this family of boats is still used as a fishing boat in the Untertrave, downstream from Lübeck. To understand its construction, imagine what could be done with a logboat in order to increase its size: that is, how could the boat be made broader than the tree trunk from which is was carved? The people near Lübeck split the log lengthwise, put one bottom plank in between and fastened these three parts together by nailing bottom timbers across them. Thus they had a flush-laid bottom of shell construction. But they were then faced with a difficult problem: at both ends there were gaps as wide as the added bottom plank, which they had to close. They managed to do this by inserting the two ends of another logboat, the so-called 'blocks', and that gave the type its name, *Blockkahn*. These blocks gave the wider boat the same shape as the logboat with which the builders had started. However, in order to strengthen

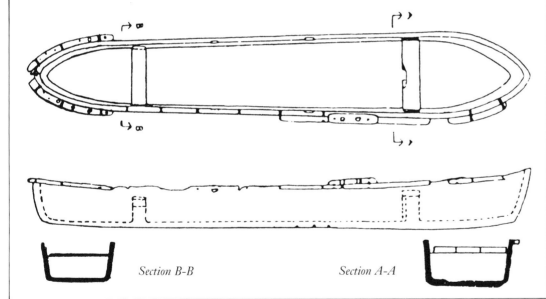

Section B-B   *Section A-A*

Middle: A cog-shaped dug out from Hasselo, Denmark, anticipating the later type in its flat bottom, steeply flared sides and raked stem and stern.

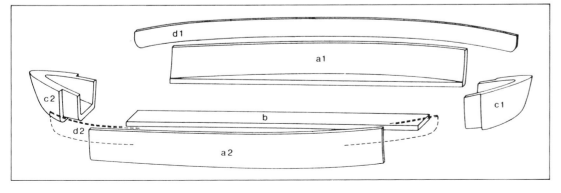

Bottom: Exploded drawing of a cog-shaped Blockkahn *from Gotmmund bei Lübeck, built in 1940. The name derived from the block stem and stern pieces.*

the construction and to get higher sides they fastened washstrakes, using clinker techniques, to the top of the sides of the boat, using iron nails which they hammered in from the outside and bent twice on the inside in order to force the points into the timber again. In the place of ribs they used bulkheads which they inserted into the complete shell to make it stiffer.

In Lake Steinhude, north of Hanover, people used another variation of this construction technique to produce a boat for fishing as well as for peat and hay transport. In trying to widen a logboat by the same method they found another way of filling the gaps at both ends. Instead of parts of another logboat they used a big solid log, triangular in cross-section, for the stempost, and at the aft end they inserted a broad transom. The other construction details are similar to those of the *Blockkahn*: there are only differences in shape. As Lake Steinhude is rather shallow, the people cut their logboats from the upper part of horizontal logs, resulting in tapering of the sides to the inside which gave the boats a trapezoidal cross-section with the widest part at the bottom. They wanted to have the underwater part of the boat as wide as possible in order to get a shallow draught. An undated logboat of this shape has been found in that lake, and the planked boat clearly follows, in all details, the shape of this type of logboat with the sides still tapering inward. Even the one solid bulkhead left in, lying across the middle of the logboat, is copied in the planked boat by an inserted piece of timber, serving as the only transverse member in a boat that, in spite of being 9m (30ft) long, has no ribs.

The ethnographical observations on cog-shaped boats of the late nineteenth and twentieth centuries are very helpful for the interpretation of medieval sources, which are not comprehensible in isolation. There are strong indications that the total design of cog-shaped boats developed from cog-shaped logboats. Unfortunately the excavated logboats of that shape are not dated, so we cannot prove them to be older than the oldest, more elaborate version of a cog-shaped boat. But the very sophisticated construction of the *Blockkahn*, with the stem and stern made like the ends of a logboat, is mentioned in a Hamburg customs document of about AD 1260 where the term *kanebloke* appears. In the medieval port of the city of Bremen the lower part of the stern portion of a cog from the early thirteenth century was excavated in 1992. The base of that cog is a logboat, on top of which additional strakes were added. The lowest part of the stempost is carved from the solid log and an iron gudgeon is nailed to it. All of these observations provide strong support for the hypothesis that the cog-type was developed from a cog-shaped logboat, traces of which are found in medieval vessels of this shipbuilding tradition, as well as in those of the nineteenth and twentieth centuries.

In Lake Steinhude, north of Hanover, fishermen use a very special steering oar in their cog-shaped boat of the *Kahn* type. The oar is called a *firrer* and is shaped like a spade with a handle in the form of a T. It has no tiller and cannot be turned. The sails are set in such a way that the *Kahn* will head into the wind when the *firrer* is raised. If the helmsman lowers the *firrer* deep into the water on the leeward side he shifts the centre of gravity astern; thus the bow of the boat turns off the wind to leeward.

To sail a straight course the helmsman only has to hold the *firrer* midway, the exact position depending on the strength and direction of the wind.

In the early Middle Ages all cogs were clearly equipped with this steering system. The oldest example is the original *firrer* from the seventh-century cog building yard on the Wurt Hessens in the modern city of Wilhelmshaven, Low Saxony. The next evidence is that of the Hedeby coins from the early ninth century, showing a cog with the blade of the *firrer*, in some cases deep in the water underneath the hull, and in other cases out of the water aft of the ship. As the coins give both extreme positions of the *firrer* it seems certain that this very type of steering oar and no other is meant by the coinmaker. On these coins the cog has a rectangular sail, much broader than it is high, stretched between the top yard and the lower boom. For steering using the *firrer*, the sail has to be set in such a way that there is sufficient side pressure on the ship, and it was impossible

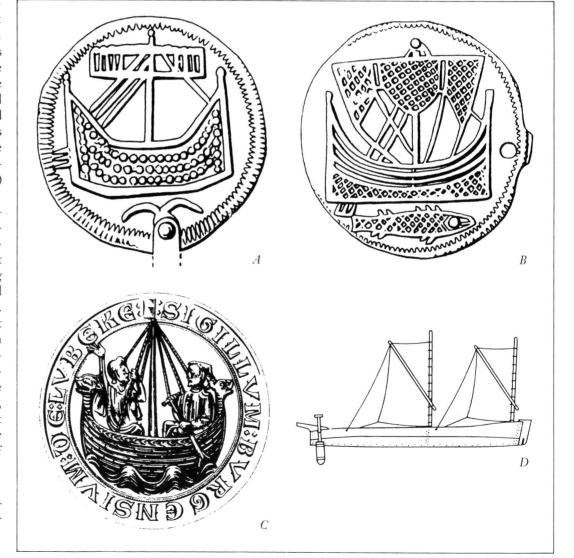

Cogs and related vessels with firrer *type side rudders:*
A   *Early ninth-century coin from Haithabu, Schleswig.*
B   *Early ninth-century coin from Haithabu, Schleswig.*
C   *Lübeck town seal from 1280.*
D   Kahn *from Lake Steinhude.*

The hull of the Bremen cog as reconstructed by the Bremerhaven museum, shortly before undergoing conservation by total immersion in 1981. (Deutsches Schiffahrtsmuseum)

to achieve that with a single square sail. In fact, on early cogs it was not the centre of the yard which was fixed to the mast; rather, the majority of the yard must have been aft of the mast. Therefore, it was not a typical square sail at all, but in reality a lug sail; it needed the lower boom. This lug sail along with the *firrer* formed a functional unit. Without the ethnographic observations of the twentieth-century *firrer* on the *kahn* of Lake Steinhude, no one could have identified the *firrer* from the Wurt Hessens or the unit of *firrer* and lug sail on the Hedeby coins.

The number of excavated cog wrecks or even typical fragments of cogs has increased dramatically. Finds have come from the east side of the Ijsselmeer, from Hanseatic ports in Germany including Bremen, Lübeck, and Rostock, and from Danish waters to the east coast of Sweden. Most of the finds have been dated to the thirteenth or fourteenth centuries. The Bremen cog find of 1962 has proven to be the key to opening several new approaches to the

development of that specific type of ship. As a result, a vast amount of new archaeological and ethnographical material has become available. Armed with this information, the images of medieval ships prove to be more reliable than previously thought, even down to the smallest details, although the proportions were obviously distorted to fit artistic forms. Last but not least, as a good knowledge of cogs themselves has been acquired, even written sources appear in a new light. In short, a completely new history of the cog now needs to be written.

The early history of the cog

The earliest evidence for this type of ship is a cog-shaped pre-Roman clay model from the Iron Age. With a flat bottom, steep sides, pointed ends and clearly elaborated, steep stem- and sternposts, without any doubt it depicts a cog. It appears almost as clumsy as cogs do on Hanseatic town seals, but without rigging. The high sides, stem- and sternposts and length:breadth ratio of 1.9:1 are details not of a

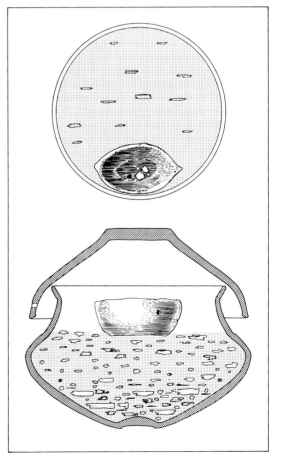

Cog-shaped clay model from an urn at Leese, Nienburg, c200 BC.

logboat but of a boat constructed from several different pieces of timber as a rivercraft which would have been punted upstream and floated downstream. The model was found in 1978 at Leese, very near to the bank of the middle Weser, south of Nienburg, in the urn of a cremation grave. It lay on top of the cremated bones of a man who had died at something between thirty and fifty years of age. The chieftains of that Iron Age port on the Weser were buried in bronze buckets, imported from Celtic tribes further south, while the rest of the population was buried in pottery urns. Among these, the man with the cog model was the only one to whom something very special had been dedicated. He was very likely the skipper of a cog-shaped river boat in which he carried the bronze buckets and other goods from the Celts from the upper part of the river Werra and brought them to his chieftain. At first glance this earliest information on a cog skipper seems to be very isolated, but there are fragments of two other clay models in the shape of cogs: one from Waltrop, a settlement of the late pre-Roman and early Roman Iron Age near the river Lippe, a tributary to the lower Rhine; and the other from Beckeln, southeast of Bremen, supposed to be of the Roman Iron Age. Above all, native-built Roman boats from the Netherlands, though not in cog shape, tell us that most of the shipbuilding techniques used in later cogs were already known in that area and period. To sum up, cog-shaped inland boats seem to have been the regional type of boat from the lower Rhine valley to the valley of the middle and lower Weser, from the pre-Roman Iron Age up to the present, as boats of the cog family are still used in some lakes of that area. As the first evidence for this kind of boat looks like a planked craft, the cog-shaped logboat from which it had been developed obviously

Roman trading ship carved on an ox bone by a German in the Lower Weser area; early fifth century.

has to be older, but it is impossible to judge how old it might be.

As all the rivers of that area flow into the North Sea, cog-shaped boats may well have been used along the southern coast of that arm of the ocean. It appears, though, that they were not used in long-term trade in the Roman Iron Age. There is strong evidence that this trade was carried on by Roman merchants in Roman sailing vessels of Mediterranean construction from the estuary of the Rhine as far as Scandinavia and the Baltic. In the fifth century, when the western part of the Roman Empire collapsed, there were no longer any Roman merchants to carry on this trade with their own ships. The breakdown of Roman trade created opportunities for the Frisians, who filled the gap by using their coastal cogs to carry Mediterranean and Merovingian products from the Rhine along their shores to southern Scandinavia, that is to the southern part of Jutland.

In contrast to their Roman colleagues, the Frisian merchants of the fifth to seventh centuries did not live in towns but in farms spread around their coastal region. One of these Frisians had his farm in the lowlands on top of an artificial hill, the Wurt Hessens, in the present navy port of Wilhelmshaven. The basis of his enterprise were his sheep, of which he kept two different breeds. From their wool a great variety of high quality Frisian cloth was woven on the farm, and the cloth became the capital base for his bartering. In the seventh century he made a slipway to repair his old cog or to build a new one for his sailing tours along the coast. The slipway and a steering oar of the *firrer* type have been excavated on the site, which suggests that the cog had a flat bottom of more than 2m (6.5ft) in width and a lug sail as counterpart to the *firrer*.

Frisians, by trading with the harbour communities in the former Roman Empire, learned to live in towns where the basis for the economy was trade and they, too, learned to use coins in their trade. At the Frankish-Frisian border in the seventh century they founded their first harbour town, named Dorestad, near Utrecht, and started to strike coins for their trade. In the middle of the eighth century their trade reached the Baltic near present-day Schleswig, where at Hedeby they founded their first trading colony on the Baltic as a bridgehead for their trade deep into that sea.

Several years later Charlemagne (768–814) incorporated Friesland into his empire and shortly before 800 started to issue coins at Dorestad which show a banana-shaped sailing vessel. This ship could be identified as a *hulk*, the outstanding type of ship in traffic between the Continent and England. The cross in the mast top corresponded to the market crosses in the ports of the Frankish empire and England to make it visible to everybody that ships and ports wanted to have peaceful trade. The Frisians at Hedeby copied those coins but they altered the elegantly rounded shape of the hulk into a box-like shape of another sailing vessel with prominent stem- and sternposts. On some coins the horizontal bottom line of this ship appears to be broken and bent upwards a little at both ends. This indicates that the actual ship depicted also had a flat bottom bent upwards at both ends, a form typical of coastal vessels on the shallow flats of the Wadden Zee. The shape allows those vessel to take the ground at low tide and to get afloat again at high water. Without the bent-up ends of the flat bottom suction might cause the ship to stick to the ground even at high tide. The flat and broad keel of the Bremen cog, in spite of being about 550 years later, is constructed from three pieces of timber forming just that broken line which appears on the coins. There can be little doubt, then, that the coins show early versions of the cog, including the steering oar of the *firrer* type.

One of the coins even shows three horizontal rows of nail-heads to demonstrate the clinker seams, with which four side strakes are fastened one to the other, and two vertical lines of nail-heads which show how these four strakes are nailed to the stem- and sternposts. Other coins just have horizontal lines instead of rows of nail-heads. Most of the issues, and probably the most accurate ones, display a flat-bottomed vessel with the four side strakes attached using clinker technique. In contrast to these early cogs, the Bremen cog has eight side strakes on top of her four bottom strakes. On top of the fourth side strake large crossbeams protrude through the side, providing a new constructional element which was to be typical for the late Middle Ages. This late cog is, so to speak, one early cog superimposed on another, with the crossbeams in between to give transverse strength to that odd construction. Compared with the Bremen cog, the four-strake sides of the early cogs on the Hedeby coins may have been no more than 1.7m (5.5ft) high amidships, which is the midship height of the ninth-century Gokstad Viking ship from keel to gunwale. This figure can only give an approximate notion of the size of early cogs, since so far no such vessel has been found. It would appear, though, that those early cogs could have been easily rowed like the Gokstad ship.

Since the people of Hedeby imitated the coins of Dorestad but changed the type of ship

The gradual improvement in the understanding of the structure and fittings of the cog is reflected in these two models built for the Bremerhaven museum. The top model represents knowledge gleaned directly from the wreck itself, whereas the later 1/10 scale model incorporates the results of research from other sources, so is able to attempt reconstructions of both superstructure and rig with a reasonable degree of reliability. (Basil Greenhill/Deutsches Schiffahrtsmuseum)

depicted on them from a hulk to the cog, it would seem that the hulk played no role in the traffic from the Rhine estuary to Hedeby. On the other hand, up to 1200 there is no evidence of a cog in England or along the coast of France, but there is evidence of cogs in ninth- and tenth-century written sources from the Netherlands and in archaeological sources not only from seventh-century Wilhelmshaven but also from Hamburg from the late ninth century onward in all eras through to the end of the Middle Ages. All these places are within the area of the shallow tidal waters of the Wadden Zee. This observation fits very well with the design of the cog, which enabled it to take the ground at low tide. So there is good reason to believe that the early sea-going cog was a ship of the Wadden Zee, sailing the relatively calm waters behind the islands and dunes and as far as possible up the coastal rivers. In Schleswig-Holstein it sailed as far as Hollingstedt, the North Sea harbour of Hedeby, from where merchandise normally had to be carried by land in carts to Hedeby on the Baltic only 16km (10 miles) away *across dry land*. Some-

Ships depicted on coins c800 AD:

A, B, C, D, Hulk – on a coin from Dorestad, from the time of Charlemagne

E, F, G, H, Cog at Dorestad; engraving from Haithabu

I, J, K, L, Viking ship at Dorestad; engraving from Haithabu

times, however, ships themselves were dragged across that small ridge between the two seas. Perhaps some skilled shipwrights from the Frisian coast settled at Hedeby and built cogs in the same way they had learnt to build them at home. At any rate, people at Hedeby minted coins with pictures of cogs, and they would not have done so if the cog were not one of the most important ship types in that harbour. Of course, the cog was not the only type of ship, and Hedeby also struck coins with Viking-type ships, but as Hedeby was a town under Danish and Swedish rule in the ninth and early tenth centuries no one should be astonished to find Viking ships on coins of the town. To find cogs as well, however, means that their role in trade must have been significant. Indeed, there is archaeological evidence from the tenth century for another cog as far east in the Baltic as Birka, near modern Stockholm. What has been found are about sixty typical cog nails among thousands of rivets from Viking ships, demonstrating that the cog was a foreigner at Birka. Even so, there can be no doubt that the strong trading connection between Hedeby and Birka was, at least to a certain extent, maintained by cogs. All in all the picture is one of expansion of traffic using sea-going cogs from the Rhine to the east, at first along the southern shores of the North Sea and its rivers and then, at least from the ninth century, reaching the Baltic at Hedeby and from that bridgehead starting to sail along the coasts of the Baltic.

When, about 1200, harbour towns began to show ships on their town seals, they depicted the most important type of ship constructed or owned by its inhabitants. Therefore, these town seals give an impressive survey, not of the total distribution, but of home ports for ship types. In England and along the opposite Continental coast, hulks and keels appear as far east as Monnikendam near Amsterdam in the thirteenth and fourteenth centuries. The westernmost seal with a cog is that of Damme, near Bruges in Belgium, and from the Ijsselmeer in the west as far to the east as Elbing (Elblag) on the Baltic there is no type other than the cog, if Scandinavia and its own ship types is excluded. The distribution of home ports for cogs along the North Sea coast in the thirteenth and fourteenth centuries is surprisingly the same as in the ninth century, whereas in the Baltic the picture had changed completely. Instead of Hedeby forming one small bridgehead, there is a long series of harbour towns founded between about 1150 and 1250 from Kiel in the west to Elbing (Elblag) in the east, which, in their seals, presented themselves as home ports for cogs. With these towns the base for shipping using cogs had been remarkably enlarged.

By the thirteenth century many construction details of the cog had changed dramatically. The cog, as depicted on ninth-century coins, was a flat-bottomed ship with four topside strakes, equipped with a special side rudder, working like a leeboard, and with a broad rectangular sail working as a lug. The next good picture of a cog is on the seal of Lübeck of 1224, but as the ships presented there and on the later seals from 1256 and 1281 have gently curved stem- and sternposts with animal heads on top, which look like the dragonheads of Viking ships, these seals have caused a great deal of confusion. Contemporary written sources say that these seals depict cogs and so historians originally thought the cog had been developed from Viking ships, but the seals themselves give three details which are never found on Viking ships, but which are typical of cogs:

1. The oldest seal clearly shows reversed clinker construction, where the lower strake overlaps the one above; with Viking ships this never occurs, but although not the rule with cogs, it is sometimes found.

2. The strakes overlap completely both stem- and sternposts, so that nothing can be seen of them but the heads. All old cog seals show this detail. The Bremen cog shows this construction, but with one specific addition: external stem- and sternposts had been added outside to close the scarf between the strakes which met in front of the inner posts. Thus the Bremen cog has inner and outer stemposts and sternposts. This constructional feature is an invention of the thirteenth century. The oldest town seal with additional external stem- and sternposts is that of Stavoren in the Netherlands from 1243. In the Baltic it is that of Wismar from 1256, whereas the seals of Lübeck from 1256 and even that of Neustadt in Holstein from 1351, showing a rather small version of a cog, lack this new invention which made the cog more seaworthy.

3. All three Lübeck seals show ships with the steering oar of the *firrer* type, which was never used with Viking ships but is typical for early cogs and cog-shaped boats. There can be little doubt that the Lübeck seals depict early cogs of a time before the stern rudder was installed on them, and therefore still closely related to the Frisian cogs of the early ninth century. The only major difference is the number of strakes, indicating that cogs had grown from four strakes in the ninth century to six strakes on the first two seals of Lübeck.

Cogs and the Hanse

It is a reasonable assumption that each town depicting a cog on its seal showed the latest stage in the development of ship construction, the state reached at the time the seal was designed. However, when Lübeckers depicted a cog with *firrer* in their first seal in 1224, that type of side rudder had already been replaced by the stern rudder, shown on the seals of all the other large Hanseatic towns. In Bremen in 1992 a fragment of a cog with a stern rudder was excavated and dated to the early thirteenth century. Even in 1281, when the Lübeckers designed the third version of their town seal, they retained the *firrer* even though in that seal they had adopted another new detail of construction: the outside stem- and sternposts, which had been introduced, at the least, more than forty years after the stern rudder. So the survival of the old-fashioned rudder on the seals cannot be taken simply as a sign of the conservatism of the Lübeckers. In fact, their seals seem to tell a specific story, one in which the old-fashioned *firrer* played a certain role, perhaps to establish for the viewer that the seal is depicting an historical situation.

Events from the past were sometimes shown on town seals. They usually indicate something about the foundation of the towns, such as events from the lives of saints whose churches became the nucleus of those towns. On the seals of Lübeck there are no saints, but two men in the ship are shown swearing an oath to one another. One of them is the helmsman and wears the typical clothes of a medieval sailor, a hooded coat called a *gugel* which was protection against bad weather. The other man on board the cog wears a coat normally used when travelling inland. Each of the men represents one of the two different groups of merchants which appear in the family names of medieval Lübeck. Those named Friso were the seafaring Frisian merchants, who sailed their cogs across the Baltic from the ninth century. The other group is named after towns in Westphalia such as Warendorf, Soest and so on. Before the foundation of Lübeck in 1159 these merchants had travelled with their horsedrawn carts to the ports of the Baltic, especially to Schleswig, the successor of Hedeby, and had traded there with the seafaring merchants who brought them the raw materials from the other side of the Baltic. These merchants who travelled on land with their carts were not able to cross the sea; they had to return from the seaports to their homes.

When the two groups of merchants founded Lübeck in 1159 they not only founded another new seaport but also invented a new way of trade. By swearing oaths they united in a new, very well-organised group for which the usual term in those days was *hanse*. In the new *hanse* of Lübeck after 1159 the seagoing Frisian merchants took their partners from Westphalia on

The earliest Lübeck cog seal, from 1224, shows the founding of the Hanseatic League: the land-based (left) and the seafaring merchants swear an oath and form a trading community.

board their cogs to the other side of the Baltic, especially to the island of Gotland, the focus of Baltic trade in those days. At first glance it might appear that the old Frisians were giving up a business advantage, since they no longer had a monopoly of seaborne trade. However, they developed a much better system. Lübeck and the Hanseatic League, simultaneously founded in 1159, coveted not only the sea routes to this port, but also the hinterland which stretched more than 400km deep into the Continent. The system was simple but effective. The former Frisian took his new fellow *hansard* from Westphalia with him to the sources of Baltic merchandise in the north and east. There, advised by the Westphalian, both were able to buy just those things for which there was a demand in Westphalia. On their return to Lübeck the partners no longer had to wait for customers since they remained the owners of the commodities of trade, which were then simply trans-shipped to carts and carried to Westphalia where they were sold at greater profit, profit divided between the two partners. The quantity of merchandise traded in both directions increased substantially under the new system, and profits developed accordingly for both groups of merchants, who found the Hanseatic League to their mutual advantage. Hanseatic sources sum up the new trading concept as trading 'across sand and sea'.

This new system of trade had several consequences. First, the Scandinavian and Russian merchants experienced the greatest adverse effect. Following the old pattern, they came to Lübeck with their ships full of Baltic cargo but then did not find enough customers who wanted to buy their cargoes in time for their trade to prove profitable. Along the excavated waterfront of Lübeck the traces of the presence of Scandinavian ships just cover the first years of the new town. After a certain time the Scandinavian merchants withdrew, and Hanseatic merchants were on their way to monopolising Baltic trade. Second, even by the fourth quarter of the twelfth century, increasing Hanseatic trade inspired a strong demand for bigger cogs. Third, Lübeck was able to convince other German seaports of the advantages of its new trading concept, and in the middle of the thirteenth century the Hanseatic League was greatly expanded, with merchants covering territory from Cologne and the lower Rhine in the west to those of the newly founded seaports along the southern coast of the Baltic to Reval in the east, including all the trading centres in their hinterlands. In addition, the Hanse established trading bases in the main seaports of foreign countries, for example at Bruges, London, Bergen in Norway, Visby in Gotland and Novgorod in Russia, to name just the most prominent.

Within three generations of its foundation the Hanseatic League's revolutionary method of business dominated trade in the Baltic and North Seas, and continued to do so for the rest of the Middle Ages. Therefore Lübeck had very good reason to show the foundation ceremony of the Hanseatic League on its town seal. With this picture Lübeck demonstrated the roots of its position in trade, and also showed that it was the head of the Hanse from the very beginning. There is hardly any other picture in the Middle Ages pinpointing so exactly the event which caused such major changes in medieval trade. The cog with the old-fashioned *firrer* shows the deep roots of the Hanse in Frisian seafaring, and the two representatives of the two different groups of merchants illustrate the new concept of combined sea and land trade with the cog as the main means of transportation. Thus the seal also shows why, after 1159, the cog became the predominant cargo vessel in the North and Baltic Seas for more than two centuries.

The new concept of trading resulted in a demand for bigger ships. As early as the 1180s written sources for the first time refer to the construction of larger vessels in the seaports of the southeast coast of the Baltic. Later town seals and cog finds indicate that the tendency was to make cogs not only longer and wider but also to give them higher sides. In 1241 a cog is mentioned with a cargo capacity of about 240 tons. The Bremen cog from 1380 with a capacity of about 80 tons is just a small version of the type. These bigger cogs could not be steered by the *firrer*, so shipwrights had to create another means of control and found it in the sternpost rudder, which they adopted from local ships along both sides of the Channel. However, from the late twelfth century the widespread employment of cogs with the sternpost rudder ensured that it became the general type of steering gear in European seafaring and has remained so up to the present day. As a result, the wide and low lug sail which was necessary for the *firrer* to function on early cogs could be altered to a high square sail, as on the Stralsund town seal of 1329. On this seal the sail consists of vertical stripes in different patterns. Wall paintings in contemporary churches show cog sails with vertical red and white stripes. Reconstructed Viking ships often give the impression that the Scandinavians were the first to use sails with red and white stripes. In fact, Viking ships had sails with lozenge or other patterns, but red and white were and are still the colours of each Hanseatic seaport. Even the different kinds of flags that appear with the cogs on the town seals were designed in nothing but red and white.

Since only a very few seals from the fourteenth century depict cogs with sails, the change from lug sail to square sail cannot be dated precisely. The oldest cog wreck, found near Cape Skagen at the northern tip of Jutland and dated about 1200, gives only a small additional hint about the pattern of the rigging, since little more than the bottom of the ship was excavated. In the bottom the position of the mast was so far forward of the centre of the ship that she could not be sailed with an ordinary square sail. Only with a lug sail could a ship with the mast in that position hope to weather Cape Skagen. Voyages doubling Cape Skagen could not employ those small, flat-bottomed 'mud-gliders' which in the ninth century sailed behind the islands and dunes through the Wadden Zee from the Rhine to Hedeby and were only able to sail from Hedeby along the shores of the Baltic. With the Cap Skagen wreck it is possible to see how shipbuilders made cogs more seaworthy. The bottom no longer meets the steep sides in a definite chine, but there is a rounded bilge that would tend to easier rolling in a seaway than the sudden jerking motion which would have been caused by an angled chine.

Last but not least, these seaworthy cogs were also more economical to build than, for example, the cog-sized ships which were being

The seal of Kiel depicts a cog with the usual features of straight stem and centreline stern rudder, but the angle of the 'square' sail suggests that possibly the sail was set rather in the manner of a lug; this inference is reinforced by the low, wide aspect of the sail.
(By courtesy of Basil Greenhill)

constructed in Scandinavia in the Viking tradition, for the following reasons:

1. Scandinavian boats were built from planks produced by the wasteful technique of splitting, whereas those used for cogs were sawn from oak tree trunks. Cogs therefore required less wood, and less skill was needed to construct them.

2. Because of the physical restriction of tree diameter, the split planks used for Scandinavian vessels were 15–30cm (6–12in) wide, whereas those used for cogs could be up to 65cm (26in) wide. Cogs therefore had less than half the number of clinker seams that were found on Scandinavian ships of the same height.

3. Carpenters and nail-makers, therefore, needed to spend much less time in finishing the outer surface. Fitting the internal timbers must also have been easier, since the smaller number of clinker seams meant there were fewer ridges over which those timbers had to fit.

As the Bremen cog from 1380 sank before it had been completed, it seems fairly certain that it was constructed in Bremen. Dendrochronological research suggests that the curved timbers used for the ribs came from the forests near Bremen. The straight oak trunks used for the keel, stem, crossbeams and so on would have been brought from the Weserbergland, probably by being floated downstream. The barrel containing tar to preserve the timbers actually seems to have been imported from Sweden. The trademark of the merchant who sold it to the shipyard can still be seen on the lid. After the barrel had been sold, notches were scored over the merchant's mark. Various tools such as a hatchet, a tool resembling a knife-like file for clinching nails, a hammer and a caulking tool were found with the ship. These, however, were only a fraction of those which would have been required to build it. Traces of work which would have been performed by other tools such as saws and gimlets are clearly visible.

Historical sources from around 1200 mention cogs with increasing frequency, in locations ranging from Riga in the east to England in the west. The English, in particular, characterised cogs as vessels used along the German or Frisian coast. The King of England himself had acquired a cog by 1210. Some of the crusaders who travelled from the North Sea to the Holy Land along the coast of western Europe made their journey by cog, so that cogs were observed in the Bay of Biscay and in the Mediterranean. In the summer of 1304 the

Florentine chronicler Giovanni Villani wrote:

Two stages in the reconstruction process of the cog at the Bremerhaven museum, showing the features of the clinker construction: relatively wide strakes, rebated frames, and through-beams notched to grip the planking strakes. (Deutsches Schiffahrtsmuseum)

then freebooters from Bayonne, in Gascony, came in their ships, which they called cogs, through the Straits of Gibraltar and into the Mediterranean, and caused much damage. Since then people from Genoa, Venice, Catalonia have also started using cogs, and have given up sailing in their large ships, as the cogs are cheaper to build, and are more seaworthy. There has thus been a major change in the types of vessel we use in our seafaring.

The extent of this transformation needs to be examined more closely, but it is certain that sailors never entirely abandoned multi-masted ships in the Mediterranean in the fourteenth century.

The local economy received a boost in each of the places to which the thirteenth-century Hanseatic merchants from the North Sea and the Baltic brought their cogs, as they would purchase the local produce in large quantities, knowing that there was a ready market in their home trading area. Huge quantities of Rhine wines were exported to England, Scandinavia

and the Baltic countries. In return, English wool was shipped to Flanders, where it was woven into high quality cloth. This, along with metal and other goods produced in Flanders, was particularly sought after in the Baltic countries. Grain and grain products, such as beer, from the hinterlands of Bremen, Hamburg and the southern coast of the Baltic, were sold in the populous areas of Flanders, England and, most importantly, in Norway. There they were traded for stockfish (dried cod), which found an almost limitless market on the Continent as a food for Catholic fast-days, as did herrings from the southwest coast of Skane. Those fish were preserved in salt from Lüneburg, which was in turn traded through Lübeck. The Swedish copper and iron mining industries were stimulated as well. Russia and the neighbouring forest areas paid for the manufactured goods imported from western areas with furs, wax and potash. Amber for rosaries and jewellery was obtained from the eastern shores, and tar from the forests everywhere around the Baltic.

It is clear from even this sample list of merchandise that each region bordering on the North Sea and the Baltic could engage in production surplus to its own requirements, and trade the surplus for imported goods. The Hanseatic merchants, the middlemen, used their cogs to ensure that supply met demand, and that both demand and supply were increased on an ever greater scale. In this way thousands of people were engaged both in producing raw materials and in manufacturing finished goods. The latter activity was performed in the towns, in the newly established artisan quarters. Whole series of new towns were founded, particularly along the Baltic coast. Existing towns mushroomed in size. Cogs thus maintained and supported the circulation of goods and associated services in the North Sea and the Baltic.

Sailing the cog

The navigation techniques employed on board these cogs left much to be desired. Neither compasses nor charts were used, and cogs had to remain within sight of the coast if they were to reach their destinations – a difficult task when sailing along a low coast with an offshore wind. While sailing against the wind was possible in theory, few seamen did so as they were unwilling to let the coast slip out of sight. If there was fog, an unfavourable wind or a storm – not uncommon, even during the sailing season, which stretched from March to October or November – there was nothing for it but to

drop anchor and wait for better conditions. Sailing along the Hanseatic routes in the reconstruction of the Bremen cog, a vessel built at Bremerhaven, has generated first-hand knowledge of how important it was to know all the sheltered bays along the coast which could be havens in emergencies. The degree to which a bay could provide protection would depend on its position and the prevailing wind direction. The worst situation of all occurred if a storm changed direction and the wind began to blow into the open mouth of the bay which had hitherto afforded protection. Most of the cog wrecks which have been discovered in Scandinavia and the Netherlands were driven on to the shore during storms. While the crew were probably saved and most of the cargo would have been rescued, the ships themselves were irretrievably lost.

The most important piece of navigational equipment was the lead-line, which was constantly used for checking the depth in coastal waters to prevent the ship running aground. The town seal of Elbing of about 1350 shows a sailor using the lead from the forecastle of a cog. The lead was used not only to gauge the depth of the water, but also to help fix position. Samples of the sea bottom were brought to the surface by means of a sticky, tallow-filled cavity in the lead. From around 1225, harbour markers of the type used in Scandinavia were introduced into the Hanseatic area as a further aid to navigation. These were tower-shaped constructions made of wood which enabled those sailing along the coast to spot the entrances to harbour towns situated in estuaries and fjords from a long way off. In the fourteenth century they were equipped with lanterns. Not all the harbours used by cogs were reached by coastal navigation alone. At certain points it was necessary to cross the open sea without remaining in sight of the coast. On these occasions the sailors would wait for a clear night and navigate by means of the pole star. For this purpose the helmsman merely had to steer the ship in such a way that the pole star remained visible above the same part of the ship. It was, of course, essential that the sea crossing should be to a coastline which could be at least dimly discerned on the horizon when the view of the pole star faded as morning broke. Islands with high elevations therefore became important navigational aids. This method of navigation was called *Nacht-sprung* ('leaping in the night') by the historian Adam von Bremen, who wrote in the eleventh century. The technique is indicated on seals dating from as late as around 1400 from England, the Netherlands and the southern coast

Sailor at the forecastle with the lead, on a seal from Elbing, 1367. The fore and after platforms may not have been initially, or entirely, warlike in inspiration: there would have been shiphandling advantages to high positions from which to conn the ship, keep lookout and perform the multifarious duties of the seaman, like swinging the lead.

of the Baltic, which depict cogs with a single star, the moon and a star, or a star-filled sky.

The disappearance of stars from seals heralds an important change in navigational techniques. Written sources from the Baltic ports first mention the compass shortly before 1400. The fifteenth-century *Niederdeutsche Seebuch*, a collection of written instructions for sailing between Cadiz and Reval and designed for the use of Hanseatic ships, only mentions compass courses. This is not dead reckoning as practised on the great voyages of discovery, but compass courses which run from one well-defined coastal position or island to the next, by means of which corrections to the course adopted could be made as and when necessary. The manual thus describes a method of coastal navigation by compass which meant that cogs no longer had to follow the coastline slavishly, but could sail in less dangerous waters away from the coast, check their position from time to time by reference to the nearest landmark, and correct their course as required.

Life on board the cogs bore little resemblance to our ideas of sea travel. The cargo was stowed below the deck while the crew and passengers remained above it, regardless of the weather. Thus, eating, sleeping, and every other aspect of shipboard life had to be carried out in the open air, whether in sunshine, rain or storm. There is no evidence of even primitive shelters on board the cogs, but sleeping bags made from hides and pelts, with the leather side facing outwards, offered a modicum

Cog with tower-shaped castle superstructure, on a seal from Danzig, 1299. At this stage the castles are not integrated with the hull. Note the star, which symbolises the importance of primitive astro-navigation in the Middle Ages.

of protection from the elements. Little is known about the food people ate at sea. It is not certain when stoves began to be used on board cogs and the various possibilities thus entailed became available. This is due to the fact that the upper part, including the decks, of most of the cog wrecks found have not survived. The well-preserved Bremen cog was unfortunately not yet complete, and possibly for that reason had no stove on board. However,

Although the Bremen cog was unfinished when lost, some intriguing fittings were recovered with the wreck. This lavatory seat was situated on the starboard side aft, under the castle deck, where the square structure jutted out over the sea beyond the curved run of the stern planking. (Deutsches Schiffahrtsmuseum)

bones from domestic cattle and a pig were found in the hull of the cog which sank off Kollerup, North Jutland, around 1200. As these bones included hooves we can assume that the animals were brought on board alive, to be slaughtered during the course of the voyage, which suggests that some sort of cooking facilities were available. The few pottery fragments found with this wreck belong to round-bellied cooking pots which would have been placed directly in the embers of an open fire. At any rate, unmistakable traces of cooking have been found near the places where cogs tied up, for example at the riverside market in early Lübeck.

There is much better information about seamanship on cogs, through pictorial sources – particularly town seals – and evidence from excavation finds. As soon as the wind was favourable and, in North Sea ports, the tide was right, the anchor would be raised by means of a horizontal windlass on the deck situated in the stern. Known as the *Bratspill*, it was turned by removable handspikes. The anchor cable ran from the hawse near the stem over the main part of the deck in such a way that the crew could use their strength to assist in the heavy work by pulling on the cable. The *Bratspill* was probably also used for hoisting the somewhat cumbersome sail. To set the sail the sailors would have had to climb up to the yard along the standing rigging, that is the stays or the shrouds. The earliest depiction of ratlines in the shrouds are those shown on the Danzig seal of around 1400. The crew would have had to sit astride the yard to let loose the furled sail. In England, ship departures were announced by a trumpet signal. It is not known if that was common practice in other ports, or whether Ger-

man cogs leaving England had to give trumpet signals too. The Bremen cog had a capstan which was also situated aft, and which could be used to adjust the heavy yard by means of braces. The helmsman at the tiller of the stern rudder, and the sailor with the lead, have already been mentioned.

Cogs had one further quality which would today appear unpleasant. The deck planks were laid at right angles to the sides, rather than longitudinally as they would be on modern vessels, and did not form a watertight join with the sides of the ship. This meant that sea spray and rain water falling on to the deck did not collect on the surface. As a result the vessel was much more stable when at sea. Even when the ship was heeling, the water on deck did not form a pond on the lower side, weighing it down still further, but instead flowed straight into the bilges, where it acted as additional ballast and provided a counterbalance. This meant that the risk of capsizing in bad weather was substantially reduced. However, when the reconstruction of the Bremen cog was being designed at Bremerhaven, it was considered important to have a water-tight deck, which meant that it was necessary to cut several large scuppers into the sides of the ship, at deck level, so that any water on the deck would flow overboard. These scuppers, of course, reduced the very height of the freeboard which had given the Hanseatic cogs their seaworthiness. The crew found that they had to reach for the

Deck view of the provisional model of the cog, showing the windlass aft on the main deck and the capstan. The windlass was probably used to raise the anchor and to hoist the main yard, but the capstan was probably a device to adjust the braces when trimming the sail. (By courtesy of Basil Greenhill)

pumps not only when leaks occurred, but also after every shower of rain or splash of sea spray, as the ship's high sides meant that it was impossible to remove the water by means of the bailer. Fragments of a wooden pump have been found on the Kalmar cog (Wreck V), which had an outlet channel in the upper edge of the aft crossbeam. The Bremen cog had not been supplied with a pump, but a chamber with the outlet leading overboard had been built under the sterncastle, so it seems logical that the intention was to install a pump.

The fact that the hold was waterlogged had far-reaching implications for the method by which cargo was stowed on cogs. All goods which could be damaged by water or which might rot in damp conditions had to be transported in water-tight containers, which, at that time, meant barrels. As a result, the carrying capacity of the hold was far from optimised. Loading and unloading the barrels was extremely heavy work, only relieved to the extent that the deck planking could be removed and barrels brought up directly from the hold. The yard, which could be rotated easily, was used like the boom on a derrick to load and unload cargo. The use of this technique in several North Sea ports in the thirteenth century led to the construction of the first harbour cranes. They looked like masts which had been installed on the quayside, each being equipped with a rotatable yard, and, on the seaward side, a chain and a hook which could be lowered into the ship. One or more ropes were tied to the landward-facing end of the yard, so that it could be lowered and the goods hanging from the hook could be swung free from the ship on to dry land. This type of crane was called a *Wippe*, a see-saw, the name coming from the movement of the yard.

It was not always possible to find sufficient cargo for a cog. The crew of the cog which ran aground at Vejby in the north of the Danish island of Sjælland shortly after 1370 had been forced to take on ballast from either the French Atlantic coast or the English Channel. The merchandise on board included fine textiles and cooking and eating utensils made from iron, copper alloys and tin, including two tin plates from the Dutch province of Gelderland – objects which were clearly intended for use in the households of townspeople. Some, at least, of the cash belonging to a merchant on board

The Deutsches Schiffahrtsmuseum in Bremerhaven has built a full size replica of the cog in order to test its seakeeping and handling characteristics. This photograph shows the vessel underway on the Weser in 1991. (Deutsches Schiffahrtsmuseum)

was found, amounting to 110 gold coins, mainly King Edward III (1351–77) nobles. From the cargo it is reasonable to conclude that this cog was sailing from northwest Europe to the Baltic for trading purposes.

The cog which ran aground at Vigsø, on the Skagerrak coast of Denmark, was also carrying goods from western Europe, including two bronze finger bowls which had been made in the area between Flanders and the Lower Rhine. They were presumably intended for a nobleman's table, where people would have used them for rinsing their fingers after eating, as forks were not yet in use and all solid food was brought to the mouth by hand. They had been ingeniously cast in the form of two people on horseback, one a Minnesinger playing the

fiddle while mounted on his steed, and the other the lady he adores. From these few examples it is obvious that the Hanseatic League was not merely concerned with trade in commonplace goods, but also in objects for use in the households of townspeople and exquisite works of art for the nobility. The merchants were always in a position to react to the demands of the market. The crews, for their part, were able to stow the various goods in such a way that even delicate objects like the finger bowls would, under normal circumstances, survive the voyage intact. They were also able to arrange the ballast so that the ship remained upright in the water and could sail with little danger.

Last but not least, the crew also had to be in

a position to carry out all necessary repairs themselves, either during the course of a voyage or, if possible, in a sheltered bay or harbour. They, therefore, had to have on board all kinds of tools and materials, including large quantities of wooden parts, iron nails, caulking clamps, moss, sailcloth and ropes. Examples of the tools used for repairing cogs have been found on some of the wrecks. The wreck at Kollerup yielded a carpenter's hammer, the narrow end of which was slit in such a way that it could be used for extracting nails. A carpenter's axe, very similar to the one on the Bremen cog, was found on the wreck at Vigsø. The tools which were used to construct the Bremen cog were, of course, also those which would be required to repair it. Cog nails and caulking clamps from the riverside market levels of early Lübeck indicate that repairs to the exterior of a ship were carried out by the crew themselves, without the vessel having even been brought into a dock. A shell auger and a crude needle made from bone found at the same location indicate the methods used for mending planks and sails respectively. Given the demanding nature of their work on board and the trials and tribulations of life at sea, it is obvious that the crews on cogs would have had little time to relax and enjoy themselves. Apart from the fact that, at the time, sailors were virtually the only people who could get to know other countries well, the various surviving sources yield remarkably little detail about leisure time activities of crew members. However, board games seem to have been popular. A wooden die and nine round, flat wooden counters were found in the cog wreck at Kollerup. Bone flutes and Jew's harps from the riverside market at Lübeck suggest that musical entertainment awaited the sailors in the port, and perhaps even some dancing, given the combination of melodic and rhythmic instruments.

The influence of war

Fragments of daggers and dagger sheaths found on the cogs at Bremen, Kalmar and Kollerup suggest that these items were carried for the personal protection of at least some of those on board, and indicate that times were by no means as peaceful as may have hitherto been imagined. Violence in the ports, and piracy on the open sea, were as much a part of a seaman's life as the use of cogs for very varied fighting. The Hanse did not have any warships as such, but in the event of war would man its cogs with large numbers of armed soldiers. The Hanseatic merchants were by no means helpless or powerless against the kings, dukes and counts

in whose lands they carried on their business, not on a diplomatic, an economic or a military plane. Merchants occupied the decision-making positions in the town councils and were, therefore, in a position to bring the entire economic and political weight of their town to bear if fighting broke out around an important trading location. If that weight proved insufficient, the remaining Hanseatic towns could be mobilised. For example, in 1234 and 1239 Lübeck used cogs in conducting two naval battles against the King of Denmark to ward off his attempts to harness the economic power of the town for his own ends.

In the early 1280s the King of Norway attempted to limit the trading activities of Hanseatic merchants in order to promote the political position, trade and sea transport of his own people. There were reprisals in the harbours, ships were seized and there was piracy at sea. All attempts at negotiations failed. Hanseatic cogs and their cargoes were openly sequestered. When, in the spring of 1284, the cog carrying the Hanseatic delegation seeking to resolve the conflict was captured, war was declared. All the Hanseatic coastal towns, with the exception of Bremen, participated. They pursued a two-fold strategy: first, no town would supply Norway with grain, or import Norwegian goods; and second, Hanseatic cogs would blockade the Norwegian ports. Lübeck alone bore 25 per cent of the costs, the remainder being shared amongst the other towns affected.

The cogs blockading the Norwegian ports were manned and equipped for war. Their purpose was to prevent ships from entering or leaving the ports and to capture all Norwegian vessels met at sea. They arrived in squadrons at the Norwegian coast and laid waste whole villages. This, however, did not affect the outcome of the war. The deciding factor was the grain embargo, which was so effective a measure that the King of Norway decided on an armistice in the middle of 1285. As part of the ensuing peace treaty all prisoners and captured merchandise were returned and the trading privileges of the Hanseatic merchants were restored.

During the blockade, Norway had been allied with England, but did not receive much assistance from that source as the King of England, Edward I, was himself embroiled in military conflict. So that they could perform their blockading activities more effectively, the cogs adopted a device which English ships had been using since the middle of the century. Tower-shaped wooden constructions with crenellated platforms were built at the fore and aft ends of

Crossbows displayed symbolically on the castles, on a seal from the Paris bolt-makers guild, fifteenth century. The ship has the characteristic banana-shaped hull of the hulk.

the deck. The first seal with a picture of a cog which was designed after the Norwegian blockade shows the high fore and aft castles and also a box-shaped topcastle at the masthead. Crossbowmen could fire their bolts much more effectively from this height than from the relatively low weather deck. Where cogs were involved, the crossbow was the most feared long-range weapon. The short, sharp-edged steel tips of its bolts could pierce any knight's armour. Furthermore, finds from the cog wrecked at Kalmar show that their wooden shafts had light, spiral fletchering. This meant that the bolts revolved in flight, the twist giving them a stable flight path not achieved with guns until the introduction of rifling in the late eighteenth century. The crossbowmen thus could be skilled and effective marksmen.

The castles on the Hanseatic cogs did not, however, retain their tower-shaped framework for long. The fighting platform itself provided a certain amount of protection from rain for the deck below. Far more protection from the vagaries of the weather was, however, offered if the space below the firing platforms was also enclosed. Eventually Hanseatic shipbuilders found a solution which pointed the way for future northern shipbuilding. The Stralsund seal of 1329 shows the first depiction of this new method. The aft platform was constructed from water-tight planking laid in such a way that it formed a type of upper deck running the full width of the ship. The rectangular castle deck right aft therefore extended on both sides far out over the planks running down to the sternpost. Below the castle deck the sides of the ship were raised by means of additional planks, and shingles, like those used in roofing, were laid between the curved hull and the rectangular deck so as to form a completely enclosed space. It was open at the centre of the stern, where the tiller projected, but the helmsman himself now had a sheltered position. The forward end of this space was also open in the centre, since that was where the indispensable windlass was located.

The decisive step in shipbuilding was to transform the *ad hoc* fighting towers into an integral part of the deck construction. That offered, for the first time on the largest trading ships in the North Sea and the Baltic, the luxury of a little comfort in a very spartan environment. This enhancement was gradually extended. Fifty years after the Stralsund seal was struck, a narrow but enclosed cabin was incorporated into both the port and starboard sides of the aftercastle of the Bremen cog. A bench seat ran along the ship's sides in the main area, for people to sit, or perhaps sleep, on. A toilet had even been fitted on the starboard side of the stern, where the castle structure projected out over that side of the hull. Its seat was so high that there was a rectangular opening above it in the castle deck so that anyone using the toilet had an uninterrupted view over the whole of the ship. It seems safe to assume that the captain himself had arranged for this feature so that he could continue to

command the ship effectively while using it himself.

The new comforts really only affected the officers and passengers in the stern. Sailors remained forward of the mast, on the open deck. Whereas their conditions had not actually worsened, those of the others had improved so much that a social distinction began to manifest itself. By the time narrow berths appeared under the forecastle for the use of the crew, the officers and passengers had long enjoyed vastly superior cabins in the aft superstructure.

Replacing the cog

The construction of relatively comfortable sterncastle superstructures represents the last stage in the development of the cog. The Hanseatic merchants may have wished for greater carrying capacity and improved conditions at sea, but these enhancements could no longer be satisfied by vessels of the cog type. Shortly before 1400 the more ambitious of those Hanseatic merchants abandoned the vessel type which had been in use since the inception of their organisation, and returned to the western European hulk which proved capable of further development and which, they found, could be fitted out to accommodate their needs. Unfortunately no medieval hulk has yet been excavated, so we cannot determine in

what respects it differed from the cog or in what ways it offered greater opportunities for development.

At present the cog is the best researched medieval ship type because there is in the Bremen cog an almost complete hull from the most advanced stage of the development of the type. It has been possible to study all its details, and thus to use the interpretation of archaeological finds along with information about small boat types which survive to the present day to help in understanding the various stages in the development of the cog. By contrast, there are only pictures and references in historical sources to help in understanding the history of the hulk and of other late medieval ship types. Therefore, it is not possible to rewrite the history of these vessels, but only to summarise current knowledge about the subject.

The seal of the English port of New Shoreham, from 1295, is the most useful starting point, as the inscription tells us that it depicts a hulk. The seal shows a banana-shaped vessel of a type which was used for trading purposes on both sides of the Channel west of the Rhine estuary throughout the Middle Ages, and which can be traced back to the region of Calais in the seventh century. Other hulks appear on coins from Dorestad from shortly before 800. The boat shown on the seal of New Shoreham still has a rudder on its port side, as have those on the Dorestad coins. Its castles rest directly on the strake ends which run almost vertically up from the wide, rounded hull construction both fore and aft, the shape of the planking being a characteristic feature of this ship type. The crenellations on the castles indicate that the hulk could also be used for naval purposes as well as carrying cargoes. The development of the hulk roughly paralleled that of the cog. Like the cog, it had only one mast and one sail, and remained confined to its region of origin until, in the case of the hulk, it began to be used by Hanseatic merchants in the Baltic around 1400. The vessel shown on the Danzig seal from 1400 is described in the

The process of integrating the superstructures into the hull is demonstrated in this Polish painting. This panel of the St Jodok altar piece is dated to about 1500, but the ship seems to be significantly earlier. The aftercastle is clearly part of the hull whereas the triangular forestage is separate, although relying on the hull for its structural support. The hull shape suggests an early carrack, and there is a second small mast on the forecastle; the position of the main mast and the shrouds makes it unlikely that the artist merely omitted any mizzen mast. (Muzeum Warmii i Mazur, Olsztyn; by courtesy of Basil Greenhill)

Seal from New Shoreham (known as Hulcesmouth in the Middle Ages) with inscription indicating that it depicts a hulk, 1295. The distinctive banana-shaped vessel is something of a mystery, since no wreck of the type has been firmly indentified, but the consistency of its representation in the iconographical sources means that the shape must have some basis in reality.

Seal from Danzig depicting a vessel described in historical sources as a hulk, around 1400. At this date the superstructures are more closely integrated with the hull.

only to the frames with characteristic flush seams. Thus at least the main framing had to be in place before the hull planks. Unfortunately there are as yet no archaeological finds from the early stages of the use of this carvel technique in northern Europe, so it is not possible to describe precisely how the shipbuilder performed his task. In 1462 a merchant from La Rochelle moored and abandoned his large merchant ship in Danzig harbour. Named the *Peter of La Rochelle* and subsequently the *Peter von Danzig* or *Das Grosse Kraweel*, it was a vessel built skeleton-first with three masts. She was fitted out for the Hanseatic war against England in 1470. The conversion work gave the Danzig shipbuilders their first experience of the skeleton-first building technique which made possible the construction of much larger vessels than with clinker building. From then on Hanseatic shipyards, decades after the rest of western Europe, began to build three- and four-masted ships of various types, using the novel method.

town's written records as a hulk and, therefore, shows the stage of development which had been achieved by that date. This hulk was equipped with a stern rudder. It is impossible to tell if the sterncastle differed in construction from those on cogs. The castle forward, positioned on the almost vertical plank ends of the rounded wooden bow, is constructed in quite a different manner from that found on cogs and has a place inside for the narrow berth, which is referred to in English, right up to the present day, as the forecastle. Here, for the first time, both castle superstructures are an integral part of the structure of the hull. This is the first stage in the evolution of the multi-storied fore and aft superstructures of the sixteenth cen-

tury. Last but not least, it is clear from the Danzig seal that each plank was secured, clinker-style, to the upper edge of the one beneath it. Unfortunately the absence of archaeological finds means that the type of clinker building employed cannot be identified. All that can be said at this stage is that the clinker seams on Viking ships were riveted together, whereas those on cogs were nailed in place.

By the middle of the fifteenth century the hulk had completely replaced the cog in the Hanseatic area. Before long, though, the same fate was to overtake the hulk itself. The last cogs had scarcely disappeared from the sea when shipwrights in the Netherlands learnt from carpenters from the French Atlantic coast how to build ships by a completely new method, in which planks were no longer fastened directly to one another but were nailed

In the meantime the development of firearms had made new demands on shipbuilders. The first firearms were taken on board Hanseatic ships approximately fifty years after they had been first used on land. They were known as *Schotbussen* and were of small calibre. In battle they were put in place over the gunwales. In the course of the fifteenth century, powder and shot became part of the normal defensive equipment on board large merchant ships, to be used for protection against privateers. For the raid against England, the *Peter von Danzig* was equipped with nineteen guns, all situated in the superstructures above the main deck.

The increasing calibre of guns certainly increased the firepower of the ships, but it also increased the weight in the superstructures high above the waterline and, therefore, increased the danger of capsizing. Somehow the heavy guns had to be accommodated as low as possible in the ship. The invention of the gunport, a flap in the side of the ship's hull, below the main deck but above the waterline, made this possible. Guns positioned below the deck could fire at enemy ships through these ports. When there was no fighting, the ports could be

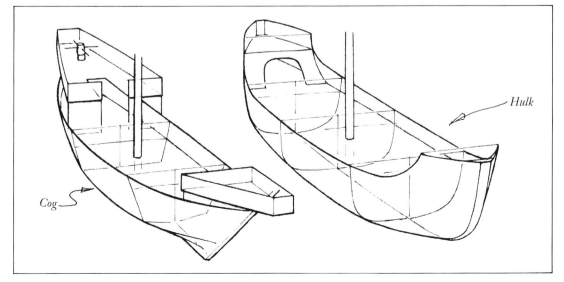

Cog

Hulk

Sam Manning's schematic comparison of the hull of a cog and that of a hulk. The advantages of the latter can be summarised as: curved bottom and round bilges for better seakeeping and for improved structural continuity between sides and bottom; fuller ends to maximise carrying capacity; ability to contain fighting platforms within the hull; and less complicated lapped seamwork in the planking. (Sam Manning, from The Evolution of the Wooden Ship*)*

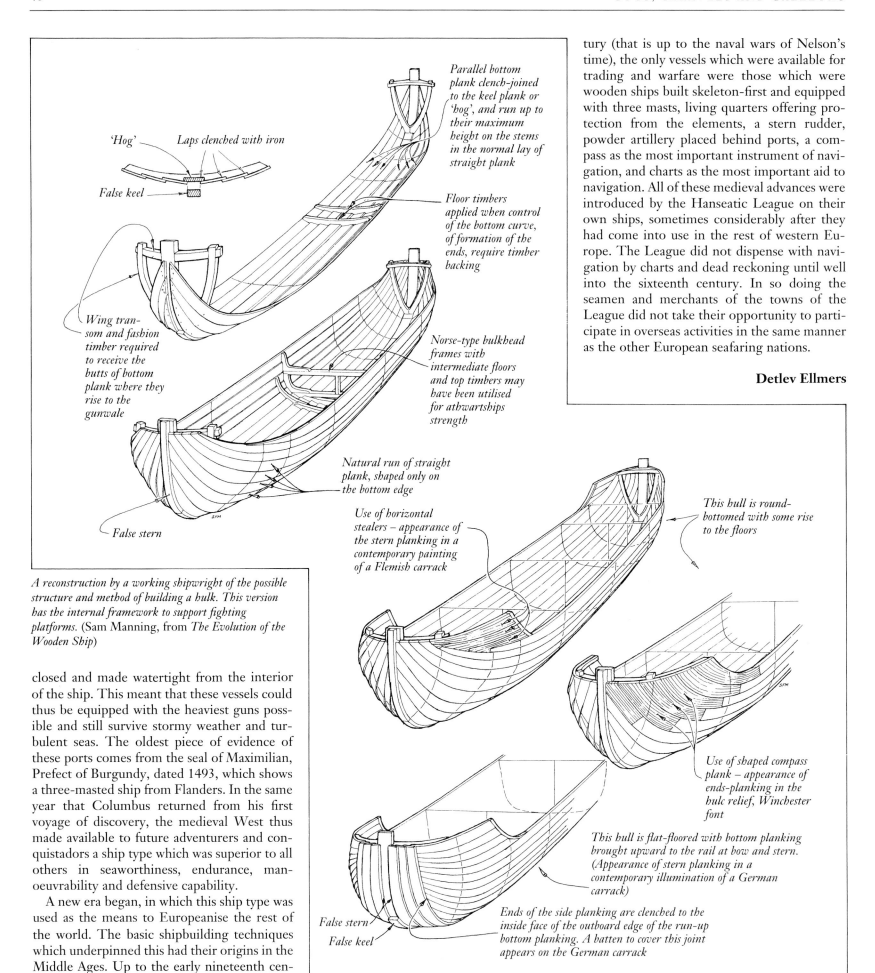

'Hog' Laps clenched with iron

False keel

Parallel bottom plank clench-joined to the keel plank or 'hog', and run up to their maximum height on the stems in the normal lay of straight plank

Floor timbers applied when control of the bottom curve, of formation of the ends, require timber backing

Wing transom and fashion timber required to receive the butts of bottom plank where they rise to the gunwale

Norse-type bulkhead frames with intermediate floors and top timbers may have been utilised for athwartships strength

False stern

Natural run of straight plank, shaped only on the bottom edge

Use of horizontal stealers – appearance of the stern planking in a contemporary painting of a Flemish carrack

This hull is round-bottomed with some rise to the floors

A reconstruction by a working shipwright of the possible structure and method of building a hulk. This version has the internal framework to support fighting platforms. (Sam Manning, from The Evolution of the Wooden Ship)

Use of shaped compass plank – appearance of ends-planking in the hulc relief, Winchester font

This hull is flat-floored with bottom planking brought upward to the rail at bow and stern. (Appearance of stern planking in a contemporary illumination of a German carrack)

False stern
False keel

Ends of the side planking are clenched to the inside face of the outboard edge of the run-up bottom planking. A batten to cover this joint appears on the German carrack

tury (that is up to the naval wars of Nelson's time), the only vessels which were available for trading and warfare were those which were wooden ships built skeleton-first and equipped with three masts, living quarters offering protection from the elements, a stern rudder, powder artillery placed behind ports, a compass as the most important instrument of navigation, and charts as the most important aid to navigation. All of these medieval advances were introduced by the Hanseatic League on their own ships, sometimes considerably after they had come into use in the rest of western Europe. The League did not dispense with navigation by charts and dead reckoning until well into the sixteenth century. In so doing the seamen and merchants of the towns of the League did not take their opportunity to participate in overseas activities in the same manner as the other European seafaring nations.

Detlev Ellmers

closed and made watertight from the interior of the ship. This meant that these vessels could thus be equipped with the heaviest guns possible and still survive stormy weather and turbulent seas. The oldest piece of evidence of these ports comes from the seal of Maximilian, Prefect of Burgundy, dated 1493, which shows a three-masted ship from Flanders. In the same year that Columbus returned from his first voyage of discovery, the medieval West thus made available to future adventurers and conquistadors a ship type which was superior to all others in seaworthiness, endurance, manoeuvrability and defensive capability.

A new era began, in which this ship type was used as the means to Europeanise the rest of the world. The basic shipbuilding techniques which underpinned this had their origins in the Middle Ages. Up to the early nineteenth cen-

3

The Cog as Warship

NORTHERN European seafarers developed a wide variety of vessel types to address their needs, but few were as successful and long-lived as the cog. The cog was not a fast sailer, but it was a durable carrier in the cold and rough waters of the northern seas. Studies of cog finds by archaeologists and ship historians since the 1960s have helped place the cog in an even more important position in the history of the evolution of the sailing ship. The inventory of features found in cogs has grown to a list of substantial size. This helps nautical archaeologists to identify finds and to look for clues concerning the modification of this vessel over time. The cog's principal features included a boxy shape suitable for carrying bulk cargo, and straight stem- and sternposts which rose at an angle from the keel. The cog was clinker-built with high freeboard. An unusual feature was the edge-joined or flush-laid planking radiating from the keel until the turn of the bilge, where traditional clinker construction began and continued to the gunwale. The flat bottom allowed the cog to beach in shallow waters without heeling, which permitted easier loading and unloading where no docks or quays were constructed. There was a single square sail carried on a mast stepped slightly forward of midships for better efficiency with a following wind; the mast step was in the keelson. Cogs had distinctive iron nails whose tips were clenched back into the planking. Moss was used in caulking, and was held in place by laths and iron clamps. There were knee-shaped bulkheads and some through-beams which ran transversely the width of the vessel, usually piercing the hull.

From merchant vessel to ship of war

The cog was very popular among the merchants of the North Sea coasts in the early Middle Ages. Frisian merchants carried much of the goods transported throughout the region. Using cogs and hulks they carried timber, furs, glass, grain and luxury goods. These early cogs were not well-suited to deep water sailing and travelled along the coasts as much as possible. Frisian trade into the Baltic in the eighth century influenced the development of the Scandinavian ports of Hedeby and Birka. The latter even had a *kugghamn*, a cog harbour, to accommodate these unique vessels. The early cog was probably powered by both oar and sail. Such features are found in a fourth-century Roman ship find at Mainz, where the mast step is made up of a notched heavy transverse frame which is similar to the mast step of a thirteenth-century cog from Jutland. The archaeological record for the early origin of the cog is reinforced by the documentary records from ninth-century Utrecht which provide the earliest use of the term 'cog'. This was followed in Germany by a reference to a *herikochum*, a vessel described as a fast warship. The origins of the cog probably even reach back to Celtic design of the late Roman period.

Steered by a side rudder (or possibly two), the early cog was an effective carrier of goods and well suited for sandy bottoms and tidal harbours. It also apparently found early use as a warship as well. The powerful Carolingian state maintained a naval force which included coast defence troops called *cokingi*. It may be that their name derived from the cogs which made up the principal part of the defensive fleet. Clearly cogs were already warships, as well as merchant ships, in the ninth century. There were many vessel types recruited for military use, but fighting vessels were typically oared.

The question of why the cog developed as

Before the adoption of the cog, naval warfare was carried on in ships derived from the Norse clinker-built boat tradition. Sometimes referred to in documentary sources as nefs, *these vessels had light structures fore and aft, and sometimes at the masthead. This model by R Quartretemps is based on the ships depicted on the twelfth-century town seals of the English Cinque Ports, but much of the detail is conjectural. (R Quartretemps)*

rate of six pence per day. The sources do not provide totals of the numbers of men employed in each special skill, but the job titles are noted.[2]

The construction and mounting of the rudder required a skilled shipwright. The centre-line rudder ran the length of the sternpost. It was heavy and the helmsman, who stood on the main deck to navigate, moved it with a tiller. The cog was soon modified so that the rudder went through an opening in the stern as the sterncastle grew and extended outboard beyond the rudder. This meant that the tiller had to pass through an opening in the stern deck, putting the helmsman below the sterncastle. A vertical whipstaff was added to the end of the tiller to enable the helmsman to stand higher and see forward. A fulcrum was added in the fourteenth century to improve the leverage of the whipstaff. Larger cogs required further modifications to accommodate heavy rudders and to provide the helmsman with a good view. When large aftercastles were incorporated in the ship's design the helmsman

The early cog on the seal of Harderwijk points up the differences with the Viking-derived nef. The cog had straight, raked ends, a centreline rudder, and despite the distortion of the form, the hull can be seen to be shorter and deeper – and hence more capacious – than the craft of the Viking tradition. Note how the forecastle sits astride the stempost while the aftercastle rests on the hull proper, unlike earlier free-standing structures. (By courtesy of Basil Greenhill)

the large bulk carrier, favoured over a modified Viking ship type, is probably best answered by noting the increased capacity of a cog. The broad flat bottom and high sides meant that it could carry much more cargo. It also was well adapted to the use of the new sternpost rudder which could improve the handling of larger ships. A cog was also cheaper to build. The simpler techniques involved in construction meant that fewer skilled labourers were needed to attach the planking to the flat bottom. Ship-builders sawed the planks rather than splitting them. The Bremen cog and some other cog finds clearly demonstrate the difference. This practice of sawing was employed from the mid-thirteenth century and had several advantages. The timber was worked more quickly, the cuts were more precise and there was less wasted timber, often an expensive commodity. Also, the construction of a cog could be done cost effectively even though the increased hull surface, decking and internal framing of the vessel demanded more wood for the job. There was a loss in strength because sawn planking is not as strong as split planking, but the advantages assured the victory of the saw over the adze and the axe for this task.

Skilled labour was still a prime requirement for the construction of a cog in the fourteenth century. Skilled craftsmen were needed to select and shape the framing timbers, knees, ribs, posts and other pieces from the available timber. Some shipyards became centres for the construction of cogs, employing labourers at

all levels. In an English shipbuilding account from 1350, two carpenters, or shipwrights, Nicholas George and William Carpenter, were hired to make repairs on the king's ships. They employed a number of assistants, which suggests that they functioned more as shipwrights or naval architects than just as hammerers or fitters. They received the unusually high compensation of eight pence per day, two pence above the standard wage of a ship master or the constable who was in charge of soldiers aboard ship. The two men worked for over a year, and removed the masts from twelve ships while erecting new ones in five ships. They repaired other vessels, caulking them. Carpenters are sometimes referred to as *calphatours* or caulkers. They used resin, varnish, animal hair, iron, rope and leather in addition to timber to make repairs.[1] The documents also refer to *borderes* (boarderers) and *helderes* (assistants) employed in construction and repair work. *Clencheres* were men whose task it was to set the clinch nails through the planking and ribs; the nails were then fitted with roves before the point was turned and hammered back into the frame. Clearly there was a division of labour among those in the shipyards whose specialities grew to include castlewrights, as distinguished from shipwrights, who were paid at the same

1. Public Record Office, London [hereafter PRO], Exchequer, Pipe Rolls, E.372/209 m.47; Exchequer, Accounts Various, E.101/2/14/5 m.4.

2. PRO, E.101/25/32; E.101/24/7 m.6.

Graffiti of cogs moored in reeds on an undated corner stone discovered at the site of Crane Godvery Manor, Gwithian, Cornwall. This evidence from the far west of England underlines the ubiquity of the type in medieval commerce. (Professor Charles Thomas, by courtesy of Basil Greenhill)

was enveloped in a room beneath the castle deck. This actually was a benefit, as it took him and the controls out of the weather and the line of fire during battle.

The combination of the increased size of the cog and the improved steering controls helped open new routes and thus markets for trade. The uncharted waters of the northern seas required an alert crew and a ship capable of quick response at the helm. New routes through the Kattegat into southern Sweden and to ports reached by transiting the Danish coast were forged by the big new cogs with sternpost rudders. The new ship with its improved sailing features and larger capacity altered the trade routes of northern Europe and would soon prompt changes throughout Europe. Cogs became extremely popular in the northern seas by the fourteenth century. A survey of ship types in England during the early phase of the Hundred Years War, 1337–1360, proved the ubiquity of the cog. Of over 1300 ships identified, cogs were the most frequently noted ship type by a wide margin. Cogs constituted 57 per cent of all vessels identified by type. Though the information was taken from crown records, most of the ships were privately owned.[3] English merchants built cogs at a steady rate in the fourteenth century, many of which were 'arrested' for royal service by the king's sergeants-at-arms. Whether carrying timber from the Baltic, or wine from the Bay of Biscay or wool to Flanders, cogs were a common sight in English ports. They were the mainstay of many trade routes and their size was well suited to the docking facilities available.

The size of most cogs early in the fourteenth century is suggested in the English wine customs accounts which reveal, for example, that of nearly one thousand ships that carried wine from Bordeaux to England between 20 January 1303 and 18 August 1304, most of them carried 100 tons or less. Accounts from the records of payments of the great custom on wine at Bordeaux indicate that 81 per cent of the ships which made this payment were under 150 tons, 15 per cent were 150–200 tons, and only 3 per cent were above 200 tons. Carrying capacity was measured by the ability to carry wine tuns.[4] Each tun, a wooden barrel, contained 252 gallons, and occupied about 33–40 cubic feet (0.9–1.1m²). It is known that mariners in

the wine trade were guaranteed, both by custom and by the Laws of Oléron, wine as a part of their meals on the return trip from Bordeaux when the ships were loaded with wine tuns. The best sailors might expect on the outbound voyage was some beer, though on some occasions before battles wine was served. This presence of wine on King Edward III's cog *Thomas* enabled celebrations after a battle. The French and Spanish carried wine as part of their stores, although with this caveat: since galleys formed a major portion of their fleets it was not thought a good idea to give wine to the rowers. However, to encourage his men in a 1406 sea battle with the English, a Spanish commander did give wine to the oarsmen.[5]

Cogs were not just limited to the role of bulk carriers. In 1360 the cog *Johan* of Yarmouth was used to pirate 30 tons of white wine from a Flemish merchant. Visitors to the Bay of Biscay included Italians who stopped en route to their markets in England and the Low Countries.[6] Italian mariners saw the large single-masted square rigged cogs and must have been impressed by their carrying ability and popularity among northern merchants. Cogs not only served pirates, but could be the objects of piratical attack. Flemish pirates attacked the *Great Cog of St Mary* of Great Yarmouth in 1308 along with the *Coga*, the *Seintmaricog* of Colchester, the cog *Beate Marie*, and the *Coga* of Valencia, the last losing wine, wheat and flour. The *Cog of Lübeck*, while passing near Berwick-upon-Tweed in 1354, was attacked by pirates who took the ship and its cargo. The *ReddeCogge* transported goods to Genoa with the king's safe conduct in 1361. The Cistercian abbot of Fourneux hired the *Maricogge* to supply victuals, and in 1368 the *Seinte Marie Cogge* of Bristol carried pilgrims to the shrine of Santiago de Compostela.[7]

The thirteenth-century Mediterranean did know a large sailing ship, described as a round

ship, which was designed to carry bulk goods (see Chapter 4). Such ships were built frame-first with edge-to-edge planking, but the major feature distinguishing them from northern vessels was the use of lateen sails for propulsion. Their rig was efficient in sailing against the wind, but awkward if much tacking was required since it was necessary to swing the yard around the mast, a manoeuvre that was dangerous and required a large crew. Either end of the yard on a square-sailed cog could be pointed toward the wind and so handled by fewer mariners. Also, lateen sails had to be changed from larger to smaller according to the weather, whereas the square sail on a cog could be easily reefed or supplemented with bonnets. The handling of the helm was easier on a cog with a single stern rudder than it was using the one, two or three steering oars typical of Mediterranean ships. This did not mean a cog was easy to handle in absolute terms, especially in heavy weather. A record from 1317 reports that the *Redecoge* taking goods to Skyburness was blown off course and unloaded at Dublin Castle instead. The master was absolved of responsibility for the diversion.[8] The cog needed only about half as many men to crew it as a comparable two- or three-masted lateen rigged Mediterranean ship, so

3. Timothy J Runyan, 'Ships and Fleets in Anglo-French Warfare, 1337–1360', *The American Neptune* 46 (1986), pp91–99.

4. Charles Higounet, *Bordeaux sous les rois d'Angleterre* (Bordeaux 1965), p242, pp254–5; Richard W Unger, *The Ship in Medieval Economy* (London 1980), p163.

5. Gutierre Diaz de Gamez, *The Unconquered Knight, A Chronicle of the Deeds of Don Pero Niño, Colunt of Buelna*, ed and trans Joan Evans (New York 1928), p162.

6. *Calendar of Inquisitions Miscellaneous* (1348–77), p109.

7. *Calendar of Close Rolls* [hereafter *CCR*], (1307–13), p446; *CCR* (1313–18), pp76, 385; *CCR* (1318–23), pp192, 256, 262; *CCR* (1313–18), p488.

8. *CCR* (1313–18), p488.

once the cog was adopted in the Mediterranean, crew sizes on ships fell dramatically.

The cog had a significant impact on the economy of the Mediterranean world, as it did on that of northern Europe. The Genoese used the large and cost effective cogs to great advantage. Their huge capacity allowed fewer ships to do the work of many at less cost. The added costs of fighting men on board to protect the ship from pirates or other enemies was not substantially greater than with other, smaller vessels. The cog with its high freeboard was not a welcome target to her enemies, who preferred to employ fast galleys. The galley was dwarfed by the high-sided cog, which also had the ability to place archers and soldiers in the fore- and aftercastles as well as the topcastle. At sea the crossbow was a useful weapon, and its effectiveness was aided by the cover and height advantage of the cog. Boccaccio records in the *Decameron* the story of two cogs that sank a privateer in the Greek islands. A well-defended cog was a floating fortress, not able to sprint away like the faster galleys, but capable of presenting a formidable challenge to any adversary.[9]

The cog did not compare favourably with a Viking ship in the sleekness of its design or speed. The mere appearance of a cog did not strike fear in the hearts of enemies as did a Viking longship with dragon heads and colourful warriors' shields along the gunwales, but it was an able fighting ship with certain advantages in war. Although the cog was about the same length as many Viking vessels, they are very different types. The Bremen cog measured 23.3m (76.1ft) while the Gokstad ship was 23.3m (76.4ft). The cog measured 7.6m (24.9ft) in beam, while the slim Viking ship was only 6.25m (20.5ft). But the biggest difference was in the height above the keel: the Bremen cog measured 4.2m (13.8ft) while the Gokstad ship was only 1.9m (6.2ft) from keel to gunwale amidships. With this amount of freeboard, clearly the cog could not be rowed. Her single mast carried a square sail that was the only means of propulsion, but she towered over the open Viking-style vessels.

It is important to note the evolution of the ship from Viking vessels like the Gokstad ship, the merchant traders found at Skuldelev and others. Those were sturdy ships made to withstand the northern seas. They shared some common construction techniques with cogs, but the results were quite different. Aside from the larger capacity of the cog, the materials utilised in the construction were different. The strakes of the Bremen cog are over twice the thickness (5cm or 2in) and three times the width (60cm or 24in) of the strakes on a Viking ship. At four or five points through-beams pierced the hull, providing further strength. The iron nails were hammered through the planking and their points bent back into the ribs in characteristic cog style. This contrasts with the riveted hulls of Viking vessels, but provided the same result – a strong ship and one which could support a broad main deck. These features, of course, made the hull of the cog more rigid and less flexible than that of a Viking ship.

English cogs and the Hundred Years War

The conflict between England and France, known as the Hundred Years War, dominates the political and military history of late medieval northern Europe. This epic struggle resulted from a complex combination of factors focused around the dynastic claim to the French throne by England's King Edward III and the attempts of the Valois monarchs, whom the English regarded as usurpers, to control France and prevent the union of the two thrones by conquest. While the roots of the conflict extend to an earlier age, the war

began in 1337 and continued until 1453. Before its conclusion most of the other states of western Europe became involved, and Spain actually served as a theatre of conflict. Because the struggle was waged primarily on the Continent, English fleets faced the formidable task of transporting and disembarking thousands of knights, squires, archers, soldiers, and support personnel for over a century. Indeed, a principal factor in the success or failure of the assaults on the mainland of Europe was the naval and logistical support provided by the English navy to its army. The navy also provided convoy escort, especially for the wine fleet, and fought important battles at sea.

The principal vessel utilised by the English was the cog. The French relied mainly on galleys, built and manned by Italians, primarily Genoese. The Castilians provided galleys and large round ships in aid of the French and for their own purposes in the war against the English.[10] Those vessels from the Mediterranean came from a very different shipbuilding tradition. Their frame-first construction and carvel building was known to northern Europeans who had studied Mediterranean vessels, but so alien were the traditions to one another that native shipwrights and carpenters were reluctant to repair, let alone construct, carvel-

9. John Pryor, *Geography, Technology, and War: Studies in the Maritime History of the Mediterranean, 649–1571* (Cambridge 1988), p154.

10. Colin F Richmond, 'The War at Sea', in K Fowler (ed), *The Hundred Years War* (London 1971), pp96–121.

The capacious, sturdy and seaworthy nature of the cog hull is evident from this photograph taken during the construction of a replica of the Bremen cog. The superstructure has yet to be added, but its superiority as a warship over the lower and lighter nef *type is clear. (Egbert Laska, Deutsches Schiffahrtsmuseum)*

Cogs were as well known for their ability to move people as to carry cargo. This manuscript of 1307, the Livre des Merveilles (Ms fr 2810, f263), shows two vessels crammed with passengers (even allowing for the medieval indifference to scale). Significantly, the vessel on the right carries a full complement of men at arms. (Bibliothèque Nationale).

built ships. Calls went out from the kings of France (but also from the kings of England) for workers who could repair the carvel-built galleys used in the war.

The king of England could summon soldiers by royal command or hire retainers for pay, but sailors were recruited in a less formal manner. The king's sergeants-at-arms travelled about the kingdom with commissions to arrest and take for military service men and ships from the various ports they were assigned to visit. Ships within the specified tonnage and approved as seaworthy were taken into the king's hand by the sergeants for royal duty. No limit was set on the period of arrest, but the wages of the mariners and captains were paid by the crown at standard rates.[11]

Along with these general commissions of arrest which applied to the kingdom at large was the contribution made to the raising of the

A manuscript illustration of cogs in action from a psalter of about 1330 (British Library, Royal Ms E 10, IV, f19). The function of the castles in battle is quite clear, but these structures were a normal feature of the ships of the period, even in merchant service. The ships closely resemble the portrait on the Harderwijk seal of some fifty years earlier, although the aftercastle is more closely integrated with the hull. (British Library)

fleets by the Cinque Ports. This ancient confederation originally consisted of Hastings, Romney, Hythe, Dover and Sandwich. These 'head ports' were the first chartered seaports which obtained liberties and exemptions from various taxes and obligations in return for their provision of ships and men for royal service. At various times throughout the period, these original five ports absorbed as associate members over thirty separate maritime communities. The best known of these are the ports of Winchelsea and Rye, which had become attached to Hastings before 1190. The portsmen were an important part of the commercial and military fabric of the realm and behaved as a political unit in defence of their common privileges.

The arrangement between the crown and the ports was that the latter would provide fifty-seven ships for fifteen days service annually. A fleet of 1299–1300 included fifteen cogs. The ships were fully manned and equipped for military service. The Cinque Ports exchanged their services for royal liberties allowing them freedom from tolls, port duties customs, suit to the shire and hundred, and jury duty, and grants for certain special favours. The extent of these liberties shows that the crown anticipated considerable returns in assistance when it called upon the portsmen. It also reflects the extent to which the monarchy would go to secure a fleet capable of transporting the instruments of war across the Channel.[12]

---

11. Travel expenses for sergeants-at-arms are recorded in the Issue Rolls (E.403) housed in the PRO, London.

12. F W Brooks, 'The Cinque Ports', *The Mariner's Mirror* 15 (1929), pp142–90; K M E Murray, *The Constitutional History of the Cinque Ports* (London 1935).

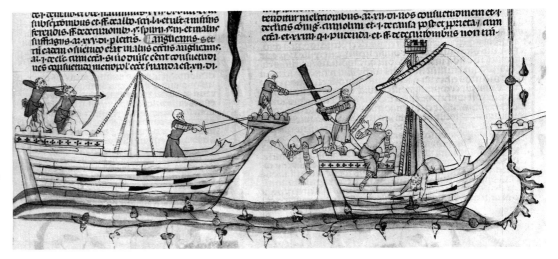

The liberties enjoyed by the Cinque Ports and the reciprocal benefits which were provided to the king contributed a considerable amount to the fighting force at sea. However, the limitations of the time, service, and numbers meant that the king had to look beyond the Cinque Ports in order to be assured of a fleet at sea on a more regular basis or to assemble large fighting forces. In the periods of protracted war with the French and their Castilian allies, both on land and at sea, this meant the utilisation of all of the ports and shipping of the realm to maintain a standing national fleet that could carry the war to the enemy.

A variety of vessel types were arrested for the royal fleet. Any ships fit for service in the royal expeditions were invariably searched out and taken over by the king's agents, but they particularly sought vessels in good condition and of the specified size, and that meant of specified tonnage, demanded by the king's writ. Generally, the writs called for larger ships, those of 100 tons or more, which usually meant cogs. Later, if the large vessels were not forthcoming, the order might encompass all ships over 50 tons, or even 20. Clearly, this depended upon the scale of the campaign and the success of the royal agents in arresting ships.[13]

While this method enabled the king to assemble a fleet, both for fighting and for transport, crown dependence upon the merchants and their ships to serve as a royal navy was quite costly for the merchants involved. It can be argued that the shipowners did well from turning their vessels over to the king: they were paid for the use of their ships, compensated for damages they sustained, and the crews were reasonably well paid, the masters at 6 pence per day and the mariners at 3 pence per day. But this is a hard case to prove. Compensation for damages incurred while in royal service was inconsistent, and whether the vessels ever came up to the original standard cannot be proved. In the Brittany campaign of 1341–43, for example, many ships were employed to carry troops and supplies. There were considerable losses due to the bad weather, and the king and council by their 'grante bonte and grace especial'

Medieval sea battles were little more than land warfare undertaken from floating platforms. Although some manoeuvring preceded combat, and there might be an exchange of arrows, darts or other missiles, the result was settled by boarding and hand-to-hand combat. This late fifteenth-century illustration, showing longbows and crossbows in use, is from Jean de Wavrin's Chronique d'Angleterre, *produced at Bruges for the library of King Edward IV, British Library, Royal Ms 14, E IV, f276r. (British Library)*

made payment to the shipowners for damages. Within a nine-month period about £1000 was paid to owners of forty-five of the ships.[14]

It is not surprising, then, that there were some shipowners who objected to this method of raising fleets and so avoided the arrest orders. The only way to manage this was to stay out of ports where agents were seeking ships for the king's service or to refuse the order, that is unless one already had an exemption. Refusal of the royal arrest order was a serious offence. It is impossible to know how successful captains and owners may have been in avoiding ports where they might be arrested. Most shipowners and masters complied with the crown's orders and allowed the arrest of their vessels. Others did the same but quit royal service the moment their assignment was

completed. Some quit a little too early, and the king called this desertion.

It was a risky business for a shipowner to have his vessel taken into royal service. Desertions occurred in 1342–43 and in 1346, reflecting the failure of the crown to come to terms with this problem.[15] In spite of the flaws in the system, however, the king was not prepared to expend the resources necessary to build his own fleet. A mercantile fleet existed, and by ancient custom he had the right to use it. The cost to him was the cost of wages, vic-

13. *CCR* (1339–41), pp370, 422.

14. PRO, E.101/24/9 (b) mm. 1–45; E.101/24/8.

15. *Calendar of Patent Rolls* (1343–45), p92; E.101/68/4f m, 72.

An illustration of the expedition of the Duke of Bourbon. This is probably a fifteenth-century version of Froissart's Chronicle, *showing three-masted carrack-like descendants of the cog; there is also a low-lying galley in the foreground. Note the decorations of the ships with shields or pavises along the topsides and castles, and the large banners and streamers.*

tuals, 'ton tight' which were payments to shipowners based on tonnage in the 1380s, and occasional compensation to the owner for loss or damage. Impressment of merchant vessels was much cheaper to the crown than the construction of ships from scratch and avoided the maintenance and peacetime lay-up problems which accompanied ownership. Nonetheless, tension continued between the crown and the shipowners. That tension should illustrate some of the further complexities of warfare at sea in an age before the organisation of standing fleets.

There is evidence of the leasing of royal ships during the fifteenth century. For example, William Catton, keeper of the king's ships, put out to hire most of the royal fleet in 1414. Ships were leased to merchants, who used them to carry wine from Bordeaux, and to sail to Newcastle for coal and to Danzig for pitch, tar, and timber. The experience proved very lucrative and over £2000 was earned on the freight charges.[16] Clearly it was advantageous to hire out the ships if such a large return could be generated and if the risk of loss or damage could be tolerated. These ships paid for themselves and offset the dock charges that would have mounted up if they had stayed in port. The critical factor in all of this, of course, was that there was very little hostility on the seas in 1413–14. When war erupted again and an expedition was launched in 1415, one which ended at Agincourt, the navy was officially accounted for by the treasurer for war and not by the clerk of the king's ships. Over £12,000 was released from the exchequer for the repair of ships and for men's wages.[17]

The crown had little need to build ships or to maintain a fleet since, given the character of contemporary ships, it could depend upon the mercantile fleet to be available for conversion to military duty. While such a conversion is impossible in a modern navy, it was practicable in the fourteenth century because of the purpose for which ships were required and materials needed for their construction. The single-masted cog could be converted to military use simply by some carpentry work. This was not always extensive, and the cost of refitting and carpentry work necessary to make a cog fit for war was modest in most instances, not all ships

being fitted out with castles fore and aft to serve as fighting platforms. However, the addition of castles atop the main mast and on the fore and after decks was usually the basic requirement. Since naval battles were little more than land battles fought at sea, there was no great problem in equipping the vessels for war.[18] The use of cannon would require additional restructuring of the ship, but though available they were not adopted at sea for some time. Bows, arrows, lances, swords, fire and heavy objects dropped from the topcastles were the usual weapons.

English cogs sailed with sufficient weapons to conduct war at sea. Accounts from the clerks of the king's ships and others list lances, crossbows, quarrels (crossbow bolts), breastplates, bows, bowstrings, arrows, armour, swords, and even some guns. Archers and men-at-arms came equipped for service in uniform. Armour was stored in the Tower of London and was released for transport to the ships, generally nearby on the Thames at Ratcliffe. Also found in the accounts are 'springalds' and 'arbalests' (types of catapult). The deck of a cog may have been suited to using an 'engine' of war to hurl stones or other objects at the enemy, but the practice is uncertain. What is

known is that such war machines were transported to France aboard ships. Cannon were ordered for the king's expedition of 1346 and several expeditions thereafter. Their use at sea was not a factor in warfare until much later, however.[19]

Ships were highly decorated for battle. The cogs *Thomas* and *Rodecog* were painted for military use with bright colours. Outfitting for war included the purchase of banners and long streamers which were lashed to the masts or rigging. Shields or pavises were usually found on king's ships and may have been placed along the gunwales to announce the arms of those aboard to the enemy.[20]

---

16. PRO, E. 364/54 and for the particulars of the account see E.101/44/24. See also Susan Rose, *The Navy of the Lancastrian Kings; Accounts and Inventories of William Soper, Keeper of the King's Ships, 1422–1427*, Navy Records Society (London 1982), p35.

17. PRO, E.364/59.

18. *CCR* (1339–41), p505.

19. *CCR* (1339–41), pp83–88; Timothy J Runyan, 'Ships and Mariners in Later Medieval England', *Journal of British Studies* 16 (Spring 1977), pp3–8.

20. PRO, E.101/392/1; H J Hewitt, *The Organization of War Under Edward III, 1338–1362* (Manchester 1966), p73.

Ships continued to be arrested on a large scale and converted to naval use by making the necessary changes to them. Also, the men continued to be gathered from wherever they could be found by the arresting officials; admirals, masters, clerks, sergeants-at-arms or other deputies. The ships were arrested and seized, *arrestandis et capiendis* being the language of the manuscripts, and the most able mariners were elected (*eligendis*) for service. The necessary quota of men was found, but the system of recruitment was not without its problems. Still, it did prove a satisfactory alternative to the creation of a large standing navy owned and maintained by the crown. The House of Commons did make some impact on the process of finding crews by its attacks on impressment and in the institution of the Navigation Acts in the 1380s, but these alterations were slight. The wholesale disposal of the royal fleet, the ships owned by the king, in 1377 and again in 1422 emphasises the dependence of the monarchy upon the merchant marine. Indeed, galleys and barges aside, cogs and other merchant vessels were the English men-of-war until the use of cannon demanded the construction of purpose-built ships.

The English did continue to build and use galleys for war in the fourteenth century, but they never built or enlisted for royal service as many as they intended. King Edward I ordered the construction of many galleys in the 1290s, but few of them were actually built. The explanation is found in the system of ship procurement and the pragmatism of commercial shipowners.

Cogs or other large sailing ships were better suited than galleys to handle the trade goods of Europe. Most of the market was in bulk commodities such as wine, wool, timber, salt, and similar cargoes. The galley was labour-intensive with its many oarsmen, which meant a large crew and high unit costs for shipping. The galley's limited space for the carriage of goods made the cog a much better alternative for merchants hoping to turn a profit on a trading venture. This principle held not only in northern Europe but also in the Mediterranean.[21]

Records from Exchequer accounts show that most galleys were either hired from abroad or built for use by the crown. Returns of the sergeants-at-arms or others empowered to arrest ships do not include many galleys. Merchants did not buy or build galleys because of their limitations as trading vessels in an economy focused on the transport of wine, wool, or other bulk cargoes. It is true that galleys might have been more vulnerable to pirates, but a solution to that threat was to travel in large convoys, sometimes with royal escorts. The Venetian government was so concerned about the loss of cogs or round ships to pirates or other enemies that sometimes it prohibited unescorted travel. On lucrative cotton voyages, Venetians used the biggest, and therefore most defensible, cogs.

The cog in action

Sea battles in the Middle Ages were frequently fought in harbours or close to shore rather than in open waters. This was due to the limitations of navigation as well as the popular use of galleys which frequently put into port for food, water and shelter. An enemy fleet might surprise them, gaining the advantage of wind and tide against a vessel confined within a harbour. This circumstance shaped the confrontation between the English and French-Genoese fleets at Sluis on 24 June 1340.

King Edward III sailed for Flanders on 22 June with a large fleet including a number of cogs. Two days later he encountered a large fleet of French and Genoese vessels anchored in the harbour at the mouth of the River Zwin. The chronicler Jean Froissart said that 40,000 men composed their forces: Normans, Genoese, and Picards. He suggested that the French knew the English were coming, and that they had passed them en route to Flanders. The French fleet was so large that 'their masts resembled a forest'. Edward III expressed surprise at discovering their flotilla, but immediately developed a battle plan. He repositioned his fleet, putting his most powerful ships in the van, but first he deployed his fighting forces within the ships. Vessels carrying men-at-arms were flanked on each side by ships loaded with archers. A flanking squadron composed of

21. Richard W Unger, *The Ship in the Medieval Economy*, pp183ff.

ships carrying archers was detached from the main force and assigned as a mobile reserve to provide help wherever it was needed. The balance of the fleet, carrying women of status travelling to visit the queen at Ghent, was not expected to participate in the battle.

Froissart's account of the actual confrontation provides a number of fascinating details.[22] The English hoisted sail and began to move against the enemy when they had the advantage of the wind on their starboard quarter. However, in order to keep the sun from shining directly into their faces, they tacked and repositioned at an angle to the sun before initiating their attack. The French thought they were retreating and began to get under way with the sounds of trumpets, horns, and other instruments. The enemy van was led by the *Christopher*, a large ex-English ship captured following the burning of Southampton in a cross-Channel raid. She was packed with Genoese crossbowmen.

Fighting began as archers and crossbowmen on both sides fired arrows and bolts as the ships closed. With the vessels grappled together with iron hooks attached to chains, men-at-arms fought in hand-to-hand combat. The *Christopher* was recovered by the English at the price of the defenders' lives; many were killed and the rest captured. At this point the English brought up vessels which transferred archers into the *Christopher* before she was sent against the Genoese. Froissart notes that sea fights were always fiercer than fights on land because retreat or flight was impossible. Bravery and fighting skills were the elements for success.

The battle lasted from early morning until afternoon. The Normans were badly beaten, and Froissart states that none escaped in the slaughter. The news of the victory spread quickly, no doubt aided by the Flemish reinforcements from Bruges, whose timely arrival helped win the battle. Froissart claims that the English were outnumbered four to one. It was a glorious victory for a king whose decisive actions suggest a considerable understanding of naval strategy and tactics. These are skills Edward would employ a decade later against the Castilians off Winchelsea. The victory celebra-

tion that night was so great a cacophony of cymbals, trumpets, drums, and cornets 'that God's own thunder would not have been heard above it'.

The victory was followed by another great triumph at sea off Winchelsea on 29 August 1350, known as L'Espagnols-sur-Mer. King Edward III commanded and fought an incredibly intense battle against a fleet of larger Castilian ships. Although he lost his own vessel in the battle, he did manage to board another, where he established his command. Froissart claims that the Iberians knew the English were waiting for them, so in preparation for combat they loaded stones and specially made iron bars to hurl down on the English ships. This implies that they knew the English vessels would be smaller and they would have the advantage in height. The Castilians also loaded projectile-throwers on some of the forty big vessels which set out from the port of Sluis.

Edward III and his chivalrous son, Edward the Black Prince, sailed out into the Channel between Dover and Calais to await that Castilian commercial fleet returning home from Flanders. Colourful streamers flew from the masts of the Castilian fleet as it approached the narrow Channel passage where the English lay in wait. Froissart fails to report any details about that formation, and suddenly the reader is into the melee at sea, which includes the king's decision to 'joust' with a large Castilian ship which was bearing down on him with a following wind. The king's ship turned into the approaching ship and would have been shattered but for its sturdy construction. As they

rebounded from the collision and passed each other, their topcastles became entwined and the mast of the Castilian ship splintered and fell into the sea, killing the men in the topcastle. King Edward's ship was taking water as a result of the collision. He resolved to grapple an enemy ship, board, and carry her before his own sank. The hooks and chains went out to snare a large ship. Fighting began as they boarded, the English troops dodging the iron bars hurled down on them. They did, in the end, carry the ship, and threw the defenders into the sea. But the day was almost gone since the battle began late.

Meanwhile, the Black Prince's ship was grappled by a big Castilian ship, which opened holes in the Prince's vessel. The Duke of Lancaster intervened by boarding the Castilian ship from astern. The Prince transferred to the Castilian ship just before his own ship sank. The chaos of battle enabled the large Castilian ship to move in and tow away the *Salle du Roi*, King Edward's household ship, but a brave soldier leapt aboard the Castilian and cut some of the rigging to the sail. Once the ship lost way, others boarded and drove the enemy overboard. The other Castilian ships escaped, but between fourteen (Froissart) and twenty-six (Walsingham) ships of the fleet of forty were destroyed or captured.[23]

The battle was a major victory for the cogs employed by the English against ships which,

---

22. Jean Froissart, *Chronicles*, ed and trans G Brereton (Harmondsworth 1968), pp62–65.

23. Froissart, *Chronicles*, pp113–19.

A fifteenth-century illustration of cogs transporting the Earl of Salisbury to Conwy Castle in North Wales. Although distorted the ships are well drawn in most details, including the stern area with the rudderhead passing through the transom. In the top hamper, the lashing of the sail to the yard, the parrel which secures the yard to the mast, and the three rows of reef points on the sail are all well defined. British Library, Harley Ms 1319, f14v. (British Library)

the chronicler Jean Froissart says, towered over the English and whose men threw heavy objects down on them. The ship commanded by the Black Prince was holed in the course of the battle. Though it is not clear that the ship was rammed, the event raises a very interesting question. It is known that the Castilians used galleys, since those oared types were very successful fighting ships in the Bay of Biscay in the 1370s. Galleys of the northern seas in the period are not well enough studied to provide much information about the placement of the ram or its structure. If a galley rammed a large cog with its high freeboard, the result could have been disastrous for both vessels. The galley might not be able to disengage from the holed ship now taking on water, and might founder with her. If the galley rammed the cog and could not immediately disengage, the crew and marines were sitting targets for the men on the cog, who could fire arrows at them or hurl objects down from their superior position. Boarding by the men of the galley was difficult because they would have had to scale the hull topside to get on to the main deck.

Since none of the outcomes of ramming a cog or other large sailing ship were likely to be successful unless the galley could ram and disengage successfully, this does not seem to have been a very satisfactory tactic. However, if Froissart can be believed, the ship was holed, and if by a galley, she did disengage, with or without the beak, which may have snapped off. Some rams were designed so that the spur could be broken off from the ship. The major advantages of the galley against the cog were manoeuvrability and firepower, if the ram was not a factor. Crossbowmen aboard a galley could be very dangerous if employed properly.

The most significant naval action upon the resumption of the war was the English loss to a Castilian fleet at La Rochelle in 1372. The disaster in Gascony was complete, with several English ships being destroyed or captured and many soldiers going to the bottom. The defeat so angered the English that increased attention and resources were directed to the navy. To shore up the fleet, temporary reinforcements were provided through the hire of ten Genoese galleys and a smaller vessel in 1373 at the cost of £9550.[24]

The French relied upon ships provided by their royal shipyard at Rouen, the *Clos des Galées*, constructed by Genoese builders in 1298. Mediterranean-style galleys were built there using southern construction methods. The Genoese dominated the yard, which produced war galleys until 1419, when Normandy fell to the English. The French destroyed the

The seal of Gdansk from about 1400 shows the developed form of the cog with fore and after superstructures more closely integrated with the hull. Another interesting feature is the inclusion of ratlines on the shrouds to give the crew access to the main yard and topcastle. (By courtesy of Richard Unger)

Clos des Galées and all ships in port to prevent the English from taking them. By then the French were hiring Genoese carracks. The war effort at sea focused on efforts to transport men and materiel across the Channel. Cogs and other large cargo ships were enlisted for this work. As evidenced by the sturdy construction of the Hanse cog found at Bremen in 1962, cogs were obviously durable vessels. Other cog finds reinforce our understanding of the type as a strong, capacious ship for its age which could withstand the internal pressures of heavy cargo and the wear and tear of its lading and unlading, and even the shovelling that was necessary after a cargo of horses had been disembarked. But the cog was also a fighting ship whose durability was important for the preservation of life and defeat of enemies. While not a purpose-built man-of-war such as the *Mary Rose*, the fourteenth-century cog was a major factor in waging war.

Naval logistics

Medieval armies depended upon a continuous supply of materials which flowed to port towns for transport with or to the expeditionary forces serving abroad. This was especially true during the Hundred Years War, when the English repeatedly invaded France. Cogs and other merchant ships served in an important logistical capacity as troop carriers and victuallers of armies operating abroad. No real conversion was necessary to put them into ser-

vice, save the construction of stalls to hold the horses ferried across in great quantities for use by knights. Since this was an age of chivalry there could be no mounted knight to lead the armies against the French and their allies without the destrier or warhorse. Between 1338 and 1359 from a few southern counties 16,000 wooden hurdles to separate the horses and 200 gangways were constructed for the shipment of horses and transported to ports of embarkation, mainly Southampton, Plymouth or Portsmouth. At least 2000 horses were shipped. However, for the king's expedition of 1359 alone, 3245 horses were shipped from Sandwich to Calais. Remarkably, the total number of horses shipped back to England from Calais was 6313. Because of the short distance it was possible to shuttle the ships back and forth to transport the men, horses and supplies. Food and water for the horses must not be overlooked in considering what a cog or other vessel was expected to carry. Hundreds of wooden tuns used to hold water were ordered for the ships carrying horses.[25] The transport of horses by ship also meant added administrative work. Since compensation was promised by the crown for horses lost or killed in the war, each animal was appraised by a military leader and a royal official. Compensation was based on this appraisal.

Loading horses on to a ship was a difficult matter. Cogs, with their high freeboard, created special problems. Horses could not be loaded directly on to the main deck save by special docking facilities, nor unloaded at a port that lacked them. Holes cut in the hull acted as doorways approached by special gangways made for the loading or unloading. Some gangways were 30ft (9.1m) long and 5ft (1.5m) wide, but most were 15–20ft (4.5–6.1m) in length. In theory, each knight had four horses, each squire three and every mounted archer two, so the transport problem becomes quickly apparent.

While a number of solutions could be employed to load and unload horses, the best option was to use ships altered to accommodate horses with appropriate gangways. For every crossing, hurdles of about 7ft by 4ft (2.1m × 1.2m) were constructed to form stalls used to separate the horses. Boards, racks, ropes,

24. J W Sherborne, 'The Battle of La Rochelle and the War at Sea, 1372–5', *Bulletin of the Institute of Historical Research* 42 (May 1969), pp17–29.

25. The volume of water carried defined the amount of time a ship could stay at sea. See T J Runyan, 'Naval Logistics in the Late Middle Ages', in J A Lynn (ed), *Feeding Mars: Logistics in Western Warfare* (Boulder 1993), pp90ff.

canvas, metal rings, nails, and large empty wooden tuns were also used for this purpose. Horses were difficult to transport by sea partly because ships needed to be purpose-built or specially altered to accommodate them, but also because of their dietary needs and the physical strain they suffered.

Assembling a fleet, refitting the ships to transport troops and horses, impressing the sailors to man the fleet, and gathering the necessary supplies was of little use to the English, however, if their fleet could not control the English Channel. After the outbreak of war in 1337, the English coastal towns were in great fear of raids and even of a general French invasion. In 1338–39 the south coast ports were hit by raiding parties and Sandwich, Hastings and Portsmouth were partially burnt, Folkstone, Dover, Thanet and the Isle of Wight were harassed, and even Southampton suffered damage. Many ships were lost through these attacks, and shipping was badly interrupted. A major invasion was planned by King Philip VI of France in 1339, but a storm scattered his fleet. Instead, Edward III commanded an English fleet that decisively overcame a combined French, Castilian and Genoese flotilla at Sluis the following year. The victory was one of the greatest of the war and the first important one, coming a full six years before the great land battle at Crécy, where the longbow worked to such advantage. What is important to notice about Sluis is that Edward III commanded from aboard his flagship in person and directed the destruction of the larger enemy force, and in doing so, helped determine the future course of the war. An English loss at Sluis would have encouraged a French invasion and shifted the battle lines more to the Channel or perhaps even to England itself. Edward's action also meant that, for a time at least, the English could safely transport the troops and supplies necessary to fight the land war on the Continent. But there were other dangers.

Merchants frequently turned pirate or suffered piracy, with the excuse that the other parties were the enemies of their own country. Truces seem to have been conveniently forgotten, and suits to the crown were often the recourse. These appeals remain as the record of piratical raids. They were, in effect, crimes of convenience with convenient excuses generated to justify plundering. The Admiralty was called upon to patrol the coasts and Channel against enemy ships and pirates on several occasions, but its effectiveness is difficult to estimate. While occasionally discouraged, the merchants never lost their desire to risk the

Great changes in sea warfare were eventually wrought by the introduction of gunpowder artillery. This manuscript illustration of 1482 shows a ship with a row of gun muzzles pointing through the bulwark and more in the forecastle. The manuscript was made for Louis de Bruges, Lord of Gruythuse, whose emblem was a bombard as shown in the margin. Bibliothèque Nationale Ms fr 38, f157v. (By courtesy of Christiane Villain-Gandossi)

voyage. The prospect of profits was too great an enticement to fourteenth-century merchant venturers.

The solution to help resolve this problem, achieved at some point in the late thirteenth or fourteenth century, was the introduction of convoys. These were especially successful in the English wine trade to Gascony. Larger fleets of merchantmen, often escorted by royal ships filled with men-at-arms, could deter individual raiders or even small pirate fleets. For protection, the transports were usually assigned squads of armed men and archers to sail with the ships and defend them from individual attack. The crew must have assisted in the fighting, and their added numbers meant that the vessels represented a considerable military challenge to pirates or enemy ships. The English ships generally sailed in convoy for added protection on both military and mercantile missions. For example, the wine carriers to and from Bordeaux regularly travelled in convoy during the war to defend themselves against French and Castilian men-of-war or pirates.[26] The threat from the latter was often enough in itself to encourage the arming of ships, or at least to seek safety in numbers. Nevertheless, not all merchants could afford, or were prepared, to tolerate the cumbersome

process of gathering a fleet at a designated port, awaiting royal escorts to join them, and then sailing a prescribed course to Bordeaux or wherever. Many shipowners preferred to push on with their trade and risk encounters with French merchants-cum-pirates. The same held true for the French, although they were not as active in the trade of wine or wool which was so important to the English economy.

Seaborne commerce was of great value to the royal income. Customs accounts and extant shipping records leave no doubt that the English trade in wine and wool was a major source of crown revenue.[27] The interruption of trade, and thus a resultant decline in customs revenue, was a matter of serious consequence to the treasury, and therefore to King Edward's ability to wage war – unless, that is, the revenue could be replaced in other ways. So-called control of the seas, therefore, is a meaningful term for this period if limited to a definition which signifies the capacity of seaborne commerce or the transport of troops to continue unobstructed by pirates or enemy fleets. Though it is often said that such control was in the hands of the English after 1340, careful review of the records reveals quick retaliation and raiding by the French. The ports on the southern coast of England were raided as they had been in the 1330s, and attacks on the shipping routes to Gascony in the Bay of Biscay continued.[28]

It is true that major expeditions by large flotillas were launched in the 1340s against the French coasts, but this did not require command of the seas. It would have taken an equally large flotilla of several hundred ships to intercept the English expeditions of 1342–43 and 1346. Focus on the resultant victories on land at Crécy in 1346 or Poitiers in 1356 can all too easily lead to losing sight of the logistical achievement involved in moving men, horses, and supplies to the Continent, which made the English victories possible.

The key to this success was the cog. More than any other vessel in English service, the cog provided for the transport of men and materiel to pursue the war on the Continent. While fighting at sea was an important factor in the course of the Hundred Years War, in the age of mounted knights and massed armies the supply of men, horses and materiel to the battlefield was critical to the successful pursuit

26. PRO, E.403/555 m. 44 on the escort of ships to Bordeaux; *Calendar of Patent Rolls* (1370–74), p204.

27. J W Sherborne, 'Shipping and Manpower 1369–1389', *Past and Present* 37 (July 1967); pp163–73.

28. PRO, E.101/24/8 for the loss from four English ships in the summer of 1342.

The military successor to the cog was the carrack, a vessel primarily noted for its size. This French manuscript, Passages Outre Mer *of the late fifteenth century (Ms fr 5594, f112), depicts a number of large carracks in the foreground, while the background shows a number of scenes of shipwreck and foundering, to emphasise the danger of sea crossing. (Bibliothèque Nationale).*

of an overseas war, and the cog was clearly the best bulk carrier of such materiel. The French could depend on galleys because they were primarily engaged in defending their coasts and raiding English shipping and coastal towns, but the English pursued a war abroad which demanded the constant recruitment of ships and mariners. Cogs were always arrested for royal service. Ranging in size from thirty to several hundred tons, the cog was sized to fit the needs of an expedition.[29]

An advantage of the cog was its ready convertibility to military use. Conversely, once the cog was no longer needed for naval purposes it could immediately resume commercial activity in the bulk trades, primarily of wine and wool. Since taxes on these goods were major producers of crown revenue, the cog helped keep the wheels of commerce turning, which generated income to be reinvested in the war effort. Galleys and other oared vessels could not do this as efficiently as the cog. Those facts help to explain why the cog was not only a mainstay of European commerce, but also of war.

Timothy J Runyan

29. An example is the expedition of 1342–43, which included over 220 ships. *Calendar of Patent Rolls* (1343–45), p92.

4

The Mediterranean Round Ship

OF THE sailing ships of Byzantium, Islam and the Latin West which plied the trade routes of the Mediterranean at the turn of the first millenium AD, comparatively little is known.[1] There are no documentary sources which give any detailed data for the dimensions, structures or rigging of such ships, and although literary sources provide occasional clues to characteristics such as steering oars, masts and sails, they permit no detailed reconstruction. Without iconographic and archaeological evidence virtually nothing would be known. Although the pictures are relatively few in number before the twelfth century, they do at least permit reasonable hypotheses concerning hull design, steering mechanisms, sails and rigging. The evidence of three important archaeological excavations provides almost all current knowledge of the structures of hulls: the Yassi Ada wreck of the seventh century, the Serçe Liman wreck of the eleventh century, and the Contarina ship of *c*AD 1300, the last excavated only with premodern techniques at the turn of the century. Its remains are now completely lost, as also are those of the Yassi Ada ship, the latter through neglect rather than ignorance. Only the remains of the Serçe Liman ship have been preserved. Other wrecks of the period have been located at various places: for example, Pelagos island in the Sporades; Mazara in Sicily; and Agay, Rocher de l'Estou, and Bataiguier off the coast of Languedoc. However, their hulls have not been excavated and reconstructed. For the High Middle Ages, *c*1050–1300, evidence can also be added from documentary sources of the thirteenth century in the contracts which King Louis IX of France made with Genoa, Venice, and Marseilles for his two Crusades of 1248–54 and 1270.

In the centuries after late Antiquity the sailing ships of the Mediterranean evolved in some

1. See, in particular, B M Kreutz, 'Ships, shipping and the implications of change in the early medieval Mediterranean', *Viator* 7 (1976), pp79–109; B Landstrom, *The Ship: An Illustrated History* (New York 1961); A R Lewis and T J Runyan, *European Naval and Maritime History, 300–1500*, (Bloomington, Ind 1985); J H Pryor, *Geography, Technology, and War: Studies in the Maritime History of the Mediterranean 649–1571* (Cambridge 1988); R W Unger, *The Ship in the Medieval Economy, 600–1600* (London 1980).

The Mediterranean world, c1100 AD. (Map by Denys Baker)

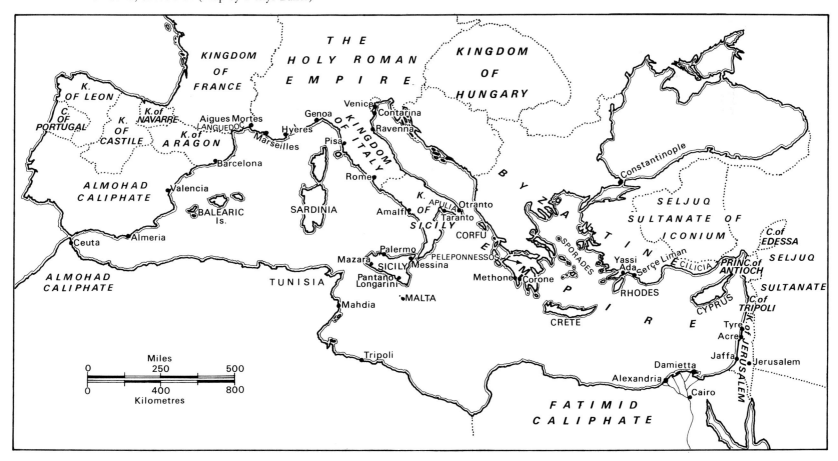

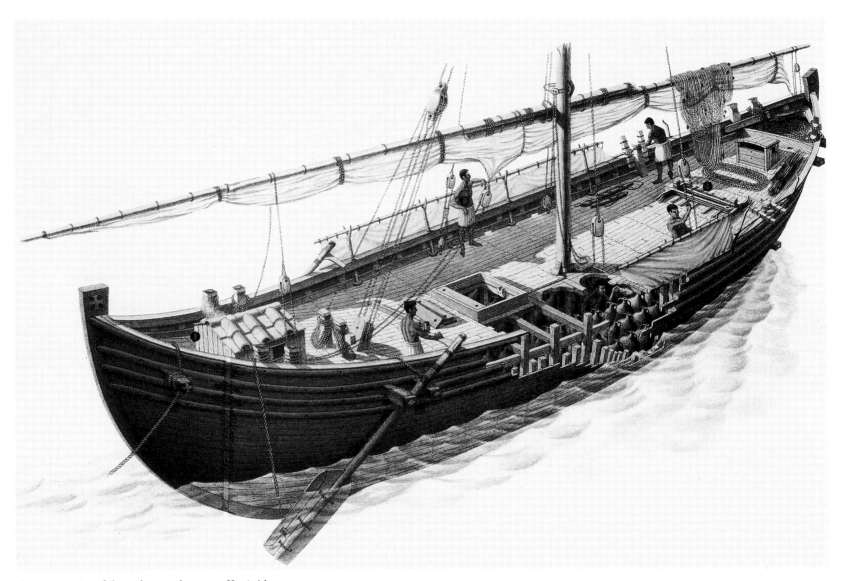

A reconstruction of the early seventh-century Yassi Ada ship based on the excavation of the wreck. Most details were determined by the archaeological evidence, but the mooring bitts and weather cloths are assumptions based on the practice of the last Greek sailing coasters. (From History from the Sea, by kind permission of Mitchell Beazley International Ltd)

of their fundamental features of construction and design to produce the peculiar characteristics of the medieval sailing ships of the eleventh to thirteenth centuries. These are usually referred to as 'round ships' because of their rounded profiles at stem and stern. Evidence from across the Mediterranean suggests that, although there were local . and regional peculiarities and some features changed with time, basic designs remained relatively constant and similar in the Byzantine, Muslim, and Latin worlds. These ships ranged in size from open boats with only half decks at best to very large ships with three decks and an overall length of 35m (115ft) or more. Their displacement tonnage ranged from the few dozen met-

ric tonnes of the Yassi Ada and Serçe Liman ships to the 800 or more of the largest transports of Louis IX. The larger, multi-decked ships had ports in the hull at the first deck through which passengers, horses, and merchandise could be loaded before they were sealed with pitch to put to sea. As Jean de Joinville wrote in his *Life of Saint Louis*:

> On the day that we entered into our ship, they opened the door of the ship and put therein all the horses we wanted to take oversea; and then they reclosed the door, and caulked it well, as when a cask is sunk in water, because, when the ship is on the high seas, all the said door is under water.[2]

The ships had straight keels but markedly convex stemposts and sternposts which gave them their rounded profile. This was accentuated by a pronounced upward rake of the gunwales from amidships towards bow and stern. At the stern they had peculiar ornamentations

of one of two types: a dual 'wing' or a 'canopy'. Some had a peculiar open foredeck beneath a recurved stempost. But all of the ships were lateen rigged, with from one to three masts, the fore mast always given a pronounced rake to the bow. They were steered not by sternpost rudders, but rather by two steering oars mounted on the hull on both stern quarters.

The seventh-century Yassi Ada ship

This wreck of a small Byzantine vessel of the early seventh century was located by Peter Throckmorton off the islet of Yassi Ada in the Chuka Channel between Pserimo and Turkey in 1958.[3] It was excavated by a team led by George Bass between 1960 and 1964. The re-

2. Villehardouin and de Joinville, *Memoirs of the Crusades*, trans F Marzials (London 1908), p167.

3. G F Bass and F H van Doorninck, jr, *Yassi Ada, Volume I: A Seventh-Century Byzantine Shipwreck* (College Station 1982).

mains of the hull were removed to Bodrum Museum where, unfortunately, they were allowed to disintegrate. Nevertheless, the seventh-century Yassi Ada ship was the first medieval shipwreck to be excavated in its entirety, and the techniques used permitted detailed reconstruction of the hull.

Even the name of the presumed master of the ship is known. A bronze steelyard found on the wreck bears the inscription: 'George the elder [or senior] *naukleros* [master/captain]'.

Between frames 12 and 13, 15 and 16, and 32 and 33, numbered from the stern, there were three through beams which projected beyond the external planking. The first two formed a box mounting outside the hull for the steering oars and the last probably braced the mast. The keel and sternpost (the stempost has been lost) were made of cypress, the frames of elm, and the hull planking of pine. Iron spikes and bolts were used to tie the structure together. The ship could carry up to 61 metric tonnes of cargo in good weather. When wrecked, she was carrying between 850 and 900 amphorae of wine, weighing some 40.03 metric tonnes. At the stern she had a cabin and a galley with a hearth of glazed tiles. From this part of the wreck many pieces of pottery which had been used for cooking, storage and eating were found, along with oil lamps, coins, and the steelyards. From the forward section of the ship eleven anchors were recovered, seven stacked in a pile at the centreline forward of the

mast and four in two pairs ready for use near the gunwales at the bow.

The really important information which the excavation of this Yassi Ada wreck yielded concerns the construction of the hull. After the keel and posts were set up, the shipwright began to build up the hull by laying strakes and adzing them to fit side by side in the desired shape, butting them edge to edge with mortise and tenon joints in the Greco-Roman way. But in this seventh-century ship there was a difference. When several strakes had been laid out in this way from either side of the keel, floor timbers were then laid inside them and fixed with iron spikes driven through the planks. The same procedure was then repeated to bring the hull up to the waterline. The frames which would carry the hull up to the gunwales were then put in place, and the hull was completed by bolting four wales to the upper frames and filling in the spaces between them with planks nailed to the frames without any mortise and tenon joints.

The excavation of the seventh-century Yassi Ada ship provided historians with conclusive evidence that, by the seventh century, a transition in construction techniques from the Greco-Roman shell technique to the medieval skeleton technique was well under way.

The eleventh-century Serçe Liman ship

In 1973 a survey team from the American Institute of Nautical Archaeology located the wreck of a ship at Serçe Liman harbour near Marmaris on the Turkish coast opposite Rhodes.[4] Coins and coin weights found aboard indicate that she probably sank in 1024 or 1025. The wreck was excavated over three seasons from 1977 to 1979. Preservation and re-

construction of the hull are still in their early stages, but new techniques used in the excavation, in particular fragment models and dioramas, have already produced important results.

The keel was made of elm but the rest of the ship of pine. When wrecked she was carrying a cargo of Muslim glassware and glass cullet as well as 110 old, reused Byzantine amphorae. Some of these bear graffito names, presumably those of the owners of their contents. Muslim pottery was also found aboard, together with fifty javelins, twelve spears and two or three swords, which appear to have been Byzantine in style, although one of them may have been curved like a scimitar. There were chess pieces of Muslim design, Muslim glass coin weights, and both Muslim and Byzantine coins. Gold earrings, a wooden comb, and bone spindle whorls indicate the presence of a woman on board. The ship carried eight anchors, five stowed at the centreline amidships, two on the port bow and one on the starboard bow. Another similar anchor with a broken shank found on the seabed nearby is probably the missing starboard anchor, and may explain why the ship came to grief.

This ship was a polyglot vessel trading between the Fatimid Caliphate and the Byzantine Empire. Whether she was in Muslim or Christian hands is impossible to say. Although some pig bones found on board may indicate Christian ownership, her construction suggests that she was Muslim built.

4. See J R Steffy, 'The Reconstruction of the Eleventh-Century Serçe Liman Vessel: A Preliminary Report', *International Journal of Nautical Archaeology and Underwater Exploration* 11 (1982), pp13–34; Various, 'The Glass Wreck: An Eleventh-Century Merchantman', *Institute of Nautical Archaeology Newsletter* 15, No 3 (September 1988), pp1–31.

Hull lines of the Serçe Liman vessel, a small trader which sank about 1025 AD. The square section amidships was the product of the partial frame-first nature of construction; this shape would not have been possible with the earlier mortised shell-first structure. From J Richard Steffy, 'The Reconstruction of the 11th-century Serçe Liman vessel', International Journal of Nautical Archaeology 11/1 (1982).

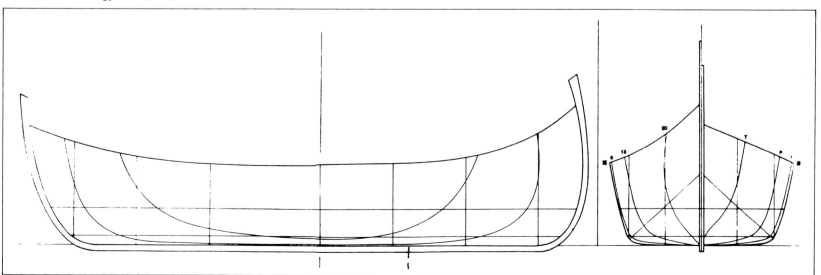

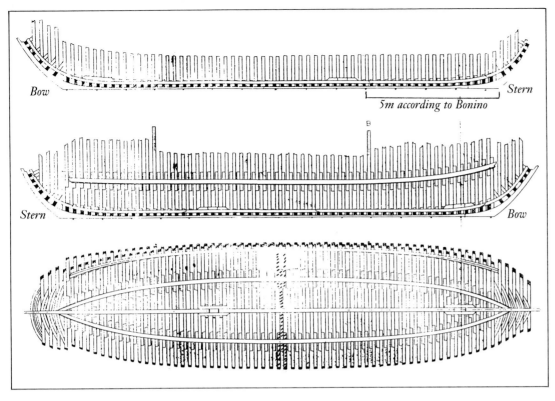

Bow ... *Stern*

5m according to Bonino

Stern ... *Bow*

A survey of the surviving structure of the thirteenth-century Contarina ship. The ship was entirely framed, with overlapping futtocks joined to the heads of the floor timbers. Longitudinal strength was provided by internal stringers and external wales at the height of the floor-futtock overlaps. The midships 'defining' timbers are shaded.

The most important revelation to emerge from investigation of the remains concerns the construction methods used to build the ship. These represent a further step along the evolutionary road from shell to skeletal construction. The keel and posts were set up first as usual, the keel being composed of three timbers scarfed together and curved up at bow and stern. Two midships floor timbers were then laid. These were short and flat to one side of the keel, but longer and with a sharp curve upwards at the bilge on the other side, being set alternately to port and starboard. Futtocks were then scarfed to their long arms. To their short arms other futtocks curved at the bilge were also scarfed. This completed two full frames. Eight other floor timbers were then added, four forward and four aft, with their long arms being set alternately to port and starboard. After that, two more frames, numbers 12 aft and 13 forward, were also probably set up with the aid of temporary construction stringers. Strakes one to five from the keel were then set up from post to post. Following that, strake ten, and perhaps strakes eleven and twelve also, were added. Setting up these strakes on the posts and midships floor timbers gave the hull its definition. At that stage the remaining floor timbers and frame futtocks

were probably set up, followed by at least three, and possibly four, wales. The remaining strakes of the sides, at least four of which did not run the full length of the hull, were then added. They were composed of various short timbers scarfed and butted together. After all the floor timbers were in place, a keelson was bolted on through the keel. Three stringers were then run across the floor timbers from bow to stern on both sides and a removable ceiling added.

No evidence of mortise and tenon joints in the planking was found. All planks were fastened to the frames with iron spikes. This was a ship built entirely frame first in that the planking was nailed to the frames and not joined edge to edge. However, it was still transitional in design in that the frames were not all set up at the start. The shipwrights worked from a

predetermined design only amidships. At bow and stern the shape of the hull was defined by the strakes and set up on the midships frames and the posts.

The remarkably flat floor amidships and capacious hull of the ship was possible only because a skeletal construction technique was used. The demands of carpentry imposed by the classical Greco-Roman shell-built, mortise and tenon technique would have made the lines of this ship impossible to achieve.

The fact that the keel was composed of three timbers rather than one long one, and the large amount of scarfing and butting together of shorter timbers to form the hull strakes, suggests that the ship was built in an environment where economy in the use of timber was important. Very possibly this may have been somewhere in the Muslim world, which was always very short of large scantling timber, rather than in the Byzantine world, which had plenty of forests and tall trees.

The thirteenth-century Contarina ship

The wreck of a small ship of the late thirteenth or early fourteenth century was discovered near Contarina in the Po delta in 1898 during the digging of a canal.[5] Contemporary techniques did not permit preservation of the ship, but the excavation was remarkably sophistic-

5. See Commissione eletta dalla R Deputazione Veneta di Storia Patria, *Sulla scoperta di due barche antiche nel territorio del comune di Contarina in Provincia de Rovigo nel gennaio 1898* (Venice 1900).

A model of the remains of the Contarina ship, which shows the flat floors, external wales at the floor and futtock timber joints. The hull is effectively double-ended. (Museo Storico Navale, Venice)

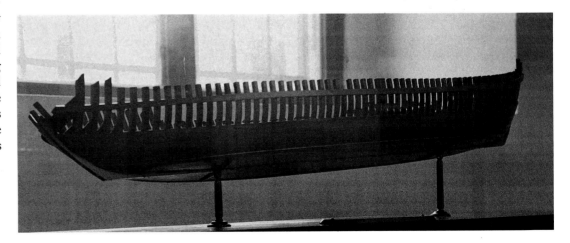

The timbers of the Contarina ship as excavated. (Museo Storico Navale, Venice)

ward, and filled between at either end on top of the keelson, thus creating mast steps about 24cm (9½in) long.

Finally, between frames 24 and 25 aft, the remains of a large transverse timber were found. The excavators could not guess at the purpose of this timber, and thought that it may have been displaced when the ship was struck during the excavation of the canal. In fact, it was almost certainly a fragment of a stern quarter through-beam used to mount the steering oars.

The thirteenth-century ships of St Louis

For his two Crusades of 1248–54 and 1270, King Louis IX of France (St Louis) made contracts with Marseilles, Genoa, and Venice for the construction and lease of various sailing ships.[6] These contracts preserve the earliest surviving detailed dimensions for Mediterranean sailing ships. The ships of St Louis represent the ultimate evolution of round ships in the Mediterranean in the period immediately prior to the appearance of the square rigged, sternpost-ruddered cog in the Mediterranean, with the qualification that all of St Louis' ships had two, rather than three, masts. They had either two or three decks, with some, but not all, having additional half-decks or gangways known as *corridoria* on the main deck along the bulwarks on either side.

Their sails were huge, the yards being much longer than the overall length of the ships and composed of two spars each, woolded together. Management of these yards and sails required large crews, even given that they had complex tackle systems to manage the standing and running rigging. Approximately one crew member per 10 tonnes seems to have been the norm, making the average crew for an 800-tonne ship around 80 officers and sailors plus some servants and ship's boys. The ships had massive steering oars and carried up to twenty-five anchors or more. They towed one large ship's

ated and well-documented for its time. Detailed measurements were recorded, plans were drawn up, and a model, which is now in the Museo Storico Navale at Venice, was constructed.

Made of oak throughout, except for stringers of larch, the ship was entirely skeleton built. It was set up on a keel composed of two timbers, stem- and sternposts, and floor timbers nailed to the keel by spikes driven from above through a keelson and clenched under the keel. The structure of three frames amidships defined the rest of the ribbing of the ship. The midships master frame was composed of a single floor timber running from bilge to bilge. To both sides of this floor timber, four futtocks, two at either end, were joined with iron nails, with an overlap of about 75cm (30in). Then an upper futtock was added on each side, fitted in between the lower two, corresponding to the floor timber, and carrying the frame to the gunwale. The first floor timber aft had futtocks abaft it and upper futtocks forward of those, corresponding to the floor timber. The first floor timber forward had futtocks forward of it and upper futtocks abaft those, again corresponding in position to the floor timber. This pattern defined the frames raised on the keel: twenty-eight towards the bow and

twenty-nine towards the stern. Forward and aft of these respectively, five and three special forked frames without floor timbers were used to raise the futtocks at the extreme ends of the stempost and sternpost.

Where the floor timbers joined the futtocks, an external wale and an internal stringer were fitted to lock the joints. Another external wale and internal stringer were used at the join of the futtocks and upper futtocks for the same purpose.

At frames 17 aft and 12 forward on the better preserved port side, peculiar upper futtocks with slots for movable planks were found. This has led to the supposition that between these two frames, over the midships part of the ship, the bulwark could be removed, perhaps to allow oars to be used when the wind failed. The ship was probably an Adriatic coastal trader which used its oars in the confined waters and shallows of the Venetian lagoons and the Po delta at the head of the Adriatic.

Perhaps the most important evidence to survive from this wreck concerns the positioning of its mast steps, since these have not been located on either the Yassi Ada or Serçe Liman ships. The steps of the Contarina wreck were composed of timbers set either side of the kelson, covering frames 7–11 aft and 22–26 for-

6. See R Bastard de Péré, 'Navires méditerranéens du temps de Saint Louis', *Revue d'Histoire Economique et Sociale* 50 (1972), pp327–56; J E Dotson, 'Jal's Nef X and Genoese Naval Architecture in the Thirteenth Century', *The Mariner's Mirror* 59 (1973), pp161–70; J H Pryor, 'The Naval Architecture of Crusader Transport Ships: A Reconstruction of some Archetypes for Round-hulled Sailing Ships', *The Mariner's Mirror* 70 (1984), pp171–219, 275–92 and 363–86; *Idem*, 'The Naval Architecture of Crusader Transport Ships and Horse Transports Revisited', *The Mariner's Mirror* 76 (1990), pp255–73.

Table 4/1: Known Characteristics of Mediterranean Round Ships

	Yassi Ada	Pantano Longarini	Serçe Liman	Pelagos	Contarina	St Louis	St Louis
Century	Seventh	Seventh	Eleventh	Twelfth	Thirteenth	Thirteenth	Thirteenth
Overall length	20.52	30.30	15.36	25	20.98	28.90	35.20
Keel: length	12	23.20	c9		16.50	18.70	22.60
thickness	0.355		0.11		0.07		
width	0.22		0.16		0.15		
Keelson: length					16.64		
thickness	0.22		0.20		0.10		
width	0.22		0.17		0.145		
Sternpost:							
thickness			0.11				
width			0.13				
Frames: thickness	0.12–0.16		0.16	0.16	0.12	0.17	0.21
width	0.12–0.16		0.11	0.18	0.12		
Strakes: thickness	0.035	0.035	0.035–0.042	0.035	0.04	0.035	0.05
					0.24?		
Through beams:							
thickness	0.19			0.30	0.24?	0.28	
width	0.32						0.34
Number of decks	1	1	1	1	1	2	3
Floor width			3.20			1.70	3.14
Maximum beam	5		5.12	8	5.20	7.75	9.50
Depth in hold	2.25		1.60		2.90	3.45	4.11
First deck height						2.06	2.91
Second deck height							2.03
Corridoria						1.57	1.76
Bulwarks						1.13	1.18
Keel to main deck	2.25		1.60		2.90	5.84	9.83
Fore mast						29.30	36.48
Midships mast						26.80	34.25
Fore mast yard						36.20	46.80
Midships mast yard						33.30	41.80
Steering oars						13.98	17.00
Beam:length ratio	1:4		1:3	1:3.125	1:4.03	1:3.76	1:3.71
Displacement tonnage (metric)	72.86	35				323	806

Note: Measurement in metres.

A modern sailing model of one of Louis IX's crusader transports, for which contemporary contracts preserve some details and dimensions. They were large ships, reaching about 115ft overall, and 800 tons displacement, with two full decks and possibly an additional level of wide gangways along the bulwarks, plus decks in the sterncastle. They could carry horses, which were loaded through large ports on the lower deck. (John H Pryor)

boat astern, carried up to three more boats on board, and had a passenger complement from a few hundred persons to over 1000. An 800-tonne ship might carry about 560 passengers. They could also carry up to 100 horses for Crusaders if their passenger load was decreased. At the first deck there were ports in the hulls which could be opened to take on horses and which were then closed and sealed with pitch before putting to sea.

The study of these ships has been bedevilled by the fact that the original manuscripts for the contracts are now lost and they survive only in unreliable transcriptions made between the seventeenth and nineteenth centuries. Nevertheless, great strides have been made in understanding them in the past twenty years, largely through the work of Bastard de Péré, Dotson, and Pryor.

The ships fell into two main classes: two-decked and three-decked. Although the three-decked ships were on average only 6.3m (21ft) longer overall, 3.9m (13ft) longer in the keel, 1.75m (6ft) broader in the beam, and 3.99m (13ft) deeper from upper deck to keel than the two-decked ships, their displacement tonnage

was a massive 806 metric tonnes, as opposed to the mere 323 tonnes of the two-decked ships. Comparatively small increases in dimensions produced large increases in tonnage when converted to three-dimensional space. A ten per cent increase in dimensions would produce an increase in tonnage of 33.1 per cent, and the addition of an extra deck of 2.03m (6.7ft) on top of that would produce a further increase in tonnage of 34.85 per cent.

The size of ships

By the early Middle Ages ships had, on average, probably become smaller than they had been during the Roman period. At the least, the huge grain transports of Rome had disappeared. It has been claimed that the cause of this was a need for speed and manoeuvrability created by the disappearance of the Roman *dominium* at sea and the development of a maritime no-man's land between Islam, Byzantium, and the West along the frontiers of the sea.[7] There may be a point in the claim as far as manoeuvrability is concerned, but not in the case of speed. Small ships do not sail faster than

large ones unless other factors are involved, such as hull design, rigging, or steering. Comparison of the length-to-beam ratios of the seventh-century Yassi Ada ship and that of a fourth-century ship found at the same site,[8] 1:4 and 1:2.9 respectively, suggests that hulls may have become more refined in a search for speed and manoeuvrability, although it should be noted that the length-to-beam ratio of the eleventh-century Serçe Liman ship was only 1:3.

The Greco-Roman world had known a plethora of smaller ships in addition to the very large grain carriers of Rome. A similar size variation no doubt continued into the Middle Ages. Evidence accumulated in recent years suggests that some very large ships continued

7. See R S Lopez, 'The Role of Trade in the Economic Readjustment of Byzantium in the Seventh Century', *Dumbarton Oaks Papers* 13 (1959), pp68–85.

8. See F H van Doorninck, jr, 'The Fourth-Century Wreck at Yassi Ada: An Interim Report on the Hull', *International Journal of Nautical Archaeology and Underwater Exploration* 5 (1976), pp115–31.

The development of mortise and tenon joinery in hull construction:

A   The fourth-century BC Kyrenia ship shows the full Greco-Roman system of tightly spaced pegged tenons.

B   The fourth-century AD Yassi Ada wreck displayed fewer and smaller tenons, less tightly fitted.

C   The seventh-century AD Yassi Ada ship had even fewer tenons, which were not pegged.

D   The eleventh-century Serçe Liman vessel had no mortise and tenon joints between any of the strakes.

From J Richard Steffy, 'The Mediterranean shell to skeleton transition…', in R Reinders and Paul Kees (eds), Carvel Construction Technique *(Oxford 1991).*

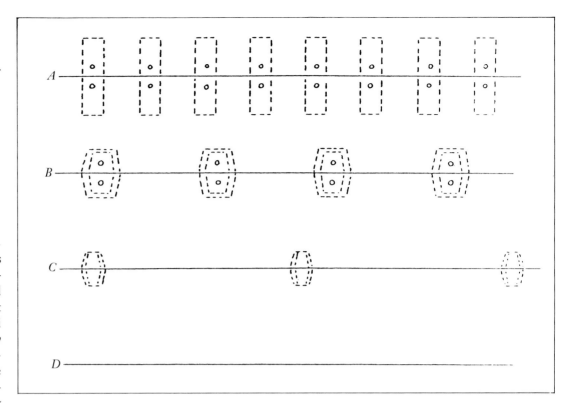

to exist up to and beyond the turn of the millenium: six ships supposedly carrying 1500 slaves each from Taranto to Tunisia and Alexandria in AD 867; seven ships of the Fatimid caliph al-Mu'izz beached at Fustat in Egypt and measured by the Persian traveller Nasir i Khusrau in AD 1046 at 150 *ârech* by 60 *ârech* (60m by 24m, 200ft by 80ft – if these dimensions are correct, they can only have been some sort of huge barges); two very large three-masted Muslim ships depicted on early eleventh-century ceramic dishes from the Balearic Islands;[9] and a large three-masted Apulian ship of the late eleventh century reported by the Byzantine princess Anna Comnena. In the absence of any reliable series of statistics, it is not possible to make any quantitative assessment of whether early medieval ships were, on average, smaller than their Roman predecessors or not. All that can be said is that very large ships designed for the specific purpose of transportation of large quantities of merchandise or large numbers of passengers between major termini most probably disappeared.

A depiction of a large three-masted Muslim ship from an early eleventh-century ceramic dish originating in the Balearic Islands. (John H Pryor)

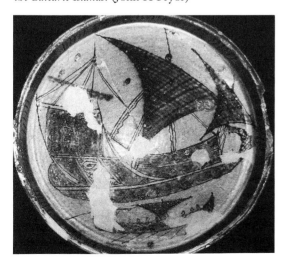

From shell to skeleton construction

Greco-Roman ships had been masterpieces of the carpenter's art. The skill and labour involved in their construction with hand tools demand admiration. Their hulls were raised on the keels and posts by laying strakes out from either side of the keel, each joined edge to edge by numerous, closely-spaced and tight-fitting mortise and tenon joints pegged with treenails. The carving of these joints with hand chisels and augers demanded a great deal of carpentry skill. The hulls were formed in shells entirely by the planks and were self-supporting. Frames were only added afterward for additional strength. Hulls so formed were immensely strong but were labour-intensive to produce and wasteful of timber. Planks had to be shaped from much larger timbers in order for the carpentry involved to become possible. Moreover, the sheer dynamics of the carpentry imposed limitations on the hull design. In particular, there were restrictions on the acuteness of the angles which could be achieved at critical points, such as the turn of the bilges amidships.

The fourth-century Yassi Ada ship showed signs of departure from these practices. The tenons in the mortises of the plank edges were smaller and looser-fitting than those of Greco-Roman hulls, and the mortises were set further apart. In the seventh-century ship the mortises were set even further apart than this. The tenons were also even smaller and looser fit-

ting, and were no longer pegged with treenails as they had still been in the fourth-century ship. These joints were now used only as guides to form the shape of the hull, not as its source of structural strength. Frames set in place after the floor strakes had been laid provided most of the structural strength and shaped the lines of the upper hull.

In the eleventh-century Serçe Liman ship, the evolutionary process had almost reached a conclusion. Twelve frames and floor timbers set on the keel before any strakes were laid provided the essential guide to shaping the hull. No mortise and tenon joints for the strakes were used at all. But this was not a ship formed entirely by its frames. Some floor strakes laid from stempost to sternpost on the twelve frames and floor timbers determined the lines of the rest of the ship. Other frames were set up only after these strakes had been laid.

Understandably in 1898, the excavators of the thirteenth-century Contarina ship did not direct their attention to the question, but there is no evidence at all that anything other than an entirely frame-first or skeleton construction technique was used in this ship. In particular, there is no record of any mortise and tenon joints between strakes. From shortly after the date of this ship, there is iconographic evidence

9. See J H Pryor and S Bellabarba, 'The Medieval Muslim Ships of the Pisan *Bacini*', *The Mariner's Mirror* 76 (1990), pp255–73.

Michael's father apparently made a fortune in shipbuilding as an unusually skilled caulker precisely at the time when the final transition from shell to skeleton construction technique occurred. Psellos's text reveals that caulking was not a simple art and that masters of it were highly prized and rewarded.

Given that the advantages of the skeleton method of construction would appear in retrospect to have been so obvious, it is remarkable that it took up to a thousand years for the transition from shell to skeleton construction to be completed. Because skeleton construction required less carpentry skill, less labour and less timber, it was far less expensive. Moreover, it permitted construction of hulls with greater cargo capacity with respect to length and beam because more acute angles at the turn of the bilges became possible. The answer to the question of why this evolutionary process took so long to reach its conclusion may lie in the geometrical skills required of shipwrights using the skeleton method. In order to shape a ship on a skeleton of frames, a shipwright had to be able to imagine the final shape of the vessel and to determine the dimensions of the frames geometrically. Apparently it took a very long time for these skills to be developed.

10. Michael Psellus, *Fourteen Byzantine Rulers* (Harmondsworth 1966), pp102–3.

from Venice that shipwrights were constructing the entire framework of ships before any planks were laid.

As the transition from shell to skeleton technique gathered pace, the profession of caulker became more important. Planks without mortise and tenon edge joining were not as tightly butted together, and caulking between the planks became much more important. Perhaps it is not accidental that the father of the Byzantine emperor Michael V (1041–2) was derided by Michael Psellos, an unmitigated intellectual snob, as a mere caulker:

> The fellow turned his attention to the sea. He had no mind to engage in commerce, or to act as navigator on a ship, or to pilot vessels at a fee when they put into harbour or sailed out to sea. However, he became something big in the shipbuilding line. Please do not imagine that he cut timber or planed off the wood they use in the ships, nor did he fit and fasten together the planks. Not a bit of it. What he did was

this. When others had done the assembling, he very skilfully smeared the assembled parts with pitch. There was not a boat, freshly built, which could ever be launched on the deep, unless this fellow, with his cunning skill had first given it the finishing touch.[10]

An illustration in a Byzantine manuscript of the sermons of St Gregory of Nazianzus is usually regarded as the oldest certain representation of a lateen sail. The manuscript itself is dated to about 880 AD, but the illustrations may be copies of earlier originals. (Interpretation by Denys Baker)

A seventeenth-century woodcut interpretation of an illustration in a late fifth- or sixth-century manuscript of the Iliad, *now in the* Biblioteca Ambrosiana *in Milan. The woodcut is from a printed version of the manuscript and follows the original miniature very closely, including details of what are clearly lateen rigged ships.* (John H Pryor)

Rigs

The most striking difference between Greco-Roman and medieval ships was in their sails. Most Greco-Roman ships, and certainly all large sailing ships, were rigged with square sails. Recent research has revealed that this was not a universal rule and that some smaller ancient ships had a variety of fore-and-aft rigs, including the lateen. Nevertheless, ancient iconography shows clearly that the square sail predominated at least until the fourth century AD. But from the ninth to thirteenth centuries there is no iconographic evidence of square sails in the Mediterranean at all. By then the lateen sail was absolutely predominant.

The yards of ancient square sails could be rotated not only in a horizontal plane but also in a vertical one so that the yard could be angled to the vertical.[11] Since the sails had brails by which they could be furled in sections, it was possible to convert a square sail to a virtual lateen when the yard was braced around for sailing close-hauled by taking up the brails at the forward end of the sail and hauling the yard downward. Sailors probably observed that

11. L Casson, 'The Origins of the Lateen', *The American Neptune* 31 (1971), pp49–51.

their ships performed better into the wind when this was done and therefore began to cut their sails accordingly. A natural process of

Right: The aerodynamics of lateen sails: air trapped at the foot of the leading edge of the sail spirals upwards to create more pressure - and hence power – at the peak. (Denys Baker)

Below: Although the lateen was more efficient than the square sail beating to windward, it was awkward when changing tack. The craft fell off the wind, when brace and sheet were loosened, and the parrel slackened to allow room between mast and yard; a crew member then hauled the yard vertical, transferred the sheet to the other side and, with the wind aft, the sail billowed out forward; as the vessel turned up into the wind again, the sheets were hauled aft, the parrel taughtened again, and the sail trimmed with tacks and braces. (Interpretation by Denys Baker, after B Landstrom, *The Ship*)

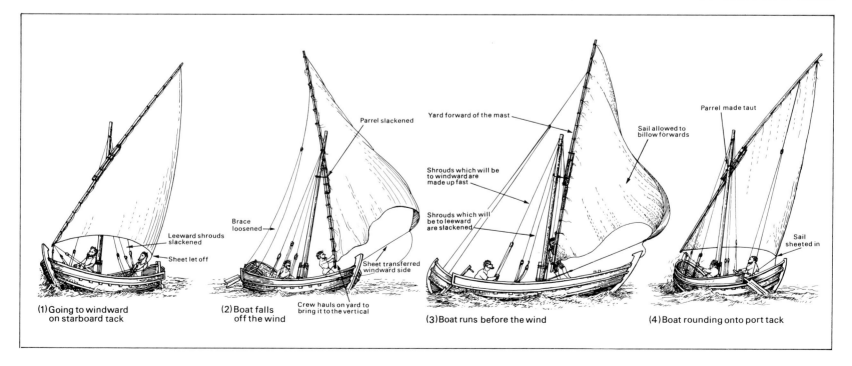

(1) Going to windward on starboard tack

Leeward shrouds slackened
Sheet let off

(2) Boat falls off the wind

Parrel slackened
Brace loosened
Crew hauls on yard to bring it to the vertical
Sheet transferred windward side

(3) Boat runs before the wind

Yard forward of the mast
Shrouds which will be to windward are made up fast
Sail allowed to billow forwards
Shrouds which will be to leeward are slackened

(4) Boat rounding onto port tack

Parrel made taut
Sail sheeted in

The early fourteenth-century St Peter Martyr relief from the Church of S Eustorgio at Milan shows two tackles attached to the blade of the steering oar: the more prominent forward tackle is designed to resist the tendency of the blade to lift due to the pressure of buoyancy; the less obvious tackle leads up into the sterncastle and was used to raise the windward oar when not in use. (Interpretation by Denys Baker)

evolution led to the characteristic triangular lateen sail of the medieval Mediterranean superseding the ancient square sail. In all probability, the first literary reference to the lateen sail occurs in Procopius's *History of the Wars*, where he states that during Belisarius's voyage from Constantinople to North Africa to open the Vandal War, he had the sails of his three command ships 'painted red from the upper corner for about a third of the length' so that the rest of the fleet could identify them and follow in bad weather.[12] This seems to indicate some sort of triangular sail with an upper corner, most probably a lateen sail.

Lateen sails are very likely shown on Byzantine dromons in a manuscript of the *Iliad* of the late fifth or sixth centuries; however, the first certain depiction of a medieval lateen sail is in a Byzantine manuscript of the Sermons of St Gregory of Nazianzus dated to around AD 880. Some art historians believe that the illustrations in this manuscript are ninth-century copies of older originals and, insofar as lateen sails are concerned, this is quite possible since it is clear that they were in use long before the ninth century.

Lateen sails gave particular advantages to ships sailing in diverse conditions. Even if square sails could be braced around fore-and-aft, lateen sails were specifically designed to be rigged fore-and-aft, whereas the former were not. For a ship beating into the wind, the closer its sails are set to the longitudinal axis of the ship the better it will perform. Lateen sails could be set much closer to this axis than could any square sail. Moreover, medieval lateen sails operated as aerofoils because of the large bag in their cut. Wind trapped at the foot of the luff of the sail spiralled upwards within the bag of the sail, creating increased pressure toward the peak.[13] Thus the yards were peaked as close to

12. Procopius, *Procopius*, trans H B Dewing and G Downey, 7 vols (London, 1968), Vol 2, p119.

13. L Dimmock, 'The Lateen Rig', *The Mariner's Mirror* 32 (1946), pp35–41.

An early pilgrim ship from the Pala d'Oro *altar screen of S Marco, Venice, suggesting little more than an open boat. It certainly has no fore or after structures.*

A model of a medieval ship based on the St Peter Martyr relief. This model was built in 1929 and more modern research might suggest some revised interpretations. A more likely version of the upperworks, for example, might well involve lighter, open lattice-work structures for reasons of both stability and windage. (The Science Museum, London)

used on some Persian and Arab ships on the Tigris and Euphrates rivers and in the Indian Ocean.

The iconography shows several alternative methods of mounting these steering oars on the hull.[15] Greco-Roman steering oars were mounted on two through beams set at different levels, but medieval steering oars were mounted on a single-level pivot. They could be either forward- or aft-mounted in an open cradle, closed in a box of through beams and side piece, fed through a hole in the hull, held by a wood or metal ring or collar on the hull, or boxed inside swing mounts. The various mountings allowed not only turning movement of the blade for steering, but also vertical movement so that the blade could be raised from the water when desired. When a ship heeled under sail, the weather quarter oar became ineffective and was raised from the water. Even the lee quarter oar was probably submerged only as much as was necessary to hold a course. To leave more of it submerged only increased drag. The St Peter Martyr relief from Milan shows two tackles attached to the blades of the steering oar. One runs forward to restrain the oar from lifting through water resistance, and the other runs up to the sterncastle to lift the oar from the water when required.

Developments in naval architecture

Although there is evidence to suggest that even in the Early Middle Ages (*c*800–1050) some very large ships sailed the seas, there is no doubt that in general the sailing ships which carried pilgrims and merchants across the Mediterranean grew larger from the time of the First Crusade. The mosaics and enamels of San Marco in Venice show this process quite clearly. The earliest of them, from the *Pala*

the vertical as possible, creating a more efficient sail. Even if an ancient square sail could be angled to the vertical, its yard was not nearly as long as that of a lateen sail and its sail could not, therefore, take as great advantage of this aerodynamic property.

The widespread adoption of the lateen sail in the Mediterranean reflects the fact that in the Middle Ages shipping tended to spread out across the sea. Ships sailed not so much between major termini using prevailing winds as to diverse destinations in variable conditions. Lateen sails improved the ability of ships to beat to windward, which suggests that they were designed to improve manoeuvrability and that there was a need for this. The only variable which history suggests could force such an adaptation was greatly increased conditions of insecurity at sea.

Steering gear

The stern quarter steering oars had not changed since Antiquity. Greco-Roman sailing ships had also been steered by them. The sternpost rudder did not make a definitive appearance in the Mediterranean until the fourteenth century, although there is some evidence to suggest that forms of sternpost rudders may possibly have been used on some Muslim and Byzantine ships.[14] There is certainly no doubt that sternpost rudders were

14. V Christides, 'Two Parallel Naval Guides of the Tenth Century: Qudama's Document and Leo VI's *Naumachica*: A Study on Byzantine and Moslem naval Preparedness', *Graeco-Arabica* 1 (1982) pp65–6; *Idem, The Conquest of Crete by the Arabs (c824): A Turning Point in the Struggle between Byzantium and Islam* (Athens 1984), pp45–6.

15. See L V Mott, 'The Development of the Rudder, AD 100–1600: A Technological Tale', (MA thesis, Texas A & M University 1991).

A twelfth-century manuscript illustration from Mt Athos in Greece depicting a small lateen rigged vessel, without superstructure. Note the hooked head to the mast, a feature of many representations of medieval lateen rigged craft; it is believed that it was intended to hold the halyard as far forward of the mast as possible to facilitate lifting the lateen yard when going about.

This increase in the size of ships accompanied a general increase in the volume of maritime traffic as ships sailing the sea both increased in number and also sailed more frequently for more destinations. This was true not only of the Latin West, for which ample documentation survives in the archives of Venice, Genoa, and other cities, but also of the Muslim and Byzantine worlds. Fragmentary literary and documentary evidence shows that Muslim and Byzantine merchant marines continued to sail the sea, and that the West did not acquire a total monopoly.

Immediately after the capture of Jerusalem by the First Crusade in 1099, huge numbers of pilgrims and Crusaders began to make the voyage to the Holy Land every year. In 1102 the Anglo-Saxon pilgrim Saewulf counted thirty large ships in Jaffa harbour. Around 1172 another pilgrim, Theoderich, counted eighty ships in port at Acre at Easter. Hundreds of ships carrying tens of thousands of pilgrims must have made the voyage from the West to the Holy Land every year. These ships carried passengers, the industrial products of the West, and money and bullion to the East. They returned with the ceramics, drugs, spices, precious cloths, glassware, and perfumes of the East which were so much in demand in the West. The stimulus which the conquest of the Holy Land gave to the maritime traffic of the West is incalculable.

It was accompanied by a simultaneous expansion of the commerce of the West into the Byzantine and Muslim worlds. Even in the eleventh century, before the Crusade, the maritime republics of the West had begun to penetrate the markets of the Byzantine and Muslim worlds. Venice concluded a commercial treaty with Basil II of Byzantium in 991 and by the second half of the eleventh century Genoa and Amalfi had opened up commercial links with Egypt. In the twelfth and thirteenth centuries Pisa, and to a lesser extent Marseilles, Barcelona and other cities, would also share in this extension of Western maritime traffic.

From the twelfth century the economies of the various regions of the Mediterranean world began to coalesce, creating an international market. Regions specialised increasingly in forms of production suited to their geograph-

d'Oro altar screen, shows an open boat with a single mast and no forecastle or sterncastle. It may well have been intended to represent a boat similar to the seventh-century Yassi Ada ship or the Serçe Liman ship. It is extremely similar to a contemporary ship illustrated in a manuscript from a monastery on Mt Athos. By the late twelfth and thirteenth centuries the ships show both forecastles and sterncastles, two masts, and more than one deck. Lines on the hull in pictures are difficult to interpret since in some cases they may have been in-

tended to represent planking. In other cases, however, they certainly represent decks, for example in the Peter Martyr relief, where the rows of through beams were deck beams. The ships from the Leaning Tower of Pisa, the *Annals of Genoa*, the church of San Giovanni Evangelista of Ravenna, and the *Cantigas de Santa Maria* of Castile all show growth in size quite clearly. By the late thirteenth century two mosaics from San Marco show ships with three masts, the first depictions of three-masted ships in the Latin West.

A large two-master from a relief on the Leaning Tower of Pisa. The horn-like extension, or wings, above the aftercastle are thought to be supports for the lateen yards which when stowed would extend well beyond the stern.

ical and human resources, selling their products on an international market. The Black Sea area and southern Italy, for example, became a centre of granaries for the growing cities of northern Italy. Cloth from northern France and Flanders found expanding markets in Byzantium, the Holy Land and the Muslim world. After the Fourth Crusade of 1202–4, a huge trade in slaves from the Ukraine and the Caucasus developed in the hands of the Italians, who sold them in the markets of Egypt and other parts of the Muslim world, as well as in Venetian and Genoese colonies in the eastern Mediterranean. All of these commercial

An illustration from the Annals of Genoa *in the Bibliothèque Nationale in Paris. The twin horned hull extensions are similar to those on the Leaning Tower of Pisa relief. From Caffaro,* Annali genovesi di Caffaro e dé suoi continuatori, *L T Belgrano and C Imperiali (eds) (Genoa 1890). (Interpretation by Denys Baker)*

developments were conditional upon the growth of merchant marines.

Larger ships needed more sophisticated technology. In order to change tack, a lateen yard had to be hauled to the vertical and dragged around the front of the mast to be released on the other side. On a small boat a few men could easily manage this task but, by the thirteenth century, the yards of large sailing ships could weigh up to 6.5 metric tonnes. To manage such yards and the huge sails hung from them, some over 800 square metres in area, required many men and complex block and tackle systems. The hooked mastheads seen in the Gregory of Nazianzus miniature, the Mount Athos miniature, and the *Pala d'Oro* enamel, disappear after the twelfth century. These mastheads obviously served to suspend the yard forward of the mast in order to make it easier to cross the mast when tacking. However, they were apparently inadequate to cope with the yards of the large ships of the late twelfth and thirteenth centuries and were replaced by block masts, known as *calzenses*.[16] These were mastheads in which pulley sheaves were housed and over which the halyards were passed. On the largest ships a *calzensis* had two sheaves. The yard was held to the mast by a truss or parral (*troccia*). The halyards were made fast to it by a strap (*paroma*) of rope lashed around the yard. Two ties (*amanti*), which ran over the sheaves of the block mast, were attached to the strap. Two tie tackles (*collaturi* or *jonchi*) were used to haul in the ties and thus to raise the yards.

Management of the steering oars must also have created new difficulties as the ships grew larger. On the three-decked ships of St Louis these were up to 17m (56ft) long and 11 tonnes

16. See Pryor, 'Naval architecture . . . revisited', pp266–7.

in weight. Although the problems of manoeuvring them would have been alleviated by the flotation effect of the water, nevertheless, the tackle systems used to control these oars must have been very complex.

Similar technological problems were no doubt encountered in the construction of ever-larger hulls. The inability to obtain trees of sufficient length for keels, stringers, wales, and planks of single timbers created a need for complex systems of scarfing and butt joining with resultant problems for structural integrity. No information survives about how medieval shipwrights learned to overcome such problems, but clearly they did so. Frames also became more complex. Whereas those of the Yassi Ada and Serçe Liman ships were composed only of floor timbers and futtocks, the

The ship mosaic from the church of S Giovanni Evangelista, Ravenna. This two-masted vessel also sports twin 'horns' at the stern.

the gap between these wings and the hull, although some show them outside them, probably through artistic misrepresentation. These wings were descendants of the Greco-Roman fan-shaped stern ornaments known as *aplustria*. Other sources, a mosaic from San Marco and the *Cantigas de Santa Maria* in particular, show a second type of stern: an equally peculiar inverted fan-shaped 'canopy' stern. These canopies swept up and back from the stern quarters on both sides to a peak at the centreline above the sternpost. They hung well over the stern and were highly decorated. Whether these canopies were structural wooden ornaments or whether they were canvas tentings is impossible to say. Ship pictures also show a third type of stern: a simple castellated stern without either 'wings' or 'canopies'.

At the bow there were also two distinct traditions. One, represented by all Byzantine ships, by Muslim ships from the Eastern Mediterranean, and by Venetian and Spanish ships, had a normal bow in which all the strakes of the hull ran into the stempost. Any forecastle was constructed above the stempost and integrated structurally into the hull. The other, represented by ships from Ravenna, Genoa, Pisa, and the Muslim Balearics and Morocco, had a very peculiar open foredeck. The bulwarks above the main deck terminated aft of the stempost, which recurved in a pronounced arc, and above which any forecastle was constructed. The open foredeck thus formed sometimes had what appear to be vertical posts mounted on it, perhaps bitts to secure the anchor cables. It is difficult to imagine how any ship with such an open foredeck could have been seaworthy. In heavy weather tonnes of water should have sluiced across the deck as the bows pitched into large waves. It is also difficult to comprehend how a forecastle poised in the air above the stempost and apparently not integrated into the hull could have been structurally sound. However, the iconography is very specific and quite extensive as to this feature of the construction of some ships.

Sailing qualities

By modern standards, the round ships of the Middle Ages were poor sailers. Their lateen sails permitted them to point into the wind fairly well, but their hull design negated many

thirteenth-century Contarina ship had a third element in its frames: an upper futtock. Some of St Louis's ships, with a height from keel to gunwale of over 12m and a beam of 10m (40ft by 33ft), probably had frames composed of even more than three timbers.

Ships all around the Mediterranean were similar in design but, nevertheless, there were

regional differences and peculiarities. Most of them, Muslim and Byzantine as well as those of the Latin West, had two peculiar curved 'wings' at the stern which swept back from the bulwarks amidships and separated from the hull at the stern. They were bridged above the sterncastle by a cross-member. Many representations show the steering oars mounted in

of the advantages gained from the sail config-uration. Because they had no deep keel and no cutwater nor gripe at the bow, there was nothing to prevent excessive leeway being made when beating into the wind. Accounts of voyages by pilgrims and other travellers reveal that such ships had extreme difficulty in main-taining a real course at ninety degrees to the wind in adverse conditions. The Muslim pil-grim Ibn Jubayr wrote of his return voyage on a Genoese ship from Acre to Messina in 1183 that:

> On Saturday the 10th of Sha'ban, . . . we parted from the coast of Crete, and made speed under a favourable north wind . . . At midnight on Sunday the 11th, the wind changed to the west . . . Strongly the wind blew and took us northward . . . Morning had scarcely come when to our misfortune we saw the coast of Crete on our left. Its mountains had (earlier) been before us, and we had left them behind to our right. But the wind had taken us from our course, and we who had thought to have passed it were mistaken.[17]

Ibn Jubayr's ship had been heading west-northwest from the south coast of Crete to-wards the Straits of Messina but was blown back on its tracks to the northeast by a strong westerly headwind. In gales ships were blown about, hither and thither, all over the sea, their yards and steering oars frequently being bro-ken. In the eleventh century, an Egyptian Jew voyaging from Tyre to Jaffa wrote after he had reached safety that:

> . . . a storm . . . drove us out into the midst of the sea, where we remained for four days, giv-ing up all hope for life. We were without sails and oars and the rudder [steering oar] was bro-ken. Likewise the sailyards were broken and the waves burst into the ship.[18]

It is not at all surprising that the average duration of voyages against prevailing winds was twice as long as those before the prevailing winds. In the Mediterranean the prevailing winds are from the northwest to northeast

17. Ibn Jubayr, *The Travels of Ibn Jubayr*, trans R J C Broadhurst (London 1952), pp330–32.

18. S D Goitein, *A Mediterranean Society: The Jewish Communities of the Arab World as Portrayed in the Documents of the Cairo Geniza, Vol. I: Economic Foundations* (Berkeley 1967), pp320–21.

A three-masted ship represented in a late thirteenth-century mosaic in San Marco, Venice. This is the earliest depiction of a three-masted vessel in the Latin West.

Table 4/2: Duration of known Voyages in Mediterranean Round Ships

Date	Person involved	From	To	Distance (nautical miles)	Time (days)	Average speed in knots
PART A: VOYAGES FROM WESTERN SOURCES						
With prevailing wind						
867	Bernard the Wise	Taranto	Alexandria	868	30	1.20
1175	Burchard of Strasburg	Genoa	Alexandria	1630	47	1.45
1183	Ibn Jubayr	Ceuta	Alexandria	2000	31	2.69
12th century	Nicholas Muzalon	Constantinople	Cyprus	955	10	3.98
1221	Peter of Albeney	Marseilles	Damietta	1740	22	3.29
1216	Jacques de Vitry	Genoa	Acre	1825	35	2.17
1248	St Louis	Aigues Mortes	Cyprus	1695	24	2.94
					Average	2.53
Against prevailing wind						
867	Bernard the Wise	Jaffa	Rome	1780	60	1.24
1184	Ibn Jubayr	Acre	Messina	1300	51	1.06
1254	St Louis	Acre	Hyères	1900	70	1.13
					Average	1.14
PART B: VOYAGES FROM SOURCES IN THE CAIRO GENIZA						
With prevailing wind						
All 11th–12th centuries		Marseilles	Alexandria	1610	25	2.68
		Palermo	Alexandria	1040	29/50	1.49/.87
		Mazara	Alexandria	1085	17/20	2.66/2.26
		Mahdia	Alexandria	1000	13/35/ 25/30	3.20/1.19 1.67/1.39
		Mahdia	Alexandria (via Palermo)	1130	41	1.15
		Tripoli (Libya)	Alexandria	935	25/20	1.56/1.95
					Average	1.84
Against prevailing wind						
All 11th–12th centuries		Alexandria	Almeria	2560	65	1.64
		Alexandria	Amalfi (via Constantinople and Crete)	2520	72	1.46
		Ras Al-Kana'is	Palermo	1040	25	1.73
		Alexandria	Mahdia	1000	40	1.04
		Alexandria	Tripoli (Lybia)	935	40	0.97
					Average	1.37

Another thirteenth-century mosaic from San Marco, Venice, showing a boat with a stern of canopied form, similar to that in the Cantigas de Santa Maria *manuscript.*

across the length and breadth of the sea throughout the year. The longitudinal axis of the sea lies from west-northwest to east-southeast. Voyages from the south to the north coasts or from east to west were against the prevailing winds. In the fourteenth century Ludolph von Suchem wrote that passengers on ships sailing from the Latin West to the Holy Land would take aboard provisions for fifty days, whereas those making the return voyage would take provisions for a hundred days. The fleet of St Louis reached Cyprus from Aigues Mortes in twenty-four days in 1248, but took ten weeks to make the return voyage from Acre to Hyères in 1254. On the outward voyage from Almeria to Alexandria in 1183, the Genoese ship on which Ibn Jubayr was travelling took thirty-one days for the run, but on its return, the next year, another Genoese ship took fifty-one days to make Messina from Acre. In the records of the Egyptian Jewish community of the eleventh and twelfth centuries which survive from the Cairo Geniza, voyages made before prevailing winds averaged 1.84kts while those against them averaged only 1.37kts.

As noted above, ships of the Middle Ages were designed to have better up-wind performance than those of Greco-Roman Antiquity. However, the historical record of voyage times shows that this improvement can only have been quantitative. Their limited performance capabilities meant that they were very much at the mercy of the winds and had to utilise local oceanographic and meteorological phenomena, such as the counter-clockwise current circulation of the sea and the daily cycles of onshore/offshore coastal breezes, to make their way to the north or west against prevailing winds. For this reason the normal route to the West from Alexandria ran east to the coast of Palestine, north to Cilicia, west to Rhodes, along the south coast of Crete and around the Peleponnesos to the Straits of Otranto, and then either north along the Balkan coast of the Adriatic to Venice, or west through the Straits of Messina to the Tyrrhenian Sea or through the Malta Channel to the Western Mediterranean.

19. R B C Huygens (ed), *Lettres de Jacques de Vitry (1160/1170–1240), évêque de Saint-Jean-d'Acre* (Leiden 1960), I.173–8 (pp77–8).

Merchant and passenger ships rarely pressed on with voyages in adverse conditions if they had a choice. They also largely avoided the squally, unpredictable weather of the winter. Except when unusual considerations overrode normal precautions, ships stayed in port between the end of October and the beginning of March. At Pisa, the twelfth-century statutes of the city forbad a master who brought his ship into port after 1 November from leaving until 1 March. In a letter written in 1216, Jacques de Vitry, bishop elect of Acre, who voyaged out from Genoa to the Holy Land, commented on the exceptional achievement of the Genoese, who had begun to navigate in winter by that time:

> However, the men of that city [Genoa] have very sturdy ships of great size, as a consequence of which they are used to crossing the sea in winter, for the reason that in that season the provisions aboard ship do not go bad easily nor the water putrefy as [it does] aboard ship in the summer.[19]

For the most part, ships of all kinds followed coastal routes around the sea. Galleys did so because their low freeboard made it unsafe for them to make high-seas crossings. Although sailing ships did not have the same problems and could make open sea crossings safely, they also tended to follow coastal routes because of human considerations. A Crusader or pilgrim ship, with no objective other than to reach Acre, might make a high-seas voyage directly from Marseilles, Genoa or Venice without making ports of call. But more generally, merchant ships, even those carrying passengers, followed coastal routes so that merchants could do business en route and passengers could break the monotony of long, slow voyages and replenish their food supplies.

Consequently, the major commercial trunk routes developed along the chain of major islands and southern extremities of the northern coasts of the sea. Strategic islands and mainland ports along this axis became markers of the maritime frontiers: Valencia, the Balearics, Sardinia, Sicily, Malta, Messina, Taranto and Otranto, Corfu, Methone and Corone, Crete, Rhodes, and Cyprus. Possession of these and other strategic positions oscillated among Byzantium, Islam and the West, both reflecting the respective politico-military strengths and weaknesses of the three civilisations at various times and also contributing to those strengths and weaknesses. When Muslims held the island chain, the frontiers were pushed close to the northern coasts. After they lost them, from Crete in AD 961 to the Balearics in 1229, the frontiers were pushed back to the North African coast.

Shipboard conditions

Travel aboard medieval ships was uncomfortable to say the least, even for the rich who could afford apartments of their own in the sterncastles. For ordinary passengers in the tween decks, conditions must have been hellish. Some 170–200 of them were accommodated on each of the tween decks of a large, 35m (115ft) 800-tonne ship in the time of St Louis. Since horses were also stabled on these tween decks when the ships carried them, the stench must have been something to be experienced. The *Statutes of Marseilles* of 1253 specified the amount of deck space allocated to ordinary pilgrims or Crusaders, their 'place' or *platea*: 0.63m by 1.64m (25in by 65in).[20] When pilgrims booked passage, the ship's scribe recorded the number of the place assigned to them and gave them a scrap of parchment with their number recorded on it. In this space they had to store their effects and sleep. There were no hammocks, of course: the passengers slept on the decks. Some were allocated places in the open under the *corridoria* half-decks on the main deck, and here they were probably given more space, although the statutes do not specify what it was. In fine weather, whenever the safety of the ship allowed the master to permit it, passengers no doubt slept in the open wherever they could find a space on the main deck.

Passage contracts entitled passengers to basic provisions supplied by the ship. Victuallers known as *cargatores* provided ship's biscuit, twice cooked bread, which was the staple diet. A contract for a projected Crusade, made in 1318 between Marseilles and Count Louis of Clermont, specified that provisions would be provided as follows for each person for 40 days:[21]

— a half a sack of biscuit
— two *millayrole* (128 litres; 225 pints) of wine
— one quarter *quintale* (10.20kg; 22.5lb) of salt meat
— one fifteenth *quintale* (2.72kg; 6lb) of cheese
— one quarter *emina* (10 litres; 17.5 pints) of beans
— one fifteenth *emina* (2.66 litres; 4.5 pints) of figs
— one fifteenth *emina* (2.66 litres; 4.5 pints) of lentils
— salt fish, onions, garlic, and other victuals, oil, rice and almonds according to the rank of the passenger.

This basic diet was similar to that of the crews of war galleys in the fleets of Venice and the Angevin Kingdom of Sicily in the late thirteenth and fourteenth centuries.[22] It consisted of biscuit and *companaticum*, that is everything one ate with the biscuit: cheese and wine plus a soupy gruel or stew made from the salt meat and legumes. It may have been adequate to sustain life, but it must have been extremely boring. Consequently, passengers normally took aboard their own supplies. In an *exemplum*, an anecdotal illustrative story, from one of his sermons, Jacques de Vitry referred to sailors who stole biscuit and other provisions

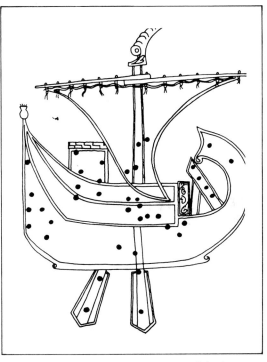

A highly stylised Muslim representation of the Argo, *from the al Sufi* Book of Fixed Stars, Ceuta 1224. *From Davia Nicolle, 'Shipping in Islamic art',* American Neptune 49 (1989).

of the pilgrims stored in the hold and who siphoned off wine from their barrels. Some ships apparently provided a commissary or pantry where passengers could buy additional provisions. Ibn Jubayr tells us that when his ship had been at sea for twenty-two days after leaving Acre, the passengers' provisions began to run out. However, they were able to buy what they wanted: 'bread, water, and all kinds of fruit and victuals, such as pomegranate, quince, water-melon, pear, chestnut, walnut, chick-pea, broad-bean raw and cooked, onion, garlic, fig, cheese, fish and many other things it would be too long to describe'.[23]

Jacques de Vitry took aboard at Genoa wine, biscuit, meat, and other food sufficient for

20. R Pernoud (ed), *Les Statuts Municipaux de Marseille* (Monaco and Paris 1949), IV.25.

21. A de Boislisle, 'Informationes Pro Passagio Transmarino', *Annuaire-Bulletin de la Société de l'Histoire de France* 9 (1872), pp253–4.

22. F C Lane, 'Diet and Wages of Seamen in the Early Fourteenth Century', in his *Venice and History* (Baltimore 1966), pp263–8; J H Pryor, 'The Galleys of Charles I of Anjou, King of Sicily: c1269–84', *Studies in Medieval and Renaissance History*, New series 14 (1993).

23. Ibn Jubayr, *Travels*, p329.

A Catalan round ship of the late thirteenth century. The original is from a painted beam now in the Museo del arte de Catalunya, Barcelona.

himself and his entourage for three months.[24] Apparently he had a very pessimistic view of how long it might take to reach the Holy Land. Of course, de Virty was not an ordinary passenger. He leased a quarter part of the upper sterncastle (*castellum superius*) as a day cabin for himself in which he could dine, study, and generally pass the time. He also leased a chamber (*camera*) in which he and his entourage could sleep, another in which to store clothes and provisions for a week, yet another in which his servants could prepare his food, and finally a space on the tween decks for his horses. The rest of his provisions were stowed in the hold, from where they were apparently brought up every week.

In an age when cooking technology was limited to open fires and charcoal braziers, it was not possible for a central galley to cook for a ship's complement running to hundreds of people. Both passengers and crew prepared their food over small fires or braziers for a few people each. The thirteenth-century Venetian maritime statutes specified the amount of firewood which passengers could take on board. Merchants and wealthy passengers had their servants prepare their food, but ordinary pas-

Mediterranean currents, prevailing winds in summer, and medieval trunk routes. (Denys Baker, based on an original by John H Pryor)

sengers, according to the *Statutes of Marseilles*, were assigned to members of the crew for messing, no doubt paying a fee for the service. When a passenger booked passage, the ship's scribe recorded in his cartulary the name of the crew member with whom he would mess. Whenever the weather permitted cooking, large ships must have resembled rafts of fires with dozens of braziers cooking for crew and passengers. The danger from fire must have been extreme. On his return from the Holy Land in 1254, St Louis assigned to Jean de Joinville the task of making the rounds each night to make sure that all fires were extinguished except the main one in the hold from which the others were lit.

The round ship replaced

In the early fourteenth century, seamen in the Mediterranean began to replace their traditional round ships with the North European cog, with its square sail, sternpost rudder, and straight keel, stempost, and sternpost. Northern seamen had sailed cogs into the Mediterranean since at least the twelfth century, particularly as part of Crusader fleets. However, the cog was a developing ship type which evolved slowly over the centuries, and it was not until the fourteenth century that its ad-

vantages over the traditional Mediterranean round ship became sufficiently apparent to persuade Mediterranean shipwrights to emulate it. By then the round ship itself had reached the zenith of its development. To compare the ship of the Gregory of Nazianzus miniature with that of the St Peter Martyr relief is to look at two different worlds. The earlier world was one of small boats of a few dozen tonnes, capable of carrying only limited numbers of passengers, and confined to coastal routes by size and technology. The later world was one of multi-decked vessels of hundreds of tonnes, capable of carrying over a thousand passengers, and for which open-sea crossings posed no dangers. Yet the Peter Martyr ship was a direct, lineal descendant of the Gregory of Nazianzus ship. Its technology was quantitatively of a different dimension, but qualitatively the same. No major technological innovation marked the transition from one ship to the other. In this respect, the centuries which lay between the two ships were a continuum, a period which maritime historians may treat as a single entity but which was separated from those which preceded and followed it by major technological innovations.

John H Pryor

24. Huygens, *Lettres de Jacques de Vitry*, I.190–91 (p78).

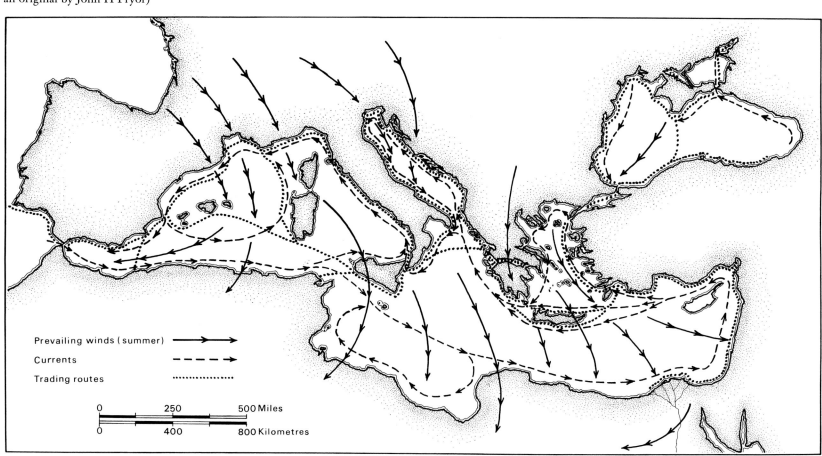

Prevailing winds (summer) ———→

Currents ‑ ‑ ‑ →

Trading routes ·············

0   250   500 Miles

0   400   800 Kilometres

5

The Carrack: The Advent of the Full Rigged Ship

ONE OF the few facts that many modern people know about aviation is that a 'jumbo jet' is a large aircraft. In much the same way, one of the few things that many people in the late Middle Ages knew about shipping was that a carrack was a very large ship. Its size was almost proverbial. In *The Canterbury Tales*, Chaucer used the width of a carrack's sail to conjure up for his readers the breadth of Satan's tail; the writer of *The Libelle of Englyshe Polycye* (*c*1436) wrote of the Genoese carracks fought by the English in Henry V's reign as being 'orrible, grete and stoute [strong]'.[1] Images of carracks, or of what are now called carracks, abound in late medieval art – great, towering vessels with high, jutting forecastles – but problems sometimes arise in trying to match modern perceptions with the historical evidence.

The carrack developed out of the fusion of North European and Mediterranean seafaring technology, some time around the late thirteenth or early fourteenth centuries. These two traditions had been separate up until that time. As outlined in earlier chapters, the typical large bulk carrier of northern Europe in the thirteenth century was the cog, a flat-bottomed vessel with high, clinker-built sides and distinctive angled stem- and sternposts. The cog had

a stern rudder and, like all northern ships of the period, a single square sail. In this context, 'northern' should be taken to mean anywhere from at least the Atlantic coast of Spain north-

wards. The northern part of the Iberian peninsula was part of the great clinker construction 'zone' of medieval northern Europe; parts of Portugal may also have been included. Clinker

---

1. F N Robinson (ed), *The Complete Works of Geoffrey Chaucer*, (2nd Edition, London & Oxford 1974), p93, lines 1687–8 (*The Summoner's Tale* in *The Canterbury Tales*); G Warner (ed), *The Libelle of Englyshe Polycye* (Oxford 1926), line 1021.

The earliest surviving North European ship picture actually named as a carrack in contemporary sources is the engraving of a ship entitled Kraeck *(Flemish for 'carrack') by the Flemish master 'WA'. One scholar has suggested that the engraver was Willem A Cruce, a Flemish goldsmith. He also suggests that the* Kraeck *engraving may have been produced as a form of guidance for the Flemish shipwrights and other woodworkers who made thirty huge 7ft (2.2m) long models of three-masted carracks for the festivities celebrating the marriage of Charles the Bold of Burgundy to Margaret of York in 1468.*

construction, square rig and the stern rudder were the salient features of maritime technology in the region.

Mediterranean ship construction and rig were very different, and served a region that was both more populous and more economically developed than the North. Mediterranean ships had been skeleton-built for several centuries: the plank-on-frame technique was cheaper and less demanding of skilled craftsmen than ancient shell construction, and is thought to have developed as a response to the shortages of materials and skilled shipwrights in the centuries following the collapse of the Roman Empire in the West. By the thirteenth century, Mediterranean vessels were being constructed that were considerably larger than any North European ship. Genoese contracts of 1268 for *naves* (ships) of three decks envisaged some ships that were over 37m in length, 9m at maximum beam, and with depth in hold of over 4m (120ft by 30ft by 13ft). A ship of this type was steered by two great side rudders, often assisted by pulley tackles, and propelled by two or more lateen sails (see previous chapter).

The lateen had been used in the Roman period, and at some time in the early Middle Ages supplanted the ancient square sail. The lateen is well adapted for sailing into the wind, and it is probable that medieval lateeners could point much closer to the wind than their square rigged contemporaries. However, the lateen can make a vessel unstable in a following wind, and in the Middle Ages it was much more cumbersome and labour-intensive than the square sail. Reducing sail in a medieval square-rigger could be achieved either by some form of reefing, or, from the mid fourteenth century, by removing a bonnet laced to the foot of the sail. The sail area of a lateener could be reduced only by taking off one sail and setting a smaller one in its place. Likewise, tacking a square-sailed ship was simply a matter of bracing the yard round from one side of the ship to the other. Tacking a lateener involved furling the sail, swinging the yard vertical, 'walking' the yard and sail round to the other side of the ship, canting the yard, and then unfurling the sail. On big ships, lateen yards could be very large and unwieldy: some of the Genoese ships mentioned above would have had yards in excess of 49m (160ft) in length.[2]

2. B Landstrom, *The Sailing Ship* (London 1969), pp72–85; R W Unger, *The Ship in the Medieval Economy 600–1600* (London & Montreal 1980), pp37–42, 130 and 161–200; J H Pryor, 'The Naval Architecture of Crusader Transport Ships', *The Mariner's Mirror* 70 (1984), pp171–219, 275–92 & 363–86.

Two early representations of the Mediterranean cocha: *a two-masted Venetian* cocha *of 1366 (top); and a two-masted Mediterranean* cocha *of 1367 (redrawn after the 1367 Portolan chart of Pizzigani). Although the originals are naive and lack detail, the lateen mizzen sail is apparent on both vessels. The bowsprit was an essential feature of the main square rig since it was necessary to give a proper lead to the bowlines, without which the ship could make little headway against any wind forward of the quarter. Neither vessel has a forecastle, but both have aftercastles.* (Interpretation by Lynn Friel)

The cog, the *cocha* and the carrack

The Mediterranean carrack developed from the North European cog. The traditional date for the adoption of the cog by Mediterranean shipwrights and seamen was given by the Florentine chronicler Giovanni Villani as 1304. He stated that in this year Biscayan (Basque) cogs were brought into the Mediterranean, and that local shipwrights started to copy them. As with most statements about technology by medieval chroniclers, this one has to be viewed with caution. Mediterranean sources of the thirteenth century were already referring to *cocas* or *coggones*, brought south by northerners. However, in support of Villani's claim it should be said that the first references to the

actual use of *coche*, as they came to be called, by the Genoese and Venetians date from the years 1302 to 1312.

There is great uncertainty as to what early Mediterranean *coche* were actually like. There are no known pictures of cog-like vessels in Mediterranean sources before the middle of the fourteenth century and, as yet, no archaeological evidence. What is thought to have happened has to be inferred from documentary sources and those first pictures. The pictures suggest that the main features of the cog, copied in the *cocha*, were the cog's square rig, its stern rudder, its capacious hull form, and perhaps its flat bottom.

Like the cog and the old Mediterranean lateeners, the *cocha* was a bulk carrier, but because the square sail, and also perhaps the stern rudder, was less labour-intensive than the lateen sail and side rudders, crewing costs were lower. The saving in crew wages was probably a crucial factor in spreading the use of the *cocha*. For example, Venetian maritime statutes of the thirteenth century stated that each sailing ship was to have one sailor for every ten *millaria* of burden (about five metric tonnes). Statutes of the fifteenth century specified only one man per 20 *millaria* (about ten tonnes), suggesting that the *cocha* type needed half the crew of a lateen rigged cargo carrier. The historian F C Lane speculated that labour shortages in the wake of the Black Death of 1348 may have helped to make the *cocha* an even more attractive prospect to shippers, although the need for larger crews for defence against pirates may have nullified some of these advantages.

The stern rudder gave better overall control than the side rudder, was easier to use, and was less susceptible to collision damage. Italian documentary sources do show that there were some *coche* with side rudders, but it is clear that the stern rudder *cocha* predominated by the second half of the fourteenth century. *Coche* described as *coche baonesche* were being constructed in Genoa before 1350, and a Genoese law of 1341 recognised that the design of these 'Biscayan cogs' allowed shippers to load them deeper than other *coche* or vessels. The *cocha* seems to have been safer, cheaper and more capacious than other types, and received a resounding vote of confidence from the Genoese. Like the Venetians, the Genoese had been sending galleys north to Flanders and England since the late thirteenth century. After 1340 the Genoese replaced all of their galleys on this long and potentially hazardous route with *coche*.

It is one of the peculiarities of the history of

the carrack that the term was seldom used in Mediterranean sources to denote a *cocha*. 'Carrack', or sometimes 'tarit', occurs in English documents from around 1350, and at first it was only applied to the Genoese ships. The origins of the word carrack are very uncertain, but it did not come from English. In the thirteenth century, *karaque* appears to have been an Arab word denoting a small vessel, but it is not known if this word had anything to do with the later term carrack. It has been suggested that the later usage originated in the Spanish language, and given the amount of Arab influence on the Iberian Peninsula in the Middle Ages, it is not difficult to see a possible connection with the word *karaque*. However, there is no evidence of a technological link between the Arab vessel type and the carrack. If the two words were connected in some way, it may just have been another example of a ship type name that meant one thing at one time and place, and something very different at another date and location. 'Carrack' survived as a definite ship type designation in English, but the usage of the term *cocha* declined in the Mediterranean in favour of the word 'ship' – *nave* in Italian, *não* in Spanish. This was no doubt a reflection of the *cocha* becoming increasingly commonplace: less an innovation, and more the norm.[3]

The earliest surviving North European ship picture actually named as a carrack in contemporary sources is the engraving of a ship entitled *Kraeck* (Flemish for carrack) by the Flemish master WA. One scholar has plausibly linked the original engraving to events in Flanders in 1468. The *Kraeck* has been dated in the past to *c*1470–80 on the basis of its three-masted rig and other aspects, so it cannot be said to have been radically re-dated, although it has been suggested that some chainwale features in the engraving were modified in 1490 or later. However, part of the importance of this new research lies in the fact that named medieval ship type illustrations are very rare: the possibility of linking this one to the 1468 events is extremely significant. This is because it would show not just what one artist thought

a carrack looked like, but what was generally thought to be the image of a carrack in the 1460s in Flanders.

The *Kraeck* has a number of salient features. It is a large, three-masted vessel, with square rigged fore and main masts, and a lateen rigged mizzen mast. The jutting forecastle sits atop a high, upcurving stem, and the forecastle is significantly higher than the aftercastle. Both the forecastle and the aftercastle have two stages. There is a stern rudder. The hull appears skeleton-built, with flush-laid planking and large longitudinal wales. The hull is very deep, and the *Kraeck* has considerable freeboard. There is an open lading port (for cargo) near the stern, about halfway up from the waterline. The presence of the port and the lines of the wales hint that the vessel has two or possibly three decks. The overall hull form is not far different from that of many illustrations of 'carrack-type' vessels from both northern and southern Europe. The large hull, the high, upcurving stem, the elevated forecastle, the stern rudder and the square sail as the main driving sail are common to all of these illustrations, making 'carrack', a reasonable description of the type, whatever contemporaries would have called them.[4]

The carrack and the two-masted rig

Pictures of *coche* from the Mediterranean can be identified as such because of their dissimilarity to the lateen-riggers, and because of their resemblance to both cogs and the later *Kraeck*. Three-masted square rig was not a defining characteristic of the *cocha* or carrack, but under both names the type seems to have played an important part in the evolution of European ship rig. The earliest illustrations of the *cocha* are also the earliest illustrations of a two-masted vessel carrying a square mainsail and lateen mizzen. The mainsail was the main

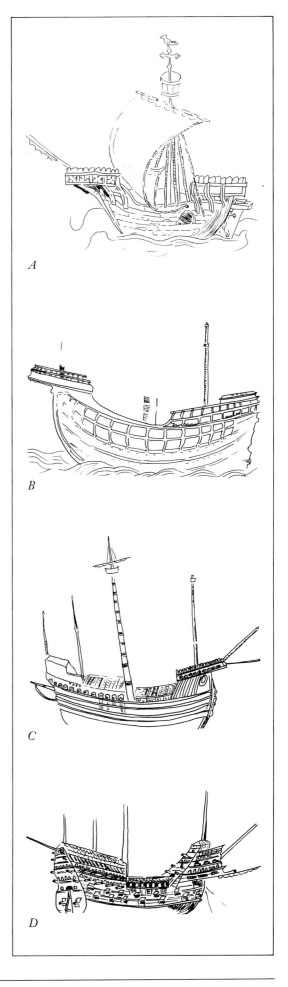

A

B

C

D

The development of hulls of carrack-type vessels, redrawn from northern and southern European illustrations of the fifteenth and sixteenth centuries (rigging and other detail mostly omitted):

A *A one-masted vessel from an English Ms of c1426 (after British Library Cotton Ms Tib. A vii, f81); note the lading port near the stern.*

B *A three-masted vessel from an Italian engraving of c1470–80 (after a National Maritime Museum, Greenwich, engraving).*

C *A four-masted carrack shown on Barbari's engraved view of Venice, 1500.*

D *The four-masted English war carrack* Henri Grace a Dieu, *after an illustration on the Anthony Anthony Roll of 1546 (original in Magdalene College, Cambridge).*

3. B Greenhill, *Archaeology of the Boat* (London 1976), pp259 & 261; P Van der Merwe, 'Towards a Three-Masted Ship', in *International Congress of Maritime Museums, 4th Conference Proceedings, Paris 1981* (Paris 1983), pp123–6; F C Lane, 'Progres Technologiques et Productivité dans les Transports Maritimes . . .', *Revue Historique* 510 (1974), p291; *Nouveau Glossaire Nautique d'Augustin Jal*, Vol 'C' (Paris 1978), p219.

4. A W Sleeswyk, 'The Engraver Willem A Cruce (WA) and the Development of the Chainwale', *The Mariner's Mirror* 76 (1990), pp347–60; Van der Merwe, 'Towards a Three-Masted Ship', p124.

driving sail. The mizzen seems to have been introduced in order to improve the vessel's manoeuvrability. Stepped close to the stern, the lateen with its better windward performance would be used to help turn the ship's head, or even, in the right conditions, to provide some extra canvas to help propel the ship in a following wind. Exactly when the two-masted *cocha* came into use is uncertain. The earliest known written reference to one is contained in a Catalan contract of 1353, which described a vessel due to sail from Barcelona to Alexandria as having a bowsprit, a main mast and an *arbre de mig*, or 'mizzen mast'.

If two-masted *coche* were sailing from Catalonia to Egypt in 1353, it is also possible that they were sailing from the Mediterranean to northern Europe at the same date. However, there is no definite evidence of this until the early fifteenth century. A Genoese ship called *La Bayard* was briefly in English royal ownership in 1372, but this was a single-master. The first two-master recorded in English sources was a Genoese carrack called *Sancta Maria & Sancta Brigida*, seized by English pirates. In 1410 this vessel was taken into English royal ownership, where it was known simply as *Le Carake*. An inventory of the carrack dating from 1411 noted that the ship had 'one great

One of the earliest known ship models that is reasonably reliable in the Western tradition is the votive ship from the Catalan monastery of San Simon de Mataro, usually dated to about 1450. The ship was probably two-masted, with a diminutive mizzen on the aftercastle to assist with steering and manoeuvring. This photograph was taken in 1980 before restoration by is present custodian, the Prins Hendrik Museum in Rotterdam. (Ian Friel)

mast' and 'one small mast'. At this point the English clearly had no specific term for a mizzen mast.[5] Within ten years they did.

Henry V came to the English throne in 1413, and renewed England's long conflict with France. To help counter the English naval threat and the possibility of invasion, the French hired some carracks from their allies, the Genoese. In the years 1416–1417, the English fleet was able to capture eight of these carracks, a considerable feat. They were large vessels, in the 400- to 600-ton range, and six of them were two-masters. The terms that the English used to describe the second mast were derived from the name they used for its sail, *mesan* or 'mizzen'. This was not an English word, and is thought to have come from Italian or Spanish. The mizzen mast was briefly referred to as the 'countermast for the *mesan*', but the term *mesan maste* was in use by 1420.

There is evidence of attempts to give a two-masted rig to six other English royal ships in the period 1416–1422, probably copying the example of the captured carracks. For the most part this rig was used either in some of the larger sailing ships in the English fleet, or on the king's balingers, which were long, oared fighting vessels. Both were types that would have encountered problems of windage from the area of hull exposed above the waterline, and would have benefited from the use of a second sail for manoeuvring purposes. There is little doubt that these carracks had a major influence on the adoption of the two-masted rig by the English.

One other rigging technique that the English learned from the carracks was an iron device called a *flaill*. In about 1417 a large apparatus, weighing 165kg (364lb) was attached to the windlass of the royal ship *Jesus*, in order to help raise the sail more easily 'in the manner of a carrack' ('*in modo carrac*'). The *Jesus* was a 1000-ton 'great ship', probably in effect a clinker-built version of a carrack. She would have had a main yard and sail easily as big, if not bigger, than that of a carrack. The *flaill* may have been a windlass pawl, or perhaps part of a Spanish windlass arrangement. Iron *siropes* (?) and *wegges* (wedges) weighing 25kg (55lb) were also bought for the windlass and the *flaill*, but how they were used is not known. Whatever its exact form, it is clear that the *flaill* was a device which made the raising of a large mainsail more efficient. It is an example of a true technical transfer, for the *flaill* was made by an English smith, and not by a man brought from the Mediterranean. Unfortunately the term is a unique reference in the sources, and it cannot be said with certainty if the *flaill* arrangement

became a regular part of the gear of large English ships.

One technique that the English certainly did not learn from the captured carracks was that of skeleton construction. By 1417–18 the crown was having to find Mediterranean shipwrights and caulkers to work on the carracks because English craftsmen did not know how to maintain them. In 1420 two of the carracks sank at anchor, and two more had to be beached in the following year. English shipwrights probably did not begin to learn skeleton or 'carvel' construction until the middle of the fifteenth century, and then perhaps by means of copying Portuguese caravels, or 'carvels' as the northerners called them. This is all the more surprising considering that, by the time 'carvels' are first mentioned in English sources, that is in the 1440s, skeleton-built carracks had been sailing to England for almost ninety years. A probable carrack-type that did play a role in the diffusion of the skeleton-construction technique was a French vessel, the 'Great Carvel' *Peter of La Rochelle*. At 700 tons this three-master was too large to have been a derivative of the caravel, but was in the size range for a carrack. The great ship was left in the Baltic port of Gdansk in 1462, following a dispute, and local shipwrights are said to have learned the technique of skeleton construction by studying its hull.[6]

The full rigged ship

The earliest evidence for the three-masted square rig dates from the period 1420–1436. The English 'great ship' *Grace Dieu* had a third mast, perhaps a fore mast carrying a square foresail. A small English balinger called the *Petit Jesus* seems to have been rebuilt as a three-master in the years 1435–36, with a mainsail, mizzen and foresail. Pictorial and documentary evidence makes it clear that the basic three-masted square rig was known in both northern and southern Europe by the mid fifteenth century, and that the main topsail had made its appearance by the mid 1460s. The

5. Van der Merwe, 'Towards a Three-Masted Ship', p125; Public Record Office, London (henceforth PRO), Exchequer, Accounts Various, E101/31/21; *Calendar of Close Rolls 1409–1413*, pp10–11, 35, 89 & 165–66; *Calendar of Patent Rolls 1408–13*, pp175, 178–79, 182 & 321; PRO Exchequer, Warrants for Issue, E404/25/208; PRO E101/44/17, m.2.

6. I Friel, 'England and the Advent of the Three-Masted Ship', *International Congress of Maritime Museums, 4th Conference Proceedings, Paris 1981* (Paris 1983); S Rose (ed), *The Navy of the Lancastrian Kings* (London 1982), pp215 & 256; Unger, *The Ship in the Medieval Economy*, p222.

An early English representation of a three-masted ship, from the mid fifteenth-century Hastings manuscript. The ship has the characteristic high forecastle of the carrack, but the aftercastle is not as highly developed as in some later vessels. There is a tall pole above the topcastle, but it is not clear if it is a true topmast or simply a flagstaff. (By courtesy of Basil Greenhill)

lateen rigged bonaventure mizzen was in used by the late 1470s. This was generally, although not exclusively, found on larger ships, its windward sailing qualities assisting the work of the lateen mizzen. Fore, mizzen and bonaventure topsails were in use by the end of the fifteenth century, along with fore and main topgallant sails.

The carrack played an important role in the development of the lateen mizzen, for the ship's size made such a sail desirable. Whilst the carrack undoubtedly benefited from many of the rigging developments of the fifteenth century, it is far less clear if these were first undertaken for the carrack. The third sail of the *Grace Dieu* was probably used to help handle such a massive ship, but a third sail was also used, within a few years, on the small balinger *Petit Jesus*. Likewise, topsails became commonplace on many vessels in the second half of the fifteenth century, and not just on carracks: the presence of topsails, or even of a bonaventure mizzen, did not necessarily mean that a vessel was a carrack.

The shape, construction and sizes of carracks

The available information on the shape and design of carracks is very limited. The one carrack hull to have received thorough study is that of the *Mary Rose*, built in 1510. The results of this await full publication.

The only surviving medieval carrack model is the famous votive ship which originally belonged to the Catalan monastery of San Simon de Mataro, and is now in the Prins Hendrik Museum, Rotterdam. The Mataro model has been dated to *c*1450, mainly on the basis of its form. The model was a two-master. It has a seemingly accurate profile, along with many impressive details. As a plank-on-frame, skeleton-built model it was almost certainly the work of a shipwright. However, it was not a scale model, for such a concept scarcely existed in the fifteenth century. The keel-to-beam ratio is almost 1:1, and when viewed from above it has the proportions of a barrel. Given this limitation, it is difficult to know how much some of the model's more unusual structural details can be taken as reflections of real shipbuilding practice. Perhaps the most unexpected feature of the model is that the ends of the two lowest strakes do not terminate at the stempost. Rather, the stem end of the garboard strake rises up to butt against the lower edge of the third strake, and the end of the second strake fits into the end-curve of the first strake. The impression is that the two lowest strakes of the hull form a sort of curved 'raft' on top of which sits the upper planking. The third strake, and those above it, all finish at the stempost. The 'raft' could be a survival from the raft-like flat bottom of the cog.

Further information can be gleaned from pictorial and documentary sources. A number of studies of the design of the carrack have been undertaken, and have produced a reasonably clear account of its development. According to pictorial evidence, the main constants in carrack hull design from the fourteenth century to the first half of the sixteenth were as follows: a hull that was large and imposing, by contemporary standards; a wide and deep hull, ideal for bulk cargoes; a high, curved stem with a marked rake; castles fore and aft, the forecastle usually higher than the aftercastle; an appreciable degree of tumblehome in the hull form; and a keel line that, when visible, was straight.

In addition, over time there was a tendency for the castles to acquire extra storeys, first as temporary additions for combat use, and later as permanent parts of the superstructure. Probable temporary additions can be seen in the bench-end carving of *c*1415 from King's Lynn. There is some evidence, from sources such as the so-called 'Timbotta Manuscript', that carracks had flat floors, at least amidships. Perhaps this was also a legacy of the flat-bottomed cog.

The Venetian 'Timbotta Manuscript' of *c*1445 contains a series of dimensions (in Venetian feet) of ships between about 125 and 625 tons (200 to 1000 *botte*). The keel-to-beam and beam-to-depth in hold ratios provide broad indices of the shapes of these vessels.

A deck view of the Mataro model, dated to c1450. Although the proportions are crude, much of the detail is convincing, and the structure of the model itself suggests that it was made by someone, like a shipwright, who understood ship structure. (Ian Friel)

A one-masted carrack, redrawn from the Timbotta Ms of c1445 (British Library Cotton Ms Titus A XXVI). The tall forestage is apparent but the aftercastle is relatively low, without the additional structures characteristic of later and larger carracks.

Table 5/1: Hull Ratios from the 'Timbotta Manuscript', c1445

Tons	Keel:Beam	Beam:Depth
625	2.50:1	2.83:1
437.5	2.59:1	2.55:1
437.5	2.50:1	–
312.5	2.90:1	2.27:1
187.5	2.78:1	3.00:1
156.25	2.93:1	2.41:1
125	3.33:1	–

By comparison, the English warship *Mary Rose* of 1510 had a keel-to-beam ratio of 2.8:1. The problem with the dimensional list in Table 5/1 is that the vessels are called 'ships', not 'carracks'. The manuscript does illustrate vessels that look like carracks, but it is very difficult to be certain if the smaller vessels in the list would have merited the description 'carrack' or 'cocha'. By the fifteenth century the term *cocha* was dying out in the Mediterranean, adding to terminological confusion. The keel-to-beam ratios may offer some clue as to one of the features that set the carrack shape apart from other types, at least in the fifteenth century. The vessels of 400 tons or more were wider in relation to their keel length than those of less than 400 tons. In fact, there seems to have been a trend for the four ships under 400 tons to become markedly narrower in relation to their keel length, the smaller they were. The data regarding beam-to-depth ratios is far less clear, and one cannot discern any pattern. Perhaps 400 tons (640 *botte*) represented the lower size limit for a carrack in the fifteenth century. Certainly the English in 1416–1417 reckoned that the Genoese carracks they had captured were no smaller than this.

The actual dimensions of ships will have been highly variable. Table 5/2 summarises information for two sizes of vessels from the same Venetian manuscript.

Table 5/2: Dimensions of Two Ships from the 'Timbotta Manuscript'

Tons	Keel (feet) (metres)	Beam (feet) (metres)	Stem height (feet) (metres)	Stern height (feet) (metres)	Depth in hold (feet) (metres)
625	96.5 / 29.4	38.6 / 11.8	51.7 / 15.8	39.7 / 12.1	13.6 / 4.1
437.5	82.3 / 25.1	31.7 / 9.7	40.9 / 12.5	23.8 / 7.3	12.5 / 3.8

The overall length over posts of the 437.5-ton carrack has been estimated to be 106.5 Venetian feet (120.9ft, 36.9m). The 625-ton ship was perhaps in the region of 140ft (42.7m) in length over posts. The flat floors of both vessels would have been quite wide, about 12.5ft (3.8m) in the case of the larger vessel and 11.4ft (3.5m) in the smaller ship. That would be either slightly under or slightly over the maximum beam, but nowhere near as flat as the bottom of a cog.

The differences in height between the stemposts and sternposts in both vessels was very marked: 12ft in the 625-ton ship (about 3.7m), and just over 17ft (5.2m) on the ship in the 400-ton range. Such an arrangement would have produced the towering forecastle so typical of carracks in medieval and sixteenth-century images. The forecastle of the large vessel would have stood over 50ft (15m) above the keel. A significant stempost/sternpost height differential was apparent even with the smaller vessels described in the Venetian manuscript, indicating that the 'carrack profile' was used in some small designs. The gradual disappearance of this profile in ship pictures of the sixteenth century is one of the signs of the decline of the carrack. Or, perhaps more accurately, it is one of the signs of the carrack's gradual transformation into another type of large ship.

Some of the war carracks of the sixteenth century were of great size. The *Mary Rose* had a

The Henri Grace a Dieu *from the Anthony Anthony Roll. Although compiled by an artillery officer, and primarily concerned with the armament of each ship, the depictions of individual vessels in the Roll vary enough to suggest at least some element of portraiture, however naively stylised. One of the largest ships of her day, the* 'Great Harry' *as she was known carried guns on the main decks and lighter weapons in the castles.* (Magdalene College, Cambridge)

keel length of 105ft (about 32m) and a beam of just over 37ft (11.4m). She is estimated to have had a draught of about 14.8ft (4.5m). A contemporary Swedish warship, the *Stora Krafvel* ('Great Carvel') or *Elefant*, built about 1532, was even larger. The ship's keel measured 126ft (38.4m), with a beam of 39ft (11.9m), a draught of 21ft (6.5m) and a height 'above water' of 52ft (16m), which may be the total height from the waterline to the forecastle. The main mast measured 122ft (37.3m) and the main yard 99ft (30.2m).[7]

The dimensions of the English warship *Regent* (built *c*1488) are unknown, but a list of masts specified for the ship in about 1512 indi-

cates that it was on a massive scale similar to the *Elefant*. The main mast was to consist of a central 'tree' of 114ft (34.8m), with four filling pieces each 72ft (22.0m) in length. The main yard was to be made of two pieces, evidently scarfed or fished together, each 31ft (24.7m) long. The principal mizzen mast was made of a single tree 93ft (28.4m) long. There were to be four other masts, of unspecified purpose, 84ft

(25.6m) long. The circumference of the single 114ft 'tree' was to be 10.5ft (3.2m) at the 'great end' (presumably at the mast step).[8] These dimensions, and the others discussed above, help to confirm the evidence from other sources that the carrack was the largest ship known to Europeans in the fifteenth and sixteenth centuries.

Crewing the carrack

The *cocha*, or carrack, was cheaper to crew than the old lateeners that it supplanted. On the basis of the Venetian laws quoted above, a 400-ton lateener would have needed a crew of 80, or one man per five tons, but a carrack of similar size could have been managed by 40 mariners. Impressive though this sounds, the evidence of the law codes should be taken more as an indication of a general degree of improvement rather than as a precise mathematical statement of the carrack's cost savings. Little is known about the crew sizes of medieval ships used on normal trading voyages. Most of the evidence for this aspect of seafaring comes from records compiled for military

7. Landstrom, *The Sailing Ship*, pp86–7; notes on the Mataro model also come from an examination of it made by the author in 1980, through the kind offices of Dr L Akveld of the Prins Hendrik Museum, Rotterdam; R C Anderson, 'The Swedish ship *Stora Krafvel* of 1532', *The Mariner's Mirror* 10 (1924), pp388–89; H Borjeson, 'The Swedish ship *Stora Krafwelen* of 1532', *The Mariner's Mirror* 14 (1928), pp149–57.

8. PRO E101/695/42.

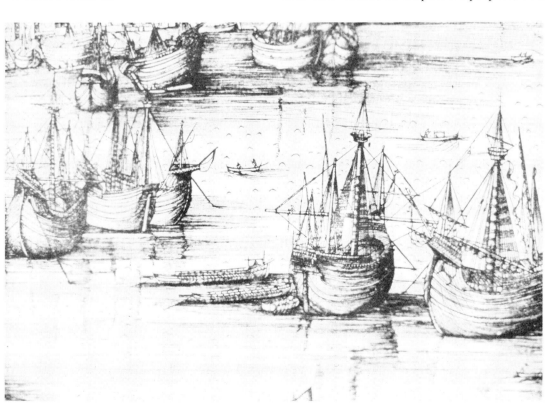

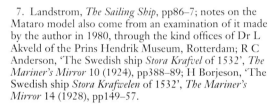

Venetian carracks of the late fifteenth century, from a panoramic engraving of Venice by Iacopo de Barbari, dated to about 1500. These are large vessels, with two mizzen masts, and the characteristic high forecastle. The detail is carefully drawn and inspires confidence in the accuracy of the artist's portrayal. (By courtesy of Christiane Villain-Gandossi)

expeditions or sea patrols, voyages in which crews are liable to have been large because of the needs of combat. Limited crewing data for three of the Genoese carracks captured by the English in 1416–17 and for a Venetian carrack hired by them in 1417 give figures of about one man per five to eight tons, somewhat better than most of the English sailing warships, which had ratios of roughly one man per three to five tons. However, this information only relates to one voyage by each of the carracks and cannot be taken as conclusive.

The great war carracks of the first half of the sixteenth century required crews of prodigious size. The increased numbers of heavy guns on board in the early decades of the century led to an increased need for professional gunners. After about 1510, 'gunners' begin to appear as separate groups in pay lists. Although they were never employed in large numbers, seldom more than one man per gun, raising many questions as to how the guns were used, they helped to swell the wage bill. For example, in about 1522 the 600-ton *Mary Rose* served as the Vice-Admiral's flagship in a war patrol. Her crew of 405 included the Vice-Admiral, the fleet Treasurer, her master, 244 mariners, 126 soldiers, 30 gunners and two surgeons. Their wages for 28 days' service came to £122 16s, enough to pay a Tudor Vice-Admiral for over thirty years! Nine years earlier, in 1513, the new royal carrack *Henri Grace a Dieu*, then called the *Henry Imperiall* and rated at 1000 tons burden, had carried a crew of 281 mariners, 20 gunners and 400 soldiers, 701 men in all. There were twelve ships of 300 tons and over serving in the English fleet in July 1513, and their man:ton ratios for mariners alone varied between 1:3 and 1:4, little different from those of a century before.

The situation regarding merchant crews was undoubtedly very different. Any medieval or sixteenth-century merchant crewing his ship on the same scale as a royal warship would have had little room to spare for cargo, and would have been bankrupted by the wage costs. The evidence is limited, but points to far lower man:ton ratios for merchant vessels. For example, the 500-ton German ship *Christopher*, on the Thames in 1545, had a crew of 36, a man:ton ratio of just under 1:14. Four other clinker-built German ships between 400 and 500 tons in London at the same time had ratios

ranging from 1:16 to 1:20. If these figures reflected a general trend, then the average trading carrack would have had four or five times fewer sailors than the average war carrack. The rig and other equipment of merchant and naval vessels was broadly similar. The main difference lay in the war vessel having an offensive purpose, and a much heavier gun armament. The larger naval crews may have been prompted by the need to use the extra men to work the ship more quickly in an emergency, but there can be little doubt that they were also there to help fight the ship. Given that all of

these warships had large groups of soldiers on board, the use of sailors in hand-to-hand combat would have been useful but not crucial. Perhaps the best explanation is that the extra sailors were there to help the small body of gunners to man their heavy cannon.[9]

9. PRO Exchequer, E364/54, E364/59 and E364/61, *passim*; British Library MS Add 89, f5; A Spont (ed), *Letters and Papers relating to the War with France 1512–1513*, Navy Records Society (London 1897), p79; M M Oppenheim, *A History of the Administration of the Royal Navy, 1509–1660* (London 1896), p171; PRO State Papers, SP204, f154.

A Mediterranean carrack from an Italian engraving that can be dated with reasonable certainty to around 1470–80. Not only is the vessel three-masted but already carries a small topsail whose sheets are belayed in the top itself. (By courtesy of Basil Greenhill)

Hull and deck details of a three-masted carrack, from a painting by the Florentine artist Sandro Botticelli (c1445–1510). Note the small deck hatches, the capstan abaft the main mast, and the two-piece mizzen yard (lying across the aftercastle). Below and aft of the forecastle is the bitt-beam, a common feature of carracks, which projected through both sides of the hull. The ends of the bitt-beam were probably used for catting the anchor.

Carracks: tonnages and trade

Large vessels such as the carrack existed to serve bulk trades. One common measure of tonnage in the Middle Ages was in terms of a ship's carrying capacity, or 'tons burden' in English usage. The tonnages of carracks could and did vary considerably. The eight Genoese carracks captured by the English in 1416–17 give some idea of the relative sizes of the type. These vessels were between about 400 and 600 tons burden, and larger than most vessels in the English royal fleet. The smallest of the four 'great ships' built for Henry V between 1413 and 1420 was of 500 tons or so, and relatively few English ships of the time exceeded 300 tons. Whilst one cannot speak in terms of a 'typical' tonnage for a carrack, it is perhaps not unreasonable to think in terms of 300–400 tons as the lowest tonnage limit for the type. As pointed out already, the ships of 400 tons and above in the Venetian manuscript seem to have been a somewhat different shape than smaller vessels. By the sixteenth century there are references to carracks of 1000 to 2000 tons, although whether these were precise estimates, orders of magnitude or mere hyperbole is difficult to say.[10]

Large though carracks were, their cargo holds were not just great voids. *Coche* or carracks had between one and three decks, and it was on these that the cargoes were stowed. Smaller vessels did possess open holds, but in larger ships there were good reasons as to why goods had to be split between various decks. Representations of carracks indicate that the deck hatches were of restricted size. They had to be, in order to make them easier to batten down, and to prevent too much water from being shipped through the upper deck. Added to this, cargo handling methods were primitive. Cranes were not common, and by their size carracks were restricted to a certain number of ports able to take vessels of their deep draught. Despite some use of tackles rigged on a yardarm to expedite loading or unloading, most cargo handling was carried out by labourers, working from deck to deck, and toiling up and down companionways with their loads. Carracks probably had fairly generous deck heights to allow for the storage of more cargo. It has been suggested that the relatively high deck spaces of the Tudor warship *Mary Rose* were an indication of her carrack ancestry.[11]

Among the most important bulk trades on which carracks were used in the Middle Ages were those from the Mediterranean to northern Europe. The Genoese were the chief users of carracks on this route, although carracks from Catalonia and Venice were also found in northern waters. The Genoese transported alum, used in fixing cloth dyes, and woad, a blue dye, to England and Flanders for use in the northern cloth industries. Their main cargoes on the journey back consisted of finished woollen cloth and wool. Whilst the woad mostly originated in northern Italy, the alum came from Genoese possessions in the Aegean and the Black Sea. Some carracks made the northern journey without touching at Genoa en route, coasting along the North African littoral. The very size of carracks made them easier to defend, and therefore more secure, than other types. Their great carrying capacity enabled them to carry adequate supplies for long voyages, without having to make time-wasting coastal stops to re-supply.

Precise data on crewing and maintenance costs for carracks are hard to come by. Some English evidence gives an idea of the scale of investment required. Only two of the eight carracks captured by the English in 1416 and 1417 were kept in fully seaworthy condition for the whole period of the time they were in royal ownership. The *George* and the *Christofre* (formerly called the *Pynele*), both of 600 tons, were two-masters taken in 1416 and 1417 respectively. The *Christofre* was sold for £166 13s 4d to a Bristol man in 1423; over the seven-year period, her maintenance costs amounted to

10. S Rose, *The Navy of the Lancastrian Kings*, pp247–52; J H Parry, 'Transport and Trade Routes', in E E Rich and C H Wilson (eds), *The Cambridge Economic History of Europe*, Vol IV (Cambridge 1967), p194; G V Scammell, *The World Encompassed* (London and New York 1981), p194; F C Lane, 'Tonnages, Medieval and Modern', *Economic History Review*, Second Series XVII (1964), pp222–3 & 229; F Braudel *The Mediterranean* (London 1975) Vol I, pp297–8.

11. Mary Rose Trust, personal communication.

some £647. The *George* was sold to two Venetians in 1424 for just over £133. Her maintenance costs, including wages paid for a voyage to Bordeaux, over the eight years reached almost £1000. This was a massive sum in contemporary terms, for £1650 would have been sufficient to build a 1000-ton English 'great ship' of the period. The use of carracks in trade clearly depended on high returns from bulk cargoes, and a high degree, in medieval terms, of safety and reliability.

An important feature of European maritime history is the marked decline in the numbers of large ships between about the middle of the fifteenth century and the second half of the sixteenth century. Various reasons have been put forward for this: spreading cargoes among several smaller ships was less of a risk for merchants than placing all of their goods in one vessel; smaller ships were able to enter more harbours, and were cheaper to crew and maintain, at least on shorter voyages. It is doubtful if any single explanation can account for this

12. Scammell, *The World Encompassed*, pp165, 171, 176–7 & 194–6; PRO E364/59, G m.2 and 2v; E364/61, H m.2; Rose (ed), *Navy of the Lancastrian Kings*, pp71–72, 77–78 & 248; G V Scammell, 'English merchant shipping at the end of the Middle Ages: some East Coast evidence', *Economic History Review*, Second Series XIII (1961), p334; Braudel, *The Mediterranean* Vol I, pp298–312; I Friel, 'Henry V's Grace Dieu – A Review of the Documentary Evidence', *International Journal of Nautical Archaeology* 22 (1993).

13. C R Boxer (ed), *Further Selections from the Tragic History of the Sea 1559–1565*, Hakluyt Society, Second Series CXXXII, (Cambridge 1968), pp56, 59–60 & Fig III; Braudel, *The Mediterranean*, pp302–3; J H Parry, *The Spanish Seaborne Empire* (London 1966), pp62 & 123; *Oxford English Dictionary*, under 'Carrack'.

Europe-wide phenomenon, but it had its effect on the carrack in that demand for great ships of most types fell, large state warships excepted. However, it took time for this to affect Genoa. In the course of the fifteenth century the Genoese were gradually displaced from the Mediterranean trade with England and Flanders by competition and piracy from the English, Iberians and others. Despite this, the Genoese clung on to their carracks until the final demise of their northern trade in the first half of the sixteenth century. In 1460 Genoa had thirty carracks, and even by about 1500 vessels of this type represented some 90 per cent of the total tonnage of the merchant fleet. Fifty years later there were only two Genoese carracks, and small vessels, that is under 200 tons, accounted for almost 70 per cent of Genoese tonnage.[12]

This was not the end of the trading carrack. A role for large bulk carriers developed in some of the transoceanic trades that opened up in the sixteenth century. The Portuguese, despite their scanty maritime resources, constructed carracks to move valuable bulk cargoes of spices and other goods from Africa, India and the Far East. The Portuguese route down the African coast and into the Indian Ocean had been pioneered by small, nimble caravels, but for all of their good sailing qualities such vessels could never bring back enough goods to make the Portuguese colonial venture worthwhile. The large, defensible carrack was the ideal vessel for this trade, although even carracks were not immune from piratical attack or shipwreck.

A survivor's account of the last voyage of the 'great ship' *São Paulo* in 1561 gives some idea of the nature of Portuguese carracks. The *São Paulo* was built in India, probably at Goa, and was described as being very strong and rock-like in all wind conditions. She sailed 'wonderfully well' in a following wind, a particular advantage in the oceanic voyages where ships relied on the prevailing trade winds; but because she was so heavy she sailed poorly when close-hauled, and was difficult to steer. A sketch of the *São Paulo* by a Jesuit artist, who also survived the wreck, depicts her as a three-master, with towering three-storey fore- and aftercastles. The *São Paulo* was wrecked on the island of Sumatra when en route from Lisbon to the Indies. As a comment on the reliability of some pictorial evidence, the woodcut frontispiece of the 1565 published account of the voyage shows a four-master: this image was probably a printer's 'standard'.

Large ships were also used by the Spanish in some of their oceanic voyages, but not in any significant way until the second half of the sixteenth century. Ships of 300 to 600 tons only began to figure in considerable numbers in the trade with the Americas from the 1560s. They were not used primarily because of their greater cargo-carrying capacities, but because they could carry heavier armament to protect themselves against attacks by pirates. Chief among these pirates were the English, to whom the word 'carrack' came to conjure up images of great wealth and became indistinguishable from the term 'galleon'. 'Carracks' were still written of in the seventeenth century, but it is doubtful if by then the term had any real technical content beyond defining a large Spanish or Portuguese ship, in the same way that 'galleon' was used in the eighteenth century.[13]

Carracks at war

It is something of a cliché – but nonetheless true – to say that medieval naval battles resembled land battles taken to sea. Whilst manoeuvres were used to bring fleets to battle, the individual ship-to-ship combats were essentially boarding actions. The larger ship in such actions generally had an advantage over a smaller opponent because it would normally have had a larger crew, would have been able to

Grassi's painting of a fleet of Genoese carracks from about 1480. By this date the type dominated the merchant fleet. Although subject to the usual distortion and exaggeration in representation, these are clearly large ships with fully developed topmasts on fore and main. (By courtesy of Christiane Villain-Gandossi)

An anonymous painting of large Portuguese carracks of about 1520. The main vessel is thought to be the Santa Caterina do Monte Sinai *and the other carrack portraits may depict the same ship from different views, as was a common later convention in marine painting. Much of the detail of sails and rigging is convincingly portrayed.* (National Maritime Museum)

rain projectile weapons down on to the deck of the enemy, and the higher sides of the large ship would have made any boarding attempt from the lesser vessel literally an uphill struggle. It is little wonder that English and other fighting instructions of the first half of the sixteenth century directed captains to set their ships against opponents of equal size.

The weaponry carried on board *coche* or carracks in the fourteenth century differed little from that found in other types of vessel. Crossbows, bows and even stone-throwing artillery were being used in the Mediterranean, although, as in the North, the hand weapons of the crew often ended up being the deciding factor in combat. The advent of cannon in the fourteenth century had very little, if any, immediate effect on the nature of sea warfare. The earliest known naval cannon was a 'certain iron instrument for throwing quarrells and lead pellets, with powder, for the defence of the ship', costing 3 shillings, supplied for an

English royal ship in the years 1337–38. Guns were used in small numbers thereafter. Despite the intensity of some of the battles and sea patrols in the years 1415–20, the fifteen gun-armed royal ships of Henry V, a minority of the royal fleet, never had more than about 43 cannon between them. Five of the eight Genoese carracks that the English captured had guns, but these numbered no more than two or three apiece. Almost all of the cannon were breech-loaders, most having one or more usually two separate breech chambers.

It is less easy to be certain of the carracks' other armament. Like most ships of the period, the topcastle was used as a fighting platform.

Bench-end carving formerly in the chapel of St Nicholas, King's Lynn (Victoria & Albert Museum, W16–1921). This carving has been dated to the early fifteenth century (c1415) on the basis of the style of carving. (The chapel is known to have been restored about this date.) The vessel has a carrack-type hull, and a lateen rigged mizzen mast. It is arrayed for war, with two-stage fighting castles and 'gads' (long iron darts) stored in the topcastle. Beyond the general date, there is no direct link between this carving and the activities of Henry V's fleet, but it is tempting to suggest that this image may have been inspired by the Genoese carracks captured by the English in the years 1416 and 1417. (National Maritime Museum)

One of the main topcastle weapons was an iron dart, called a 'gad' by the English, which was hurled down on to the decks of enemy ships, doubtless with lethal results. Bundles of long 'gads' can be seen protruding from topcastles of many ships in medieval illustrations. Ammunition was run up to the topcastle by a small winch system called a 'crane'. 'Cranelines' were purchased for various of the carracks. A winch

and 'crane bags' can be seen attached to the main top of the *Kraeck* in Master WA's famous engraving. The carrack *Marie Sandwich*, captured in 1416, was equipped with a *sesyng grapnell* by the English. This was carried at the bow, and used to secure the carrack to an enemy vessel. Again, a similar device can be seen in the *Kraeck* engraving. The *Marie Sandwich* grapnel was a formidable device, with a chain sixteen fathoms long (about 96ft, 29m), weighing 370lb (168kg).

There is evidence that the English, in the reign of Henry V, constructed clinker-built versions of carracks. Between 1413 and 1420 four 'great ships' were built for the king: the *Trinity Royale* (about 540 tons), the *Holigost* (about 760), the *Jesus* (1000 tons) and the *Grace Dieu* (1400 tons). They were probably the largest vessels ever built in medieval England, and among the largest in the Europe of their day. The author of a poem on sea power, *The Libelle of Englyshe Polycye* (written *c*1436–37), was in no doubt as to why Henry had had these vessels built:

> It was not ellis that he caste to be
> Lorde rounde aboute environ of the see . . .

In other words, Henry was said to have been aiming to secure control of the sea, specifically the English Channel, to allow his forces to cross to France. The poem, part nostalgia and part polemic, goes on to refer to the defeat and capture of some of the Genoese carracks in 1416.[14]

The Genoese carracks, operating with the French, posed a serious danger to English shipping, and this makes it likely that the four 'great ships' were conceived, in part, as anti-carrack weapons. At least two of the great ships, the *Trinity Royale* and the *Holigost*, took part in the Channel battles in which the carracks were captured. Exactly how such battles were fought is not easy to say. The vessels might have been laid alongside each other, as some medieval illustrations suggest. However, the great height of a carrack's bow and forecastle, and pictorial evidence of the 'seizing grapnel' at the bow, could indicate that a carrack attempted to come bow-on to the side of

an enemy vessel. The detailed contemporary woodcut of the battle of Zonchio (1499) shows two Venetian carracks attacking a Turkish carrack, with the attackers at angles to their target, their forecastles projecting over the waist of the Turkish vessel.

Between 1400 and the middle of the sixteenth century large carracks became the typical 'prestige' state warships of various European kingdoms. Henry V's four 'great ships' saw only limited use. The *Grace Dieu* never saw action. The naval war with France was effectively over by 1420, and the four big vessels were laid up. Another large *Grace Dieu* was build in the late 1430s, apparently as a private venture, but later came into royal ownership. The tonnage of this vessel is unknown, but she was evidently of some considerable size. An inventory of this *Grace Dieu*, taken in 1485, shortly before she was broken up, shows that she was a four-master.

Despite having only a small navy for much of his reign, Henry VII of England invested in two large prestige warships, the *Sovereign*, probably about 800 tons and completed *c*1488, and the *Regent*, about 1000 tons and completed *c*1490. There are no illustrations of these vessels. A French poem of *c*1513 has a drawing purporting to show the *Regent* ablaze when she

was destroyed in action with the French warship *Cordelière* in 1512, but the image is rather stylised. However, the inventories of the *Regent* and *Sovereign* make it clear that they carried many guns. As these inventories predated the invention of the gunport, the only places in which these guns can have been disposed were either on the open deck in the waist, or in the superstructures. By inference, these ships must have had very large castles. In 1495 the *Sovereign* carried 141 guns, of which only 20 were in the waist. Even allowing for the fact that these were mostly small weapons, it gives some credence to sixteenth-century illustrations that show carracks with massive castles, bristling with guns. The *Regent* had 225 guns, but as was typical of major warships of the time she also had a full complement of hand weapons, consisting of 200 bows, hundreds of arrows, 248 bills (pole-arms) and 100 spears.[15]

14. J S Corbett (ed), *Fighting Instructions 1530–1816*, Navy Records Society (London 1905), pp15 & 24; PRO E101/20/27, m.1v; L G Carr Laughton, 'The Cog', *The Mariner's Mirror* 46 (1960), pp69–70; PRO E364/54 and E364/59, *passim*; PRO E364/59, G m.1; Warner (ed), *The Libelle . . .*, lines 1018–19 and 1021.

15. M M Oppenheim, *Naval Accounts and Inventories of the Reign of Henry VII*, Navy Records Society (London 1896), ppxxi, xxii, 36–47, 194–5 & 274.

A close-up of the famous Cowdray engraving of the Anglo-French battle of 1545 in which the Mary Rose *was lost (the topmasts of the sunken ship are just visible, top left). Although this eighteenth-century engraving, after a lost painting, is crude in its depictions of the ships, the* Henri Grace a Dieu *shows the gunports low in the hull – one gun is being fired at the leading French galley, to the left.*

An engraving of the 'The Embarkation of Henry VIII at Dover, 1520', painted by an unknown artist, c1545. This is not a realistic representation of the actual event: the ships used in Henry VIII's crossing to France in 1520 were smaller. However, this collection of three- and four-masted carracks may well have represented some English warships of the 1540s. Whilst most have some lidded gunports in the hull, none has them in any great number, suggesting an early stage in the development of the gundeck. (The Science Museum, London)

A comparison of the weapons inventories of Henry V's ships and those of Henry VII clearly points to a massive increase in the numbers of guns carried at sea. However, as the *Regent* inventory and also the mass of hand weapons recovered from the wreck of the *Mary Rose* show, the proportion of 'conventional' projectile and hand weapons was high. Increased numbers of guns, at this stage, chiefly contributed to making boarding actions noisier and more murderous. It took the invention of the gunport to enable the gun to develop into a destroyer of ships.

The invention of the gunport has been traditionally attributed to a French shipwright from Brest named Descharges, in 1501. No-one ever seems to have adduced any original evidence to support this claim. The furthest it can be traced back is to nineteenth-century French sources. As pointed out many years ago by the British historian L G Carr Laughton, the idea of putting a port, with a hinged watertight lid,

close to the waterline of a ship was by no means new. Loading ports, such as that to be seen in the *Kraeck* engraving, had been in use for many centuries. The technology of the gunport existed. Any innovation lay in cutting gunports in rows on a deck below the weather deck. This enabled ships to carry more heavy guns. Hitherto, heavy guns could not be used in large numbers because, placed on the weather deck or in the castles, they would have made a vessel very unstable. They posed much less of a stability problem when placed close to the waterline. The deck on which they were mounted became a true gundeck, from which only heavy cannon were fired. Hand weapons could be and were fired from the weather or castle decks.

The chronology of the development of the gunport and gundeck is very uncertain. It is fairly safe to say that modern warships built in the late 1480s, such as the *Regent* and *Sovereign*, did not have them. The English warship *Mary Rose*, lost in 1545, had them in highly-developed forms. The *Mary Rose* was built in 1510, and underwent some major repairs or refurbishment in the 1530s, but on the basis of published evidence it cannot be said if the main gundeck and gunports were constructed in the 1530s or in 1510. This information would be crucial in dating the development of the gunport. Documentary sources are unclear, and it is difficult to find any ship picture, securely dated to the period 1500–1530, that clearly shows rows of lidded gunports. The painting of

the Embarkation of Henry VIII at Dover in 1520, once thought to date from *c*1520, has now been dated to *c*1545. What can be said with reasonable confidence is that lidded gunports and enclosed gundecks do not seem to have been in use around 1500, but that they had been developed by the mid 1530s and were in use in at least one major unit of the English royal fleet. The Anthony Anthony Roll, the famous illustrated list of the English fleet completed in 1546, shows that by the 1540s gunports were commonplace.

The development of the gundeck did not have an immediate effect on naval tactics. Large ships carried batteries of heavier guns, but many decades were to pass before sea battles began to change from being a series of boarding actions to being stand-off artillery duels.[16] As is well known, the *Mary Rose* carried a large contingent of soldiers, a mixture of bowmen and other infantry, the latter equipped with pikes, bills and other hand arms. In other words, the *Mary Rose* was ready for fighting at close range or by boarding, in much the same way as carracks of a century or even two centuries earlier.

Before the *Mary Rose* had been fully excavated and studied, the depiction of the ship in

16. A Jal, *Archéologie Navale* (Paris 1840), under 'Sabord'; Carr Laughton, 'Early Tudor Ship Guns', *The Mariner's Mirror* 46 (1960), pp250–51; C Lloyd and S Thurley (eds), *Henry VIII: Images of a Tudor King* (Oxford 1990), p120.

the Anthony Anthony Roll as a traditional, towering carrack, had led many scholars to suppose that her design was top heavy. Analysis of the hull remains has produced a reconstruction with much lower superstructures, a sleeker, more compact vessel closer in appearance to the English war galleons of the 1570s and 1580s than to the lumbering carracks of the fifteenth century.[17] Parallels to this can be found in ship pictures of the mid sixteenth century, but it is difficult to say whether or not the *Mary Rose* evidence represents the carrack somehow beginning to 'evolve' into the

'race-built' galleon. The problem is partly that of terminology. The word 'carrack' was certainly used in Tudor England, and sometimes served to describe royal warships, but it was far more common for such vessels to be called simply 'ships' or 'great ships'. Documentary and pictorial evidence does indeed suggest that the large old 'great ships' were dying out in English naval use by the 1570s. The main units of the English fleet in 1588 were probably a good deal more weatherly and manoeuvrable than their predecessors of fifty years before. It is not unreasonable to think that the *Mary Rose* represented a move in this direction.[18]

However, the *Mary Rose* evidence does not mean that all the large carrack-type English vessels were built in the same way in 1545, and it is known that high-castled carracks were still

A view of a modern model of the Mary Rose, *based on research by the Mary Rose Trust. This represents the hull and main armament as they were when the ship was lost in 1545.* (National Maritime Museum)

being built in other countries, such as Portugal and Sweden. Carracks were the major sailing warships and bulk carriers of Europe between the fourteenth and sixteenth centuries, with an influence on economic and military affairs out of all proportion to their numbers. However, for all that, the carrack was a specialised vehicle, needing either high trading returns or a state budget to support it. Its very size and expense made the carrack much more vulnerable to changing economic, technical and military factors than smaller types of vessel.

Ian Friel

17. M Rule, *The Mary Rose* (London 1983), pp29–38 & 149–83.

18. Friel, 'England and the Advent of the Three-Masted Ship', pp131–4 and Friel, 'Henry V's Grace Dieu'.

6

The Caravel and the Galleon

The Caravel

More than any other vessel, the caravel is intimately linked with the Portuguese and Spanish explorations that led to the opening of a sea route to the East Indies and the conquest of the New World. Its use, however, went well beyond the overseas ventures. From the 1440s on, caravels quickly propagated throughout Atlantic Europe and the Mediterranean, becoming adapted to local seafaring practices and gaining popularity as small to medium size cargo carriers, warships, patrol or dispatch boats, and corsair vessels. Their heyday lasted almost a hundred years, until the trend favouring lighter craft began to ebb in the 1530s. After a period of eclipse, Iberian caravels made a partial comeback in the late sixteenth and the first half of the seventeenth century, but outside the Portuguese and Spanish sphere other ships had taken over the caravel's functions.

Given the importance of the ship type, it is ironic that less is known about the construction of caravels than about that of Viking ships or medieval cogs. No extensive, well-preserved and securely identified remains of a fifteenth-

1. J M Silva Marques (ed), *Descobrimentos portuguêses: Documentos para a sua história*, Vol 1, (Lisbon 1944), pp7–8, 190; Silva Marques, *Descobrimentos . . . Supplemento* (Lisbon 1945), pp10, 16–17; Rosa y Bouret (ed), *Las Siete Partidas del Rey D Alfonso el Sábio* (Paris 1861), Partida II, Título XXIII, Ley VII.

Three-masted lateen rigged caravels, a detail of an ivory Virgin and Child sculpture (late fifteenth-century Provençal or Catalan). From a private collection in Canada. (By courtesy of Martin Elbl)

or early sixteenth-century caravel have yet been found, and the first geometric drawings and construction specifications date only to 1571–1616. Our current knowledge is largely based on unsatisfactory artistic renderings, and on fragments of information culled from the accounts of early explorers, chronicles, dockyard supply lists, a few fifteenth-century con-

tract specifications and building or refitting accounts, and sixteenth-century treatises on navigation and shipbuilding.

Before the age of exploration

The earliest known Iberian caravels date to the thirteenth century. At that point, the name attached to an offshore fishing boat also employed in coastal trade and probably related to the *caravo* or *qãrib*, a lateen rigged craft used by the Muslims of the Iberian Peninsula and western North Africa well into the fifteenth century. By 1255–58, caravels were used in northern Portugal both for carrying goods and for fishing off the Galician coast, and at the same time a mention of caravels found its way into the *Siete Partidas*, the Castilian law code of Alfonso X the Wise. By 1286, fishing caravels appeared in central Portugal, at the mouth of the river Liz. All these were very light craft: The caravels of the Liz carried about five men each, which in terms of some fifteenth-century small ship manning ratios would make them around 20 metric tons burden or less. In a Portuguese document of 1388, such vessels were mostly assumed to be open boats, whose yards were hoisted without using heavy tackle.[1]

Caravels with crews of nine, possibly up to

Single-masted fishing caravels drawn as part of the signatures of Spanish fishermen. The original is in the Archivo de Indias, Seville.

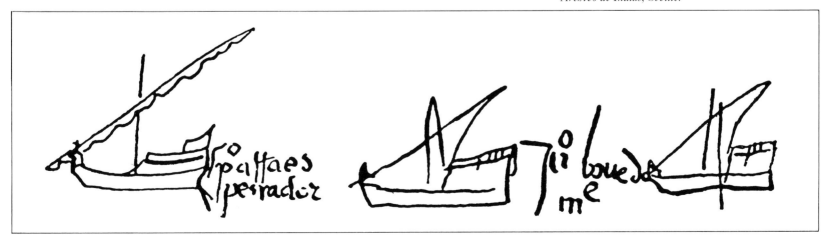

30 tons, still appeared in Biscayan waters in 1307, but after this no more is heard of the ship type until the early 1400s. The first mention, apparently dating to 1408–9, comes from Seville.[2] Next, the *Chronicle of D Pedro de Meneses* by the Portuguese court chronicler Azurara, completed in 1464, refers to a caravel captured by Muslims near the Andalusian port of Tarifa in 1417. Still later, some sources claimed that a storm had driven Portuguese caravels to the Canary Islands in 1416. Whatever the value of these testimonies, caravels were common among the Lisbon fishermen by 1434, the year when a Portuguese caravel was arrested in Valencian waters for having earlier captured a Catalan barque and taken her to Cartagena. In a description of a flood in Seville in 1434, a Castilian royal chronicle also mentions a caravel. In 1437, many Portuguese fishing caravels sailed to the failed conquest of Tangiers, and that same year there were caravels in Tarifa.[3] The ship type was thus well known in the Iberian south by the time of the Portuguese voyages down the African coast.

The caravels of discovery

There is no evidence that the Infante Dom Henrique of Portugal, better known as Henry 'the Navigator', improved the caravel, let alone

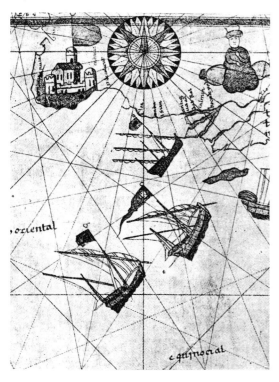

Two- and three-masted Portuguese caravels from the chart of Juan de la Cosa. Shown off Calicut, the three-master has sail furled whereas the other two are under sail, close-hauled. All three have long quarterdecks, but no forecastle.

invented it. Although from 1419 and the re-discovery of Madeira to the late 1430s the only explicitly identified exploration vessels were the barque and the *barinel*, caravels were certainly available by 1433–34 and served the Portuguese crown. The Venetian merchant adventurer Cadamosto (1455) claimed that caravels had always played a role in the African enterprise, and that by 1433 they took part in raids against southern Morocco. While the latter part of Cadamosto's claim seems plausible, the Azurara's more authoritative *Chronicle of the Conquest of Guinea* suggests, however, that caravels were not used for exploration until 1440. The apparent delay remains to be explained, but the timing coincides with the first instances of caravels being adopted outside of Portugal and Andalusia. At this point the original fishing boat had obviously become large enough and ranged far enough afield in sufficient numbers to be noticed as useful. It is the service rendered by caravels at Tangiers in 1437 that may have really brought them to Prince Henry's attention.

From 1440 to the death of Prince Henry twenty years later, over eighty caravels sailed south into the Atlantic, and from 1448 to 1460 hardly any other ships are mentioned. Our knowledge of the earliest exploration caravels is limited, but the evidence suggests craft from about 18 to 60 tons burden. In 1455, Cadamosto used a caravel of about 58 tons. This matches the known tonnages of the caravels that supplied the fortress of Ceuta in Morocco around 1450, namely 19 to 58 tons. No reliable contemporary evidence exists concerning the dimensions of these ships, although later fifteenth- and sixteenth-century depictions convey an impression of their general appearance. The smallest caravels were open boats and had only one mast. Fully decked Portuguese caravels stepped two or three masts with lateen sails and their length-to-beam ratio may have been around 5 : 1. They had no forecastle, and the low aftercastle might run almost to the foot of the main mast or a little forward. The caravels' main advantages were speed, manoeuvrability, and shallow draught. Light and sensitive, they could point higher—as close as 45 or 50 degrees (four to four and a half points) to the wind according to some estimates—while their low sides reduced windage, and hence leeway. This made them ideal for inshore work and better able to return north from West Africa against the contrary winds and currents.

The caravel's characteristics might make it seem obvious why the earlier barque and *barinel* were so abruptly abandoned by explorers,

but that would mean dismissing these vessels too easily. Even less is known about the barques of the early explorations than about caravels. Like the northern barges, many Portuguese barques probably hoisted one or two square sails, and may have also used oars. On the other hand, Mediterranean barques of the early 1400s carried up to three masts and were usually lateen rigged. Which type prevailed in Portugal in the 1420s and 1430s is a moot point. The barques that supplied Ceuta in the 1450s were of 40 to 70 tons burden, while 15- to 70-ton barques abounded in the Mediterranean from 1400 to 1450. Barques still jostled alongside caravels in Porto in 1460, and in 1498 a Portuguese barque carried 176 tons of Madeira sugar to Istanbul. Mediterranean barques of 100 to 150 tons also continued to ply the Levant and Flanders routes in the early 1500s.[4] There can be little doubt about the sound sea-going capabilities and versatility of the barque.

The Portuguese *barinel*, as evidence from Valencia (1426) and Portugal (1445) shows, was the same ship as the Atlantic *balener*, the workhorse with which Basque, Galician, and Portuguese mariners successfully broke into the Mediterranean carrying trade from the 1420s. It also resembled the English balinger. The northern balingers of around 1420 were still probably shell-built, unlike their skeleton-built southern counterparts, but they were beginning to adopt the rig of the southern *balener*. At first, a square main sail was combined with a lateen mizzen, and by the mid 1430s the basic three-masted square rig began to appear (square main- and foresail and lateen mizzen). Often equipped with both sails and oars like the barque, the Portuguese *barinel* was nonetheless heavier, between 60 and 90 tons. In the Mediterranean, where the *balener* was quickly adopted, there were *baleners* of 90 to 130 tons in 1420–1439, and Catalan, Castilian, Portuguese, and Italian *baleners* of 110 to 180 tons by 1440–1459. Like the barque, the *balener* survived into the early 1500s, and as late as 1495–

2. A Boscolo, *Saggi di Storia Mediterranea tra il XIV e il XVI secolo* (Rome 1981), p188.

3. Martin M Elbl, 'The Portuguese Caravel and European Shipbuilding: Phases of Development and Diversity', *Revista da Universidade de Coimbra* 33 (1985), pp551, 553; Carla Rahn Phillips, *Six Galleons for the King of Spain* (Baltimore 1986), p37.

4. H L de Mendonça, *Estudos sobre navios portuguezes* (Lisbon 1892), pp11–16; Elbl, the Portuguese Caravel . . .', p556; H Bresc, *Economie et société en Sicile*, 1300–1450 (Rome 1986), pp297, 299, 301; E Salvador, *La economía valenciana en el siglo XVI* (Valencia 1972), *passim*; M Sanuto, *I diarii di Marino Sanuto* (January 1496–June 1535), Vol 1 (Venice 1879), p916.

The caravel in its role of African exploration vessel: two are shown off the Gold Coast trading fort of Sao Jorge da Mina, established in 1482. The full rigged ship on the right would seem to place the illustration in the sixteenth century.

1499 a *barinel* sailed between Lisbon and the Gold Coast.[5]

The Portuguese lateen caravel seems to have won over the barque and the *barinel* by offering a fortunate combination of features at the right time, during the African phase of coastal exploration. She sailed closer to the wind. She mounted a sternpost rudder, unlike the Mediterranean barques, which in the early 1400s continued to use steering oars. She remained lighter and more shallow-draughted than the *barinel*. And she was first and foremost a good sailing ship, although caravels were known to use oars or sweeps, as the chronicler Damião de Góis shows.[6] Nonetheless, the fabled ability of the lateen caravel to gain against wind and current should not be overrated: sources ranging from Azurara to Columbus show this well. The experience of beating to windward south of Cuba with the *Niña* and two lateen caravels in June–July 1494 prompted Columbus to write: 'the great currents which run there in the same direction as the wind so make it that nobody attempts to struggle close-hauled, for in one day they would lose what they gained in seven; nor do I except caravels, even Portuguese lateeners.'[7]

The lateen rig was also less than ideal for long downwind passages. The answer was to put square sails on the fore mast and even the main mast. Thus Columbus rerigged his *Niña* square for the outbound voyage of 1492, and the caravels in Vasco de Gama's fleet of 1502 sailed east under square rig, reverting to lateen sails only in the Indian Ocean. Various east-bound caravels continued this practice later on. The lateen rig presented other drawbacks as well. Tacking briskly required a larger crew, and in heavy weather the rig was unforgiving to the novice, and fickle even toward those who knew it well. Not all mariners took kindly to it, as the Sevillian sea captain and experienced Atlantic navigator Juan Escalante de Mendoza stressed in 1575, anticipating a later Provençal saying about the lateen sail: 'Sé mi counouisès pas, mi toquès pas'—'If you do not know me, do not touch me.'[8]

Although the lateen caravel remained the Portuguese caravel *par excellence*, its drawbacks were felt by the 1480s. The design trend that set in after the voyage of Bartolomeu Dias to the Cape of Good Hope ultimately produced the Portuguese *caravela da armada* of the sixteenth century, with two square sails on a forward-raking fore mast and lateens on the three remaining masts. This type answered the need for a more capacious cargo carrier and a more effective warship, while retaining some of the speed and capacity to sail close to the wind. Saving manpower was undoubtedly a consideration. Outside of Portugal, however, square rigged caravels appeared much earlier. A caravel built in 1438–39 for Philip the Good of Burgundy—interestingly enough by Por-

tuguese shipwrights—and refitted near Nice in 1443, seems to have hoisted a square main- and foresail and a lateen mizzen. The Catalan caravel of Gracía Amat (*c*1465) carried a square main course and a lateen mizzen.[9] In Andalusia, square caravels (*caravelas redondas*) were found at the latest by 1476, although lateen caravels were quite common.

Until the early sixteenth century, Iberian explorers and caravels, lateen or square, went together. Caravels accompanied the Portuguese in charting the coast of Africa from Sierra Leone to the Bight of Biafra and down to the Cape of Good Hope. They took part in all four of Columbus's voyages, from 1492 to 1504, and they served as scout ships in the early East India fleets, for instance under Pedro Álvares Cabral in 1500–1501 and under Vasco da Gama in 1502. Many parts of the north and east coasts of South America, including the great estuaries of the Río de la Plata and the Amazon, were reconnoitred by caravels. And half a world away, a caravel was one of the three ships sent from Malacca in 1511 to find a route to the spice-rich Moluccas. In 1519, the 75-ton caravel *Santiago* accompanied Magellan's expedition and met her fate north of the entrance to the Strait of Magellan. By then, however, caravels were progressively giving way to small full rigged ships as the mainstay of exploration fleets. On the ever longer voyages, the beamier full rigged ship offered the important advantage of a relatively greater payload of supplies, presented fewer risks in handling the sails, and with the use of bowlines she too could sail reasonably well to windward.

5. Ian Friel, 'England and the Advent of the Three-Masted Ship', *International Congress of Maritime Museums, Fourth Conference Proceedings* (Paris 1981), *passim*; Elbl, 'The Portuguese Caravel . . .', p549, 556; Bresc, *Economie et Société . . .*, pp301, 305.

6. Damião de Góis, *Crónica d'el Rei D Manuel* (Coimbra 1936), Part 2, Chap XIX.

7. Samuel Eliot Morison, *The Great Explorers* (Oxford 1978), p463.

8. Juan Escalante de Mendoza, *Itinerario de navegación de los mares y tierras occidentales* (Madrid 1575), in Cesáreo Fernández Duro, *Disquisiciones náuticas*, Vol 5, (Madrid 1876–1881), p460.

9. Jacques Paviot and Eric Rieth, 'Un compte de construction de caravelas portugaises à Bruxelles en 1438–1439', *O Arqueólogo Português*, Ser IV, 6/7 (1988–1989), p317; Elbl, 'The Portuguese Caravel . . .', p571.

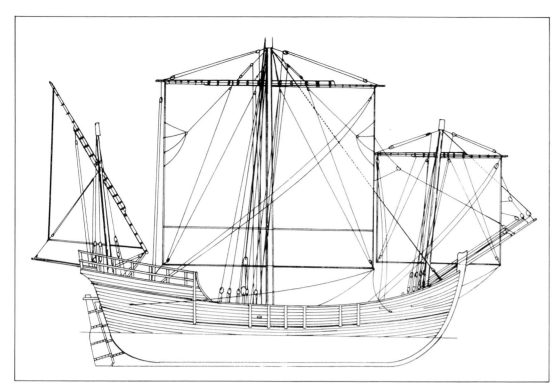

A conjectural reconstruction of Columbus' caravel the Niña *as modified with a square rig. The small drawing shows the probable sail plan as a lateener. Drawings by Xavier Pastor, from* The Ships of Christopher Columbus.

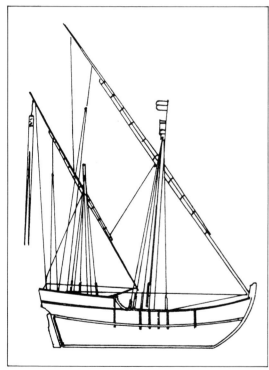

The Iberian workhorse

For all its qualities, the caravel was not specifically designed for exploration. The vast majority of all caravels ordinarily toiled at common trade and fishing, or served as escort and patrol ships. The Moroccan and West African fisheries were one of the caravels' main and oldest haunts. By 1448, Portuguese caravels worked the Saharan coast down to the Río de Oro, and later on down to Arguim, where caravels continued to fish as late as 1601. Andalusian fishermen likewise frequented the West African coast by the early 1450s, and in 1487–89 the mariners from Puerto de Santa María, Lepe and Cartaya who contracted for access to the fisheries with the Portuguese crown were forbidden to send down lateen caravels, being allowed only *caravelas redondas*. Following the Corte-Real voyages of 1500–1502 the range of the fishing caravels expanded as Portuguese ships flocked to the Newfoundland cod grounds. In the first half of the sixteenth century about 100 caravels from Viana, Aveiro and other Portuguese ports sailed each year to the 'Terra Nova do Bacalhau'. In the Iberian home Atlantic fishery, caravels likewise remained commonplace throughout the sixteenth century, while *caravelões*, small caravels that had first appeared in 1484 in the Gulf of Guinea trade, constituted the backbone of the Algarve spring tuna fleets in the 1570s.

Caravels not only caught fish, but distributed the catch to European markets. New heavier caravels were being built by 1456 at the estuaries of the Lima and the Ave to carry Portuguese sardines to the Mediterranean. Their shallow draught was a boon to those ports that were silting up, and their speed made them a more elusive prey for corsairs. Other caravels, from Viana, Ponte de Lima, and Vila do Conde, took salt to Ireland once or twice a year and brought back cloth. By 1552, salt and fish were still among the staple cargoes of northbound Portuguese caravels. But the ships also carried more glamorous goods. In the Atlantic islands they loaded cane sugar, and in West Africa gold, malaguetta (the seeds of *Aframomum meleguete*, a pungent African spice popular in many parts of late medieval Europe), and tailed pepper. The 1509 Regulations of the Lisbon *Casa da Mina*, the Portuguese crown agency administering trade with Africa, provided that twelve caravels, at the rate of one a month, were to carry gold each year from the Gold Coast to Lisbon. After the opening of the sea route to India, caravels took spices from Lisbon to Flanders, and from the 1520s to the 1550s they shipped their fair share of gold, pearls, and later on silver from the Americas to Spain. As late as 1580–1620, light caravels were the tools of trade for the *peruleiros* who smuggled Spanish silver and gold from the Río de la Plata to Brazil. To these commodities must be added an infamous but no less important one—slaves, for from the very beginning of the African enterprise caravels had served as slave ships.[10]

In short, until about 1550 and then again in the late sixteenth and early seventeenth centuries, caravels helped to move goods along all the far-flung lanes of Iberian trade. The expanding commercial and overseas interests also called for aggressive support, however, and here too the caravel served untiringly, in roles that ranged from short-range supply carrier and troop transport to regular warship. Caravels ferried men, horses, and supplies to the endless North African campaigns, from Tangiers in 1437 to the conquest of Arzila by the Portuguese in 1471 for instance, or that of Oran by the Spanish in 1509. Patrolling Iberian coastal waters and policing the seas were tasks to which caravels were likewise quickly put with notable success, even in the Mediterranean where the job would remain with the galleys for a long time yet. The caravel armed by the city of Barcelona that captured the notorious Florentine corsair Pierozzo de' Pazzi in July 1454 could hardly have netted a greater prize. In the Bay of Biscay, the crown of Castile maintained a patrol squadron of one carrack and several caravels as early as 1453.

Armed with guns, the fast and manoeuvrable caravel became in the later fifteenth century an

10. Vitorino Magalhães Godinho, *Os descobrimentos e a economia mundial* (Lisbon 1987), Vol 1, pp163, 171–178; Vol 2, pp63, 96, 102; Vol 4, pp124–143.

A drawing based on one of the three-masted lateen rigged caravels on an Atlas attributed to Pedro Reinel (1516). The original is in the Bibliothèque Nationale in Paris.

or kill the renegade Count of Penamacor, who had attempted to organise interloping expeditions to Guinea. On a more frivolous but no less important note, when the wedding of the Portuguese prince D Afonso with the Infanta Isabel of Castile was being prepared in 1490, a caravel was entrusted with taking to Italy the agents of King D João II and the gold to pay for brocades, silks, and precious stones.[13] In November 1533, when the news of a Turkish squadron about to enter the Indian Ocean required rapid action, a Portuguese fleet of nine caravels, two galleons and one *nau* made India in less than seven months at sea.[14]

The New World interest in Columbus has ensured that the caravel has been much studied, and a number of replicas have been built. Perhaps the best researched to date is the Santa Clara *(Niña's original name) built in Brazil for the 500th anniversary of his first voyage of discovery. The research was carried out by John P Sarsfield for the American Columbus Foundation. This photograph of the preparations to step the main mast shows the fine lines of the hull. (J M Nance)*

effective instrument of war. By 1494, King D João II of Portugal had heavy guns successfully mounted on board caravels built to guard the Portuguese coasts and the Straits of Gibraltar. The small 40- to 50-ton caravels or *caravelões* of the sixteenth century carried light armament only—two falcons (5 to 7pdrs) and four *berços* or breech-loading swivel guns. Some very heavily armed large caravels mounted up to 30–40 pieces, but the normal artillery complement was 14 to 18 pieces. The caravel of 160 tons described in the anonymous *Livro Nautico* of *c*1570–95, a Portuguese manuscript miscellany of shipbuilding specifications, mounted 18 pieces: 6 *berços*, 6 falcons, 4 light perriers (firing a stone projectile), and 2 *esperas* (in this case probably 3pdrs). In 1513, 16 to 20pdrs called *selvagens* were considered unsafe for use in caravels because of their weight and size.[11]

Caravels armed for combat assumed patrol, interdiction and convoy duties both in distant waters and on the Atlantic approaches to the Iberian Peninsula. From 1516 to 1530, caravels showed the Portuguese flag along the coasts of Brazil and attempted to keep open a Portuguese stake in the Río de la Plata. Closer to home, as the threat of French corsair attacks increased in the 1520s, a squadron of escort caravels would meet every year, in the Azores,

ships returning from all parts of the Portuguese maritime empire. Similarly, Spanish caravels struggled to keep the home reaches of shipping lanes clear of enemies—and often paid the price. In 1548, a particularly unlucky patrol squadron lost two ships in a squall, and two others were ambushed off Faro. While some Spanish escort caravels, like the Portuguese ones, picked up their charges in the Azores, in 1549 two ships remained on offshore patrol while four sailed all the way to the Indies to shepherd back six merchantmen.[12]

Finally, caravels, like the frigates of later times, were ordered out on special assignments or when speed was required. In 1488, a wellarmed Portuguese caravel was sent to England with the cloak-and-dagger mission to kidnap

11. *Livro Nautico ou Meio prático de construção de návios e galés antiga*, Biblioteca Nacional, Lisbon, Ms 2257; Quirino da Fonseca, *A caravela portuguêza*, (Coimbra 1934), p461; João Manuel Cordeiro, *Apontamentos para a história da artilharia portugueza* (Lisbon 1895), p61.

12. V M Godinho, *Mito e mercadoria, utopia e prática de navegar* (Lisbon 1990), pp472–473; Ernesto Schäfer, *El Consejo Real y Supremo de la Indias* (Seville 1947), p368.

13. Rui de Pina, *Crónica de el-Rei D João II*, (Coimbra 1950), Chap XLIV, p116; Garcia de Resende, *Crónica de Dom João II*, (Lisbon 1973), Chap LXXIIII, pp108–109.

14. Godinho, *Descobrimentos*, Vol 3 (Lisbon 1987), p44.

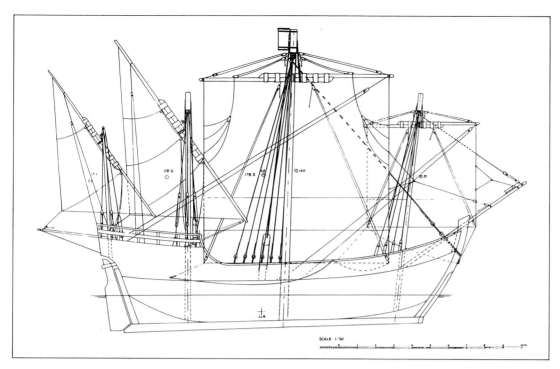

The sail plan for the Santa Clara, *drawn by J M Nance. It was based on the recent discovery by Eugene Lyon of a document called the* Libro de Armadas *which included an inventory of equipment on board the* Niña *in 1498. This noted a 'counter-mizzen' sail, which suggested the ship may have stepped four masts, although shrouds were listed for only three. As built the ship had a single-piece fore yard, and a single martnett. (J M Nance)*

The century of the caravel

The period from the 1430s to the 1530s was, however, not only an Iberian but a more broadly European century for the caravel. Within two decades either side of 1450, the ship type began to be adopted and adapted by one maritime region after another, from Brittany and England to Sicily. This was part of a trend that favoured smaller, more versatile, and faster ships that spent less time loading and had access to a greater range of ports. The same trend also brought to prominence the balinger and the *saetta*. The shipping slumps of the 1430s and 1440s eroded the fortunes of the great carracks of the early fifteenth century, and the depressions of the 1470s and 1480s, together with the loss of the great alum trade by the Genoese, sealed the victory of the small ship. By 1478, Andrea Satler, a correspondent of the German Ravensburger Company, was able to write from Bruges, 'The small ships have quite displaced the large ones'.[15]

As early as 1438–39, Philip the Good of Burgundy had a small caravel built in the Flemish port of Sluis by a Portuguese shipwright, and two other caravels at Brussels, on the river Senne. One of them joined the small Burgundian squadron sent to Rhodes in 1441. She was stationed and refitted at Villefranche near Nice in 1442–43, sailed to Constantinople in 1444, and then took part in pirate raids in the Black Sea. Her crew numbered twenty-one, which might make her around 50 tons. In Sicily, the first few Catalan-owned caravels, of about 60–70 tons, are reported in the late 1430s. The

ship type quickly found favour with Sicilian shipwrights, and by 1440–50 local caravels of 60 to 170 tons burden were seen alongside Catalan, Genoese and Tuscan ones in the island's ports. From the mid 1450s, both Sicilian and Catalan small caravels of 15 to 45 tons plied a risky trade along the Libyan shore, exchanging grain for African gold or slaves.[16]

In Majorcan records, caravels begin to appear in the 1440s, and in Catalonia locally built caravels are documented by 1452. From the very first, they worked all the main shipping routes of the Western Mediterranean, and by 1454 their destinations included the Levant. The average Catalan or Valencian caravel was around 50 tons or less. The Barcelonese caravel of Graciá Amat (1465) offers a good example. A vessel of about 53 tons burden, she was 18.5m (60.7ft) long, 4.5m (14.7ft) wide, and 1.7m (5.6ft) deep in hold, had a single deck, a low aftercastle, and carried two masts and a bowsprit. Interestingly enough, she mounted both a sternpost rudder and a pair of steering oars, unlike other Catalan caravels, for instance the *Santa Maria i Sant Jaume* of 1456, which had only a sternpost rudder. Caravels bound for the Levant were considerably heavier, and so were those destined for the Atlantic routes: to carry grain to La Rochelle and Bordeaux, a caravel of 90 tons, with a crew of fourteen, was chartered in 1483. Sizeable caravels nonetheless made an early appearance even on shorter runs: the *Santa Maria* of Barcelona, chartered in 1455 for the Barbary Coast, was of 135 tons burden.[17]

There were Genoese caravels going to coral

fisheries in Algeria by 1456, and from 1460 onward the ship type became increasingly frequent in Genoa, as the great carrack fleet declined. In the Adriatic and in the Venetian dependencies, caravels were common by the end of the century. The Venetian mobilisation lists of 1499 mention a total of forty-two caravels, including sixteen Dalmatian ones of about 130 tons each, with crews of thirty-five to fifty, and six Cretan ones of 39 to 162 tons. Greek and Turkish caravels are documented in the sixteenth century.[18]

Portuguese trade with England and Ireland brought caravels north in a leap bypassing south-west France, where the ship type did not take hold until the late 1460s. In English sources, caravels are first mentioned in 1448, when a safe conduct was delivered to a caravel of Porto of about 80 tons burden. From 1448 to 1455, eight or nine Portuguese caravels were taken at sea by the English or the Irish, and in 1454 the mariner Affonso Fernandes of Lisbon was punished for having bartered his caravel for a small *naveta* in an English port. The caravel became a vehicle for transplanting skeleton or carvel construction north, and gave rise to the northern *carvel*, a three-masted full rigged vessel foreshadowed by the already mentioned caravel of Philip the Good, refitted near Nice in 1443. The English *Particulars of Customs Accounts* record forty-six English *carvels* and one Irish between 1461 and 1500, and

15. Fernand Braudel, *The Mediterranean and the Mediterranean World in the Age of Philip II* (New York 1972), p301.

16. J Paviot and E Rieth, 'Un compte de construction . . .', *passim*; Bresc, *Economie et Société . . .*, pp301, 304–306, 308.

17. Elbl, 'The Portuguese Caravel . . .', pp562–563; Mario del Treppo, *I mercanti catalani e l'espansione della corona d'Aragona nel secolo XV* (Naples 1972), pp451, 555, 608–727, and *passim*; N Coll Julià, 'Aprotación al estudio de los patrones y de la propiedad de las naves en Cataluña en la Baja Edad Media,' *Homenaje a Jaime Vicens Vives*, Vol I (Barcelona 1965), pp377–393.

18. Elbl, 'The Portuguese Caravel . . .', p564; J Heers, *Gênes au XVe siècle* (Paris 1961), pp637–638; A Delatte, 'L'armement d'une caravelle grecque du XVIe siècle, d'après un manuscrit de Vienne', *Miscellanea Mercati*, Vol 3 (1946), pp490–508.

Scottish *carvels*, including one of 140 tuns belonging to the bishop of Aberdeen, were seen in Sluis by 1464.

The northern leaders in *carvel* building, however, were the Bretons. Between 1450 and 1475, Breton *carvels* heavily outnumbered all others in the Channel, North Sea and Bay of Biscay ports. In the 1460s and early 1470s, between 40 and 80 per cent of the *carvels* entering the ports of Exeter, Dartmouth, Poole, or Royan (at the mouth of the Gironde) were Breton, and in the single year of 1464, forty Breton *carvels* passed through the port of Sluis. English, Norman, Portuguese, Basque and Scottish caravels or *carvels* trailed very much behind. As to Holland and Zeeland, they seem to have adopted the *carvel* only relatively late in the 1460s.[19]

The Santa Clara *under full sail, lacking only the main 'drabbler', an addition to the foot of the sail used in fair weather. As far as the best modern research can determine, this is what a square rigged caravel looked like around 1500.* (J M Nance)

End of the line

In his *Arte da guerra do mar* of 1555, Fernando Oliveira complained that caravels were made too narrow, with a length-to-breadth ratio of more than 3 : 1, and carried but little cargo.[20] By that time, however, the development of the caravel had already culminated in the four-masted *caravela de armada*, documented in the first surviving detailed specifications of the *Livro Nautico* miscellany of 1570–1595. Carrying a square spritsail, fore sail and fore topsail, and three lateen sails, the heavy fighting caravel of 140 to 170 tons had a length-to-beam ratio of only 2.9 : 1, and was a hybrid of round ship and caravel. It offered a better artillery platform, but undoubtedly lacked some of her precursors' finer characteristics. Oliveira's complaint about narrow caravel hulls was, however, justified in the sense that smaller and more finely proportioned caravels had not disappeared. The 'old-style' small caravel of around 95 to 113 tons, described in the same manuscript and rigged like a *a caravela de ar-mada*, was closer to earlier caravels with her ratio of 3.3 : 1. The two-decked caravels measuring 11 and 12 *rumos* on the keel (16.5m and 18m), of about 85 and 114 tons respectively, documented in Manuel Fernandes's *Livro de traças de carpintaria* (1616) had length-to-beam ratios of 3.6 : 1 and 3.8 : 1. The smallest of caravels, of some 16 to 20 tons, called *mexeriqueiras* in Portugal and used for carrying dispatches, were still common in the 1580s and cannot have differed very much from caravels of a century earlier.[21]

Fernando Oliveira and other advocates of the full rigged man of war as the ship of the future despised the hybrid *caravela de armada*. But they had an equally unfavourable opinion of the full-blooded lateen caravel, arguing that

19. Elbl, 'The Portuguese Caravel . . .', p560; J Pavito and E Rieth, 'Un compte de construction . . .', pp318–320.

20. Fernando Oliveira, *Arte da guerra do mar* (Coimbra 1555), pp42v–43v.

21. Fonseca, *A Caravela portuguêza*, Chap 9 and 10.

In this engraving of the arrest of Columbus at the end of his third voyage, the caravels in the background are all shown with square rigged fore masts and lateens on the other two masts.

The Galleon

The galleon has often been misunderstood in standard reference works on ships and the sea, a situation that relates in part to the name itself. Venice used large oared ships called *gallioni* for river patrols in the fifteenth century, and the word for 'galleon' in diverse European languages would seem to derive from the Venetian *gallioni*. Moreover, certain characteristics of the *gallioni*, including the use of oars, appeared on many examples of the evolving galleon of the sixteenth century. The classic galleon of the late sixteenth and seventeenth centuries abandoned oars, however, while retaining a name that related to its oared past.

Several European peoples used ships called galleons in the sixteenth and seventeenth centuries, most notably Spaniards, Portuguese, and Venetians. Although versions of the ship could differ considerably from one another, all of the ships called galleons had certain features in common. Those same features, however, were shared by ships of other European peoples who rarely if ever called them galleons.

she was prone to heel too much, and that the absence of a forecastle excessively exposed her deck, and the tiller under the poop deck, to direct enemy fire. The caravel of course also had its defenders, whose admiration is reflected in the lavish praises sung by Jerónimo Osório (1571).[22] Wherever the truth might have lain, however, the age of the caravel was coming to a close. In the 1530s, the number of caravels in the port of Valencia, for instance, declined sharply, and at the same time caravels gradually began to disappear from the *Carrera de Indias*, the Spanish shipping route to the Americas. Demand for shipping space and the development of the galleon as an increasingly specialised warship worked against caravels, and so did Spanish government policy. The 1552 regulations for the *Carrera de Indias* barred from the trans-Atlantic passage ships below 100 tons and with a crew of less than thirty-two men, and in 1587 the tonnage requirement was raised to 300 tons.

When small ships flourished again in European waters from the 1570s onward, the caravel reappeared, but she was being rapidly supplanted by a revitalised barque, the *saetta*, the *patache* (a vessel under 100 tons, similar to the northern full rigged three-masted pinnace of the same period), and the *bergantín*. Under a

different name and with somewhat different characteristics, however, the *saetta* carried on the heritage of the caravel. In the days of Pantero Pantera, captain of the Papal galleys and author of the *Armata navale* (1604), the *saetta* of 50 to 100 tons, with its light and long hull and three lateen rigged masts, was the largest of the new small Mediterranean lateeners. The full rigged *saetta-polacra*, in turn, continued the tradition of the *caravela redonda*.

Martin Elbl

22. Fernando Oliveira, *Arte da guerra da mar*, pp43–43v; Jerónimo Osório, *Da vida e feitos d'el-Rei D Manuel*, Vol 1, (Lisbon 1804), pp192–193.

Caravela de armada, *from a chart of the Azores by Abraham Ortelius of Antwerp (1584). This form represents the final development of the caravel type.* (By courtesy of Martin Elbl)

Large Spanish ships after Pieter Breughel, thought to date from the 1550s. The lefthand ships have the main features of the carrack, but the vessel on the far right shows a narrow stern, a much lower forecastle and a low beakhead that came to characterise the galleon. The vessel second from right is something of a hybrid with carrack-like after superstructure, but with a forecastle and bow shape more reminiscent of caravels; note the primitive fore-runner of the beakhead.

Most significant in this regard were the Dutch, whose pinnances, whalers, and early East Indiamen shared many characteristics with ships called galleons elsewhere. In marine paintings of the early seventeenth century – the heyday of the galleon – many ships with similar features are virtually indistinguishable. Only their flags and the titles of the paintings identify them as, for example, Spanish galleons, English warships (sometimes called galleons), or Dutch pinnances and whalers. Setting aside distinctions based solely on nomenclature, this chapter is devoted to the history and salient features of galleons, and the warships and fast sailing ships that looked like galleons, from the early sixteenth century to about 1650.

Very little systematic scholarship exists on comparative ship design for that crucial period, compared with the fuller information available after 1650. Given the paucity of serious scholarship on galleons and their counterparts before 1650, some confusion regarding their nature and characteristics is understandable. Moreover, many twentieth-century works on naval affairs and competing European empires have been tainted by nationalistic prejudices that cast doubt on their conclusions. Current scholarship shares that taint to the extent that authors rely uncritically on those early works. Apparently, national variants of the galleon developed in response to national needs, though it is difficult to judge whether one variant was preferable to another. Diverse Europeans adapted the galleon to suit the characteristics of their home ports, sailing itineraries, and requirements for trade and defence. Consequently, each variant of the galleon succeeded or failed according to how well it suited a nation's needs. In their heyday, galleons and other fast sailing ships of the Mediterranean and the Atlantic were characteristically used for military purposes. Often, however, they were not dedicated warships like the naval vessels of the eighteenth and nineteenth centuries. Instead, their hull and rigging made them adaptable to various assignments, including merchant voyages and whaling expeditions.

A strongly-braced hull seems to have been one of the most characteristic features of the galleon, enabling it to withstand hard and continual use on the open ocean, especially in the Atlantic and the Pacific, but also in the Mediterranean, the Baltic, and the Indian Ocean. Other features characteristic of the galleon included a beak below the bowsprit, the most visible reflection of the galleon's descent from the medieval war galley that had used its prominent beak for ramming enemy vessels. Although the Dutch did not call their own ships galleons, they used the word 'galjoen' to describe the beak of their large vessels, as was the case in various German states.

Overall, despite the galleon's name, its beak, and the presence of oars on some sixteenth-century vessels called galleons, it owed more to the sailing ships of the fifteenth century than to the oared galley. The blending of characteristics from northern and southern European vessels in the fourteenth and fifteenth centuries produced the full rigged ship that was the most direct ancestor of the galleon, as well as many other ocean-going vessels. In general, the full rigged ship of the fifteenth century had three masts, the fore mast and the main mast with square sails, and the mizzen mast with a lateen sail. It was steered with a sternpost rudder. Large ships of this type were commonly called carracks, and in contemporary artwork they were usually depicted with a capacious rounded hull, a high, protruding forecastle, a smaller after castle, and a deeply-cut waist in between. However, in the fifteenth century the hull forms of sailing ships and their rigs did not follow rigid definitions. From its basic design, the full rigged ship developed along several paths, each hull form aiming toward the solution to a particular set of needs and circumstances. One of those paths led to the galleon.

The origins of the galleon

Neither the origins of the galleon as a sailing ship nor its evolution is clear. Vessels called *galeones* were used as early as the thirteenth century on the southern and eastern coasts of the Iberian Peninsula. Moreover, in addition to the oared *galleoni* used by Venice, full rigged varieties of galleons were used by both Italy and Spain before 1530. Spanish *galeones* participated in fishing fleets off the Cantabrian coast in 1513. Several *galeones* appeared on a list of ships sailing for the Spanish crown in 1526; presumably they were used in a military capacity. Although it is not clear what the vessels looked like, there is no indication that they were new or unusual. Early sixteenth-century documents from Bordeaux in southern France mentioned galleons as feared warships from Spain, which also suggests that they were in common use in Spain.

The famous 1529 'Carta Universal' of Diego Ribero, cosmographer to Charles I of Spain, depicts several ships that appear to be full rigged caravels or galleons. The caravel in its most characteristic form was a small, agile ship

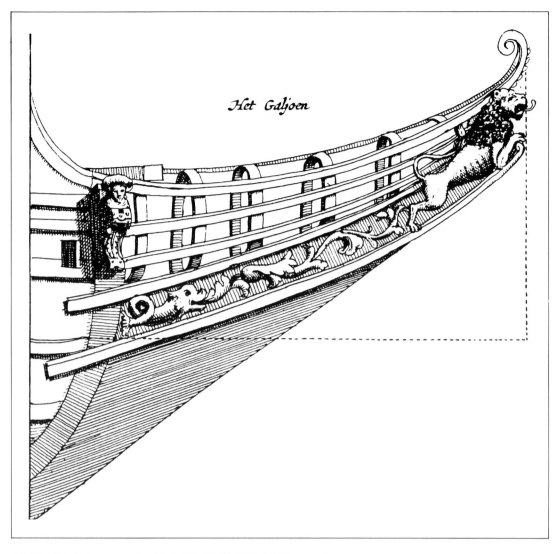

Het Galjoen

A characteristic feature of the galleon was the low beakhead below the bowsprit. This feature was called a galjoen *in Dutch, shown here in an illustration from Nicholaes Witsen's* Architectura Navalis et Regimen Nauticum *of 1671.* (The James Ford Bell Library, University of Minnesota)

with one deck and two lateen sails, although Spanish caravels often carried a full rig, and some caravels might carry four masts with various combinations of square and lateen sails. The forecastles of some of the ships on Ribero's map are much lower than the after castles, a characteristic feature of both caravels and galleons that contrasted with the high castles fore and aft on carracks and some other merchant vessels. Ribero's ships also display a 'square tuck' or flat stern, a feature designed for speed that distinguished both the caravel and the galleon.

Matteo Bressan is usually credited with designing and building Venice's first sailing galleon around 1528. According to Frederic Lane, arguably the foremost expert on Venice and its seapower, a Venetian great ship of the new type called a 'galleon' distinguished itself at the battle of Prevesa in 1538, using its gunnery to fight off surrounding Turkish galleys.[23] Yet subsequent Venetian attempts to produce effective sailing ships called galleons evidently failed; the next successful Venetian galleons date from 1570 onwards.

Craftsmen's traditions governed ship construction in the sixteenth century and gave way very slowly to a more rigorous approach. The few manuscripts on ship design that have come to light for the sixteenth century show striking similarities, whether they originated in Venice, Portugal, Spain, or England. They all shared a concern to find the ideal dimensions and proportions for ocean-going ships, blending theory with practical experience and moving a bit farther down the long road toward making shipbuilding more a science than an art. The ideal would vary nation by nation, however. Where shallow coastlines dominated, designers shaped the hull to create a shallow draught. If they aimed for speed, they narrowed the hull and sacrificed cargo capacity. Every choice required compromise, even within the same broad framework of evolving

23. Frederic C Lane, *Venice: A Maritime Republic* (Baltimore, Md 1973), p361.

Detail showing ships that could be either caravels or small galleons, from Diego Ribero's 'Carta Universal' of 1529. The original is in the Biblioteca Apostolica Vaticana, Vatican City. (Carla Rahn Phillips)

A four-masted ship, one of a number decorating a chart (dated 1555) by a Huguenot seaman Guillaume Le Testu. Many of these vessels have the high narrow stern of galleons but the bow perhaps shows a transitional stage from the carrack, with a cut-back version of the many-decked forecastle and a deep solidly built beak structure. (Peter Kirsch)

seventeenth centuries. In addition to its planked decks, the developed galleon was fitted with additional braces and beams, but no planking, below the lowest planked deck in order to fortify the hull. This unplanked deck was called the 'empty bows' (*baos vacíos*) in Spanish usage, and the 'false orlop deck' in English usage.

Tonnage

Two formulas for calculating tonnage generally held sway in Spain in the late sixteenth century, one for ships sailing on merchant voyages and the other for ships fitted out and equipped for military duty. The formulas first calculated the square measure of an average cross-section of the ship, assuming that the average was half the size of the cross-section at the ship's maximum breadth or beam. For a military voyage, 5 per cent was subtracted to account for the space taken up by additional bracing timbers. The average cross-section was then multiplied by the length on the first deck (the keel plus its extensions fore and aft), giving a total measure for the hold in cubic *codos*. The figure for cubic *codos* was divided by 8 to yield *toneladas*, or tonnage. For military voyages, 20 per cent was supposed to be added to the calculated tonnage to allow for the additional lading of guns, munitions, and soldiers, but in practice even warships were often gauged by the simpler formula for merchant ships.

Scholars vary in defining the *codo*. Most Spanish authors prefer 574–575mm; others use 557–559mm. The 1618 ordinances on shipbuilding issued by the Spanish crown printed an official ruler line labelled a 'quarto de codo' (fourth of a *codo*) that measured 140mm. In other words, the full *codo* for measuring ships, often called the *codo real* or royal *codo*, would have measured 560mm in 1618. For simplicity and consistency, that is the preferable figure to use for Spanish ship measurements during the early modern period.

ship design. When it is possible to compare cross-sections of the hull from various nations, we can discuss how the designs differed from one another, and speculate on their likely strengths and weaknesses, but we should judge the overall success or failure of a design only in relation to its full historical and geographical context.

Galleons were built using the method of skeletal construction pioneered in the Mediterranean. By the sixteenth century, variations of this method were used all over Europe for large ships. The length of the keel and the angles formed between the keel and its stem- and sternpost extensions varied according to local shipbuilding traditions, but even before the keel was laid the future owner, the master builder, and the master carpenter would already have in mind the proportions for the finished ship. Tradition and mathematical proportions dictated each vessel's principal dimensions, from the length of the keel and its extensions fore and aft, to its maximum breadth or beam, to the depth of the hold and the width of the floor. The estimated or calculated capacity (tonnage) of a ship was based on those measures, and ships with quite similar measurements could have notably different tonnages and sailing characteristics.

In typical skeleton construction, the shape of the hull derived from the largest and fullest pair of frames or ribs, located slightly forward of the ship's mid-section. Experts on European ship construction debated the optimum curve

and placement of these 'master frames' for centuries. Other frames were placed at even intervals to fill in the skeletal framework. The hull of a galleon had more ribs and bracing than ships designed solely to carry cargo, in order to withstand the weight and shock of firing the artillery. Many authors have assumed that the typical galleon was quite sleek, with proportions of length-to-beam commonly four or even five to one. That is a mistake. Though a few galleons were undoubtedly that narrow, they seem to have been dangerously unstable. Successful galleons for which measurements exist were generally no more than 3.5 times longer than they were broad, the length being measured along the lower of their two planked decks. In general, the classic galleon had two fully-planked decks that carried artillery, plus a half-deck, a quarterdeck, and a poop deck aft of the main mast, some of which might carry artillery. The forecastle was always lower than the structures aft, giving the galleon a distinctive, low-slung crescent profile. The high structures aft of the main mast enhanced the defensibility of the galleon in the era when grappling and boarding were common tactics of naval warfare. As many contemporary experts acknowledged, without defensible superstructures the only refuge for a ship's defenders lay below decks, where they could not mount an effective counterattack.[24] The Mediterranean galley was particularly vulnerable to the galleon, a lesson driven home in many marine battle paintings of the late sixteenth and early

24. See the remarks of the English mariner William Monson (b1557/58; d1642/3), in *The Naval Tracts of Sir William Monson*, M Oppenheim (ed), 6 books in 5 vols, The Navy Records Society (London 1913), Vol 4, pp91–2.

The English navy of Henry VIII is represented by a comprehensive, if naively illustrated, fleet list compiled by the artillery officer Anthony Anthony around 1545. The king experimented with a number of unusual warships (including a Mediterranean galley), but in terms of the development of the galleon the main interest lies in a number of medium-sized vessels, like the Anne Gallant *shown here, which were much lower than contemporary carracks. This profile may well anticipate the 'race-built' galleons of his daughter Elizabeth's reign. Note the early form of beak, which the Anthony Anthony Roll suggests was a widespread feature of Henry's fleet.* (British Library)

National variations in galleon design and employment

Classic galleons and their equivalents, by whatever name, seem to have carried three masts – the fore mast, the main mast, and the mizzen mast – plus a bowsprit. Some galleons were four-masted, with a bonaventure mizzen aft of the mizzen. The fore and main masts carried large trapezoidal ('square') mainsails (or 'courses') and topsails, and in the seventeenth century topgallants as well. The mizzen, and the bonaventure mizzen, carried large lateen sails, sometimes with a trapezoidal topsail as well. The bowsprit carried a trapezoidal spritsail, a spritsail topsail, and sometimes a spritsail topgallant.

The average length of time any ship could remain serviceable varied widely according to the nature of its service. Although a few ships on strenuous runs might last fifteen years or more with frequent refittings, careful studies have revealed surprisingly short lifespans for ocean-going ships – only five to ten years. Similarly, the galleons that escorted Spanish merchant fleets to the Indies rarely served more than four round-trips across the Atlantic, even with frequent careenings and refittings. Thereafter they were generally assigned elsewhere if they were royal ships, or sold off for easier service in local trade if they were privately owned. Even in the mid eighteenth century, French officials planned naval construction using an average lifespan of twelve years, 'an arbitrary figure based on estimates that well-built ships constructed of carefully selected timbers lasted ten years in the Atlantic and twenty years in the Mediterranean.'[25]

As the Spanish galleon developed in the early sixteenth century, it took features from the galley, the caravel and the *nao*, the large merchant ship of the medieval Mediterranean that was strengthened and streamlined in the early sixteenth century to meet the requirements of transatlantic navigation. Confusingly, Spaniards and Portuguese used the word *nao* to refer both to streamlined merchant ships and to enormous ships with large superstructures which others called carracks. Portuguese carracks with high castles both fore and aft differed considerably from galleons, and much of the confusion about the nature of the galleon can be attributed to confounding carracks, *naos*, and galleons. Spaniards made a consistent distinction between these ships and specialised cargo bulk carriers (which they called *urcas*), the most famous example of which was the Dutch *fluit*.

A central point of confusion about the galleon has to do with its functional definition in various European contexts. The Portuguese and the Dutch distinguished between the vessels they used for commerce and those they used for warfare. In the Portuguese case, galleons for warfare were usually smaller than carracks used for commerce and lacked the carrack's prominent forecastle, although both types of ship were strongly built. In the Dutch case, the warships that evolved in the late sixteenth century were much more heavily built than the famous cargo *fluits*, with more sail area and decks designed for gun batteries. The Dutch often called their military vessels *pinnassen*, but they were quite different from the small vessels usually associated with the name 'pinnace'. The Dutch *pinnas* had a half-deck, a quarterdeck, and often a poop deck like the Spanish galleon, but unlike the Spanish galleon the *pinnas* was supposedly never used for cargo. By reputation *fluits* and *pinnassen* were both very long in relation to their width, but apparently the Dutch measured a ship's length at the farthest extension of the rakes over the keel. If the length were measured just above the water-line, as was the practice elsewhere, these ships would not have been appreciably narrower than large galleons elsewhere.

In Venice, as in the Netherlands, galleons seem to have been used exclusively as warships. Venetian shipwrights were even lent to King Sigismund August of Poland in 1570 to build a warship that the Polish documents called a galleon. Venetian merchant carracks in the Mediterranean evidently carried only light armament. In the late sixteenth century they were often preyed upon by a ship type that Frederic Lane calls 'a "defensible merchant-

---

25. James Pritchard, *Louis XV's Navy, 1748–1762: A Study of Organization and Administration* (Montreal 1987), p126.

An illustration of a Spanish galleon of about 1600 from the Atlas of Gerard Mercator, published at Amsterdam in 1628. Its nationality is fixed by the characteristic Vizcayan flag of crossed red harpoons on a white field. (The James Ford Bell Library, University of Minnesota)

man" which was more like a galleon, essentially the same type of vessel with which the English were preying on Spanish shipping. Although relatively small, they were strongly built and carried formidable batteries.'[26]

Because Spanish galleons were nearly always sailing for the crown, or had sailed for the crown at some time, historians have often tended to regard the Spanish galleon as a specialised warship. In fact, the distinction between Spanish cargo carriers and warships was not clear. Even in the seventeenth century the same ship might serve as a galleon and then as a merchant vessel on consecutive voyages. Throughout its history the Spanish galleon could serve both for military purposes and for carrying cargo, as the situation required. The confusion between merchant and war vessels was particularly acute in Spain's transatlantic fleets, which arguably employed more galleons and merchant ships in the sixteenth century than any other nation could muster. Very few

of the hundreds of ships going to the Spanish Indies in the first half of the sixteenth century were identified by type, but of those identified, 35.4 per cent were galleons. In an average Indies fleet of 1551–1600, 44 per cent of the ships of known type were identified as either galleons or *naos*.[27] Early galleons in Spain could be considerably smaller than pure merchant ships; the same situation occurred in France. In addition, they often carried oars as well as sails for better handling near ports and along difficult coastlines.

The speed and manoeuvrability of the galley as a war machine inspired several Spanish attempts to develop large sailing ships that could also be oar-propelled. Beginning in 1540 the Spanish nobleman and mariner Don Alvaro de

26. Lane, *Venice*, p388.

27. Pierre Chaunu and Huguette Chaunu, *Séville et l'Atlantique*, 8 vols in 12 (Paris 1955–59), Vol 8(1), pp159–68.

A Portuguese galleon as depicted in the Atlas Civitates Orbis Terrarum by Braun and Hogenberg (1576). A prominent bow-chase gun emphasises one advantage of the low beakhead and also serves to reinforce the idea that it developed from the projecting ram of the late medieval galley.

Bazán experimented with a combined use of oars and sails, producing 'galleons of new invention', designed to be true heirs to medieval war galleys. In his proposal to the crown, Bazán called his vessels *armada* (literally 'armed') ships rather than merchant vessels and provided them with heavily reinforced and braced hulls, improved layout of the artillery, loftier topmast yards, a shallower draught, and oars as well as sails. The oars proved useless and were abandoned in later designs, but his other innovations were adopted to good effect by Spanish galleons. The profile of a French galleon called *La Roberge*, sketched in 1565, also shows the hybrid nature of some sixteenth-century galleons; the vessel had three masts and one bank of oars.[28]

Extrapolating from prior experience, Pedro Menéndez de Avilés, a Spanish official in Florida, built eight small galleons or *galizabras* in Vizcaya in 1568. The ships had keel-to-beam ratios of about 2.5:1 and length-to-beam ratios of nearly 3.7:1. Because of this, Menéndez is often credited with lengthening sailing vessels for the Atlantic. Unfortunately, the ships handled badly and were too small – about 200 *toneladas* – to compare usefully with the larger galleons that were the workhorses of Spain's Atlantic fleets. Later galleons would succeed in combining greater length and carrying capacity with stability and acceptable speed. Galleons as

large as 700 *toneladas* were registered in the province of Guipúzcoa in the 1570s, although the average would probably have been about 350 *toneladas*. Galleons could also be smaller and carry less crew and artillery than merchant ships, though both types of ship tended to grow larger in the later sixteenth century, a development encouraged and subsidised by King Philip II. Nonetheless, the largest ships in the Indies armadas were rarely over 600–700 *toneladas*, so that the few leviathans of 1000 or even 1200 *toneladas* were always worthy of note.

By the late sixteenth century the Spanish galleon had acquired its classic shape, displaying a high sterncastle, usually consisting of a half-deck, a quarterdeck, and a poop deck; a square stern, at the top of which was painted the ship's namesake; a low, set-back forecastle; a beak below the bowsprit; and full ship rig, complete with topsails on the fore and main masts. It was faster, more manoeuvrable, and better able to sail to windward than earlier galleons, but it was not a dedicated warship. A certain amount of speed and agility had been sacrificed for carrying capacity, meeting the needs of the Spanish empire for multi-purpose vessels.

Since other nations developed versions of the galleon as well, though the vessels were not always called by that name, a good deal of

effort has been expended in claiming primacy or superiority for the ships of one nation or another. Effort would be better spent in analysing the diverse maritime needs of each nation and trying to determine how, and how well, ship design met those needs. Many continental European governments owned far fewer ships in peacetime than they needed in wartime. They embargoed and refitted merchant ships to fill out their fleets when at war, saving the expense of maintaining a large permanent fleet, and encouraging or forcing private industry to consider military needs when building ships.

Instead of relying so heavily on merchant shipping, the English crown developed a permanent navy earlier than its neighbours on the continent. Royal ships were rarely used except in wartime. This saved considerable expense because the outfitting and crewing of a ship, even on a single voyage, could cost more than the ship itself. In the long run, peace was the English navy's worst enemy, as even the minimal cost of a royal fleet that sat idly at anchor created strains between the crown and parliament.

From a design standpoint, by using royal ships almost exclusively for periodic military purposes, English galleons could sacrifice cargo space and hull strength for speed and manoeuvrability. The English privateer John Hawkins, who was knighted and made an admiral for his efforts against the Spanish, developed an improved vessel after 1570 that eliminated the high forecastle of the carrack, an innovation that had already occurred on many warships in southern Europe. Although very little rigorous work has been done on English ship design, Hawkins's ships were reputedly strong and agile, so perhaps the small English galleons that preyed on Venetian merchant shipping in the Mediterranean were of this type.

28. José Luis Casado Soto, *Los barcos españoles del siglo XVI y la Gran Armada de 1588* (Madrid 1988), p192, a sketch from the Archivo General de Simancas, Mapas, Planos y Dibujos, XIX–87.

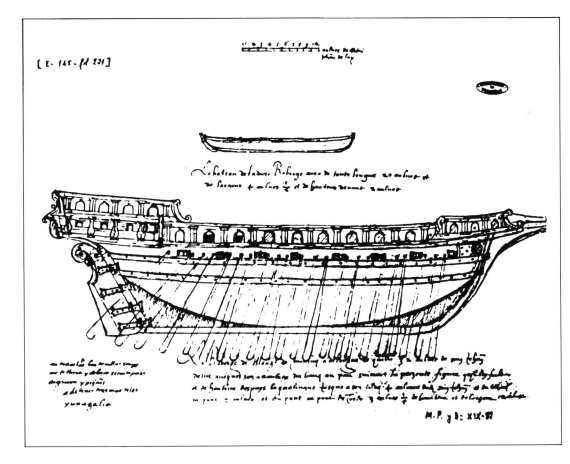

The origin of the galleon is interwoven with the history of the galley, even if only etymologically. There were numerous attempts to combine sail and oar successfully – Venetian galleases and Henry VIII's 'row-barges' amongst them – but in general such ships proved suitable only for sheltered waters or relatively light conditions. The Spanish made similar efforts, which may have had an influence on the design of galleons, although their primary requirement was for ships capable of meeting Atlantic conditions. This is a Spanish drawing of a French oared 'galleon' called La Roberge, *dated 1565. (Archivo General de Simancas)*

A coloured drawing of a small English galleon, from the manuscript work usually called 'Fragments of Ancient English Shipwrightry' and attributed to the Elizabethan master shipwright Matthew Baker. The ship may be regarded as representative of the new lower 'race-built' English style so often credited to John Hawkins or his influence. (Magdalene College, Cambridge)

Galleons of the Armada campaign

The 'Great Armada' sent by Spain to invade England in 1588 and the English fleet gathered to defend against that invasion provide the best opportunity available for studying the range of ships that represented galleons. The most careful summaries of those fleets list 130 ships on the Spanish side and 197 ships on the English side. The Spanish fleet included not only galleons and *naos* built mostly on Spain's Cantabrian coast, but also ships that the Spanish called galleons, built in Portugal, France, and around the Mediterranean. Most of the ships in the fleet, many of foreign origin, were embargoed by the crown and rented for the duration of the campaign. The royal bureaucracy kept very detailed records of the dimensions and calculated tonnage of each ship, in part to figure the rental fees owing to the vessels' owners.

If English historical sources could provide the same detail as Spanish ones, it would be possible to compare the size and configurations of ships in both fleets. Unfortunately, measurements have been found for only thirty ships in the English fleet, including only nineteen roughly comparable with the principal vessels in the Spanish fleet. However, the methods used for measuring and describing the English ships differed markedly from the methods used in Spain and elsewhere on the continent. The differences are daunting enough to have discouraged many serious scholars from any attempt to compare the fleets. Nonetheless, over the centuries writers have not shrunk from making qualitative judgments about the ships, sometimes based on little more than nationalistic preferences. Some English authors have ridiculed the Spanish ships as large and clumsy. Spanish authors have observed that many of the English ships were designed and used for corsairing rather than for peaceful trade, and thus would understandably have been lighter and more agile than many of the vessels used by the Spanish fleet. The burst of publications inspired by the four-hundredth anniversary of the Armada campaign in 1988 has shed some light on this perennially fascinating and contentious topic, but not enough to lay the controversy to rest.

Despite the difficulties involved, a crude attempt can be made to compare the configurations of the largest ships in both fleets by using the official measurements for each list of ships and by supplementing the English list with other information. Virtually all of the 130 ships in the Spanish fleet were measured officially before the Great Armada set sail, including 20 designated as galleons and 29 designated as *naos*. Galleons formed about 15 per cent of the Spanish fleet, about equally divided between Spanish and Portuguese galleons, plus a very few from other countries. The rest of the fleet was composed of *naos* armed for battle, cargo hulks, and small support and dispatch vessels of several kinds. Each ship was listed by beam, depth in the hold, and length, the three measures used by the Spanish to calculate tonnage.

Of the 30 ships out of 197 with measurements recorded in the English fleet, 19 were listed at 400 'tons and tonnage' or larger. They were not designated by type, however, and only their keel, beam, and depth measures were provided, not their length. A list dated 1602 contains fuller information for ships that may have served in the 1588 fleet, though it is possible that those ships had been rebuilt in the interim.[29] In England, a ship could be taken apart and rebuilt completely, often with different proportions, and administratively still be considered the same ship with the same name. The 1602 list provides measurements for the extension, or rake, of the hull forward and aft of the keel. It is not clear if those extensions were measured from the lowest planked deck, or at the farthest extension of the hull over the keel. Only if the extensions were measured at the lowest deck would the keel plus its extensions equal what Spaniards called length (*esloria*). It is assumed that the Spanish tonnage formula can be applied to the English ships, taking the keel plus its extensions as equivalent to *esloria*. When that is done, what the English called 'tons and tonnage' comes very close to the tonnage calculated by using the Spanish formula for merchant voyages.

According to the measurements of ships in the Spanish fleet in 1588, the galleons from Portugal had a ratio of length-to-beam of 3.35:1, and a ratio of depth-to-beam of 0.53:1. In other words, they were about three and one-third times longer than they were wide, and just over half as deep in the hold as they were wide. The large galleons made on the Cantabrian coast of Castile were slightly longer and deeper, with average ratios of 3.5 length-to-beam and 0.65 depth-to-beam. The smaller Castilian galleons had ratios of 3.6 and 0.63,

29. Michael Oppenheim, *A History of the Administration of the Royal Navy and of Merchant Shipping in Relation to the Navy from 1509 to 1660 with an Introduction Treating of the Preceding Period* (London 1896), p124.

One of a series of engravings by the Dutchman Claes Jansz Visscher, purporting to be the English galleon Griffin *which took part in the Armada campaign. Doubt has been cast on their authenticity as portraits since they were undertaken long after the event, but at the very least they probably represent the general design practices of the very early seventeenth century.*

making them longer and shallower than their larger equivalents from Castile, but deeper in the hold than their Portuguese counterparts. The one French galleon had ratios of 3.75 and 0.58, and the one galleon from Florence had ratios of 3.85 and 0.62. In the Armada campaign without exception, the *naos* were considerably wider and deeper in the hold than any of the galleons. The twenty-one Cantabrian *naos* had an average length-to-beam ratio of 3.07 and a depth-to-beam ratio of 0.67. Eight *naos* built in various places in the Mediterranean had ratios of 2.87 and 0.6 – in other words, they were wider and shallower than the Cantabrian *naos*.[30]

Overall, the English ships in the Armada campaign seem to have been somewhat longer and shallower in the hold than Spanish ships of roughly the same tonnage, assuming that the figures in the 1602 English list reflect the dimensions of ships in the 1588 fleet, and further assuming that the keel and its extensions were equivalent to the Spanish *esloria*. The 800-ton/*tonelada Victory* and *Ark Royal* had ratios of length-to-beam of 3.77 and depth-to-beam of 0.49 and 0.41 respectively. The 600-ton/*tonelada Hope* had ratios of 3.98 and 0.39, and the 500-ton/*tonelada Nonpareil* had ratios of 4.25 and 0.54. Some at least of these ships would have been 'race-built', with lower superstructure than Spanish galleons or their English equivalents. The smallest of these ships had been built for speed, and even the

largest would likely have been faster than their tonnage equivalents in the Spanish fleet. The notion that the primary fighting ships in the English fleet were sleeker and faster seems borne out. As long as the English were able to use their cannon to good effect and avoid being grappled and boarded, the greater defensibility of the galleons in the Armada did Spain little good.

The English won a geat victory in 1588, thwarting the invasion of their homeland and inflicting considerable damage on the Spanish fleet. Yet that damage has often been overstated. Based on official documents recently analysed in detail, the Spanish fleet lost 34 or 35 vessels of their total of 130, mostly on the stormy homeward journey up and around the British Isles. The heaviest losses occurred to ships designed for trade in the Mediterranean, the North Sea, or the Baltic. Few Spanish-built ships were lost – only 20 per cent of their overall tonnage – and no Spanish galleons or their auxiliary craft.[31]

In 1575 Juan Escalante de Mendoza noted that, in the course of the sixteenth century, the various European nations had developed ships that best served their needs. The Spanish crown and its overseas empire required medium to large vessels that could withstand hard use and serve for trade and defence at the same time. Galleons were called upon to defend Spain's sea lanes, but they also carried passengers and some cargo on nearly every voyage

across the Atlantic. Even galleons on purely military missions had to carry provisions and supplies for long voyages. Their design was a compromise between the military needs of speed, agility and power, and the mercantile requirement for cargo space and stability. The Spanish also employed a diversity of specialised craft to carry out other functions.

The English crown centred its fleets on royal vessels designed for military use and generally kept them idle in peacetime to save money. Ships owned by the crown for coastal defence could rely on home ports for resupply and could devote nearly all the ship's capacity to the men, guns, and limited supplies needed for brief forays out to sea. Royal shipbuilders could therefore aim for speed and agility in their designs, sacrificing carrying capacity for sleeker, faster ships. The private vessels embargoed under extraordinary circumstances developed as their owners' needs required, although the crown paid a bounty to those who built private ships adaptable for military use. Many distinguished mariners made their careers as privateers, preying on the Spanish Empire and its fleets in order to garner a share of the transatlantic trade claimed by Spain. They, too, favoured sleek, fast ships.

The galleon in the seventeenth century

With the advent of the seventeenth century, England pulled back from open confrontation with the Spanish Empire and consequently gave less attention to its fleet. Peace with Spain, concluded in 1604, and growing concern with problems at home took attention away from England's role as a seafaring power, even before internal tensions led to civil war in 1649. Nonetheless, royal interest in the fleet continued, and under James I the royal navy acquired several new and many rebuilt ships.

30. Casado Soto, *Barcos españoles*, pp186–199. The names and measurements of each ship appear on tables, pp209–221.

31. José Luis Casado Soto, 'Atlantic Shipping in Sixteenth-Century Spain and the 1588 Armada', in M J Rodríguez-Salgado, and Simon Adams (eds), *England, Spain and the Gran Armada 1585–1604. Essays from the Anglo-Spanish Conferences London and Madrid 1988* (Savage, Md 1991), p122.

The most important shipwrights of the time were Matthew Baker, the famous designer of Elizabeth I's reign, who lived until 1613; William Burrell in the reign of James I; and Phineas Pett, member of a distinguished shipbuilding dynasty and the pre-eminent shipwright in the reign of Charles I.

Patronage and personal animosities at court and in the dockyards influenced the awarding of official contracts in the early seventeenth century, to the detriment of naval affairs in general. A major financial scandal in 1618 led to widespread criticism of the way that ships were built and refitted. To remedy the situation a board of twelve Navy Commissioners was appointed for five years, responsible to the Lord Admiral, to supervise ship construction. The Navy Commission aimed to maintain a fleet of about thirty royal ships, building two

new ones each year to replace those too old for service. In 1618 the commissioners issued general guidelines about the ideal size and configurations for the new ships, which were to have a keel-to-beam ratio of 3.0:1 and dispense with 'too lofty upperworks, which overcharge many ships and make them loom fair but not work well at sea.'[32] The new ships were to have three decks, the lowest deck beneath the waterline, and artillery on the two upper decks. English experts, like their counterparts elsewhere, continued to grapple with the issues of proportions and upperworks. The high afterdecks of the galleon still had many proponents in England, because of their undoubted benefits in warfare. Actual ships built or rebuilt during the reign of James I followed the official guidelines specifying keel-to-beam ratios just under 3:1. Lower superstructures seem to have improved their stability.

In the early seventeenth century, naval powers all over Europe consolidated and assimilated the rapid changes made during the

sixteenth century and looked for the ideal combination of beam, keel, length, and depth that would provide ships with the characteristics they needed. The most successful alterations in the proportions of ships were introduced deliberately and incrementally. Whereas England stayed with a basic hull design for warships that was long in relation to its beam, in Spain designers sought to retain a large cargo capacity as well as adequate speed and agility for military purposes. Insufficient work has been done to trace this development in detail for all of Europe's maritime powers, but the case of Spain is well documented. As John Fincham noted in his pioneering study of naval architecture in 1851:

> as the science of naval architecture was formerly encouraged more in Spain than

An illustration by Juan de la Corte of Spanish galleons in action off the coast of Pernambuco, Brazil, in 1635. Archivo Museo del Viso del Marqués, Cuidad Real. (Museo Naval, Madrid)

32. Oppenheim, *Administration of the Royal Navy*, p205. See pp194–215 for discussion of the Navy Commission and its work.

principal ships involved in transatlantic voyages. The rules proposed a keel-to-beam ratio of averaging 2.6:1, and a length-to-beam ratio of 3.5 (much narrower than traditional sailing ships) and a maximum size of 567 *toneladas* (much smaller than some merchant ships in the late sixteenth century). Although the rules were not to take effect until March 1609, merchant shipbuilders complained that they mandated ships more suitable for warfare than trade, with far too little cargo space. Several shipbuilders even criticised their value for warships, arguing that the new ships would be so long, with so little depth in the hold, that they might roll too much on the open sea, especially during storms. They warned that even a small surge could flood the lower gunports on ships with so little depth. The critics also noted that experience had shown the military value of ships that sat high in the water because their fighting men were at an advantage in both boarding and firing guns at an enemy. The critics conveniently ignored the fact that Spanish gunnery in the Great Armada campaign had been ineffective in firing at lower English ships, but old wisdom died hard.

Before the rules went into effect, the Spanish crown answered its critics by naming a panel of 'persons practised in navigation and the fabrication of ocean-going ships, to try to amend some defects that experience has found in the General Ordinances of 1607 on the making of ships of war and of commerce.'[34] The search for acceptable multi-purpose vessels engaged mariners, shipbuilders, merchants and theoreticians in a common enterprise lasting several years. One of the many participants, Juan de Veas, an experienced mariner and shipbuilder, suggested an alternative both to traditional measures and to the 1607 rules, advocating ships similar to shallow-draught and flat-bottomed Dutch designs. Veas's pro-

elsewhere, the ships of that country were before those of the more northern nations of Europe, in possessing the excellence of form from which both fast sailing and other good qualities result.[33]

After Spain made peace with its various adversaries between 1598 and 1609, the crown's total tonnage afloat declined, but a permanent navy remained. Even in peacetime, squadrons of galleons were needed to protect merchant fleets on the transatlantic run. During the reign of Philip III (1598–1621) the Spanish monarchy exercised close control over the shipbuilding industry, keeping private construction in line with public needs. As always, the crown sought to ensure that merchant shipping could be adapted for military duty if hostilities resumed. Not only were the sizes

and configurations of ships regulated, but the crown specified where ships were to be built and where materials and labour should be found. By regulating ship construction, the crown maintained a reserve of vessels suitable for military use at the expense of private shipowners, but it was forced to consult those shipowners in shaping the regulations. Three major sets of shipbuilding ordinances appeared during the reign of Philip III – in 1607, 1613, and 1618 – accompanied by lively government-sponsored debate. Royal policy showed a willingness to experiment, not only with methods for the procurement of ships, but also with their size and configuration, searching for the ideal compromise between merchant vessels and warships.

An ordinance of 21 December 1607 specified for the first time the dimensions for the

33. John Fincham, *A History of Naval Architecture: To Which is Prefixed, An Introductory Dissertation on the Application of Mathematical Science to the Art of Naval Construction* (London 1851), p47.

34. Cesáreo Fernández Duro (ed), *Disquisiciones náuticas*, 6 vols (Madrid 1876–81), Vol 5, p378. For the 1607 rules and documents from the subsequent debate, see Vol 5, pp50–55, pp376–78; and Martín Fernández de Navarrete (comp), *Colección de documentos y manuscriptos compilados*, Julio Guillén Tato (ed), 32 vols (Nendeln, Lichtenstein 1971), Vol 23(1), doc 45, pp559–63, and Vol 24(2), doc 49.

This overhead view of Mayflower II *under construction clearly shows the beakhead that characterised the galleon. Its practical value included providing a platform for handling the head sails, but since it jutted out over the sea, it was also a convenient position for the crew's latrines – to this day marine lavatories are called 'heads' because of a long standing association with this area of the ship.* (CMP)

posed design aimed to combine speed with ample cargo space, a seemingly ideal combination, yet Tomé Cano, another member of the royal commission, pointed out that such ships were hard to handle and had a tendency to pitch and roll even in light seas.[35] As debate proceeded, the crown continued to subsidise large private ships suitable for warfare, providing incentives for merchants to fall into line with government regulations.

A new set of rules in 1613 proposed a ratio of length-to-beam that was still higher than traditional ships, but lower than the 1607 rules required, averaging between 3.2 for galleons of about 1100 *toneladas* and 3.55 for galleons of about 380 *toneladas*. The depth in the hold was reduced to half the beam because the lengthened keel would presumably have allowed for more cargo with less depth. In addition, the aftercastle was supposed to be reduced for greater stability, and external platforms, often used to increase cargo space, were banned. Despite compromises from the crown to provide for more carrying capacity in the vessels, merchants still complained that they would be shaped more like warships.

The guild of merchants and shipbuilders in Seville tried to stall the implementation of the 1613 regulations, claiming that ships' carpenters feared no one would buy their vessels if they followed the mandated proportions. Self-interest undoubtedly motivated both merchants and shipbuilders: the new rules diminished cargo space in the interests of speed and manoeuvrability. Nonetheless, the crown exempted existing ships from the new rules. Surprisingly, given the vehemence of merchant opposition, when royal officials surveyed all the ships in Seville and Cádiz in February of 1614, they found thirty-three of the seventy-six ships surveyed to conform substantially to the new rules, and another twenty that could be remodelled easily. They found only twenty-three that should be retired after one more voyage,

35. Tomé Cano, *Arte para fabricar y apareiar naos* (1611), Enrique Marco Dorta (ed) (La Laguna, Canary Islands 1964). Though the book was published in 1611, it was substantially complete in 1608.

Felix Castelo's painting 'The Recapture of San Cristóbal Island in the Caribbean, 1629' shows a number of Spanish galleons in action. (Prado Museum, Madrid)

either because of their condition or their unsatisfactory proportions.[36]

On 16 June 1618 the Spanish crown published a new set of ordinances for ship construction, establishing longer, shallower vessels with less superstructure that would be faster, easier to handle, and more manoeuvrable. Nevertheless, they were still supposed to be good cargo carriers, and the crown made noteworthy concessions to the commercial community in that regard. Although the rules by no means gained universal approval, merchants accepted them as the best compromise they were likely to get. Besides stating detailed mathematical proportions for ships on Atlantic voyages, the new ordinances specified a length-to-beam ratio of about 3:1 for ships of 1000–1100 *toneladas*, and about 3.4 for medium sized ships of 300–400 *toneladas*. Depth in the hold was to be about half the beam in ships of all sizes. The maximum size for merchant ships was set at 624 *toneladas*, small enough to pass the sandbars at Sanlúcar de Barrameda and at San Juan de Ulúa on the Mexican coast. Increased cargo space in the new design supposedly reduced the need to stow cargo in the superstructures. Even galleons built for the Indies run had to follow the 1618 rules, which made them wider than Spanish galleons of comparable size in the Great Armada of 1588, and therefore more suitable for cargo.

With the publication of the 1618 ordinances, the major naval legislation of Philip III's reign was completed. As long as international peace treaties held, the king and his advisors continued a policy of promoting private shipbuilding rather than building up the royal navy. When warfare resumed in 1621, that strategy proved inadequate and the crown began to contract for galleons from private shipbuilders, guided by the 1618 ordinances. More specialised warships, such as small frigates, were built at the same time by the Spanish government, but the galleon and the *nao* remained multi-purpose vessels. The frigate would eventually grow in size and replace the

36. Navarrete, *Colección de documentos*, Vol 24(1), docs 11–14, pp93–131.

A large Dutch galleon from an engraving by Barentsoen dated 1594. Although it may not be a specific portrait, the details are believable for a ship of the period, even if the Dutch are known to have built few vessels of such size for their own purposes.

This anonymous painting of the fireship attack on the Spanish Armada (7 August 1588) was probably produced in the Netherlands not long after the event. The ship portraits are reasonably detailed, although the proportions do not always inspire confidence. Nevertheless, the English ships are generally less lofty than their Spanish opponents. In the foreground an English galleon is bearing down on a galleass, which is attempting to escape under oars. (National Maritime Museum)

galleon as a major warship, but in the early seventeenth century it usually remained in an auxiliary role to heavier ships such as the galleon.

The Dutch also favoured multi-purpose vessels in trading areas where they were likely to encounter hostilities, and a ship built and crewed lightly would not suffice. In addition, during the early seventeenth century Dutch warships strongly resembling galleons also served on whaling expeditions in the Arctic. It seems that the designation of Dutch ships was as flexible as that for Spanish vessels, with the role of a ship on a given voyage defining it as a warship, an East Indiaman, a whaler, a support vessel, or some other type, rather than a particular hull form or rig. The Dutch also built galleons for other nations, including Sweden and France.

In the early seventeenth century the Venetians favoured medium-sized galleons for warfare and seem to have continued making a fairly sharp distinction between commercial vessels and warships. Some Venetian galleons in about 1620 carried 20–30 guns, the same firepower as contemporary Spanish galleons of 330–540 *toneladas* built to protect Spain's Atlantic shipping. Because Spanish galleons habitually carried less artillery than their tonnage seemed to warrant, the Venetian galleons were probably smaller than their Spanish counterparts, perhaps about 325–350 *toneladas*. In 1641 Robert Dudley, an Englishman working for Venice, proposed a reformed galleon that he claimed would be able to carry more men and armament than traditional galleons, as well as being faster and more manoeuvrable. He freely admitted, however, that it would not be a good cargo carrier.[37]

The Portuguese, who were governed by the Spanish Habsburgs from 1580 to 1640, retained a distinction between merchant vessels and galleons used for warfare, although armed merchantmen were also common in Portuguese trade. The manuscript manual of ship carpentry by Manoel Fernández in 1616 discussed and illustrated several different types of vessels, including a four-decked merchant *nao*,

galleons ranging from 200 to 500 *toneladas*, and *navíos* ranging from 100 to 1200 *toneladas*. The enormous merchant *nao* had a keel-to-beam ratio of 1.87, and a length-to-beam ratio of 2.77, with an impressive amount of cargo space in the hold. It measured about 1700 *toneladas* according to the Spanish tonnage formula for merchant ships. The largest Portuguese *navíos* listed by Fernández had very similar proportions to the *nao*, but those from 900 *toneladas* down had keel-to-beam ratios above 2:1, and length-to-beam ratios above 3:1. *Navío* seems to have been used as a generic term at that time, although in the eighteenth century it would come to denote a ship of the line. The galleons discussed and illustrated by Fernández had an average keel-to-beam ratio of 2.2, an average length-to-beam ratio of 3.24, and an average depth in the hold (*pontal*) of 0.34.[38] Fernández's galleons were much sleeker and more apt for warfare than the large *naos* and *navíos* in his treatise. Compared with the offi-

37. Robert Dudley, *Arcano del mare* (Florence 1646), tome 1, lib 4, p7.

38. Manoel Fernández, *Livro de traças de carpintaria, 1616* (facsimile ed, Lisbon 1989). Tables of contents are located at fol 1–1v for the text and fol 69–70 for the drawings.

An undated painting by Cornelisz Verbeecq (c1590–1635) of an engagement between Dutch and Spanish galleons. The ships depicted probably reflect the practice of the early decades of the seventeenth century, and apart from decorative differences, there is little to distinguish the design of each nation's fighting ships. The largest ships in the centre of the picture – one Spanish and one Dutch – have elaborately decorated panels above the stern galleries; this part of the stern became known as the 'taffrail' in English, from the Dutch word for a picture, suggesting that the Dutch made a feature of such sterns even if they did not invent them. (National Maritime Museum)

cial Spanish rules for Atlantic shipping promulgated in 1613, Fernández's proposed galleons were considerably wider in relation to their length, but shallower in the hold. Compared with several Spanish galleons actually built in the 1620s, Fernández's galleon designs had a shorter keel, a more pronounced forward rake, and slightly less depth in the hold, but similar length (esloria) in relation to the beam.

In England, the government of Charles I (1625–49) worked to revive England's naval power after two decades of peace. Charles's demands for funds to pay for the navy contributed to his fatal clash with Parliament and the civil war. Many of the thirty ships that comprised the royal navy in 1625 were aged and unfit for immediate service, so that the ineffectual fleet sent to attack Cádiz that year in-

In England the large galleons of the Elizabethan era were expanded into the 'great ships' of the succeeding Stuart dynasty. This painting by H C Vroom depicts the return of Prince Charles from Spain (5 October 1623), providing portraits of the principal vessels of the fleet. Leading is the Prince Royal, *the prestige flagship of James I's navy and effectively a three-decker (probably the world's first). Built in 1610, she was a stage nearer the ship of the line, with its emphasis on gunnery duels rather than boarding tactics. Nevertheless, the upper deck amidships was still stepped to force boarders to fight their way up and out of the waist. The ships astern are the slightly later flush-decked* St Andrew, Defiance *and* Bonaventure *of 1615–18. All look somewhat topheavy and ungainly, partly because of the cut-down winter rig without topgallant masts. (National Maritime Museum)*

cluded only twelve royal ships and seventy-three hired merchant vessels. Stung by the failure of the expedition and the inability of English ships to combat Flemish privateers and pirate vessels in the Channel, the government embarked on an ambitious plan of naval construction. Over two dozen ships were built during the reign, including six from 478 to 875 gross tons in 1632–34, and eight from 341 to 471 gross tons in 1646–47.

The ships built in 1632–34 had an average keel-to-beam ratio of 2.97. The set of smaller ships, or frigates, built from 1637 to 1647 had an average keel-to-beam ratio of 3.35. The depth-to-beam ratio averaged 0.42 for all of the ships regardless of the tonnage. The 1522-ton *Sovereign of the Seas*, built in 1637, and the 1187-ton *Prince Royal*, rebuilt in 1641, were the largest ships in the royal navy, but they were widely considered to be ineffective for anything but show.[39] Quite small ships were built for specific purposes as well. Private shipbuilders, encouraged by the crown, continued to favour ships that could be armed and defended. Many large English merchantmen and warships in the first half of the seventeenth century can be considered galleons; contemporary artwork shows ships with English flags that bear a close resemblance to Dutch, French, Portuguese, and Spanish galleons, although artistic plagiarism renders the images questionable. English warships of the time were reputed to be strong, an advantage in artillery battles, but slow, a disadvantage against privateers. They were generally longer in relation to their beam than many continental galleons, anticipating later developments in warships, but that did not necessarily make them faster or more seaworthy. English naval experts and shipwrights, like their counterparts elsewhere, continued to experiment with pro-

portions in search of the ideal. They sometimes went badly wrong. The 823-gross ton *Unicorn*, built in 1633, was deemed 'dangerous and unserviceable' by the admiral in command of her sea trials, though other ships of similar size and configurations sailed well.[40]

The most striking cautionary tale of early seventeenth-century ship design concerns the *Nya Wassan* or *Vasa*, a Swedish galleon built by Dutch shipwrights. Reputedly featuring proportions ordained by the King of Sweden himself, the *Vasa* had a length-to-beam ratio of over 4:1 and a depth-to-beam ratio of about 0.41:1. In other words, she was extraordinarily long and shallow and could not be ballasted properly without flooding her lower gunports. With sails set the ship was so unstable that she capsized and sank in Stockholm harbour on

39. The *Sovereign of the Seas*, according to Michael Oppenheim, 'until she was cut down, was the largest most ornate, and most useless ship afloat'. *Administration of the Royal Navy*, p252, note 1. Ship measurements appear on pp202, pp254–55. During the First Dutch War, the ship was called the 'Golden Devil' by her opponents, who obviously did not share the historian's view.

40. Oppenheim, pp257–58.

The only survivor of the galleon era is the Dutch-designed Swedish ship Vasa *(or* Wasa*) which sank in Stockholm harbour when brand-new in 1628. A superb underwater salvage effort has raised the ship and preserved almost every original detail for public display. The high, narrow stern and low forecastle and beakhead give the ship the classic galleon profile, but two flush gundecks look forward to the broadside-to-broadside tactics of the ship of the line. (Wasavarvet, Stockholm)*

her maiden voyage in 1628, taking more than a hundred people to their deaths. Thanks to pioneering techniques of underwater salvage and wood preservation, the *Vasa* was raised and restored for display in the 1960s. Ironically, although her proportions were literally disastrous, she remains the best-known of all seventeenth century galleons. Yet the Dutch were clearly capable of building excellent galleons for their own use and for others.

From galleon to ship of the line

The classic galleon evolved from the late fifteenth century in response to increasing European commercial and military needs, and quickly gained a reputation as a warship. However, each nation that developed versions of the galleon adapted it to their own particular requirements, which often included the ability to carry cargo as well as fighting men and armament. Regardless of their varied uses, the fully-developed galleons of the late sixteenth and early seventeenth centuries displayed common features that suggest a structural, as well as a functional, definition for the galleon. Those features included a beak below the bowsprit and a crescent profile, with a low forecastle and a half-deck, quarterdeck, and often a poop deck aft of the main mast. The galleon generally had two full decks above the waterline upon which to mount artillery, and three or four masts plus the bowsprit. Square sails were carried on the fore mast and main mast and lateen sails on the mizzen (and bonaventure mizzen, if the ship carried a fourth mast). The hull was heavily built and braced to withstand continual use and the hazards of battle. The galleon generally ranged from about 300 to about 1000 tons in capacity, measured by either Spanish or English methods. Its ratios of length to beam generally ranged between about 3.2:1 and nearly 4:1, with narrower versions sacrificing carrying capacity for increased speed.

Gradually the nature of warfare changed as artillery improved, and grappling and boarding an enemy ship gave way to gunnery duels at greater distances. Castles fore and aft, no longer needed to defend against boarding, were abandoned in favour of nearly flush decks; the sail plan rose to new heights; hulls became more streamlined and lower in the water, with consequent improvements in sailing qualities. By the end of the seventeenth century the galleon faded in importance. Some of the last large galleons were launched in Spain at the very end of the seventeenth century, presumably because their versatility still made them

Table 6/1: Selected Galleons of Various Nations, with Probable Dimensions

Name	Nation	Year	Approx tonnage*	Beam (metres)	Keel-to-beam	Length-to-beam	Depth-to-beam
REVENGE	England	1577	500	9.7	2.88		0.50
SAN MARTIN	Portugal	1580	720	10.4		3.35	0.53
SAN MATEO	Portugal	1580	540	9.5		3.35	0.53
SWALLOW	England	1580	360	8.2	3.26		0.52
ELIZABETH BONAVENTURE	England	1581	600	10.7	2.27		0.45
SAN CRISTOBAL	Portugal	1581	260	7.4		3.35	0.53
SANTA ANA	France	1581	240	6.8		3.75	0.58
SAN CRISTOBAL	Spain	1583	620	9.0		3.50	0.66
SAN FELIPE	Portugal	1583	570	9.6		3.35	0.53
SANTIAGO EL MAYOR	Spain	1584	470	8.6		3.60	0.63
SAN LUIS	Portugal	1585	600	9.8		3.35	0.53
SAN MARCOS	Portugal	1585	570	9.6		3.35	0.53
SANTIAGO	Portugal	1585	380	8.4		3.35	0.53
SAN JUAN	Portugal	1586	780	10.7		3.35	0.53
SAN BERNADO	Portugal	1586	260	7.4		3.35	0.53
NONPAREIL	England	1590	500	8.6	3.04	4.25	0.57
ARK ROYAL	England	1602	800	11.3	2.70	3.77	0.41
VICTORY	England	1602	800	10.7	2.71	3.77	0.49
HOPE	England	1602	600	10.1	2.85	3.98	0.39
(built for crown)	Spain	1603	780	10.5		3.22	0.58
(built for crown)	Spain	1603	480	9.1		3.22	0.55
PRINCE ROYAL	England	1610	1200	13.3	2.64		0.41
DEFIANCE	England	1612	700	11.3	2.62		0.41
DREADNOUGHT	England	1612	450	9.5	2.71		0.42
CONSTANT REFORMATION	England	1619	750	10.9	2.98		0.42
HAPPY ENTRANCE	England	1619	580	10.0	2.94		0.43
GARLAND	England	1620	680	10.1	2.82		0.48
TRIUMPH	England	1623	920	11.3	2.97		0.46
MARY ROSE	England	1623	390	8.2	3.07		0.48
VASA	Sweden	1628	800	11.9		4.15	
...BEGONA	Spain	1628	540	10.1	2.44	3.15	0.47
SAN JUAN BAPTISTA	Spain	1628	450	9.5	2.47	3.15	0.47
SANTIAGO	Spain	1628	340	8.5	2.50	3.26	0.47
UNICORN	England	1633	820	11.1	2.94		0.41
LEOPARD	England	1634	510	10.1	2.88		0.38
COURONNE	France	1636	2000	14.8	2.62	3.28	0.47
SOVEREIGN	England	1637	1520	14.2	2.73		0.42
PROVIDENCE	England	1637	300	7.9	3.46		0.38
...ENCARNACION	Spain	1646	540	9.6			
DRAGON	England	1647	410	9.2	3.20		0.40

Note:
These figures denote the general order of magnitude, from various sources. They should not be taken as exact tonnage calculations.

useful, although they were narrower than their precursors. During the seventeenth and eighteenth centuries, the galleon's military function was gradually assumed by the dedicated warships that came to be called ships of the line. With much-reduced superstructure, multiple gun-decks, and longer hulls, all to increase speed and firepower, the new warships retained few features of the galleon, except its hull strength, along with a shortened and stylised beakhead – a vestigial reminder of the medieval *galleoni* that were their distant ancestors.

Carla Rahn Phillips

7

The Fluit: Specialist Cargo Vessels 1500 to 1650

I
N NORTHERN Europe in the sixteenth century, shipbuilders developed new types of cargo ships which would prove revolutionary, not so much in the design innovations as in the effect the new, more efficient carriers would have on commerce, communication and on maritime history. The new types came from an assimilation of the major advances of the fourteenth and fifteenth centuries and from experiments with the limits of those advances. The most important breakthrough of the previous period without doubt was the development of the full rigged ship. By the end of the fifteenth century full rigged ships with three masts, the mizzen at the stern carrying a lateen sail, were familiar throughout northern Europe. Over the long term the critical modifications shipbuilders made were in sail plan and in hull construction. Those modifications in time led to the development of a highly efficient bulk carrier, the *fluit*.

The configuration of the sails on the full rigged ship was imitated, but also improved. Already by 1500 captains were increasing the number of sails while decreasing the size of the largest sail, the main sail. The greater division of the sail plan made it easier for them to deploy canvas effectively. Such division also decreased the size of the crew, since men could work on each sail in turn and the number of crewmen needed to handle a sail decreased with its size. The process of experiment with sail sizes and with different types of sails continued through the sixteenth century, as did experiments in hull construction.

Northern European shipwrights had seen ships built using skeleton-first construction as early as the thirteenth century, if not before. The method of building, long practised in the Mediterranean, was embodied in ships that made regular visits to the North in the fourteenth century. But, even in the late fifteenth century, shipwrights in the North were still having trouble adopting what to them was a novel technique. Skeleton-first ships had planks abutting one another (carvel construction) with the strength of the hull coming from the internal frames rather than from the hull planks as with their traditional method of clinker building (in which the planking is fastened along an overlapping edge). To build vessels using the novel method, shipwrights had to learn not only the technicalities of carvel construction, but also the process of conceptualisation before construction. In clinker vessels the hull shape was determined by the

A drawing of fluits *getting underway by the great Dutch marine artist Willem van der Velde. It shows the main features of the type as developed by the mid seventeenth century - round bulbous hull with steep tumblehome (the curving in of the upper hull), a round tuck stern with a very narrow taffrail above and a standard three-masted rig. Some have a straight stem and some a beakhead while the size of the rig varied, but the essential characteristics of the hull were shared by all. (National Maritime Museum)*

A four-masted carrack with high castles and deep waist, the typical cargo carrier of the early sixteenth century. An anonymous woodcut of the ship of St Stonybroke (St Reynuut), c1520. (By courtesy of Richard Unger)

operating the vessel, that is for paying the crew. Safety and reliability were more pressing matters for the captain and crew, though no shipper wanted to lose a ship with its cargo. There was always a type of vessel which offered the lowest cost of transporting particular goods through specific waters. In the North the greatest use was for bulk carriers to connect ports around the Baltic and North Seas with each other and with the ports of the Atlantic front of western Europe. It was precisely in those trades, exchanges which expanded rapidly in the sixteenth and even in the seventeenth century, that the *fluit* proved most efficient. The design of the Dutch *fluit* of the early seventeenth century made significant advances on all of its predecessors competing in the carriage of relatively bulky goods. The use of the *fluit* could and did lower costs to levels similar to or below that of smaller vessels. It lowered costs to such a level that it was not necessary to build monstrous ships in the search for increasing savings with greater size. The *fluit* could avoid all the problems of very large wooden vessels, and at virtually no offsetting disadvantage. The *fluit* proved that it was commercially effective on a wide variety of routes. The design of that cargo ship over the course of the seventeenth century did prove highly flexible, and easily subject to modification so that shipbuilders could produce specialised designs specifically for certain trades or routes, which in turn produced even more efficient carriage of goods. The *fluit*, first developed in the province of Holland in the Low Countries, along with its many variants proved to be the basis for the prosperity of Dutch trade in the seventeenth century, but also of intra-European trade in the same period and beyond.

The bulk carrier of northern Europe in the fourteenth century had been the cog. By 1400 that vessel was modified by combination of its design with that of another vessel with Celtic origins, the hulk.[1] That cog-hulk combination was the design which faced the challenge created by the appearance of the carrack from the Mediterranean. Descendants of Viking ships had long since disappeared from long distance trades, that is with the rarest of exceptions. They remained in place in a number of re-

process of adding strakes, which allowed for some modification and adjustment as construction proceeded, but with skeleton-first vessels the profiles of the frames set the shape and this had to be decided in advance; therefore the technique encouraged conscious 'design' rather than trial-and-error methods. By the early years of the sixteenth century, northern shipwrights had acquired in part if not in whole the ability to build a hull in the way their counterparts did in the Mediterranean. With that skill mastered and full rig understood, for shipbuilders in Europe and especially in northern Europe the sixteenth century was a time of testing, of trying to find out how best to exploit the more reliable and more effective vessel.

When carracks from the South visited English, Low Countries and German ports they undoubtedly generated a curious reaction. When such vessels came to stay, either by accident as happened at Gdansk with the *Peter of La Rochelle*, deserted by the owners because of debt, or by plan, as happened in the Low Countries when Spanish ships were leased for use, they offered examples which could be studied and even copied in part or in full. Those vessels joined a broad range of other types already in use in northern Europe, from fishing boats to coastal traders and sea-going cargo ships to river boats descended from Celtic or Viking craft, all subject to modification and development through the Middle Ages. The injection of skeleton-first building in the form of the carrack certainly created new op-

tions and new challenges for northern European shipwrights, but they did not abandon or ignore the established designs which they had been using for centuries. The cog and hulk might be the typical choice for bulk carriage in the fifteenth century though ports still had many keels, descendants of vessels of the Vikings, barges and balingers, most carrying some oars but still having the ability to sail, and a variety of smaller craft with a myriad of local names. Builders modified each type in the course of the sixteenth century in light of the new skeleton-first building techniques. In some cases the modifications were not enough to keep a place for the model, and types all but disappeared from use. The great scope of options and the modifications of those designs served as prototypes or sources of design in one way or another for the highly efficient cargo ships which emerged by the end of the sixteenth century.

The *fluit*: a cost effective cargo carrier

The *fluit* was to be the product of a broad range of types, the culmination of a mass of experience. The goal of shippers and the men they employed to build their ships had long been the production of an efficient cargo carrier. Their understanding of efficiency was in terms of costs. They wanted to see the lowest outlay for the ship, that is for its construction but also for its maintenance during a long and productive career, and the lowest outlay for

1. Richard W Unger, *The Ship in the Medieval Economy, 600–1600* (London 1980), pp163–171.

gional and local trades and in coasting. Though capable of carrying bulky goods such as grain, such vessels were increasingly reduced to a minor role, that is in the carriage of goods but not necessarily in their influence on the design of other ship types. The carrack, which arrived from the Mediterranean in the years around 1400, had a number of advantages. It took a century or more for those advantages to be appreciated and accommodated to northern conditions. By the early sixteenth century,

The Lastage, *the shipbuilding area of Amsterdam. The long buildings are ropewalks. Details of bird's-eye view of Amsterdam by Cornelis Antoniszoon, 1541.* (By courtesy of Richard Unger)

shipbuilders had made some modification to the massive carrack and it evolved into the common heavily-built cargo ship with tall castles and a deep waist that, in the form of the *urca* or the *nao* or just the 'ship', was to be the dominant vessel on major trade routes in Europe through the next hundred years. Though it too was subject to modification, perhaps influenced by developments in the design of the galleon, that vessel was the bulk carrier during the years of rapidly expanding trade in the sixteenth century. It was into the context of such long distance bulk carriage that Dutch shipbuilders thrust the *fluit* in the closing years of the century.

Sources of information on cargo vessels

Knowledge about the cargo ships of the sixteenth and seventeenth centuries comes from records of shippers and shipbuilders and from records of governments which taxed and regulated shipping. Over the period, surviving records grew in number and in variety. So too did depictions of ships. Artists made seascapes, in the train of landscapes, part of the body of subjects they painted. Their products sold well on the rapidly growing market for objects to hang on walls of homes in the expanding towns of seventeenth-century Europe. Added to in-

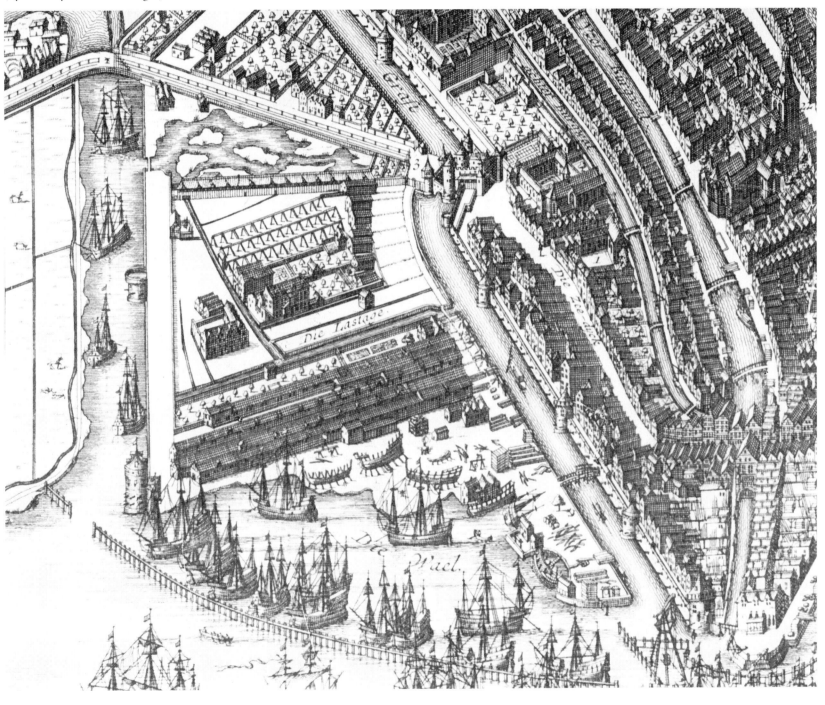

An overview of an excavated wreck (NOP G 37) in one of the IJsselmeerpolders. The vessel is from the fourteenth or fifteenth century and about 17m (56ft) in length. Bow and stern are badly eroded. A portion of the clinker-built side has fallen back over the hull on the lower right. (Rijksdienst voor de IJsselmeerpolders)

formation from those sources is a growing body of data from archaeological investigations, most notably from the reclaimed land of the former Zuider Zee in the Netherlands.[2] Two books written in the second half of the seventeenth century, one by a prominent Amsterdam politician and the other by a shipbuilder from Dordrecht, provide detailed information about construction methods in the Dutch Republic.[3] Those works were based on experience with building ships at Dutch yards. Despite some serious shortcomings[4] they offer an effective commentary on the masses of seventeenth-century illustrations of ships and of shipbuilding.

An equally, if not more valuable source comes from some records of construction. From the late sixteenth century onwards, more and more agreements or contracts between buyers and sellers of new ships survive, though they undoubtedly existed earlier, even if they were not committed to paper. These written records, called *bestekken* in the Low Countries, set the principal parameters of construction. The name of the ship type might appear, but there certainly would be a list of the main dimensions of the ship, the agreed price and the delivery date. By the time the Amsterdamer, Nicolaes Witsen, published the first edition of his book on shipbuilding in 1671 he could produce a series of model charters or contracts for different types of vessels.[5] The buyers of ships were typically a partnership, each buyer own-

ing a share in the new vessel. The partnership usually hired an agent to act for them, to oversee the construction of the ship, to make progress payments to the shipbuilder and to present to them at regular meetings a full accounting of expenditures.[6] Together, all the material gives an excellent idea of not just the principal features of cargo ships, but also their principal dimensions and the principal deviations and variations in both design and construction.

The origins of the *fluit*

These are to be found only partially in the large sixteenth-century cargo carriers which were descended from the carrack. Though it was their task that the new *fluit* was to assume, shipbuilders looked to other and different vessels for design features. Much of the inspiration for the *fluit* came from small vessels, inland craft, and from the fishing boats of the coastal provinces of the Low Countries. The true source of the design of the *fluit* was the merger of indigenous designs for small, highly functional craft with the design of the dominant sea-going trader and bulk carrier which had evolved in the course of the sixteenth century. Along the shores at the southern end of the North Sea, in part because of the various conditions, shipbuilders produced a variety of craft and with them a variety of options for use in other designs.

By the early fifteenth century, boatbuilders in the Low Countries had probably already discovered the spritsail, that extremely efficient rig which was to hold sway on small boats for centuries with only slight modifications. On a single mast they put a sprit or boom which went diagonally from the lowest point on that side of the square or rectangular sail stretched to the mast up to the outer upper corner, the peak. In the course of the sixteenth and early seventeenth centuries spritsails came to be replaced very slowly by gaff sails. For those sails the canvas was simply set from a yard at the top of the square or rectangular or even trapezoidal piece of cloth. Both the spritsail and the gaff sail were true fore-and-aft sails with one edge of the sail attached along the mast. To the fore-and-aft sail could be added a triangular fore staysail which was set from the fore stay, a line running from the top of the mast to the bow or, on larger vessels, a bowsprit. The stay was there to support the mast, but served as a convenient hoist for an additional sail, one which could be handled with ease – one man could handle a small version of a boat with a staysail and a fore-and-aft sail, just like a modern sailing dinghy. Such vessels proved highly manoeuvrable, a critical factor on lakes, streams and canals. The example of a rig which was flexible and required little crew served as a basis for innovation in larger coastal traders.

The boyer from the middle of the sixteenth century appeared in rapidly growing numbers

2. A series of occasional reports, under the title *Flevoberichten*, is published by the Rijksdienst voor de IJsselmeerpolders, Lelystad, describing in detail results of excavations in the polderland reclaimed from the IJsselmeer; See also, G D van der Heide, *Scheepsarcheologie* (Naarden 1974).

3. Nicolaes Witsen, *Architectura Navalis et Regimen Nauticum ofte Aeloude en Hedendaagsche Scheeps-bouw en Bestier* (second edition, Amsterdam 1690 [first edition, 1671]), pp94–176; Cornelis van Yk, *De Nederlandsche Scheeps-bouw-konst open Gestelt* (Amsterdam 1697), pp52–112.

4. A J Hoving, 'A 17th-century Dutch 134-foot *pinas*', *The International Journal of Nautical Archeology and Underwater Exploration* 17/3 (1988), pp212–216.

5. Nicolaes Witsen, *Architectura Navalis . . .*, pp176–187, 189–195.

6. Richard W Unger, 'Selling Dutch Ships in the Sixteenth Century', *Maritime History* 3 (1973), pp135–140.

A full rigged ship with features of the later fluit *(round tuck stern and narrow taffrail) on the left and on the right a boyer, off the north Holland port of Enkhuizen. An engraving by Frans Huys after Pieter Bruegel, 1565. (By courtesy of Richard Unger)*

A view of Amsterdam seen from the north bank of the River IJ, from an engraving of Pieter Bast, 1599. On the right is a single-masted boat with a spritsail and staysail, handled by one man. The larger ships have the standard small galleon type hull of the period. (By courtesy of Richard Unger)

boats and local coastal craft. For the former it would be another type which borrowed from the boyer and from fishing boats that would supplant it in long distance trade.

The technical changes of the late fourteenth century made it possible to catch and preserve herring at sea, freeing fishermen from immediate ties to the shore.[8] With the new method of curing, men on board gutted the fish right after they were hauled on board and then packed them in brine-filled barrels. Vessels had to have capacious holds for the barrels and deck space for fishermen to work on the catch. The large drag net used to catch the fish required a steady pull when it was spread in the sea. Shipbuilders met these requirements by developing, in the course of the fifteenth century, a different type of sea-going fishing boat, the *buss*.

The name *kongebuss* was applied to a high medieval variant of the Viking cargo ship, but the connection with the fifteenth-century Dutch fishing boat may be no more than in the name. The buss was bluff-bowed but with a square stern, at least up to about 1600. The rudder was hung from a sharply curved sternpost. In contrast, bilges were sharply angled, which gave a squared cross-section and so a good deal of space for the many barrels needed to carry salt to the fishing grounds and cured fish home. By the end of the fifteenth century builders of busses had gone over to

in ports in the Low Countries and north Germany, as well as on the east coast of England. It was never large but was able to compete with bigger ships because of the limited manning requirements — limited because of its more efficient rig. Though it probably started

Possibly a boyer, but lacking the typical spritsail; the artist's intentions regarding the main sail are not clear but he may have intended to show a staysail (jib) before the main. The ship appears as decoration in one of the charts in Lucas Jansz Waghenaer's Spiegel der zeevaerdt, *published in two volumes at Leiden by Christoffel Plantijn in 1584–1585. The collection appeared in English as* The Mariner's Mirror. *Using copper plates the cost of the charts was sharply decreased and so they became more readily available.*

as a river boat, by the mid sixteenth century the boyer had built-up topsides and a complex sail plan. In addition to a spritsail and a triangular fore staysail, the main mast carried two square sails, the smaller topsail above the main sail. There was also a second mast, a mizzen at the stern, with a lateen sail. This experimentation with sail plans suggests dissatisfaction with the single square sail rig, and the better balance of the sails must have made the boyer good at going to windward – good by the standards of the day, at least. Boyers of around 100 tons were the most common size in the second half of the sixteenth century, which would have made them smaller than even the cogs of the fourteenth century, but boyers had the advantage of needing few crewmen. A ton:man ratio of 20:1 was well within their range, a ratio rarely reached by any ships of the day.[7] Larger boyers ran to 20m (65ft) in length with a breadth around 6m (20ft). They had sides built up to protect cargo and, in larger versions, a full deck. In this form boyers had their greatest success in coastal trades of the North Sea. That made the boyer a threat both to the large ship and to the keels, still around from the time of the Vikings. For the latter, the boyer served to demote them even further to the role of fishing

A buss from about 1570 with square sails on all three masts, a square topsail on the main mast and a rack to support the yards and masts when struck down during fishing. From a sketch in a book of the town records of Dordrecht, Holland. (By courtesy of Richard Unger)

7. G V Scammell, 'Manning the English Merchant Service in the Sixteenth Century', *The Mariner's Mirror* 56 (1970), p132.

8. Richard W Unger, 'The Netherlands Herring Fishery in the Late Middle Ages: the False Legend of William Beukels of Biervliet', *Viator* IX (1978), pp335–356.

Koopvaardijbuss, *a buss adapted for use as a general cargo carrier. The ship has simple square sails on fore and main and could set a third from the mizzen. An illustration from Lucas Jansz Waghenaer's* Spiegel der zeevaerdt, *1584–1585. (By courtesy of Richard Unger)*

putting up the skeleton first and giving the hull that flush appearance with planks abutting instead of overlapping (carvel rather than clinker construction).

What made the buss different was that it combined that relatively large cargo space with relatively great length. During fishing the buss had to control the net. The rig helped. The buss was three-masted, each mast carrying at least, and usually only, one square sail. Two of the three masts were struck during fishing and stowed on a rack. The remaining mast carried a sail which remained set, giving the necessary steady pull on the net. Manoeuvring with the net strung out and the single sail rigged was difficult, and having a relatively long boat proved a great asset.

Busses, then, had length-to-breadth ratios of 4:1 and even 5:1, much longer than cargo ships of the Middle Ages and of the sixteenth century. Busses could reach as much as 200 tons, but the more common figure was around or somewhat below 100 tons with lengths up to 25m (82ft).[9]

9. Richard W Unger, *Dutch Shipbuilding Before 1800: Ships and Guilds* (Assen 1978), pp29–30.

10. J Kuyper, 'Pieter Jansz. Liorne en de Nederlandse Scheepsbouw', *West-Friesland Oud en Nieuw* 24, pp60–75; Theodorus Velius, *Chroniick van Hoorn . . .* (third edition, Hoorn 1648), pp271–272. The chronicler did not mention the construction of the first *fluit* in the first edition of 1604, but did in the second of 1617.

11. P C van Royen, 'The First Phase of the Dutch Straatvaart (1591–1605): Fact and Fiction', *International Journal of Maritime History* 2, 1 (June 1990), pp101–102.

12. Richard W Unger, *Dutch Shipbuilding Before 1800*, pp35–38.

The next step was to translate that experience from fishing boats to large cargo carriers. The *buyscarveel*, which came out of shipbuilding yards in the Low Countries as early as the close of the fifteenth century, combined skeleton-first building, a full rig of square sails on the fore and main masts and a lateen mizzen, and the essential features of buss hull design. Such vessels also received a full deck and a low-slung bow. In that modified form the buss formed an ideal example of a ship that could handle bulkier cargoes, and one which Dutch shipbuilders used in the second half of the sixteenth century in creating the type that would come to be called the *fluit*.

The 'invention' of the *fluit*

The development of the *fluit* is one of the few cases in the history of ship design, indeed of any technology of pre-modern Europe, where there is a report of an invention, of a man who came upon a new idea and put it into practice. The problem is that the story of the invention is almost certainly inaccurate. The inventor, according to the single chronicler who mentions the event, was a shipbuilder from the town of Hoorn just north of Amsterdam on the Zuider Zee, one Pieter Jansz Liorne.[10] He built and launched in 1595 the first '*gaings of fluyte*'. It had a length-to-beam ratio of 4:1, had shallow draught but was still a good sailer. The design enjoyed immediate success and was copied very soon in other parts of Holland. Within eight years of the first launching, the chronicler claimed, there were already eighty *fluiten* in service.

What is in dispute is not so much the improvements made by that builder on that date, as how novel this new type was. It is true that freight rates fell in the decade after 1595,[11] but the fall may have been due to a broad range of factors which have nothing to do with improvements in ship design. Many of the principal features of the *fluit* were already being incorporated into cargo ships before the last decade of the sixteenth century. The most obvious of those features was the relatively great ratio of length to breadth. Borrowing possibly from the *buss*, the *fluit* quickly rose to ratios of 5:1 and even 6:1, far above those of large cogs or carracks. But already in the second half of the sixteenth centuries *verlangers* – literally lengthened ships – were coming out of Dutch shipbuilding yards. Builders were obviously experimenting with the possibility of greater length while keeping many of the better features of existing ships.

Another thing they experimented with was

redesigning the castles. At the bow they were decreasing or eliminating the upperworks. At the stern they were narrowing the aftercastle. Stern-on, that gave the impression that the afterworks looked something like a thinly-shaped glass, a flute, which may be the origin of the name. Already in the 1550s the Flemish artist Pieter Breughel the Elder showed, in the same print with a boyer, a cargo ship with a fluted stern and many of the features that would typify the *fluit* of the next century. So rather than being a product of invention, the *fluit* was more likely the product of gradual evolution in the design of cargo ships. Whatever the source, by the first years of the seventeenth century Dutch shippers were finding that the design gave them an advantage over competitors.[12] They also found ways, in co-operation with captains and builders, to modify the basic design, producing ships which were more reliable and better suited to specific tasks.

The *fluit*, with its relatively long but shallow hull, nearly flat bottom, sharp turn to the bilges and sharply angled stem- and sternposts, gave the interior appearance of a box. The design furnished a greater carrying capacity than other contemporary vessels of equal length. The bow was low. There was a through deck, at least on larger versions, and the bigger *fluiten* would have had a half-deck and even a poop deck at the stern, each narrower than the one below, giving the fluted shape to the stern. On those larger versions there was a wing transom above a rounded hull and even a second through deck. The rig was more limited and simpler than that of earlier big cargo carriers. The fore mast, stepped far forward, carried a single square sail. The main mast carried one square sail on smaller and two on bigger *fluiten*. The topsail (where there was one) on the main mast was small relative to the main sail. The mizzen mast carried a lateen and, on larger versions, a square topsail. There was also a spritsail slung under the bowsprit. Some carried staysails, or at least a fore staysail. That type of sail, borrowed from smaller inland craft, was simple to handle, required little work and hardly any extra rigging. The *fluit* carried less canvas than other types of the same size; the rig was kept simple, and the sails relatively small. As a result the *fluit* was slow. The goal was to build an effective bulk carrier, and speed did not matter as much as handling qualities. By building a ship that was reliable and manoeuvrable, and by adding labour-saving devices on board like blocks and tackles to help with handling the sails, designers kept down crew size.

Fluiten were typically of 200 to 500 tons.

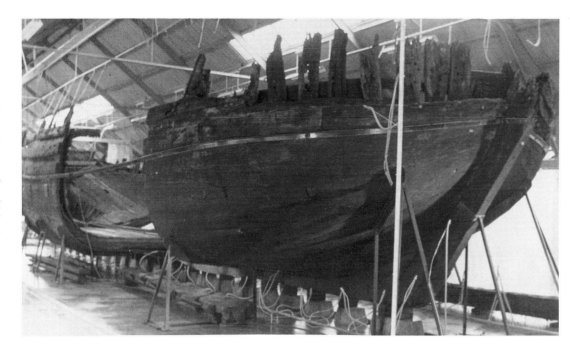

A seventeenth-century cargo ship, showing the typical cross-section of a bulk carrier, excavated from the floor of the former Zuider Zee in the Netherlands and here undergoing preservation at the Museum Ketelhaven. (Rijksdienst voor de Ijsselmeerpolders, Museum Ketelhaven)

When they were first introduced they were smaller but more efficient than other contemporary cargo ships. They supplanted those earlier vessels and in the second half of the sixteenth century probably reduced the average size of trading vessels in northern Europe. *Fluiten* grew in the last years of the sixteenth and beginning of the seventeenth century. By the 1630s Dutch cargo carriers were probably on average about 50 per cent larger than a half-century earlier, and larger than the vessels of traders from other parts of northern Europe who less commonly used *fluiten*.[13] For the largest versions square topsails were added to the fore mast and even to the mizzen. The main topsail also grew in size both absolutely and relative to the main sail. Designers exploited the advantages of an increasingly divided sail plan, again as always keeping down crew requirements.

Nicolaes Witsen said that a *fluit* 28.3m long and 6.2m broad (92.8ft by 20.3ft) would be rated at 200 tons, one of 32.5m in length and 6.65m broad (106.6ft by 21.8ft) at 300 tons and one 35.1m long and 6.8m broad (115.2ft by 22.3ft), that is with a length-to-breadth ratio of 5.17:1, at 400 tons.[14] *Fluiten* could be as large as 800 tons or more, but very rarely exceeded 500. Dutch builders, in the course of designing an efficient bulk carrier, found the optimum size of a sailing cargo ship to be somewhere between 400 and 500 tons. Smaller vessels did

not carry enough to make them competitive, while larger ones involved too great a loss if sunk and too many delays waiting in ports to fill the hold. The limits discovered in the early seventeenth century for what would become the sailing 'tramp' held until technical changes as well as a rise in the total volume of commerce in the nineteenth century made larger vessels practical.

The principal result of simplicity in rig and hull form was to keep down crew size. 'The secret of the flyboat's cheap operation was in the smallness of its crew in relation to its carrying capacity.'[15] Even smaller *fluiten* easily reached ratios of 20:1 for tons served per crew-

man. Seven men and a boy could handle a *fluit* of 150 tons in the Norwegian trade, and the size of the crew did not rise as rapidly as the tonnage. Many features of the design helped to keep numbers down. In addition, the *fluit* was lightly built. Wherever possible, shipwrights used pine in place of oak to make the hull lighter. The choice made construction cheaper since pine was easier to get, cost less and was easier to work, which decreased expenditures on labour. The choice also made the *fluit* less durable and increased maintenance and repair work. Nevertheless, a twenty-year lifespan seems to have been the norm for such ships. Lack of armaments was another major reason for small crews and low operating costs. A *fluit* typically had few guns and in many cases none. The type was known to be lightly armed and even defined that state. A warship in the eighteenth century which sailed without guns or with guns in the hold, was said, both in French and English, to be armed *en flûte*.

13. Aksel E Christensen, *Dutch Trade to the Baltic About 1600: Studies in the Sound Toll Register and Dutch Shipping Records* (The Hague 1941), pp99–104, 444–445.

14. Nicolaes Witsen, *Architectura Navalis . . .*, p178.

15. Ralph Davis, *The Rise of the English Shipping Industry in the Seventeenth and Eighteenth Centuries* (London 1962), p49.

'Dutch merchant ships, commonly called fluiten*', an etching of 1647 by Wenzel Hollar. The fully developed* fluit *stern is evident but the bow views still show beakheads whereas many small versions had a plain stem.* (By courtesy of Richard Unger)

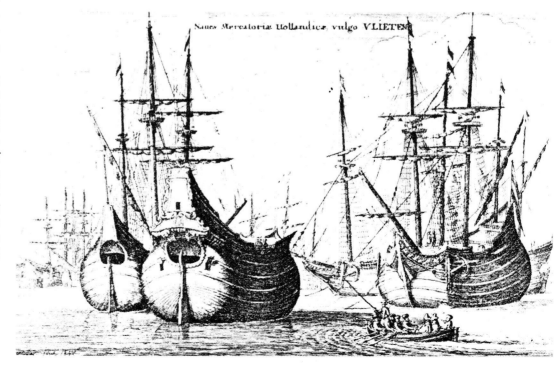

Specialist warships and cargo carriers

The *fluit* could escape from heavy construction and armament for two reasons. First, the type in its purest form was used for voyages to the Baltic and Norway, peaceful trades where piracy and indeed violence of any kind was relatively rare. Second, the Dutch, and in their train other Europeans, differentiated warships from cargo ships. The development of the galleon and the related Dutch type, the pinnace, created vessels which could protect cargo vessels. Travelling in convoys guarded by heavily armed vessels, the *fluiten* did not have to carry guns with powder and shot, and crew to man them. Such expenditure could increase operating costs a third or even a half. Under the circumstances shippers were willing to pay convoy charges and, later, import and export taxes to government agencies which in turn covered the cost of protecting cargo ships. In the Low Countries the relatively defenceless *busses* had travelled together in convoys since the fifteenth century, and there was a well-established tradition of fitting out heavily

armed vessels to accompany fishing fleets, the costs being paid by contributions from owners of the fishing vessels.

In the seventeenth century specialisation in design became more extreme. By that time the design of the galleon was already widely used. The Dutch version of the northern European galleon, the pinnace, was different from its counterparts, largely because of the borrowing of some design features from the *fluit*. Narrower decks and a cross-section like that of the cargo ship, matched with greater sail area for each ton and deeper draught, made the pinnace as good as the galleon for the job of convoying cargo ships.[16] The Dutch, before and more fully than any of their contemporaries, used *fluit* and *pinas* together, the specialised warship convoying the specialised cargo ship. Whether or not the origins of the practice were in the herring fishery and whether or not experience there explains the early and heavy commitment to convoying, the results were greater efficiency and lower costs for the Dutch merchant marine. The presence of and continued development of the *fluit* made that commitment to convoying possible and even pressed and promoted further the differentiation between warship and cargo ship.

The distinction also gave a new function to government. Admiralties found themselves with the task of administering protection for commercial fleets, and the principal function of the Dutch navy in the wars of the seventeenth century came to be convoying what was a highly vulnerable and very large merchant and fishing fleet. They were not always successful.

Busses on fishing grounds operating with masts lowered and long nets deployed. In this engraving by an anonymous artist from about 1600, the fishing boats are escorted by two armed three-masters. (By courtesy of Richard Unger)

The *fluit* could not be used as a warship. The design and crew size determined speed and defensibility of the type, which in turn determined the need for convoys. In peacetime that was a small price to pay for the greater efficiency and so lower cost of transport. Convoying also made it possible for designers to concentrate their efforts even more on lowering the crew size of *fluiten*, reducing costs, all without having to be concerned with defence.[17] Other navies and merchant marines throughout Europe followed the same pattern in the seventeenth century.

Construction

For the new cargo carriers of northern Europe of the late sixteenth century, like all but smaller coastal and inland craft, shipwrights used skeleton-first construction. Northern shipbuilders had trouble adjusting to the novel method of building ships, and initially relied on men brought from the Mediterranean to teach them. They also relied on the increasing number of examples which appeared in Northern ports from the South to guide them. The result was the adoption and adaptation of those Southern methods, but with variations and differences. Shipbuilders are reputed to be very conservative, a logical attitude given the high cost of error. Shipbuilders in Holland were re-

16. A J Hoving, 'A 17th-century Dutch 134-foot *pinas*', pp218–220; Richard W Unger, *Dutch Shipbuilding Before 1800*, pp46–47.

17. Jonathan I Israel, *The Dutch Republic and the Hispanic World 1606–1661* (Oxford 1982), pp110–117; Richard W Unger, 'Warships and Cargo Ships in Medieval Europe', *Technology and Culture* XXII (1981), pp233–252; Bob Oosting, 'Preliminary Results of the Research on the seventeenth-century Merchantman found at LOT E81 in the Noordoostpoldes (Netherlands)', in R Reinders and K Paul (eds), *Carvel Construction Technique: Skeleton-first, Shell-first* (Oxford 1991), pp72–75.

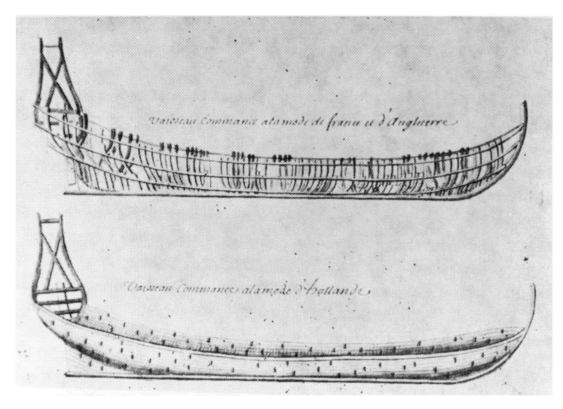

A sketch by the French spy Arnould, an agent of Jean-Baptiste Colbert, comparing English building methods (top), where frames are erected first and connected by ribbands, and Dutch building methods (bottom) with planking up to the waterline in place before a rib is set up. (By courtesy of Richard Unger)

temporary illustrations, it has been argued that the hybrid method was in use in the northern part of the province of Holland while in the southern part shipbuilders were much earlier converts to the complete skeleton-first way of carrying out the work. While by the years around 1700 it appears that most Dutch shipbuilders had gone over to the by-then-normal method of building, the exact date that the unique hybrid way of putting together a hull was abandoned simply cannot be discovered.[19] It is unclear whether the determining factor in the choice of building method was the part of the province, the type of ship being built, the experience and inclination of the builder or some other factor or factors. The survival of the compromise method, retaining some features of older procedures, suggests that the

luctant to change over to skeleton-first building and so borrowed the new technique in part. For the *fluit* that meant a hybrid form of building.

Precise investigation of ship construction suggests that such hybrid methods and hybrid types of vessels were and are typical. Experiment with novelty almost always entailed retention of portions of traditional ways. For the *fluit* that meant the laying of the keel and then the erection of stem- and sternposts. The next logical step with skeleton-first building was to put in place the principal frames. In Holland, however, builders attached a few of the bottom strakes on either side of the keel. It was a practice left over from the earlier shell-first construction and may have remained because of long experience with building flat-bottomed cogs. With the *fluit* the bottom was very close to being flat, so the connection in building procedure could have been made easily. The next step was the erection of the principal frames, held in place by long ribbands, and then the insertion of the remaining frames before the hull planking was fastened to the frames. In the late seventeenth century, Dutch builders

still put together their slow-moving box-like cargo ships in that way. Contemporaries in France and in Sweden knew this way of building as uniquely Dutch, though the practice may have been copied elsewhere.[18]

On the basis of what authors said in contemporary books on shipbuilding and of some con-

18. Richard W Unger, 'Dutch Design Specialization and Building Methods in the Seventeenth Century', in Carl Olof Cederlund (ed), *Postmedieval Boat and Ship Archaeology* (Oxford 1985), pp153–164.

19. A J Hoving, 'A seventeenth-century Dutch 134-foot *pinas*', pp216–218.

One of a series of sixteen etchings from around 1700 by Sieuwert van der Muelen called Navigiorum Ædificatio *which depicted the life history of a ship. This one is titled 'A start is made with the ship's planking', and it is obvious that the bottom garboard strakes are fitted before the frames are set up. (By courtesy of Richard Unger)*

An etching of 1638 by Salomon Savery of a fluit *in starboard profile with topsails on all three masts and six guns to a side. The ship has a spritsail topmast perched at the end of the bowsprit; although very vulnerable, this sail supplied considerable turning momentum during manoeuvring and was a feature of large ships for over a century, despite its precarious fragility. (By courtesy of Richard Unger)*

combined method had some advantages. Going ahead in that form may have added to the reliability of the hull and almost certainly contributed to the square cross-section of the *fluit* which, of course, helped to increase carrying capacity.

Standardisation, reliability and technological conservatism

In general the design of the *fluit*, in its various forms, appears to have been highly reliable. Shipbuilders seem to have been able to predict the performance of such vessels even before they were launched. They could be built on the understanding that the principal dimensions laid down in the contract would yield a serviceable ship. With contemporary warships there were tests and shakedown cruises followed by refits, often with 'furring' at or near the waterline to improve or adjust stability. All that work was carried out even before the ship was allowed to go to sea. With *fluiten* there are no such stories of necessary adjustments. Admittedly difficulties with cargo ships were less likely to be documented than those with warships, but surviving records leave the undeniable impression that the *fluit* that came out of a shipbuilding yard in the seventeenth century, because of the soundness and simplicity of the design, was ready for sea with, at most, minor adjustments to suit the user. Unlike warships, the design of the *fluit* did not press the limits of existing technology. The design was very much contained and familiar. It was also, from early in the seventeenth century, by pre-industrial measures of such things, highly standardised. This even went so far as the use of parts of the same design, shape and measure in a number of ships. Though it is wrong to interpret this as the use of interchangeable parts, still less as mass production, nevertheless the moves in that general direction made the resultant ships more predictable. The approach was far distant from producing identical copies, but employing known and tried features did typically make *fluiten* more reliable. The approach also contributed to keeping down the cost of constructing the ship.

Contemporaries were unquestionably im-

pressed by the low cost of the *fluit*. It caught their attention as much or more than the reliability and effectiveness of the design itself. An English report of 1669 claimed that Dutch merchant ships costs about 40 per cent less to build than similar English cargo vessels.[20] Dutch shipyards kept costs down by having low cost supplies, brought by *fluiten* from throughout northern Europe. That was true of iron from Sweden, wood from the Baltic and Norway and canvas from northern France, among other supplies. They kept costs down by having agents for the buyers who oversaw construction at the shipyard, making sure that the new owners' interests were being seen to. Those same agents managed all sub-contracts, such as the supply of sails, nails, anchors, and even spars and ropes. Often an experienced seaman, the agent could judge quality but also had the time and the purpose of seeking out the best supplies and suppliers.[21] Dutch shipbuilders kept down costs by concentrating the construction of *fluiten* and other sea-going ships in one district, in the Zaanstreek just north and west of Amsterdam, where taxes were light and the cost of land low. They also kept costs down by standardisation, but even more by the large scale of the industry. The design of the *fluit* and its derivatives proved so effective and popular that there was a brisk market in the seventeenth century for such ships.

Shipwrights gained a great deal of experience with the design and so became better at executing it. They also kept costs down by using machinery to replace men. Visitors to Dutch yards were impressed by the number of labour-saving gadgets they found on the slips. The many, often small, cranes and the pulleys made moving wood faster and easier, and so decreased labour requirements. However, the most effective labour-saving device was the wind-powered sawmill, used to cut the timbers for the ships. From the end of the sixteenth century virtually all planks were sawn; splitting trees was almost unknown. The savings in wood implied by sawing also suggested more physical labour, increased by the growing size of vessels; this made the individual parts, the hull planks and, even more, the timbers which made up the frames, big, difficult to handle and even harder to saw. Turning the task over to an inanimate source of power implied a great difference in the effort required from the workers. It also allowed builders to work to narrower tolerances when cutting the constituent parts for these cargo ships. Therefore it was not just the design of the *fluit* which made

20. Violet Barbour, 'Dutch and English Merchant Shipping in the Seventeenth Century', *The Economic History Review* 2 (1930), p275.

21. Richard W Unger, 'Selling Dutch Ships in the Sixteenth Century', pp.138–141.

for the success of that type and its variants, but also innovations in shipbuilding yards, which lowered the capital costs of the shipping industry.

Developments of the *fluit*

Modifications in the basic design of the *fluit* were made up to and after 1650. What emerged was a series of related specialised types suited by design for specific tasks. For certain trades and for carrying some goods the *fluit* still proved superior. For Dutch *fluiten* going to the east or the north there were few adaptations. There the waters were relatively safe. The *fluit*, especially if used in trade to the Baltic, ran to between 30m and 40m (100ft to 160ft) in length. With a length-to-breadth ratio of 5:1 ot 6:1 the beam was about 6m (20ft) though there was a marked tumblehome to the sides, the width at the waterline being considerably greater than at deck level. The relatively narrow decks were to make working the ship easier, but also to decrease toll charges that

A Straertsvaerder *(left) for voyages through the Straits of Gibraltar and a vessel for trading to France which the artist, Reiner Nooms (c1650), describes as a* kat *despite the armament and abundant canvas. Nevertheless, the Mediterranean trader is more heavily sparred and much more powerfully armed.* (By courtesy of Richard Unger)

Baltic traders had to pay to the agents of the King of Denmark on their way through the Sound. Since the masts were short and the *fluit* never carried much canvas relative to its size, the tumblehome presented no problems for stability and the narrow decks became a distinguishing feature of the *Oostervaerder*, as the Baltic trader was called. Those vessels came back with grain, often loaded loose in their holds and not even put in sacks or barrels. They brought the grain from ports like Gdansk and Riga but they also, because of the shallow draught of the ships, brought it from smaller ports along rivers and inlets where traders could buy directly from landowners and eliminate payments to wholesalers and tax collectors. In addition to grain, *Oostervaerders* loaded trees, wood and other sylvan products such as potash.

Variants of the Baltic trader, called the *Noortsvaerder*, were modified for the Norway timber trade. That trade in wood generated considerable transport problems and forced some significant design adjustments. Tall pine trees, intended for masts and spars in shipbuilding, might even be towed behind the sailing ships, but more often they were loaded through ports at the bow. Having such openings made it possible to carry very long poles, but the openings threatened the integrity of the hull. Once the trees were on board, the

openings were covered and the seams around those covers heavily caulked.

The *Straetsvaerder*, the variant used in the Mediterranean, acquired a low-slung bow, a beakhead like a galleon, and lost the bluff bows of other *fluiten*. It was also much more heavily built, even more heavily than the ships used down the Atlantic coast of Europe. The *fluiten* that traded to France and Spain went for salt loaded on board in barrels. In time, to that basic cargo a range of other goods was added, many of them from outside of Europe, which went to the Low Countries where they were trans-shipped for carriage in the holds or on the decks of ships headed to the Baltic. Vessels going into the Mediterranean carried foodstuffs but faced greater dangers from pirates than ships travelling in the Atlantic, and so faced dramatically higher costs because of the guns (and gun crews) they had to carry. In terms of costs, the design of the ship counted a great deal, but so too did the area where the vessel was employed. Nevertheless, the *fluit* with or without modifications was efficient enough to act as a bulk carrier in the Mediterranean, bringing in grain and taking out fish or olive oil or even stone. The *Straetsvaerder* was strongly built to support the guns necessary for self-protection, and always carried more guns than its counterparts in the North.

However, as early as the first decade of the

An Oostervaerder *(left) for shipping to the Baltic and a* Noortsvaerder *designed for the Norway wood trade. The print of about 1650 is by the reliable Reinder Nooms, 'Zeeman' (seaman). The Baltic trader has a main topgallant and a few guns on the quarter, but is otherwise similar to the Norway-man.* (By courtesy of Richard Unger)

seventeenth century, Dutch shippers were able to get the cost of moving goods from Amsterdam to the Mediterranean down to a level for each ton similar to that for moving goods to other parts of Europe, even to the Baltic.[22] Dutch ships made great inroads into southern European commerce, beginning around 1590 carrying grain to Italian ports. For the movement of such bulky cargo the *fluiten* of the North were adequate. The dangers were such in the Mediterranean though, that as early as 1607 the Dutch government set minimum crew numbers of ships of specific sizes to guarantee safety. It appears, though, that such regulations had little effect, and shippers continued to use *fluiten* only slightly modified, equipped with a number of guns which were more to deter than actually to damage a potential attacker. Even so, tons served per man rarely exceeded seven between 1591 and 1605, well below the typical levels for *fluiten* in the North.[23] Those *Straetsvaerders* carried luxuries and goods of high value in both directions as well as grain, and the trade in luxuries increased over time, though Dutch shippers were

at a disadvantage because the goods they had to offer, other than grain, did not find a ready market in the South in the years around 1600. Rather quickly, however, Dutch traders found ways to compete in the carriage of more valuable goods. The modifications made in *fluiten* seem to have eroded the competitive advantage enjoyed by English shippers, who typically used more strongly built derivatives of the galleon in the dangerous trades. In times of war, which was most of the time in the Mediterranean, though, English shipping through the seventeenth century proved more successful.[24]

The same fine bow of the Mediterranean traders was typical of variants used in the whale fishery. Those types were also built with planking of increased scantling to reinforce the vessel, but with the whalers it provided protection from ice rather than gunfire. The *katschip* was a smaller and even simpler version of the *fluit*. The *katschip* in the seventeenth century carried no topsails at all and the mizzen had, instead of a lateen, a gaff sail. With pole masts and that true fore-and-aft sail on the mizzen no sailor ever had to leave the deck to handle the canvas. Draught was shallow at 1.1–1.4m (3.6ft–4.6ft) so there was a great deal of freeboard. The *hekboot* was another bulk carrier of the seventeenth century which, like the *katschip*, proved better for some uses than the *fluit*. The *hekboot* typically had a single deck, was between 19m and 27m (62ft–89ft) long, and carried three

masts. The lateen mizzen was replaced toward the end of the seventeenth century by a gaff sail. The stern was square, the bilges sharply angled, but there was little tumblehome to the sides so decks were not as narrow as on a *fluit*.

Fluiten even made it to the Far East, though it was extremely rare for the Dutch East India Company to send out the relatively slow type. *Fluiten* certainly had the technical capability of making such long voyages over the open ocean. What they did not have was the ability to defend themselves in the dangerous waters through which they had to pass in the Atlantic and Indian Oceans. To make them fast enough and defensible enough required modifications so extensive that it was more effective to use modified galleons, pinnaces and, later, East Indiamen, *retourschepen*, than the virtually flat-bottomed *fluit*. The variants, whether for use in bulk trades in the North, for the whale fishery or for more dangerous trades to southern Europe or the Far East, all kept the same principal characteristics of the original design developed in the second half of the sixteenth century.

22. P C van Royen, 'The First Phase of the Dutch Straatvaart', pp88–93.

23. P C van Royen, 'The First Phase of the Dutch Straatvaart', pp94–98.

24. Jonathan I Israel, *Dutch Primacy in World Trade 1585–1740*, pp54–56, 97–101, 149–156, 202–205, 224–230.

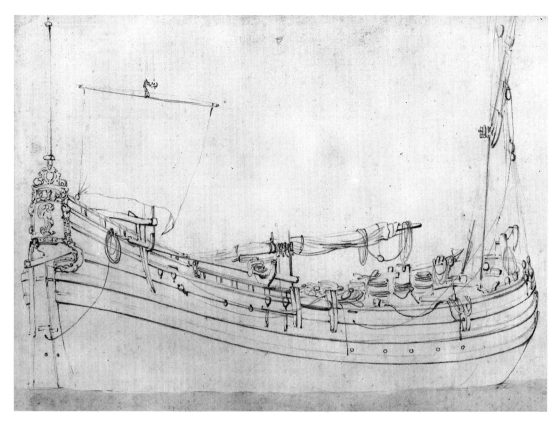

The significance of the *fluit*

The *fluit* grew out of earlier efforts in medieval and Renaissance Europe to develop an effective sailing ship. The emergence, slowly and tentatively at first, of the three-masted full rigged ship solved the major navigational problems that had limited and confined medieval shipbuilders and sailors. The balance of sails gave masters much greater control. Having square sails to drive the ship and a lateen sail to manoeuvre made sailing to windward much easier. The diversity of the sail plan made ships much more reliable, better able to deal with a range of different and difficult circumstances. It was that sail plan which shipbuilders simplified to its bare essentials in the late sixteenth century, creating the efficient cargo carrier that emerged as the *fluit*. That simplified rig was married to a hull design which borrowed from earlier flat-bottomed Northern coasters and relatively long fishing boats. The result was bluff bows, a rounded stern, a squared-off midship section, stability and relatively higher carrying capacity.

Below: The Golden Age of the Netherlands: the harbour of Amsterdam in 1606, the bottom half of an engraving by Pieter Bast. The variety of ships is dominated by three-masted and single-masted vessels, the latter mainly sprit rigged. The shipbuilding area has greatly expanded since the 1541 groundplan reproduced on page 117. (By courtesy of Richard Unger)

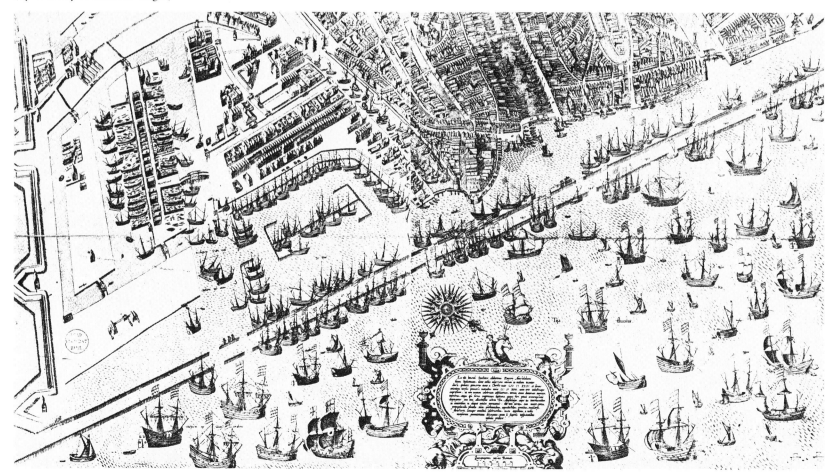

The fifteenth and early sixteenth centuries mark a period of rapid improvement and refinement in ship design, with shipwrights throughout Europe pursuing different avenues to establish what could be done with the three-masted ship rig. The general evolution of naval architecture produced a variety of ships capable of going almost anywhere in the world and getting back. The *fluit* proved to be one of the most successful of that collection because it offered a solution to the most pressing commercial problem of the seventeenth century, the movement of bulky goods at lower cost. Just as the galleon met another set of requirements for speed and defensibility, the *fluit* was well-suited to peaceful waters and carrying goods where transport costs made up a large portion of the delivered price. The two types comple-

mented each other extremely well. Shipbuilders and buyers modified both so that the two types became even more specialised over time.

The *fluit* in all of its forms and variants established the principal lines of development in ship design and in intra-European shipping, with modifications of course, for the 200 years after Dutch shipbuilders launched the first example of the type. The gains in shipping in the seventeenth and eighteenth centuries were to come not from dramatic advances in design but rather from better organisation of shipping, a greater volume of commerce, a decrease in piracy, the more efficient exchange of more information and, above all, shorter turnaround time with vessels spending less and less time in port waiting for cargoes.[25]

Fluiten in all their forms opened new possibilities for European shipping. That they could move goods at lower cost than their predecessors permitted the intensification of exchange along existing routes. The *fluit* came to dominate along itineraries formerly plied by

cogs, hulks and later carracks. In addition, since the design of the bulk carrier meant little loss of manoeuvrability and improvements in reliability, the *fluit* also opened new routes to trade. It was not so much to new parts of the world that the *fluit* found its way as to existing lesser and under-utilised ports in Europe. As a result, the type generated a more diverse and therefore more flexible trading network.

The economic success of the Dutch in the seventeenth century, the 'golden age' which made the Dutch Republic the envy of other European states, was connected in the minds of contemporaries with the *fluit*. The close connection between the *fluit* and trade to the Baltic and Dutch prosperity in fact understates the importance of the design. The *fluit* was, after all, a product of a long period of development.

25. Douglass North, 'Sources of Productivity Change in Ocean Shipping, 1600–1850', *Journal of Political Economy* 76 (1968), pp959–962; Gary Walton, 'Sources of Productivity Change in American Colonial Shipping, 1675–1775', *Economic History Review*, Second series 20, 1 (April 1967), pp73–77.

A major employer of fluiten *was the whaling industry, represented here by this painting by Abraham Matthys (1581–1649). Although the ship in the centre has the full stern galleries of a warship (and is probably the escort), the other vessels are all* fluiten. (National Maritime Museum)

It was not just one single simple type, but rather part of a range of variations on a basic concept, vessels with many features suited to special uses which came out of Dutch yards. It was not just a type built in the province of Holland and not just a type sailed by Dutch captains and crews. Sailors from all parts of Europe used the *fluit*. As early as the end of the sixteenth century Dutch builders found a market for *fluiten* in the merchant marine of Venice. French shippers and governments bought cargo ships as well as warships from Dutch yards in the first half of the seventeenth century. In the second half the government made strenuous efforts to develop the ability to build ships just like the *fluit*.[26]

In England, shippers bought Dutch ships because of their efficiency, but the more common method of acquisition, especially from the middle of the seventeenth century, was seizure. The capture of ships in wartime by naval vessels, or more frequently by privateers, was a common way for ships to move from ownership in one country to another. The figures for captures were sizeable, the English losing more than 300 ships in war with France and Spain from 1624 to 1629. It was in the Anglo-Dutch wars of the second half of the century, though, that the greatest exchange of vessels occurred. English privateers found the largely defenceless Dutch cargo ships easy targets, and their exposed central position, with many trades funnelling into a small region, made it easy for the marauders to find those ships. Between 1652 and 1654 the Dutch lost between 1000 and 1700 ships, with around 500 lost in each of the subsequent wars in 1664–67 and 1672–74. In those latter two wars, though, the Dutch took at least 360 and about 400 English merchantmen respectively.[27] The captured ships were sold at auction and so entered the English and Dutch merchant fleets, making them less homogeneous and giving them a broader range of designs. The addition of hundreds of *fluiten* must have enhanced the competitive position of English shippers and given English ship-

builders examples to follow. Though there is no direct evidence that the actions of privateers led to the building of *fluiten* or ships like them in England, overwhelming circumstantial evidence suggests that by 1670 for certain, and perhaps even earlier, this was indeed the case.[28] At the end of the seventeenth century the design concepts of the *fluit* had been adopted for the sailing 'tramps' that carried goods throughout European waters.

The *fluit* was the culmination of a development which started by putting a lateen sail on a cog, presumably somewhere in the Mediterranean at some time in the fourteenth century. The *fluit* was the culmination of what could be done with the full ship rig to make an efficient cargo ship. But also the *fluit* was the culmination of efforts, starting with the earliest seafarers, to create a reliable cargo ship powered by the wind which could move goods at low cost. There would be changes and improvements, modifications and variations to suit specific trades, to suit specific captains, to suit developments in construction. There were still many ways in which sailing cargo ships could be made more effective, both for the shipper and for the men who sailed them. With the experiments and the solutions found in Dutch yards at the end of the sixteenth century, though, shipbuilders reached a plateau, a higher level of design than in the past, and defined the parameters for European merchant shipping and shipbuilding for many years to come.

Richard W Unger

Appendix: Proportions of Dutch Ships

In 1671 when Nicolaes Witsen set about writing his book on ancient and contemporary shipbuilding practice, *Aeloude en Hedendaegsche Scheeps-bouw en Bestier*, and again in the second edition published in 1690, he included the principal proportions of a number of ships. In Chapter 9 the figures were for warships recently built in Holland; in Chapters 12 and 13 he offered a much more extensive list of sample building contracts which contained the principal measures of a series of different types seagoing and inland cargo ships respectively. With the cargo ships of both types the figures were idealised and did not represent real ships. The theoretical dimensions, though, presumably reflected both written contracts and what Witsen was told was common practice of the day.

It is impossible to generalise from the limited data, but Witsen's numbers show warships to be longer – in some cases much longer – and

also wider than cargo ships. The *Pinas* and the *Ooster-vaarder* of 28.30m and the same types of 35.38m offer clear comparisons. The carrier going to Norway, according to Witsen, could be expected to be deeper than the vessel going to the Baltic, another 0.55m in a vessel 28.30m long. Yachts, although wider relative to their length than smaller cargo ships and inland vessels, were still narrower, relatively, than large warships which they were designed, in part, to emulate. The cog was the direct descendent of the large sea-going cargo ship of the Middle Ages, changed and smaller but still in use in inland and coastal waterways in the seventeenth century. Witsen reported the measures in Amsterdam feet (1ft = 0.283m) and inches (1in = 0.0257m, that is 13in = 1ft), and the figures below are converted to metres.

Table 7/1: Selected Dimensions of Seventeenth-Century Dutch Ships

Ship type or Name, date	Length over the posts	Width	Depth of hold
Warships			
Pinas	28.30	7.08	2.83
Pinas	35.38	8.49	3.40
Pinas	36.79	9.62	3.82
Pinas	39.62	9.91	4.10
Warship	42.45	11.04	4.25
Dirk Raven (Pinas), 1627	31.70	7.36	3.25
Prins Wilhelm, 1630	44.43	10.47	3.68
Mauritius, 1637	36.22	7.92	3.68
Graf Enno, 1642	35.80	7.92	3.47
Eendraght, 1660	37.64	8.31	3.54
Vreede, 1667	48.11	12.45	3.82
Warship, 1669	45.28	11.32	3.68
Zwermer (Fregat), 1681	27.31	7.15	2.97
Sea-going Cargo Ships			
Common *fluit*	36.79	7.50	3.81
Fluit	33.96	6.23	3.25
Ooster-vaarder (Baltic trader)*	28.30	6.23	3.11
Same	32.55	6.65	—
Same	35.38	6.79	3.40
Noorts-vaarder (Norway trader)	28.30	6.23	3.68
Katschip	32.83	6.51	3.40
Boeijer (Boyer)	24.34	5.66	2.62
Galjoot	24.06	5.94	3.11
Buis (Buss)	14.72	3.83	2.26
Egmond Zee-pink	9.91	3.40	0.85
Inland Cargo Ships			
Smal-schip	16.98	4.53	1.98
Wydt-schip	19.81	5.66	2.32
Vlot-schuit	19.81	4.10	1.27
Sloep (Sloop)	11.89	2.55	1.56
Kaag (Cog)	13.30	3.55	1.70
Speel-jaght (Pleasure yacht)	11.89	2.65	1.06
Large *Jaght* of the West India Co	18.68	5.38	1.70

*The three sets of dimensions for the *Ooster-vaarder* are for vessels of 100, 150 and 200 lasts (about 200, 300 and 400 tons) respectively.

26. Richard W Unger, 'Dutch Design Specialization and Building Methods . . .', p157; Richard W Unger, *Dutch Shipbuilding Before 1800*, p112; Frederic C Lane, 'Venetian Shipping during the Commercial Revolution', *American Historical Review* 38, 2 (1933), p234–237.

27. Ralph Davis, *The Rise of the English Shipping Industry*, pp50–52, 315–316; J R Bruijn, 'Dutch Privateering during the Second and Third Anglo-Dutch Wars', *Low Countries History Yearbook 1978 (Acta Historicae Neerlandicae XI)*, pp79–81, 88–93.

28. Alan McGowan, 'The Dutch Influence on British Shipbuilding', in David Proctor and Charles Wilson (eds), *1688: The Seaborne Alliance and Diplomatic Revolution* (Greenwich 1989), pp90–95.

8

Coastal Shipping and Navigation in the Mediterranean

EVER SINCE Phoenician times, the Mediterranean has been a hospitable sea, allowing easy contact between the cities of the Greek world dotted around its shores. The steep slopes on its northern coasts combined with the difficulties of transportation by land, notwithstanding the extensive network of Roman roads, made the Mediterranean the most effective link between these coastal cities. The Middle Ages inherited innumerable maritime traditions from Greek and Roman times, this great wealth of experience and observations mainly relating to ways of building ships and the practice of navigation by estimation. Extensive fishing throughout the Mediterranean, the salt trade in Venice and compulsive wars against the Saracens led to major advances in seamanship and, from the tenth century onwards, Italian cities found themselves in the vanguard of a revival in seafaring. This is how Italy came to be one of the most powerful countries in the region. Italy seemed to be the source of everything: not only was she responsible for the major inventions, but she then spread the use of these inventions, firstly in the direction of the western basin of the Mediterranean, and later, from the thirteenth century onwards, towards the Atlantic coasts of Spain and Portugal.

The diaspora of Italian merchants and navigators towards the border regions of Atlantic Europe led to a most profitable marriage – one between the inventiveness of the North and

For a large part of the period covered by this volume, the maritime trade of the Mediterranean was dominated by the Italian coastal city states, and in particular Venice. This highly detailed panoramic engraving by Iacopo de Barbari dates from about 1500. The Arsenale, the largest industrial enterprise of the medieval West, dominates the eastern (righthand) end of this view, visible from the serried ranks of galley sheds around the basins and canal. (By courtesy of Christiane Villain-Gandossi)

the practical, if ancient, skills of the South. It was this union that was to provide the basis for the great discoveries of the late fifteenth century. However, during the Middle Ages, navigation in these parts was still subject to certain limitations which were essentially those of the Mediterranean Sea itself. It was a region where landmarks such as promontories and islands, and the enforced use of certain channels, made navigation easy, and sailors were reluctant to let the coast slip from view. The distinction between sea-going and coastal navigation was completely artificial. Mediterranean ships rarely ventured far from the coast. In fact, their voyages largely consisted of moving from one natural landmark to the next. For the most part they relied on points on the coastline that seafarers had come to know from tradition and experience, and which had been noted down in portulans and charts. Navigation in the Mediterranean was mainly of the coastal variety, and was also fundamentally empirical: it still felt able to ignore, or disregard, the skills of astronomy that were already considered essential to navigation in the Atlantic.

It would therefore be a mistake to try and

differentiate between the designs of vessels used for trade along the coast and those of ships fitted out for slower voyages on the high seas. Small and medium-sized vessels normally used for short journeys voyaged throughout the Mediterranean just as much as cogs and great galleys, although the latter were also utilised for the kind of coastal tramping work that was mostly done by small craft and *linhs*. It should not be forgotten either that maritime terminology varied substantially from one region to the next, and even from one town to the next. In fourteenth-century Barcelona a cog was a small decked ship; at the very same time, however, a vessel of the same name was being hailed as the finest of all the Genoese merchantmen, without question the largest vessels of their type in the entire Mediterranean. In fact, the word 'cog' was used to describe a wide range of quite different craft over a period of only a few decades. Another example of this is the thirteenth-century *navis* which, with its lateen sails, had little in common with a fifteenth-century vessel of the same name which was equipped with a stern rudder and square sails. Comparisons can be very con-

Among the many ships depicted in mosaics in Venice's Basilica of San Marco is this open boat in the story of St Mark. The boat in this thirteenth-century mosaic may seem none too specific but is probably based on contemporary local types and bears some resemblance to later Venetian local types like the Caorlina. *(By courtesy of Christiane Villain-Gandossi)*

fusing. The choice of ship was dictated by its destination and by the type of goods it was to transport. Commerce on the high seas and coastal trading fundamentally complemented one another, and the rise in the importance of more localised forms of trade foreshadowed a highly favourable commercial conjuncture.

Historical sources throw more light on the main shipping routes of the Mediterranean than on more humble coastal voyaging. Moreover, archaeology provides more information on the ships of Antiquity and the Renaissance than on medieval vessels, the latter being less easily identifiable on the sea bed as they did not carry amphoras or artillery. Later on, iconography also took more interest in ships that plied the high seas than in coastal craft, and certain art forms proved more adept at tracing the general development of ship design than in depicting what was really happening at any given point in history.

Written documentary sources are difficult to interpret. For one thing, lawyers rarely drew up contracts for the construction of small boats or *lembi*; by contrast, contracts signed by Louis IX with Genoese shipbuilders include every imaginable detail relating to the building of the ships and galleys that he was to use on his crusades. Other surviving written evidence includes a few surviving deeds authenticated by notaries, customs registers, maritime statutes, commercial letters, and above all ship's registers and accounts of voyages and pilgrimages. This abundance of information does not come anywhere near telling the story of the entire Mediterranean basin, but it does enable us to determine how ships were built and what types of ship actually existed. It also explains what purposes the vessels were used for in both coastal trade and high commerce, thereby illustrating the economic importance of shipping in the Mediterranean during the latter centuries of the Middle Ages.

Shipbuilding centres

We do not need to emphasise the importance of the proximity of wooded hills to the shipyards. Maurice Lombard has already done this most competently. It is a link that explains why those Mediterranean provinces that backed on to forest-clad hills and mountains prospered, while countries that had no wood at all declined. Shipbuilding yards in the Islamic world – they were called *dar açina'ah*, from which we get the word 'arsenal' – were also close to forests. Eventually, however, Hisn at-Tinat in the Gulf of Iskanderun, Acre, Tyre, Tripoli, Beirut (which profited from the Lebanon's short-lived forestry resources), Alexandria, Damietta and Tinnis in Egypt were all obliged to seek supplies beyond their borders and to ask for the help of the great Italian merchant republics. And, in addition to the arsenals attached to the great ports, there were any number of smaller yards erected on forgotten foreshores, and which survived for only short periods of time. Similarly, in the Byzantine world, the heroic maritime traditions of the seafaring peoples of Asia Minor explain why every small town and village along the coast had its own shipyard. These yards built fishing boats and *caramoussals* which took provisions round the Aegean, or else were used for smuggling corn when the islands eventually fell to the Ottoman Turks.

In the West, the link between the closeness of available wood and the rise in the importance of shipyards began to loosen as the economic power of the major ports was established. From the thirteenth century onwards, Genoa and the other Ligurian shipyards began to exhaust the limited resources of the Apennines, which were by now becoming rapidly deforested. They then had to rely on wood that was imported thanks to agreements signed by the Commune. The Venice Arsenal was the largest industrial enterprise in the medieval West, occupying a site of almost eighty acres at the eastern extremity of the city, and it imported its supplies of wood from the mainland territories and from the Dinaric Alps. Further west, the shipwrights of Barcelona, Blanes, Palamós and San Felíu de Guixols found the hills of Montseny ideal for their needs but, as time went by, even they found themselves obliged to exploit the wooded slopes of the distant Pyrenees. Improved organisation freed the shipyards from the narrow restraints of the immediate environment.

From now until the end of the Middle Ages, it became common to find small shipbuilding sites springing up at some distance from the great public yards. At the western end of the Mediterranean, for instance, the northern coast of the Maghreb and the area round the Gulf of Sidra had only a few scattered shipyards. Elsewhere, however, every beach, every natural shelter along the coast had its *scario*. In Catalonia, small fleets of oar-propelled craft were built on the *ribera de mar* (seashore) or on the *platja* (beach), while galleys were constructed in the arsenal at Drassanes. Each tiny yard had piles of wood that were stocked by merchants, and this wood was used by master carpenters who had been recruited, usually on the basis of a verbal contract, to build the hull and ensure that it was properly supported until the ship was finally launched. In Liguria there were the great yards at Genoa, at the mouth of the River Bisagno near the pier, and at Sampierdarena; however, there was also much shipbuilding activity at Varazze and Savona to the west, and at Sori, Recco and Sestri Levante to the east. Most of the boats constructed in these harbours were small coastal vessels, but galleys were also built whenever the Commune was preparing for war. Other places noted at the time for their shipwrights included small ports in Campania, Apulia, Istria, Dalmatia, and near the Bocche di Cattaro. There was even more shipbuilding on the Venetian islands and at the mouths of the River Po, where the boatmen transported huge quantities of Venetian goods on their *burchi* and other small craft.

Shipyards also sprang up in the eastern basin to provide links between the many ports along

A portrait by Antonio Pisano (1380–1455) of a burchio, one of the many local types used in and around the Venetian lagoon. From a fresco in the church of S Anastasia in Verona, details such as the masthead sheave for the halliard inspire confidence in the artist's knowledge of his subject. (CMP)

the Balkan and Asia Minor coasts. In this region, the sea was a much safer means of travel than the mountainous and dangerous land routes. People living on the Ottoman coast had inherited long maritime traditions from the Greeks, and they built *schirazzi* and *caramoussals* to carry on contraband business amongst the islands of the Aegean. We have documentary evidence of Venetian shipyards on Candia (Crete), and of Genoese yards on the island of Chios and at Famagusta in Cyprus. Prior to the fall of Constantinople in 1453, the Genoese colonies had turned their most important eastern outposts into major naval shipbuilding centres; their purpose in so doing was to respond to regional needs rather than to retain links with the metropolis. After 1289, *linhs* began to be constructed in one of the arsenals at Pera, a quarter of Constantinople, possibly as a replacement for the old Byzantine Exartysis. Indeed, in the list of compensation claims presented to Andronicus

The classic sailing merchantman of the early medieval Mediterranean was a lateen rigged 'round ship' of one or two masts, usually steered by a pair of oars over the quarters (see Chapter 4). This mosaic from San Marco in Venice represents such a vessel. (By courtesy of Christiane Villain-Gandossi)

II by the Genoese ambassador Nicola Spinola, the *linhs*, *vachete*, *barche* and *taridas* (which had undoubtedly been constructed by local builders) attracted much more attention than the galleys and carracks which came from the capital. Around about this time, a shipyard or *scario* near the customs house at Kaffa (Theodosia) is known to have been building small boats such as *taridas*, *linhs*, *galleazae* and *brigantins*. One function of these craft was the defence of the Genoese colonies themselves; another was the transportation of produce from the Black Sea region, and the importation of the grain, salt and wood which the arsenal itself needed. There were also other outposts in the Crimea such as Cembalo (Balaklava) and Soldaia (Sudak), and ports on the Danube including Kilia, Licostomo and Moncastro, which accounted for a substantial amount of shipbuilding.

Mediterranean ship types

Despite the chronic shortage of wood along the coastal areas of Syria and Egypt, documents in the Genizah in Cairo show that a huge range of vessels were constructed in these parts. A description by al-Bakri of a voyage from Mahdia in Barbary to Alexandria – it involved forty-five stops and landfalls – demonstrates how commerce was normally conducted using coastal navigation techniques. Commerce made use of a wide variety of vessels, though, and there are over two hundred

names for Arab craft alone. The best known of these, the *markab*, the *qarib*, the *qunbar* and the *khitti*, may well have resembled the boats depicted on ceramic dishes imported by Pisa from the Maghreb, and which are now displayed in the Museo Nazionale di San Matteo, Pisa.

The vessels referred to in the Genizah documents are tiny; they also carried a very small crew, and they relied totally on the wind for propulsion. Normally, they travelled in convoys: in 1060, over thirty boats are known to have left Alexandria for Tunis in the space of ten days in two successive convoys. For the most part, Moslem ships were smaller than those found in European Antiquity; moreover, they were less solidly constructed, they were propelled by lateen sails, and they never ventured far from the coast.

A revival in seafaring activity which started in the western basin at the end of the tenth century led to major changes in shipping practice in the Mediterranean as a whole. And within a few decades the shipbuilders of the Italian maritime republics were to demonstrate their absolute supremacy throughout the region. Considerations of space prevent an analysis of the causes of the upheavals brought about by the introduction of new shipping routes between the western and the eastern ends of the Mediterranean, and by the resurgence of coastal navigation which was so essential to trade.

Commerce in the Mediterranean relied on

two kinds of ship, and these dominated the fleets of the main maritime towns. The first of these was a 'long ship' or galley, mainly driven by oars, but also boasting one or two masts with lateen sails; the second was 'round' and was propelled solely by sails. The design of these ships, whose traditions F C Lane traces back to the Phoenicians, evolved rapidly during the Middle Ages, particularly between the end of the thirteenth century and the early years of the fourteenth century. In the West, the medieval 'nautical revolution' radically improved the means of propulsion and the way in which ships were steered. As a result, the productivity of sea transport was greatly increased.

As far as the history of long ships is concerned, the evolution of the early galley is described in another volume in the series, but some details are included here for completeness. The contracts signed in the thirteenth century between the Commune of Genoa and the emissaries of King Louis IX refer to a galley about 40m (130ft) long and 5½m (18ft) wide (*ie* a length-to-breadth ratio of 7.2:1). It had two lateen rigged masts, a platform forward protected by armings or weather-cloths, and a castle round the main mast. This ship was a bireme, but was propelled by a system of two men to an oar, rather than by two rows of oarsmen one above the other, as had been the practice in Antiquity. Not only did oar propulsion give these ships great manoeuvrability at the entrances and exits to ports; it also enabled them to make headway in a calm sea. Moreover, the lateen sail meant that they could make reasonable progress to windward. In 1278 these galleys were transporting an average of 20½ tons of merchandise and a crew of 140 men – in other words, a seventh of a ton per man, hence the high cost of transporting freight.

The construction of galleys underwent important changes at the beginning of the fourteenth century. The laws of the *Officium Gazarie* published in Genoa between 1330 and 1340, and the *Ordo galearum armatarum* published in Venice in 1321, set out regulations covering building standards. These publications also began to distinguish between the light galleys known as *sottili* and large galleys called *galea grossa* (great galley). The former

enjoyed the advantages of being light and speedy, and this meant they could be used not only as warships, but also for transporting light, expensive goods. The builders of the *galea grossa* went to great lengths to combine the advantages of the galley with those of round ships (including the capacity to carry large loads) so as to increase the overall productivity of sea transport. A light galley described by a Genoese *ordo* of 1333 was 40.19m (131.8ft) long, 5.024m (16.5ft) wide on average at the *bocca*, and a maximum of 2.066m (6.8ft) high (*ie* a length-to-breadth ratio of 8.0:1). A regulation set out by the *Officium Gazarie* of 1340 refers to a large galley with the same overall length, but with a breadth of 5.954m or 19.5ft (*ie* a length-to-breadth ratio of 6.7:1). These figures refer to galleys for the 'Romania' (Byzantium) trade and built in Venice – overall length 40m; breadth 5m; freight capacity about 130 tons. Galleys on the Flanders run were even bigger: they could be as much as 50m (164ft) long and 9m (29.5ft) wide and, by the fifteenth century, they could carry almost 250 tons. These merchant galleys were ideally suited to coastal trade around shallow ports and estuaries. The use of a single rudder became common during the fourteenth century, as did the fitting of two masts. From the sixteenth century onwards, these galleys each carried a crew of about 200 men and they were equipped with substantial artillery. Eventually, they gave way to round ships which began to dominate the transport market from about

1540; at about the same time, the merchant galleys, which had hitherto been used on the routes controlled by the celebrated *mude* system, were reconverted to warships.

There are several other kinds of vessel that derived from galleys, and are normally categorised under that heading. The *galleazza*, a large Venetian vessel, was different from the ordinary galley in that it was slightly smaller and carried a smaller crew. This was certainly the practice in Genoa; as for Venice, F C Lane is of the opinion that it was equivalent to the larger galley. The *galleotta* is much less confusing. This was a small bireme galley with 16–22 banks of oars, two masts and two side rudders. Construction of this type must have been very quick: in 1454, a master carpenter in Blanes, Catalonia, undertook to complete one in less than two and a half months.

The *saete* was very different from the ordinary galley. Genoa boasted a wide range of *saetes*, ranging from light 14-oar boats to more substantial vessels propelled by eighty oarsmen; a mast with a lateen sail and the ship's overall slender design enabled these small vessels to travel at high speed. It is not clear whether this kind of craft was known in Venice. According to J-C Hocquet, the ships that transported cargoes of 12–15 tons of salt from the salt marshes of Cagliari in the fourteenth century were large decked vessels. In the eastern end of the Mediterranean, one small craft type was the *xandalum*, a successor to the Byzantine *sandalion*. The word was initially used

Square rigged shipping at Venice about 1500 in the detailed engraving by Iacopo de Barbari. These large carracks took over the carrying trade of Venice from the lateen rigged 'round ship' and the large merchant galleys of earlier centuries. (By courtesy of Christiane Villain-Gandossi)

to describe a small dromon (a galley widely used by the Byzantine navy), and later on a large fishing boat, and this type of vessel was known to transport up to 200 tons of grain across the Black Sea from Kaffa to Trebizond. From Byzantine times to the period of Italian supremacy, the word *xandalum* was used to describe a wide range of craft. This resulted from the fact that ships continued to evolve rapidly, but the words that people of the time used to describe them did not always keep pace with the progress being made in the shipyards.

The variety of round ships, or cargo ships, was no less great, and their evolution is discussed in Chapter 4. Much of our information on thirteenth-century shipping comes from descriptions of Venetian vessels like the celebrated *Roccaforte*, which measured 38.19m (125.3ft) in length, 14.22m (46.7ft) in breadth and 9.35m (30.7ft) in height amidships. Other precise measurements have come down to us from the orders given by Louis IX to the Genoese shipwrights. These sources tell us of round ships with two or three decks that were elevated at the extremities to form a raised forecastle and poop; aft, this deck was itself surmounted by a platform containing cabins for passengers of rank, and forward by a crenellated and bratticed castle. These heavy vessels, which set lateen sails from very long yards and were steered by two side rudders, required a crew of over a hundred men to perform the interminable task of handling the sails; this made running costs, and particularly the crew's wages, a very onerous charge.

The medieval 'nautical revolution' was marked by the replacement of the lateen rig with square sails; the latter were first seen in Genoa in 1286 and in Venice in 1312. However, Genoese designs grew to a huge size (one particular vessel had three decks and a length-to-breadth ratio of 3.6:1) and were used to carry heavy cargoes, particularly alum from Phocaea; by contrast, the Venetian model could transport only medium-sized loads. Even the version constructed in Barcelona was extremely small. It was not until the end of the fourteenth century that Venice decided on a design that had a tonnage in the 500–800 *botti* range. By contrast, Catalonia remained faithful to the *nao*, which had a single centreline rudder (known as a 'Bayonne' rudder), one or two

decks, and a tonnage of 300–700 *botti*. By the early fifteenth century the Italian cog had become the merchant ship *par excellence*, to such an extent that the word *cocha* had disappeared and was replaced by the more generic term *navis*. This vessel then began to acquire the characteristics of late fifteenth-century carracks, or of the galleons that sailed across the Atlantic during the following century.

The *lignum* was the best known of all medium-sized and small ships, and it was to be found throughout the Mediterranean. Another type of ship was the *leny* which, in Catalonia, was a medium-sized craft propelled by oars; in Venice, on the other hand, the *leny* was a large vessel of burden, the largest models being capable of transporting up to 150 tons of salt from Ibiza to the Adriatic, rather like the *linhs* which went from Amalfi to load up with salt from Sardinia. Genoese ships included the *ligna de bandis* with raised gunwales similar to those found on round ships, the *ligna de orlo* which were equipped only with weather-cloths, and the *ligna de teriis* which closely resembled contemporary galleys. The *lignum* was equipped with thole pins to which the rudder's strops were attached. In fact, the word *lignum*, on its own, is a rather imprecise word for a medium-sized or even light vessel that is not a nef, a cog or a galley. It is also sometimes used as a synonym for the *panfile* and the *tarida*. The *panfile*, which was a successor of the Greek *pamphylos*, was looked upon as a ship of burden in the western Mediterranean; its extremities were

curved upwards and it had sails as well as carrying rowing slaves. The *tarida* sometimes had large ports cut in the hull to facilitate the transportation of horses; in Venice and Catalonia it was a large round ship, having been lateen rigged in the thirteenth century before adopting the square sail. One *tarida* is known to have unloaded 476 tons of salt at Venice.

Other regional or locally imported vessels played a major role in coastal navigation. These include the Genoese *bucius*, a ship of burden similar to the lateen nef but smaller, *fustes* and *lembi*, all of which catered for local needs. The ancient *chiatte* still survived in the Adriatic for coastal transportation, but the beginning of the fourteenth century saw the appearance of the *marano*, which initially served to transport stone from Istria, although it was later used for a variety of quite different purposes. Eventually, in 1469, the Venetian Senate noted that *marani* could reach a capacity of 700 *botti*. The *marsiliane* was even more successful in that it remained part of the Venetian merchant fleet for almost four centuries. This was a broad, full hulled, flat-bottom vessel with sheer, that had a flat bow and several square-sailed masts. It could sail up rivers into the plain of the Po, but it was equally capable of proceeding down to Apulia, and even to ports beyond the Straits of Otranto with loads of 70–80 tons of merchandise.

During the sixteenth century, Venice adopted ships from foreign states. These included the galleon and the *barza* from the Iberian

Peninsula, the English *bertone*, the *orcha* from the Hanseatic towns, and above all the caravel which enjoyed such a brilliant, if transient, career in the Venetian marine. The caravel is known to have played a major part in the discovery of the Americas, and is also well known from Father Fernando Oliveira's *Livro da Fabrica das Naves*. It was a relatively long sailing ship with a length-to-breadth ratio of 3.3–3.8:1, and was easy to manoeuvre if the square driving sail and the triangular lateen sail were used in conjunction. The effectiveness of the square sails was enhanced during the sixteenth century thanks to the introduction of bowlines, which enabled the caravel to sail closer to the wind. The caravel was able to stay at sea for long periods of time and in all weathers and, as it drew so little water, it could easily penetrate river mouths and sail in shallow waters. It was as well suited to explorations of the New World coastline as to Adriatic commercial activities in the channels that ran between the islands of Dalmatia.

Navigation

After that far-from-exhaustive survey of the various types of ship that existed between the eleventh and sixteenth centuries, we now need to take a look at the technical matter of navigation. The medieval nautical revolution was not just about changes in the types of ship that were built; it also concerned a major change in the art of navigation that saw the old, purely empirical, methods of Mediterranean seamanship that had been handed down for two thousand years replaced by more refined techniques based on the use of compass, charts and trigonometry tables. The importance of the magnetic pointer had been well known since the end of the eleventh century, despite the fact that it was still a fairly crude instrument made of needles rubbed against a lodestone and floating freely in a liquid. It is also known that the Arabs had been using compasses since 1243, but it was not until the beginning of the fourteenth century that it proved possible to make a casing called a *bussola* or compass, and to place the magnetic needle inside it on a centre pin. This needle was linked to a dial which first had eight, then sixteen, and later thirty-two radial lines. The centre pin ensured that the instrument gave continuous readings, and the needle made it possible for a ship to follow a specific course.

The first nautical maps, or portulans, appeared during the thirteenth century. Joinville, the chronicler of Louis IX's crusade, describes how, when the king was on board a Genoese ship on the high seas off Sardinia, he had the route described to him on the map. At the time, charts were portulans studded with stars, and with rhumb lines linking ports. The various indentations of the coastline and the positions of towns along the shore were indicated with the use of the thirty-two rhumb lines. Here again, Italy was an innovator. Following the *Carta pisana*, the Genoese school of portulan draughtsmanship distinguished itself mainly through Pietro Vesconte (with maps from 1311–1320 surviving) and Perrino Vesconte (whose maps from 1320–1327 have also been preserved). Soon afterwards, the Catalonian and Majorcan schools of cartography were in the ascendant, largely through the work of Angelino Dulcert (died 1339).

Another advance was made in the measurement of latitude; this posed the problem of magnetic declination. After Pierre de Maricourt published his treatise *Du Magnétisme* (1269) in which he noted the divergence between the pole star and the celestial pole, a start was made during the fourteenth century on resolving the problem of magnetic declination with the help of *martelogio* tables; these were trigonometry tables used by sailors. The word *martelogio* appeared in a Genoese document dated 1390, although it had been used extensively throughout the fourteenth century. The supreme achievement of pre-astronomic navigation was the practice of aiming the quadrant at the horizon, the sun or the pole star as a way of calculating latitude. Mariners first had

A Genoese chart of 1457 showing an early three-masted ship. The vessel seems to set three square sails, without bowsprit, topsails or lateen mizzen. There are examples of such an apparently odd rig from northern waters, but the hull form seems to be Mediterranean in origin. (By courtesy of Christiane Villain-Gandossi)

to wait for certain calibrations to be carried out on land, in the course of the Portuguese explorations of the African coast; then, and only then, were they able to obtain more reliable measurements than the dubious calculations that were made by aiming from a ship's deck rocked by the waves. We know from a treatise entitled *Regimento do Astrolabo e do Quadrante*, published in Lisbon in 1509, that the use of the quadrant and the astrolabe was not common practice until the beginning of the sixteenth century. This invention, originating in the Mediterranean but perfected in Atlantic Europe, opened up an age of calculated, scientific navigation. The consequences were to be the key to the success of the century's great discoveries. For example, Christopher Columbus used charts and a quadrant, he rediscovered magnetic declination, and he was also able to choose with certainty the correct latitude to take him towards Cipangu (Japan) and Cathay (China), although he hoped to reach these parts by sailing towards the west.

Trade and trade routes

In the course of the closing centuries of the Middle Ages, the great maritime cities of Italy and Spain continued to improve the organisation of shipping on the high seas. As early as the end of the thirteenth century, the Venetian Senate had established the system of *mude*, or state galley voyages sailing within fixed periods so as to ensure the safety of maritime transport and the regular functioning of the markets; they employed convoys of armed galleys that were hired to patrician families. There were *mude* in the trades with Romania (as the Byzantine Empire was known) and Flanders in the thirteenth century, to Alexandria and Beirut in the fourteenth century, to Aigues-Mortes in 1412, and to Barbary in 1436; succeeding decades also saw the rise of the *al trafego* voyages from Tunis to Alexandria. In this way, the two ends of the Mediterranean were linked up by a chain of staging posts which were regularly served by the Venetian marine.

There was nothing like the same degree of systematic organisation in the ports of Genoa and Barcelona, although there is some evidence of merchant ships departing for the east *in conserva*, that is to say in twice-yearly convoys – one in the spring, the other in the early autumn – as a precautionary measure against pirates. These navigational lines spread throughout the entire Mediterranean basin, from the Spanish coast to the shores of the Black Sea. This was particularly true after 1277, when the Genoese were the first to

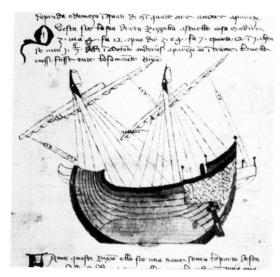

The more inquiring attitude to the world that in the West came to be called the Renaissance was manifest early in the business practices of the Italian city states. Their success was dependent on superior organisation, particularly of finance, and individual merchants often committed to paper the fruits of their experience. This fourteenth-century workbook, by a Venetian called Zibaldone da Canale, includes such information as the time trading ventures took to specific destinations by ship and overland. It is enlivened with sketches, including this representation of a typical two-masted lateen rigged 'round ship'. (CMP)

establish regular links between the Mediterranean and Flanders passing through the Straits of Gibraltar. However, it would be wrong to exaggerate the amount of shipping that passed between east and west. In the fifteenth century, no more than about ten Venetian galleys arrived each year in Alexandria, and only three or four Genoese or Catalonian ships; other maritime states of the western Mediterranean such as Ancona, Ragusa, Marseilles and Montpellier sent ships only very irregularly. To the official shipbuilding programme, we must add the private construction of galleys and ships. The Venetian Senate was very enthusiastic about this when it could find no takers for the great galleys, or else there were not enough of them to pick up the merchandise waiting at the staging posts. We know very little of this form of shipping as it was not recounted accurately by archival sources.

These trade routes played an essential role in the establishment of a Mediterranean-wide economy based on exchanges between the two coasts. Not only cloth and fabrics were exported from the west to the east, but also wine, oil and fruit. In their turn, the great Italian and Iberian ports of the west were well supplied with spices, silks, cotton, alum, leather and animal furs. Furthermore, there was fiercely competitive trade in cereals, now in one direction,

now in the other, according to the economic climate of the moment. All of these exchanges were dominated by Italian and Catalonian shipowners and merchants, who alone were in a position to invest the vast sums (around 600,000 ducats every year in Venice alone) that sea trade in the eastern Mediterranean demanded towards the end of the Middle Ages.

All that remains is to describe the economic role played by small and medium-sized ships, the vessels that were mainly, though not exclusively, responsible for coastal navigation in the Mediterranean. As F Braudel has recalled, 'When large ships set out on their own, the prospects were gloomy. When they set out in the company of large numbers of sailing vessels, the prospects were often favourable.' There appears to be plenty of evidence to support this position. The rise of the small ship was a sign of a substantial increase in the amount of trading in a wide range of commercial products, and coastal shipping took over responsibility for plying the main routes on behalf of the major maritime towns. On the other hand, the shorter a boat's range, the more likely it was to go in for unmixed cargoes, the owner having a vested interest in losing as little time as possible while loading and unloading. It is therefore possible to speak of a degree of specialisation in shipping in respect of the distances to be covered and the type of goods to be carried.

Galleys, nefs and cogs of many types could all be used for coastal navigation. Ships' registers that have come down to us tell us of the Genoese galleys of Paganino Doria (in 1351) and of Silvestro de Marinis (in 1382) clinging to the coast, and heaving-to for the night in the shelter of a promontory, or in a port where the crew could negotiate the purchase of fresh produce and other merchandise. Voyages undertaken by galleys towards the east were interrupted by stops that were less due to military or economic considerations than to the vessels' reliance on the right weather conditions. The Venetian Senate's organisation of mude was based more on economic imperatives than on anything else, and political deliberations determined exactly where the ship had to call. The same applied in Catalonia. We have details of a chartering contract dated 5 February 1393, relating to a nef bound for Flanders and owned by one Miguel Martinis. It provides for a ten-day stopover at Majorca, a popular meeting-point for shipping routes, twenty days at Valencia, ten days at Cadiz, and a similar amount of time at Pontevedra or Muros. A contract for a voyage to Alexandria dated 1450 fixed calls at Alghero, Cagliari, Gaeta, Naples,

A rare representation of a full rigged ship under sail from Carpaccio's 'St George and the Dragon', in the Scuola di S Giorgio degli Schiavoni, in Venice. There are numerous noteworthy features of the rig including a spritsail under the bowsprit, a small topsail sheeted into the top, and very curious triangular 'save-all' light weather sails between the main yard and its lifts. The painting is dated to the end of the fifteenth century. (By courtesy of Christiane Villain-Gandossi)

Palermo, Messina, Syracuse and Rhodes. The Mediterranean therefore used its huge network of shipping routes to benefit each of the major maritime cities.

Small and medium-sized vessels played an essential role in this network throughout the east and the west of the Mediterranean. In fact, coastal fleets were particularly active in Genoa's overseas colonies. The compensation demands submitted by the ambassador Nicola Spinola to the emperor Andronicus II relate not only to the thirty owners of boats or galleys, but also to eighty-three linhs captured by Greek pirates in the Black Sea and along the coasts of Greece and Asia Minor. Mention was also made of a few taridas, vachettes and even larger vessels sailing around the Sea of Marmara or amongst the Aegean Islands. By the end of the thirteenth century, smaller ships slightly outnumbered larger vessels. They typically set off from Kaffa to load up with merchandise (salt, fish, grain, animal furs, wax and honey) at the mouths of the Danube at Tana, La Copa and Ciprico, before taking it on to Pera, Simisso, Sinop or Trebizond. These small craft enabled Genoese living overseas to acquire huge influence. They became well-known figures in the market place, but also succeeded in establishing themselves in international commerce circles in regions which, without the energetic involvement of the Italian merchants, would have continued to operate lethargically at the level of a subsistence economy. The disappearance of small Italian ships from the Black Sea during the fifteenth century foreshadowed a lasting crisis, and was the prelude to the Ottoman conquest.

What was true of shipping in the east applied even more to activities in the west. Seville, Valencia and Barcelona boasted fleets of coasters which sailed to small harbours along the Iberian coast to pick up cargoes of wool, alum, jars of oil, casks of wine and dried fruit. The big Italian and Catalonian merchants then exported them throughout the Mediterranean, and even as far afield as the seas around Scandinavia. The coasts of Languedoc and Provence, too, teemed with fleets of ships transporting Languedoc wool and salt from Hyères, and redistributing products from the east that had been imported by Genoa or Marseilles. These big ports needed large trading zones for all the goods that they were acquiring, and this was especially true of the *contado* of Genoa, which owned very little agricultural land to speak of. Wine and oil from the Mediterranean 'rivieras' was brought in on ships, too, but there was also an unending succession of small vessels that sailed to pick up salt from the Maremma, Campania and even Sicily, cheese from Corsica, and wool and salt from Sardinia; as they did this, they moved along the Tyrrhenian coast redistributing spices and animal furs, Iberian fruit, and cloth and linen from northern Europe. Coastal trade clearly sustained the

activities of the major maritime states by forcing the entire coastal region of the Mediterranean to take part in commerce.

The same went for the Adriatic. It has been observed that the capacity and number of vessels developed in opposite directions: the shorter the distance to be covered, the larger the number of ships and the smaller their capacity. Coastal shipping was in the ascendant in Venice, as it was from here that small vessels went to load salt in Zara (Zadar), Cervia, Pola (Pula), Piran, Pago, Corfu and Sebenico (Sibenik). Between 1596 and 1600 as many as 68 sailing ships were counted in the Bay of Levkimmi on Corfu – 13 *barcas*, 2 *grippi*, 9 *saettas*, 16 marsilianes, 16 galleons, 11 nefs, and 1 *bertone*. Other vessels came to the Bocche di Cattaro to pick up supplies for the Montenegro caravans. Meanwhile, an unceasing flow of marsilianes, galleons, brigantins and frigates – not to mention caramoussals and *schirazzi* accompanied by fleets of small coastal vessels from Chioggia, Cattaro and Perast – filled the sea routes throughout the length of the Dalmatian coast. As many as 398 vessels were identified between 1563 and 1591. On the western Adriatic coast, ships transported cereals from the Romagna and Marches ports of Pesaro, Fano, Senigallia, Fermo, Pescara, Ortona and Vasto up to Venice. Further south, marsilianes were used to bring oil up from Apulia; Apulian oil accounted

for almost a tenth of all of Venice's foreign trade in the seventeenth century. However, these barcas, saetes and *marani* also carried almonds, figs, carob beans, lentils, broad beans and cheese – in short, everything that Venice needed for survival. Despite its conquest of the mainland territories, a lot of Venice's supplies still came from overseas. The use of small ships reduced the entrepreneur's costs; it also greatly facilitated trade which was less dependent on seasonal factors that the prevailing winds of the Adriatic imposed on large-scale commerce.

This picture of coastal navigation would be incomplete without some reference to the upheavals which were brought about by piracy and the arrival in the Mediterranean world of foreign competition. Piracy took the form of hostilities amongst Christians, or between Christians and infidels. The former pitted the Genoese against the Catalonians or Venetians, or the Dalmatians and Slavs against the merchants of the Venetian Republic; the latter was marked by the ability of the Barbary pirates to spread into the entire western Mediterranean basin.

At all events, piracy threw the traditional commercial patterns into disarray, and at the same time created new ones. For one thing, booty had to be resold before being reintroduced by one method or another into the market, subject only to the deductions made by intermediaries. A much more serious situation was created when seafarers from the north – Englishmen and Dutchmen – arrived in the Mediterranean in the early seventeenth century. They took over the trade in raisins, and in oil from Djerba and Apulia, and they brought with them not only corn, rye and casks of herring, but also manufactured products which they sold at lower prices than comparable Venetian textile products. The careful balance that had survived up to the end of the sixteenth century was now threatened, particularly as the northerners, by entering the eastern spice markets by direct voyages, were taking over the distant commercial outlets of the Mediterranean. An entire system of commercial exchange that had been based on a close working relationship between coastal trade and large-scale commerce had been shattered. Two centuries were to pass before Mediterranean coastal trade returned to being a coherent economic entity.

Michel Balard

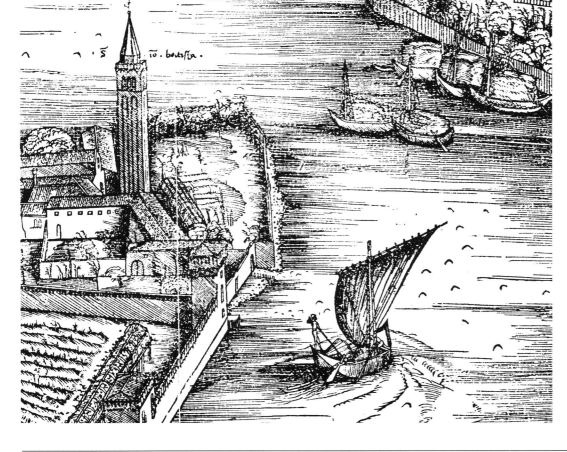

Another Venetian local craft represented in Iacopo de Barbari's engraving is the rascona. *Somewhat similar in hull form to the* burchio, *it had only one mast.* (CMP)

Guns and Gunnery

9

THE FIRST European gunfounders, and the gunners, sailors and shipwrights who sought to use their products not long after the turn of the fourteenth century, faced daunting technological and tactical challenges. Though the process was a gradual one and some four and a half centuries were needed to realise the full potential of the materials available, they and their successors were to face and overcome those challenges with surprising technological and tactical elegance, a matter of no small consequence. To understand how this came to be, a basic understanding of the unique characteristics of gunpowder, or black powder, is necessary. It should be noted at the outset.

Black powder

The behaviour of black powder differs from that of modern, nitrocellulose-based propellants in ways so fundamental as to render insights gained from knowledge of guns and gunnery in the age of smokeless propellants irrelevant or misleading. The initial focus will thus be on internal ballistics, what went on inside the gun between charge ignition and the exit of the projectile. That depended on the chemistry, thermodynamics and physical composition of black powder, a subject which remains poorly understood to this day. Except where noted otherwise, references to black powder are to corned powder with more or less spherical grains made to modern proportions, not all that different from modern sporting black powder, though with larger grains when

intended for use in heavy ordnance. After a cursory discussion of the parameters affecting cannon design and manufacture, the discussion will address external ballistics, what happened to the projectile in flight, and terminal ballistics, the interaction between projectile and target. The chapter will conclude by tracing the salient changes in the design, construction and use of naval ordnance and the way in which it affected ship design.

Black powder is by definition a mixture of saltpetre (KNO_3), charcoal and sulphur, finely ground and mixed together. The very earliest European gunpowder was probably mixed to a ratio of 1/1/1 by weight, and recent experiments indicate that gunpowder of these proportions can, if tightly confined with a wooden plug, expel a projectile from a gun with useful velocity.[1] Gunners quickly realised that the optimum proportion of saltpetre was much higher, and recipes soon began to converge on an approximate ratio of 75/15/10, generally taken as the modern recipe. The ratio was anything but constant, medieval gunners believing

that a lower proportion of saltpetre was desirable in large ordnance. Whether they were right or wrong is unclear, and in fact the final and most sophisticated black powders for large ordnance, compounded in the 1880s and '90s on the basis of extensive experiments, were comparatively rich in saltpetre.[2] In any event, the propellant qualities of black powder were remarkably tolerant of variations in the recipe.

Black powder, unlike modern nitrocellulose-

---

1. European gunpowder recipes specified ingredients by weight from the beginning, but cannot be accurately compared with modern recipes since the purity of the sulphur and, particularly, the saltpetre is unknown. Niccolo Tartaglia, writing about 1540 in *Three Books of Colloquies Concerning the Arte of Shooting . . .* (London 1588; original Italian edition, 1546), believed that the very earliest gunpowder was mixed to a ratio of 1/1/1. J R Partington, *A History of Greek Fire and Gunpowder* (Cambridge 1960), pp73–75, comes to similar conclusions with his analysis of Roger Bacon's late thirteenth-century recipe, which calls for proportions of 7/5/5.

2. Perhaps the most sophisticated of these powders, British Prism Brown, had proportions of 79/18/3; HM Stationery Office, *Treatise on Service Explosives* (December 1895), p51.

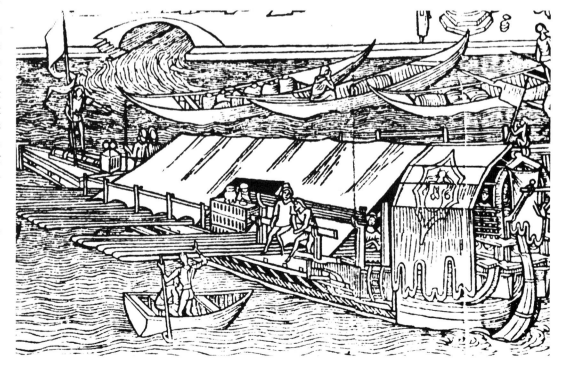

Among the first naval vessels to use heavy guns at sea were the galley fleets of the Mediterranean, although the design of the oared vessels made it difficult to mount many. The usual position for the heaviest was forward in a fixed position, as shown in this woodcut of a Venetian galley of about 1486. This centreline piece is wrought iron and bedded in the bows, the gun being trained by turning the ship. It is not clear if the gun represented is a muzzle- or breech-loader. (By courtesy of John F Guilmartin)

Early guns were built up of hoops and staves like a barrel. This Portuguese example from the late fifteenth or early sixteenth century reveals the lines of the staves inside the muzzle. (By courtesy of John F Guilmartin)

edges and impart a glaze.[5] The result, corned powder, appeared during the first quarter of the fifteenth century and was more uniform, more stable, and safer to handle than serpentine. It was also more powerful, a puzzle since the chemical energy resident in equal quantities of corned and serpentine powder made to the same proportions is identical. In fact, serpentine and corned powder behaved very differently for reasons which merit attention.

Knowledge of black powder internal ballistics relates almost entirely to corned powder. Powder can be ignited with a red-hot wire, a spark or an open flame. The most common method involved the application of the smoldering tip of a length of slow match, that is cord soaked in saltpetre and then dried. Once ignited, the burning rate within a grain of black powder is about 0.20fps (0.06m/sec). By contrast, the spread of the reaction between grains progresses at about 30fps (9m/sec), one and a half orders of magnitude higher. Since burning takes place at a constant rate and only on the surface of the grain, the rate of gas evolution is a function of surface area. Since surface area is an inverse function of grain size, charges of

based propellants, is a simple mixture rather than a chemical compound. Whereas modern propellants yield only propellant gases and small amounts of water vapour, a majority of the decomposition products of black powder, some 57 per cent by weight, are solid particles. This had important technical ramifications and tactical consequences. A hard coating of solid particles quickly formed inside bores, which had to be periodically swabbed, washed and scraped clean. The solid particles produced clouds of thick smoke which limited visibility in battle, particularly in high humidity and light winds. Finally, and most important ballistically, the high molecular weights of the decomposition products combined with the chemical and thermodynamic characteristics of the decomposition reactions to limit muzzle velocities.

Black powder decomposed by means of three mutually dependent chemical reactions, one exothermal and two endothermal, which proceeded in parallel, cancelling one another out thermodynamically. In consequence, the rate of gas evolution was effectively independent of changes in pressure and temperature. The constant burning rate combined with the high molecular weights of the decomposition products to impose an inflexible limit on muzzle velocities of about 2000 feet per second (fps) or 610 metres per second, though values of 1200–1400fps (366–426m/sec) were probably more representative.[3] This also meant that increasing the lengths of cannon barrels beyond a relatively modest amount had no

beneficial effect on muzzle velocity or range. Just what that amount was is beyond precise reconstruction, but late nineteenth-century experimental data suggest that a charge of black powder imparted 95 per cent of the attainable velocity to a cannonball by the time it had travelled eight to ten feet from the face of the charge. As gunfounders and gunners approached the structural and ballistic limits of black powder and cast iron from the mid eighteenth century on, the barrel lengths of smooth bore naval ordnance corresponded increasingly closely with this value.[4]

Gunpowder's physical form was a critical determinant of ballistic performance. In the earliest gunpowder, called serpentine, the ingredients were ground dry to a fine powder and mixed together. Serpentine was ballistically docile when handled properly, but the components tended to segregate in storage and had to be re-mixed before use, a dangerous procedure which raised clouds of noxious and explosive dust, as did the normal procedure of loading with an open ladle. Charges of serpentine had to be carefully tamped, and, if a stone ball were used, had to be confined with a wooden plug. These problems were overcome by grinding the ingredients together in an aqueous slurry, perhaps with an admixture of urine or wine, a procedure introduced as early as the late 1300s. After grinding, the slurry was pressed wet through a screen and left to dry in grains, or – the definitive procedure – dried in sheets, broken into grains, sieved and segregated by size and tumbled in drums to wear off the rough

3. John F Guilmartin, Jr, 'Ballistics in the Black Powder Era', *British Naval Armaments, Royal Armouries Conference Proceedings* 7, Robert D Smith (ed) (London 1989), pp76–77, 93. The above values are representative for black powder with more or less spherical grains. These limits were exceeded in the 1880s and '90s with powder pressed into shapes whose geometry promoted progressive burning, specifically perforated hexagonal plates. Since the grains burned partly from within the perforations, the net burning area, and therefore the rate at which propellant gases evolved, increased as the charge burned. Velocities of the order of 2500fps (762m/sec) were obtained using such powders, of which Prism Brown was one. Designed for use in large armour-piercing naval and coast defence guns, these powders were the ultimate development of black powder.

4. Guilmartin, 'Ballistics in the Black Powder Era', pp77–78. The point is demonstrated by examining a cutaway scale profile of the midsection of a late eighteenth-century or early nineteenth-century ship of the line showing the guns, *eg* Fig 190 in Jean Boudriot, *The Seventy-four Gun Ship*, Vol 2 (East Rotherfield, Sussex 1986), p157: the lighter guns of the upper decks are considerably longer relative to their bore diameters than the lower deck guns. The convergence toward a common maximum barrel length regardless of bore diameter continued to the end of the black powder era.

5. The above passage describes eighteenth-century practice and probably the most advanced of the sixteenth century, though it is unclear when tumbling became common. Methods were anything but uniform, and serpentine continued to be used into the 1600s.

The hooped external appearance of the early wrought iron breech-loader is evident from this verço *(verso) in the Museu Militar in Lisbon. (By courtesy of John F Guilmartin)*

in the 1570s, said that the ball should be 10 per cent smaller than the bore, that is 10 per cent lighter than a ball equal in diameter to the bore, a more or less typical value for the early modern period.[8]

Windage permitted the ball to rebound from side to side, or *ballot*, as it travelled down the bore, departing at an unpredictable angle. Whatever spin the ball acquired in the process was at an angle to the long axis of the bore, causing the ball to deviate from the trajectory dictated by velocity, mass and initial direction, in the manner of a hooked or sliced golf ball. Relatively little spin was imparted to the ball, but that was the problem: non-spinning or slowly spinning spherical projectiles are inherently inaccurate aerodynamically, having a

smaller-grained powder evolve their propellant gases more rapidly.

Medieval gunners believed that optimum grain size was related to the size of the gun, preferring large-grained powder for heavy ordnance, fine-grained powder for pistols and priming, and so on. Though they had no way of proving it, their preference had beneficial results with regard to heavy ordnance, the most demanding and dangerous use of gunpowder. Larger-grained powder releases its propulsive gases more gradually, giving the projectile time to start moving down the bore as the pressure begins to rise, resulting in lower peak pressures for the same propulsive force, less strain on the gun and a reduced chance of bursting. This, however, was demonstrated experimentally only in the 1850s. Ironically the medieval gunner's pragmatic appreciation was in advance of the scientific ballistics of the eighteenth century, when armies and navies standardised on fine-grained musket powder for heavy ordnance, based on its better performance in short-barrelled éprouvette mortars and powder testers which did not give coarse-grained powder time to develop its propulsive force.[6]

The extent to which the above generalisations applied to serpentine powder is unclear. Late nineteenth-century British experiments showed that the presence of dust in a charge, that is small particles of powder worn off through shaking in storage, slowed the net burning rate by impeding the spread of the

The breech end of the Portuguese wrought iron guns reproduced in the previous illustrations. (By courtesy of John F Guilmartin)

reaction from grain to grain.[7] In any event, it is clear that a properly-rammed charge of serpentine decomposed more slowly than corned powder and put less stress on the gun.

The essentials of external ballistics are more easily dealt with. The relevant tactical issue is accuracy as a function of range, almost entirely restricted to spherical projectiles fired from smooth bores, an inherently inaccurate combination. To prevent the projectile from sticking in the barrel, clearance, or windage, between ball and bore was necessary to allow for irregularities and inaccuracies in ball and bore and to account for fouling. In addition, cast iron shot expand as they rust, a particular problem when operating near salt water. The first of these problems could be reduced by improved manufacturing techniques, but the second two were inherent to black powder smooth bore ordnance. Luis Collado, writing

6. Powder testers were small, usually hand-held devices in which a measured charge of powder was ignited in a short barrel, usually pointing vertically upward. The open end of the barrel was sealed with a flat metal plate mounted on a hinged arm held shut by a strong spring. The arm was fitted with a ratchet which held it at the highest point of ascent after firing, and the further the arm rotated against the spring the stronger the powder was considered to be. Eprouvettes were small, short-barrelled mortars which expelled a heavy ball with a small powder charge, the strength of the powder being gauged by the distance the ball was thrown. These devices were useful for detecting deterioration from moisture, etc, in a given batch of powder, but measured only the propellant force generated before the lid opened or the ball exited the barrel. They yielded highly inaccurate results with slow-burning, large-grained powders since the lid opened or the ball exited before the charge could develop its full propulsive force.

7. HM War Office, *Treatise on Ammunition*, 8th ed (London 1905).

8. Luis Collado, *Platica Manual de Artilleria* (Milan 1592; Italian ed, Venice 1586), pp43–44, p48.

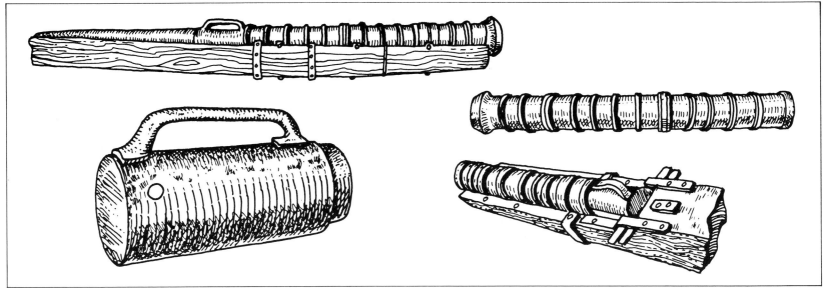

tendency to 'float' or wobble, deviating unpredictably from the line of flight.[9] Given the limitations of gun carriages and the difficulties of aiming accurately from the moving deck of a ship, it is probably safe to say that the best late medieval and early modern naval gunners had little hope of hitting their targets with any precision beyond about 300yds (275m) under all but the very best of conditions.

Once the ball left the bore, velocity diminished rapidly and in an irregular and unpredictable manner. The prime culprit, though by no means the only one, was a sharp decrease in the coefficient of drag as velocity dropped from supersonic to subsonic speeds. Since muzzle velocities were typically in excess of the speed of sound, 1096fps (334m/sec) at sea level and 0°C (32°F), this meant that aerodynamic drag could not be expressed as a simple squared or cubed function of velocity. Mathematicians could accurately describe the ballistic trajectory in a vacuum from Galileo on, but were unable to account for the effects of aerodynamic drag in any systematic way until the twentieth century.[10] In consequence, the angle of elevation needed to achieve a given range could be found only by trial and error, and most of the so-called range tables compiled in late medieval and early modern times were fanciful where long ranges were concerned. This was true even of tables compiled by careful gunners. In his *Platica Manual de Artilleria* published in 1592[11] the Spanish artillerist Luis Collado connected angles of elevation and ranges out to about 800yds with remarkable precision, confirmed by modern ballistic calculations.[12] Beyond 2000yds, however, Collado's ranges could have been achieved for the angles of elevation indicated only with muzzle velocities clearly unattainable with early modern ordnance, and other range tables were even more fanciful.[13] More to the point, attempts to predict the fall of a projectile at long ranges were, for the most part, tactically irrelevant because an inert projectile falling at a steep angle was unlikely to do much damage, and because the inherent inaccuracy of smooth bore ord-

Sketches of a fifteenth-century breech-loader recovered in 1847 from a wreck off the Danish island of Anholt. The gun is strapped to an oak stock, which was the usual method of mounting these early guns. The chamber, which held the powder charge, is shown separately. If there were numbers of these per gun, they could be loaded in advance to give the gun a relatively high rate of fire. (CMP)

nance made it unlikely that anything worth hitting would be hit.

Conversely, gunners were quite capable of extracting useful accuracy from their pieces at ranges where they could be expected to do serious damage to the hull of a ship or a fortress wall by aiming along the top of the barrel, by the line of metals, as it was called. Since cannon were generally thicker at the breech than at the muzzle, this imparted a slight positive angle of elevation. The ball would rise through the line of sight and then drop back through it within several hundred yards, depending on the geometry of the piece, and targets within that distance were said to be at point blank range, from the Spanish *punto de blanco*, pointed at the target, that is without elevation. Long, or ran-

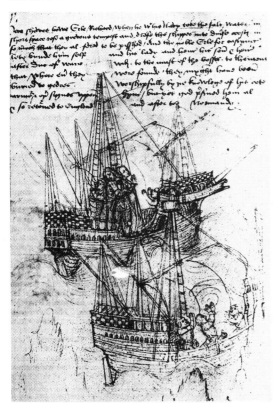

Before the introduction of the watertight gunport in the hull at the beginning of the sixteenth century, guns at sea were mounted to fire over the waist of the ship or, in the case of smaller calibres, through small openings in the castles fore and aft. The English carracks from this late fifteenth-century manuscript known as the Warwick Roll show both.

9. Sir Howard Douglas, *A Treatise on Naval Gunnery* 4th ed (London 1855; reprinted 1982), pp86–7.

10. Sir Alfred G A Greenhill, 'Ballistics', *Encyclopaedia Britannica*, 11th ed (London 1911), Vol III, pp271.

11. Milan; originally published as *Practica Manuale di Artiglieria* (Venice 1586).

12. John F Guilmartin, Jr, *Gunpowder and Galleys: Changing Technology and Mediterranean Warfare at Sea in the Sixteenth Century* (Cambridge 1974), Appendix 2, 'The External and Internal Ballistics of Sixteenth Century Cannon', pp277–283. Collado's data were examined for the author by Charles H Legegern and Joseph W Kochenderfer, Firing Tables Branch, US Army Aberdeen Proving Ground, Maryland.

13. For example, Diego Prado y Tovar, *Encyclopedia de Fundición de Artilleria y su Platica Manual* (Madrid 1603).

dom, shots were tried on occasion to bring down a crucial piece of rigging in order to disable a fleeing prize or pursuing enemy, but by and large long-range accuracy was not the gunner's main concern.

The physics of terminal ballistics present mathematical problems of daunting complexity, but come down to a simple problem: the ability of an inert ball of stone or cast iron to penetrate a wooden hull or perhaps cut a crucial spar or piece of rigging, more a matter of gunnery and luck than ballistics. An inert ball could do serious damage to the wooden hull of a ship, but only at relatively high velocities and acute impact angles, which is to say at comparatively short ranges. By the late fifteenth century, if not before, the best ordnance afloat was quite capable of putting a stone or cast iron ball of moderate weight, say 12lb or more, through the hull of a ship at perhaps 200–300yds; the shorter the range the more lethal the effect. In addition to piercing planking and smashing or damaging frames and spars, penetrating balls tore out long splinters on their way through, inflicting horrendous injuries on the men behind. This happened relatively infrequently until well into the seventeenth century – John Hawkins's fight with the Spanish fleet off San Juan de Ulloa in 1568 was very much the exception. That this was the case is more a commentary on the gradual evolution of carriage design, ship design and gun drill than on the power of the guns themselves. The dichotomy between light 'man killers' and heavy 'ship smashers' is more a product of modern scholarship than pre-modern gunnery, but multiple anti-personnel projectiles of various kinds fired from rail-mounted swivel guns, and not infrequently from larger pieces, particularly in galley warfare, played a major role in combat afloat which gradually diminished as naval ordnance became heavier, handier and more common.

The earliest naval guns

Just when and where gunpowder was first used at sea is unclear, but with regard to weapons whose technological offspring were to play a major military and economic role in world affairs, the evidence suggests that it was in Euro-

pean waters early in the fourteenth century. Gunpowder was known in China by the eleventh century and the earliest depiction of a cannon is Chinese, dating from c1128.[14] Technical development stagnated, however, and guns had no observable impact on the conduct of war in Asia until reintroduced by Europeans in the sixteenth century. The systematic exploitation of the explosive properties of gunpowder to drive inert projectiles against military targets with increasing force, frequency and efficiency date from its appearance in Europe during the thirteenth century, probably as a result of the Mongol invasions. References to guns and their projectiles were relatively common in European documents by 1300, and the ancestors of the basilisks, bombards, culverins and cannon which spawned the gunpowder revolution of the fifteenth and sixteenth centuries were European. Underlying these developments was the appearance of the Catalán forge around the beginning of the fourteenth century, permitting the production of unprecedented quantities of wrought iron of high quality.

There is some evidence that primitive cannon, or *gonnes*, were carried aboard war galleys as early as the first decades of the fourteenth century, though it is unclear whether they were intended to be fired afloat or were transported for use ashore. What these earliest examples of shipboard ordnance – if indeed that is what they were – looked like and how they were used is conjectural. The earliest European depictions of guns are contained in the Walter de Milemete manuscript dating from about 1327 and show small, vase-shaped pieces fired by

applying a red-hot wire to the touch hole.[15] The projectiles were oversized crossbow bolts nearly as long as the gun, and contemporary documents suggest that they were made of metal, probably wrought iron. The guns are shown simply resting on trestle tables, so recoil and power were no doubt modest, and efficiency was not helped by the considerable difference in diameter between bore and projectile shaft, which was probably wound with a leather strap to seal the gap.

Guns of the kind depicted in the Milemete manuscript gave way only gradually to cannon firing spherical projectiles of stone, iron or lead, first with tapering bores and then – the key development – with tubular bores which gave the propellant gases time and space to accelerate the ball to meaningful velocity. No doubt in part because of the high price of gunpowder, the earliest guns tended to be very small: forty-seven 'large cannon' made for Richard II of England between 1382 and 1388 had barrels weighing an average of 380lb (172kg).[16] Then, toward the end of the century, gunfounders began to make larger pieces of wrought iron with serious military potential.

---

14. L Gwen-Djen, J Needham and P Chi-Hsing, 'The Oldest Representation of a Bombard', *Technology and Culture 29*, 3 (October 1988), pp594–605.

15. Assuming that the humans depicted with them are to scale, the larger was some 8ft (2.25m) long and about a third that in diameter, and the smaller was 3½–4ft (1–1.25m) long and half that large across, or perhaps a bit more; see Gwen-Djen, Needham and Chi-Hsing, 'The Oldest Representation of a Bombard'.

16. Philippe Contamine, *War in the Middle Ages* (New York 1984), pp140–41.

Details of the breech of a wrought iron verço *(verso) in the Museu Militar, Lisbon, probably of late fifteenth- or early sixteenth-century origins. Note the removable powder chamber and the holes in the sides of the receiver through which a wedge was hammered to seal the chamber to the barrel. (By courtesy of John F Guilmartin)*

An extremely large wrought iron bombard (right) and a small cast bronze verso (verço, left) in the collection of the Museu Militar, Lisbon. They probably date from the early and mid sixteenth century respectively. Note the heavy lifting rings on the bombard. It also has trunnions though they are elaborately decorated and not perfectly cylindrical, thus suggesting that it was founded during a period of technical transition. (By courtesy of John F Guilmartin)

pieces firing from the castles and upper decks, was common on European ships. Bronze guns seem to have seen less sea service, perhaps because of their greater cost and concentration in siege trains. Generally speaking, the larger

17. For the remarkable facility of gunfounders with wrought iron and an analysis of fifteenth- or early-sixteenth-century blacksmithing technique, Joe J Simmons, III, 'Wrought-iron Ordnance: Revealing Discoveries from the New World', *The International Journal of Nautical Archaeology* 17, 1 (January 1988), p31.

18. Robert D Smith, 'Port-Pieces: The Use of Wrought-Iron Guns in the Sixteenth Century', *Journal of the Ordnance Society* 5 (1993), pp2–5.

19. Smith, 'Port-Pieces', pp5–6, note 5, for the confusing and unclear English terminology; Simmons, 'Wrought-iron Ordnance', for Spanish terminology and a description of the ordnance of a vessel dating from 1495–1515 recovered by underwater archaeology from Caribbean waters. Technical terms applied to ordnance were generally very similar in the major Mediterranean languages; see Henry Kahane and Andreas Tietze, *The Lingua Franca in the Levant: Turkish Nautical Terms of Italian and Greek Origin* (Urbana, Illinois 1958).

20. Clifford J Rogers, 'The Military Revolutions of the Hundred Years' War', *The Journal of Military History* 57, 2 (April 1992), pp266–71.

Generically called lombards or bombards, these came into widespread use during the fifteenth century and, with their smaller offspring, remained the most common ordnance at sea through the sixteenth. Constructed of hoops and staves like a barrel, they were initially almost all breech-loaders, perhaps because of the difficulty of forging a long tube sealed at the end, and had one or more separate breech blocks, or halls.[17] Carriages consisted of long wooden stocks or sledges into which the barrel was chamfered and bound with iron bands. There was an open recess for the hall and provisions for wedging it tightly against the barrel with a wrought iron wedge, apparently sometimes supplemented with a T-shaped wooden piece called a *forloke* or *forelok* which was dropped into the carriage behind the hall.[18] There were many variations on this basic theme, including long, narrow breech-loaders of modest size – 3 to 6pdrs were probably typical – called *pasavolantes*, *cerbatanas* and fowlers, and even smaller swivel pieces called *versos* or bases.[19]

Our first solid evidence of shipboard ordnance dates from the fifteenth century. Not coincidentally, it was then that gunpowder ordnance was first used with decisive effect on land, when cannon were used from the 1420s to breach fortress walls with low-trajectory fire rather than to lob projectiles over them.[20] Mills for the production of corned powder appeared at about the same time, reducing cost through the use of water power. By the mid 1400s wrought iron ordnance, mostly small

The Battle of Zonchio, 1499: the Turkish galleys' bow guns are wrought iron swivel pieces on wooden stocks. Note that all three carracks are armed with considerable numbers of wrought iron pieces firing over the rails. Two Turks are shown discharging some sort of pyrotechnic devices from the tops, but none is shown with shoulder arms. Conversely, two Venetians are shown firing proto-arquebuses.

pieces threw balls of cut stone, descendants of the trebuchet projectiles of an earlier age. Smaller pieces fired balls of cast iron, and the smallest shot pellets of lead, the choice of material being driven by internal ballistic considerations. Denser projectiles accelerated more slowly, causing higher chamber pressures and placing greater strain on the gun. Gunfounders understood this empirically, and stone throwers, or pedreros, had thinner and shorter barrels than iron throwers and typically weighed a third to a half less than pieces designed to fire an iron projectile of the same weight. Terminal ballistics also played a role. A stone ball made a larger hole than an iron ball of the same weight, and a preference for stone-throwers for naval use manifested itself. Composite shot, made of a cube of wrought iron cast within a lead ball, was used in pieces of moderate size, combining lead's malleability with iron's lesser density.[21]

Naval mounts and carriages became increasingly specialised, though they continued to show their ancestry as simple stocks or sledges. By the mid 1400s the stocks of smaller pieces were fitted with trunnions and suspended from wrought iron yokes in swivel mounts; a Venetian woodcut of the Battle of Zonchio in 1499 shows pieces of this sort on the bows of Turkish galleys. It was probably aboard Mediterranean war galleys during this period that heavy ordnance was first used routinely and with effect at sea. This was in the form of the main centreline bow gun, at first rigidly embedded in the structure of the bow, firing straight ahead and aimed by manoeuvring the entire galley. Main centreline guns could be quite large. In Spanish service by the 1540s 24pdrs to 50pdrs were common. They were supplemented by smaller forward-firing flanking pieces and still smaller swivel guns, mounted on posts and railings at the bow and stern.

Less is known about mounts and carriages aboard sailing vessels. Wrought iron breech-loading deck guns were fitted with eyelets atop

A very long 12pdr Spanish sacre (saker) in the collection of the Turkish Army Museum, Istanbul, cast by a German founder in 1518 (right): 16ft 3in long, it had a bore diameter of 4.4in. The extremely long bore, some 41 calibres in length, was far longer than the ballistic optimum. This was characteristic of the best guns in the culverin class of the early sixteenth century. (By courtesy of John F Guilmartin)

their halls and chambers, into which wrought iron rings were let. Precisely what purpose these served is unknown. The rings on chambers were no doubt used to transport them from loading point to gun, but the function of those atop barrels is obscure. Prior to the development of the hinged, watertight gunport, heavy ordnance could not be permanently mounted low in the hull and was ordinarily stowed in the hold for reasons of stability and brought up only when needed. The rings atop the barrel were therefore surely used as lifting lugs to move the piece, as well as a means of

21. Simmons, 'Wrought-iron Ordnance', pp31–33.

securing it to the deck and gunwales. By the sixteenth century some deck carriages were fitted with a pair of wheels. *Versos* had lost their wooden stocks and were made entirely of wrought iron with integrally forged trunnions set into a yoke for rail mounting and a long tiller for aiming. These were widely used both on war galleys and sailing ships and were probably the most common ordnance afloat. Bore diameters of the order of 2in (50mm), barrel lengths of 3–3½ft (1–1.5m) and total lengths about twice that were typical.

Cast bronze guns

By the last quarter of the fifteenth century, wrought iron ordnance was giving way to pieces of cast bronze, cannon and culverins, as Europe's premier heavy gunpowder ordnance. The ascendancy of cast bronze introduces an apparent anomaly, for the late medieval gunfounder and gunner believed that there was a positive correlation between quality and length, and by extension between quality and effective range. In fact, they were right, but for structural rather than ballistic reasons. As nineteenth-century experiments were to prove, there is a positive correlation between the strength of bronze and its density. Density within a casting varied as a function of the height of the column of molten metal above it as it cooled and solidified. Since guns were cast breech-down in pits, making the gun longer had the beneficial effect of making it stronger at the breech, where strength was most important.[22] By the end of the fifteenth century, founders and gunners seem to have appreciated that longer pieces were, all else being equal, safer. Gunnery was an esoteric craft practised by an elite imbued with an aura of mystery by their ability to harness secret and dangerous forces. The best gunners tended to get their pick of ordnance, and no doubt gravitated to long pieces of bronze for demanding tasks, 'long shots' among them. Note, however, that they had no comprehensive theory of stress and strain in bronze castings against which to test their beliefs. Indeed, the structural dynamics of cast bronze ordnance still defy precise quantitative explanation. The modern theory of stress and strain in thin-walled tubing specifies that any increase in wall thickness beyond a quarter of the bore diameter results in no increase in strength at all, yet medieval and early modern founders routinely cast their pieces with wall thicknesses approximately equal to the bore. Moreover, individual founders cast their pieces to the same proportions with great precision, and barrel thick-

nesses and lengths gradually and systematically decreased with time as foundry practice improved, yielding obvious benefits in handiness and cost. By the last quarter of the sixteenth century the best English pieces of cast bronze were being made to proportions not very different from those which prevailed to the end of the smooth bore, black powder era.

As foundry practice improved, the labour needed to forge large wrought iron pieces and cut the stone cannonballs they fired became more expensive relative to the considerably greater capital investment which bronze ordnance entailed, at least in the West. The ease of maintenance and longevity of corrosion-resistant bronze was no doubt also a consideration. Better bronze pieces used at sea might remain in service for a century and a half.[23] Perhaps most important from the gunner's standpoint, a sound cast bronze muzzle-loader charged with corned powder and firing an iron ball could do more damage to the hull of a ship or the walls of a fortification, pound for pound and shot for shot, with less risk to gun and gunner than any other combination save a cast bronze pedrero, and stone shot were far more expensive than cast iron. That having been said, wrought iron ordnance endured through the sixteenth century and into the seventeenth, no doubt largely for economic reasons.

By the beginning of the sixteenth century, muzzle-loading cast bronze culverins and cannon had replaced wrought iron breech-loaders as Europe's premier heavy ordnance. Cast with integral trunnions to secure the barrel to the carriage and facilitate adjustments in elevation, heavy bronze ordnance had assumed the basic form which it was to retain until rendered obsolete by rifled iron and steel breech-loaders late in the nineteenth century. By mid century wrought iron was giving way to cast bronze at sea, and wrought iron ordnance of any size was considered dangerous when fired with corned powder or an iron ball.

As cannon grew in size and power, and as rates of fire increased, carriage design evolved to meet the challenge. Though the evidence is thin, this probably began with the development of sliding carriages for the main centreline bow guns of Mediterranean war galleys toward the end of the fifteenth century. Designed to absorb recoil by sliding beneath the corsia, the raised walkway between the rowing benches, these seem to have looked very much like truck carriages without wheels and were probably their precursors. By the beginning of the sixteenth century the best heavy ordnance on land, French for the moment, was mounted on trail carriages with dished wheels which dif-

fered from their successors over the next two centuries only in their relatively greater bulk and weight. Mobile heavy ordnance on the new pattern forced major changes in land warfare, notably in forcing the development of the *trace italienne* fortress with angle bastions and sunken profile, and developments at sea were not far behind. Foremost among these was the development of the hinged, watertight gunport. This is traditionally dated to around 1500 and credited to an anonymous French shipwright, but the origins of the watertight gunport are obscure. The appearance of port pieces, large wrought iron breech-loaders intended for use afloat, in English naval ordnance inventories in the late 1510s[24] supports the traditional date. What is certain is that the development of the watertight gunport made it possible to mount heavier guns lower in the ship, dramatically increasing firepower without sacrificing stability. By mid century naval gun carriages were evolving into the basic forms which they were to retain until the second half of the nineteenth century. The pivotal development was the emergence of the four-wheeled truck carriage in England and Portugal around mid century.[25] By the turn of the seventeenth century, the sophistication and efficiency of naval guns and carriages equalled or surpassed that of their equivalents on land, and increasingly heavy ordnance was taken to sea. Warships and merchantmen armed with batteries of heavy guns mounted behind watertight ports on gundecks low in the hull were the norm. Broadside batteries had combined with tumblehome largely to neutralise the threat of boarding from low-lying vessels. Swivel guns and railing pieces had diminished in size and importance to relative insignificance.

22. For an eighteenth-century appreciation, Carel de Beers (ed), *The Art of Gunfounding: The Casting of Bronze Cannon in the Late 18th Century* (Rotherfield, East Sussex 1991), p136. Bronze gunfounding technique remained unchanged in basic principles from the fifteenth century through the nineteenth, but the appearance of stasis is misleading. Quality, measured by success in passing proof and in the steadily decreasing bulk and weight of cannon barrels relative to the weight of the projectile, improved steadily.

23. John F Guilmartin, Jr, 'The Guns of the *Santissimo Sacramento*', *Technology and Culture* 24, 4 (October 1982), pp586–87, p595.

24. Smith, 'Port-Pieces', pp5–6.

25. Colin Martin and Geoffrey Parker, *The Spanish Armada* (London 1988), pp50–51, pp208–210. When the book went to press, Martin and Parker had no evidence of four-wheeled truck carriages outside of England prior to 1588, but Parker subsequently found a contemporary Portuguese depiction of such a carriage; information to the author.

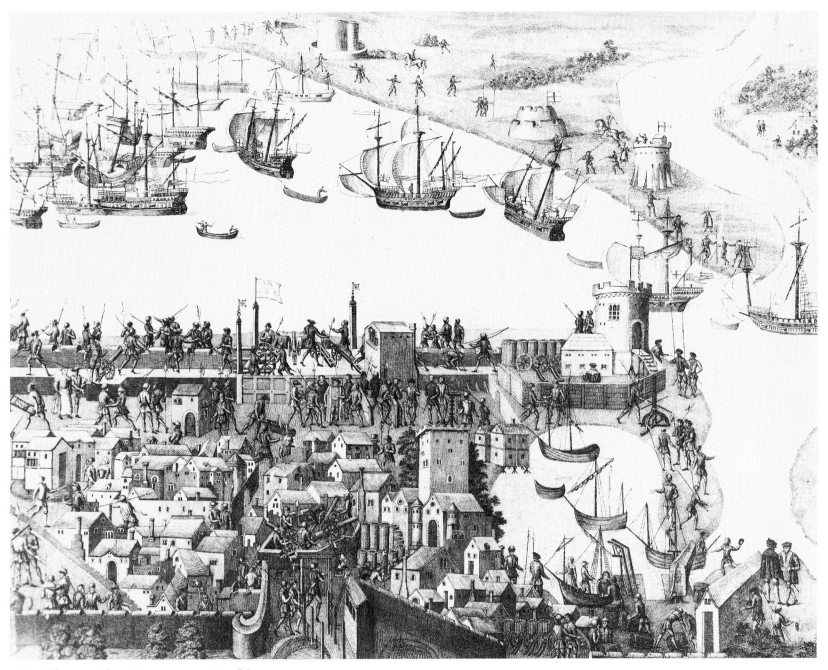

A detail from an eighteenth-century engraving of the action in which the Mary Rose *was lost in 1545. Although the representation is crude, it is based on a now-lost painting executed very soon after the event. The variety of English warships is clear, and the larger ones all have gunports cut in the hull. Contemporary artillery can also be seen among the coastal defences, and similar carriages were used at sea – although there was already a move towards the four-wheeled truck carriage familiar from later centuries. (CMP)*

The Mary Rose

On 19 July 1545, as King Henry VIII's fleet sortied from Portsmouth harbour under light winds to confront the French fleet, one of his largest and most heavily armed warships, the carrack *Mary Rose*, was caught by a sudden freshening of the breeze. Cleared for action under a heavy press of canvas, with her lower gunports open, the lids lashed up and her guns run out, the ship began to heel. Before the crew could react, water poured into the lee ports, swamping the vessel. Within minutes she was on the bottom, carrying virtually everything on board with her. Of the crew of 500–600, fewer than 40 survived, but tragedy for them and the King's fleet was to prove a boon for students of naval architecture and ordnance of a later age.

Some ordnance was apparently removed shortly after the vessel went down, but salvage efforts were otherwise fruitless. Lying on its starboard side at an angle of 60 degrees to starboard, the hull filled with sediments and silt as the years passed. Exposed upper parts decayed and collapsed inward or were carried away by the current and tides. The rest became a time capsule to be recovered by underwater archaeology between 1971 and 1982.[26] Today, the surviving structure and artifacts, not least among them the ordnance, are on display in the Mary Rose Museum, Portsmouth, and what we have learned from them has made a major contribution to our knowledge of naval

26. The basic source is Margaret Rule, *The Mary Rose: The Excavation and Raising of Henry VIII's Flagship* (London 1982); see also Ernie Bradford, *The Story of the Mary Rose* (New York 1982). Both works went to press before the hull was raised; however, Bradford, pp193–202, has a full discussion of recovery and preservation methods.

Part of the Mary Rose *Exhibition housed in Portsmouth Dockyard's No 5 Boathouse. A magnificent cast bronze gun recovered in 1979 rests on a wooden replica gun carriage made by craftsmen at the Weald & Downland Museum, West Sussex. In the background is a reconstruction of two of the* Mary Rose *gundecks.* (Mary Rose Trust)

vessels and ordnance during a pivotal period of transition.

A major question which study of the *Mary Rose* is helping to answer involves the timing of the introduction aboard the King's ships of a main battery of heavy ordnance mounted low in the hull on a continuous deck behind lidded ports. The lidded, watertight gunport is generally believed to have been introduced about 1500. *Mary Rose* was laid down in 1509 and extensively rebuilt in 1536. Examination of the hull suggests that some parts, at least, were originally planked clinker fashion and later rebuilt carvel style so that gunports could be fitted. The evidence is not conclusive, since the tell-tale notches cut into frames to accept clinker planks may be evidence only of the use of timbers salvaged from another ship.[27]

The evidence suggests, however, that the *Mary Rose* may have been fitted with a continuous main gundeck with lidded ports from the start. The argument hinges on the types and weights of guns listed on successive inventories and on the identity of a wreck excavated in 1912 at the site of the Woolwich Power Station in London. The earliest, 1514, inventory of the *Mary Rose*'s ordnance includes an impressive number of heavy guns which would have been difficult to mount in any other way

An English demi-cannon cast in 1571 by Thomas Owen in the collection of the Museu Militar, Lisbon. The best English founders at this time were casting some of the finest bronze ordnance extant: they were shorter and lighter for the weight of ball thrown, and the metal was generally denser, than Dutch and Spanish pieces. (By courtesy of John F Guilmartin)

without compromising the ship's seaworthiness. Tentatively identified as the *Sovereign*, built in 1488, the Woolwich Power Station wreck was clearly rebuilt from clinker to carvel style at a later date, presumably so that gunports could be fitted. Comparison of the *Sovereign*'s ordnance inventories of 1488 and 1514 shows a shift from a battery of 141 light guns suitable for mounting in the waist and castles to 84 heavier pieces.[28] If the wreck is, in fact, the *Sovereign*, evidence that she was replanked before 1514 reinforces the hypothesis that *Mary Rose* had lidded gunports from the beginning.

The most remarkable aspect of the *Mary Rose*'s ordnance is its diversity. Before the recovery of the *Mary Rose*, it was known that the armament of the King's ships – let alone private vessels – in the sixteenth century was an unstandardised mix of the modern and the archaic, but the degree to which this was so was not appreciated. No record survives listing the ordnance on board when she went down, but an inventory on the Anthony Anthony Roll showing the ship after her 1536 rebuild includes six bronze pieces of considerable size – two cannon, two demi-cannon and two culverins – which were surely mounted on the main gundeck. Before the vessel's recovery, we would probably have placed the six demi-culverins there as well, and concluded that the twelve wrought iron port pieces were smaller guns for the upper decks. Some of the largest pieces on the *Mary Rose*'s gundeck, however, were massive wrought iron breech-loaders on two-wheeled sledge carriages, almost surely port pieces; interestingly, several of the carriages in question had large spoked wheels typical of land service ordnance. One of the ship's finest guns, a magnificent 8pdr bronze demi-

---

27. Rule, *Mary Rose*, p152.

28. Rule, *Mary Rose*, p152.

culverin cast in 1537 by Robert and John Owen, was recovered from the upper castle decks.[29] To complete the picture of heterogeneity, some remarkably archaic pieces were recovered, including a small cast iron hailshot piece with an oblong bore, and the ship's armament included a considerable number of longbows and their associated arrows and quivers.

Cast iron ordnance

Perhaps most important in global repercussions, muzzle-loading ordnance of cast iron, heavier than bronze and more prone to burst but far cheaper, was cast in England from 1543 onwards. Cast iron guns were considerably heavier than bronze pieces which threw the same weight of ball, but cost only about a third to a fourth as much, a disparity which increased with time, the cost of iron ordnance falling to an eighth that of bronze England by the 1670s.[30] The relative lightness of bronze continued to be of pre-emptive importance on land, and it was at sea that cast iron ordnance made its mark. Heavy capital investment was required in hulls, spars, sails, rigging and fittings, but heavy ordnance could be moved more easily and cheaply by sail than by draught animal, largely negating cast iron's disadvantages in bulk and weight. It was far easier to manhandle a heavy gun on the smooth deck of a ship than on rocky, rough or muddy ground, all the more so since the shipboard gun was securely lashed to deck and bulwarks by heavy, adjustable tackle.[31] It was within this technological context that cast iron's cost advantage was decisive. Bronze remained the material of choice for naval ordnance when it could be had, but iron's cheapness made it possible to arm ships on an unprecedented scale, and the nations which could cast and purchase iron ordnance in quantity enjoyed a steadily increasing advantage in the struggle to control the commerce of the world's oceans.

The increasing use of ordnance afloat from the mid sixteenth century was accompanied by steady, incremental improvements in carriage design and foundry practice. By the end of the sixteenth century, guns mounted on truck carriages and firing through hinged, watertight ports were the core armament of all but the smallest European sailing vessels. Gunfounders working in both bronze and iron were gradu-

ally approaching optimum proportions in their cannon, casting them progressively lighter and shorter for the weight of ball. This was an empirical matter, driven by the cost of materials and the great handiness of shorter pieces. There were complicating factors, not least among them the qualities of available iron ores, and the perceived connection between barrel length and range persisted in the minds of many. This was no doubt partly due to the connection between length and strength, but long barrels served other purposes as well.[32] They helped to keep muzzle blast clear of flammable rigging, particularly when firing through shrouds and backstays at sharp angles of traverse. Nevertheless, though systematic optimisation would have to await Benjamin Robins' invention of the ballistic pendulum in the 1740s, by the mid seventeenth century the barrel lengths of first class naval ordnance were converging on the optimum length of eight to ten feet (27m–30m) from the face of the

powder charge. The biggest guns afloat became larger, and efforts were made to standardise the size, bore diameters and proportions of guns. The *Sovereign of the Seas*, launched in 1637 with a full lower battery of cast iron cannon-of-seven (that is 42pdrs) was a

---

29. Rule, *Mary Rose*, pp156–62.

30. Carlo Cipolla, *Guns, Sails and Empires: Technological Innovation and the Early Phases of European Expansion 1400–1700* (New York 1965), p42, note 3; Frank Fox, *Great Ships: The Battlefleet of King Charles II* (Greenwich 1980), pp163–64.

31. The weight advantage of bronze remained a vital factor on land to the end of the black powder era: the smooth bore, muzzle-loading 12pdr Napoleon gun-howitzer was the premier field artillery piece of the American Civil War, 1861–65, enjoying important tactical advantages over the more cumbersome iron rifled pieces which threw significantly smaller projectiles for the same weight.

32. See Brian Lavery, *The Arming and Fitting of English Ships of War, 1600–1815* (London 1987), Ch 17 'The Proportions of Guns', pp92–7, for a useful discussion.

The breech of the 1571 English demi-cannon, showing the founder's inscription. The distinction between form and function, beauty and utilitarian value was less clearly delineated than it came to be later on. (By courtesy of John F Guilmartin)

benchmark in this regard.[33] The cannon-of-seven was to remain the largest gun commonly mounted aboard ships of the line almost until the end of the smooth bore, black powder era.

European production of naval ordnance increased to meet the demand created by the emergence of a global maritime economy and the armed struggle for its dominance. Though quantitative data are lacking, it is clear that the increase was almost entirely in cast iron. By the end of the sixteenth century the production of cast iron ordnance had spread to the Netherlands, Germany, and, above all, Sweden, and by the middle of the seventeenth there was a

The culmination of the naval gunnery revolution was the ship of the line with its multiple batteries of uniform-calibre guns on flush gundecks. This is the lower deck of the Swedish Wasa, *lost in 1627 and now recovered and restored in Stockholm. The gun carriages show a marked resemblance to those of the* Mary Rose's *cast guns nearly a century earlier. (Wasa Museum, Stockholm)*

massive international trade in cast iron guns. Cast iron ordnance had become the standard and increasingly available means of defence and offence afloat, and was to remain so until the end of the black powder era. Efforts were made to standardise on a limited number of calibres, and the weight of ships' batteries increased substantially during the first half of the seventeenth century, particularly on warships; this was true both of the total weight of ordnance carried and of the weight of individual guns. All of these developments rested on the ability of shipwrights to accommodate heavy guns within their designs. The ability was well-developed by the 1650s and was to prove so robust that a 20 per cent increase in the weights of English cast iron pieces in the 1670s was easily accommodated, albeit with a reduction in firepower.[34]

By the eve of the Anglo-Dutch Wars, European shipwrights and gunfounders were well on the way to determining by trial and error

and practical experience the optimum design of armed, deep-sea vessels attainable with hulls of oak, masts and spars of pine and fir, cordage and canvas of hemp, fittings of wrought iron, and ordnance of cast iron and gun carriages of elm and oak. In the case of armed merchantmen, they had come very close indeed with the *fluit*, and the English, French and Dutch warships of the 1650s are clearly the direct ancestors of the 74-gun ships of the line and frigates of the next century, the final, elegant, solutions, of how best to harness the power of the wind and black powder at sea.

John F Guilmartin, Jr

33. Lavery, *Arming and Fitting*, p98.

34. Lavery, *Arming and Fitting*. The reasons for the increased weight are obscure; changed production technique to accommodate inferior ore is the most likely candidate.

10

Ship Construction: Tools and Techniques

UNTIL the modern era, wood was the most important material for all forms of construction throughout the world. In shipbuilding, its dominance was complete. Nothing else could offer the same combination of qualities: a strong, light material which was flexible and easy to work and which could be provided in large dimensions and quantities at relatively low cost. It was therefore wood, its qualities and availability as well as the technology used when working it, that in practice determined the development of the ship.

Timber for shipbuilding

Europe is not climatically very homogeneous. Along the Mediterranean coast the climate is subtropical and in the far north it is Arctic. As a result the character of the woodlands and the species represented in them are just as variable. Changes not only in latitude, but also in longitude mean different conditions for the forests. The east has warm, dry summers which sharply contrast with bitterly cold winters, while the west is dominated by the humid, Atlantic climate. Thus ship carpentry never enjoyed the same circumstances throughout Europe, but had to adjust to local and regional conditions.

It was not only climate and soil that decided the character of the woodlands. Man also had his effect by using them for grazing, timber and firewood, or by clearing them for agriculture. In vast areas of Mediterranean and western Europe, the efforts of man radically changed the forests and reduced their extent prior to and during the Middle Ages and the Renaissance. Shipbuilding played a role in this development and was influenced by it as well. Trade in timber was one answer to the problem of failing supplies, technological changes another. Both

are well represented in the history of European shipbuilding.

The timber trade is a phenomenon almost as old as seafaring in the Mediterranean. Lebanese cedar was imported by the Egyptians, partly to be used by their highly skilled ship carpenters. Millennia later, Asia Minor was still exporting timber for shipbuilding, although the focus had now shifted from the decreasing supply of cedar to another softwood, cypress. Cypress is very fast-growing under good conditions and control of cypress-producing Crete has actually been seen as one of the major strategic advantages which finally tipped the naval balance between the Arabs and the Byzantines in favour of the latter.[1] Cedar and cypress were probably the two best species

for shipbuilding which could be found around the coasts of the eastern Mediterranean. Although they are only moderately strong, they are light and malleable and easy to work. Furthermore, they have one very important quality for ship timbers: they are less likely to suffer from dry rot and so are very durable. The now almost extinct Lebanese cedar could probably reach very large dimensions like other cedar species, with lengths of 50m (164ft) and diameters of more than 1.5m (5ft), but the cypress seldom grows to more than half those dimensions.

After the change from shell to skeleton con-

1. R W Unger, *The Ship in the Medieval Economy* (London 1980), p55, note 21.

This medieval illustration of Noah building the Ark (from the Nuremburg Chronicle), although naive in its representation of the ship, does show a number of the shipwright's tools of the late fifteenth century. (By courtesy of Richard Unger)

struction techniques in the Mediterranean in the early Middle Ages, softwoods were used mostly for the planking of ships. As they were easy to work and easy to fit to the curved lines of a hull, there was no reason to replace them with woods harder to work and perhaps less accessible, such as oak. Oak had been in use since antiquity for the most stressed parts of ships like keels and stem- and sternposts, but with the change to skeleton construction it became necessary to use stronger timbers in the frame system as well. Oak and other hardwoods, such as elm, became increasingly important during the Middle Ages, a fact which must have favoured the city states in today's northern Italy and the north-western coasts of the Mediterranean in general, where oak grew. Due to climate, plentiful resources of good quality oak were not accessible in the regions on the eastern and southern shores of the Mediterranean. From the thirteenth century onward, oak turns up as the most dominant wood in some of the wrecks excavated in the western Mediterranean, although different sorts of pine did play an important role as material for planking.[2]

In early medieval northern Europe, the

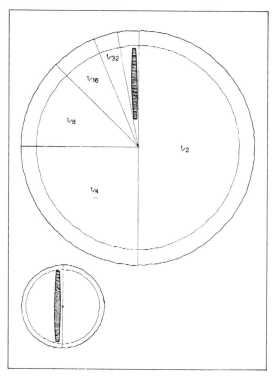

The splitting techniques. Large, high quality oak logs could be radially split into sixteen or more blanks, each producing an extremely strong plank 2.5–4.0cm thick. Tangential splitting produced only two planks from each log, but of almost the same high quality. The method was suitable for smaller logs only, and was used to produce fir planks in the northern districts even in the seventeenth century. After Crumlin Pedersen.

situation was completely different. Apart from the northernmost parts of Scandinavia, oak was the shipbuilding wood par excellence and was used for most features of a ship. Sometimes, compromises were made and other hardwoods like ash or elm were used, but those cases were rare. The major alternative in the north was the pine, *pinus sylvestris*. It is stronger and a little heavier than the Mediterranean softwoods, but like the southern pines, it lacks that critical resistance to dry rot, a quality which oak has because of its high tannin content. Oak has other qualities which explain its popularity as a shipbuilding timber. It is very strong and when grown in forests it typically develops a long, straight trunk with few knots. Furthermore, it is easily capable of producing a log 1.2 metres (4ft) thick. This would not have been an advantage at a time when land transport was still very difficult if it were not for the fact that oak splits extremely well. Oak logs were split in halves, quarters and so on, until they were converted to sixteen or more planks, each having a width less than half the effective width of the parent log. As the split would follow the grain of the wood, only a minimum of fibres were cut in the process, thus providing ship carpenters with a building material at that time unequalled for the purpose. Ash and elm split very poorly and no other hardwood has the durability of oak. Therefore it was never challenged in its position as the primary shipbuilding timber in the early medieval period. It was also never challenged seriously later on when it was no longer important to be able to split the timbers to make planks.

During the high Middle Ages the radial splitting technique lost its importance partly because of its own drawbacks. The method had two serious flaws: it demanded large logs of high quality in order to produce planks of even a modest width, and any increase in thickness meant an increase in the required diameter of parent log. Such trees took 150 years or more to grow and were always attractive for many different purposes. Furthermore, the waste proportion during the splitting process was high: up to 75 per cent. In deforested and densely populated areas there was little hope of finding woodlands capable of producing oaks of the desired dimensions. There was even less willingness to accept so high a proportion of waste. As shipping and the demand for shipbuilding materials increased, the splitting technique had to be abandoned in favour of methods which consumed less material. Only in the densely forested pine districts in the northernmost areas of Europe did splitting continue to be used, here in its extremely

wasteful tangential variant for smaller trunks which produced only two planks per log. It is hardly a coincidence that in subsequent centuries the main stronghold of the clinker-building tradition, also adapted to the high quality planking of the splitting techniques, continued to be the same districts.[3]

Other timber species were used for special purposes in shipbuilding, demonstrating the intimate knowledge of their qualities among ship carpenters. For example, willow was used for the wedged wooden nails connecting planking and frames in the eleventh-century coastal trader found at Skuldelev in Denmark. This use reflects two of the willow's characteristics very well: the difficulty of splitting it and of breaking off its fibres. This level of expertise is not surprising at a time when wood was used for almost any type of construction and had been for millennia.

Timber conversion

Ship carpentry was becoming increasingly specialised and moving toward becoming a separate trade during the Middle Ages, but the tools of the shipwright were not specific to his trade alone, as they are not today. Most work in the medieval shipbuilding process was directed to converting logs to planks or timbers, just as in most other large wood construction projects. The methods of assembling and fastening the constructional elements to each other were also hardly specific to shipbuilding, since the use of both iron nails and wooden pegs were common for other building purposes. The special demands which the ship carpenter faced over and above those of others working in wood were accuracy and control, so that they could make the curved shape of the hull symmetrical. Measuring tools and tools for bending and keeping the timbers in place were, therefore, the ones likely to be specific to shipbuilding. Another important demand placed on shipbuilders was to make and keep the hull watertight, even when it would be flexed by the waves and by deliberate or accidental grounding. The solution to this problem was likely to produce trade-specific tools as well. Apart from those special tools, the content of the shipbuilder's tool chest differed very little from that of other carpenters, as far as can be established from the meagre historical and ar-

2. Unger, *The Ship in the Medieval Economy*, p126; M Gurout, *et al*, *Le Navire Genois de Villefranche* (Paris 1990), pp151f.

3. A E Christensen, 'Boat Finds from Bryggen', in *The Bryggen Papers*, Main Series, Vol I (Oslo 1985), pp213ff.

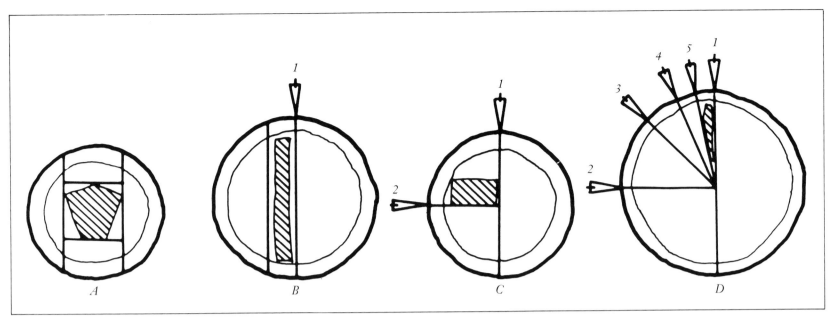

Conversion techniques for elements of typical Viking ships:
A   for keel, stems, frames
B   long and wide planks & stringers
C   beams and stringers
D   cloveboards
After Ole Crumlin-Pedersen. (By courtesy of Richard Unger)

chaeological sources which survive. There were some differences, if not between ship carpenters' and other carpenters' tools, then between the tools of ship carpenters working within different traditions and with different materials.

Along the shores of the Mediterranean, the early medieval shipwright used few tools not used by his Roman predecessor. Even the shapes of the tools varied only slightly from their classical precursors. The most important tool was the one today known as a 'pit-saw'.[4] A framed plank-saw, it was the basic instrument for converting the square-hewn logs of cypress or other softwoods into boards. The tool consisted of a straight blade kept stretched in a rectangular wooden frame, the short ends of which also served as handles. Smaller timbers were sawn with one end resting on the ground and the timber laid over a trestle. To facilitate the sawing of larger timbers, they were placed horizontally by means of a trestle and crutches which could be moved as the sawing pro-

ceeded. The trestle would have had steps which served as a ladder for the top sawyer. For such sawing a handle would be fixed to the frame at the upper end of the saw, and eventually at the lower end as well. The tool had changed little from its Roman form and was to change little throughout the Middle Ages. It probably survived the introduction of water-

powered sawmills in the fourteenth century due to its flexibility. For small-scale production it was easier to bring the saw to the wood than

4. W L Goodman, *The History of Woodworking Tools* (London 1964), pp131f, has pointed out the inaccuracy of this term in a medieval context, as the use of saw-pits seems to be a post-medieval technique.

The framed plank-saw, or pit-saw. The use of saw-pits is not known from the medieval period; instead the timbers were lifted from the ground. The saw could be improved by adding one or two handles, making the working position more comfortable for the top or bottom sawyers. From a mosaic in the Monreale Cathedral, last quarter of the twelfth century.

vice versa. That type of saw was still found in use in Europe in the beginning of this century.[5]

The use of the framed saw in early medieval Europe was restricted to the Mediterranean area. It can hardly be wrong to claim a connection with the use of softwoods for planking in the same region. The softwoods are much easier to cut with a saw than oak, partly because of their structure and partly because of their size. Therefore, the saw did not come into use in northern Europe until the supply of large, high-quality oak trunks had been exhausted. There, framed plank saws begin to appear in pictorial material from the thirteenth century on, although they were probably in use somewhat earlier. The early thirteenth-century cog wreck from Kollerup shows only axe marks on the tangentially split oak planks, while a late thirteenth-century wreck of a small trading ship found in southeastern Denmark is partly built of sawn planks. The major portion of the planking, though, is radially split and hewn with axes.[6] In the Bremen cog from 1380 only sawn planks were used, and analyses of the wood has shown that it was imported from forests 200 kilometres south of the construction site on the river Weser. Not long before the Bremen cog was built, powered sawmills started to be built in western Europe. The oldest known example is mentioned in 1322 in Augsburg, southern Germany. During the fourteenth and fifteenth centuries such mills became more common, but it is not until 1530, for example, that the first evidence of sawmills in Norway appears.[7] Developments in metallurgy may have been equally important in contributing to the change to the use of saws. Early thirteenth-century improvements in iron smelting techniques made it possible to produce cast iron, and thereby steel, by indirect reduction instead of the traditional direct reduction method. This meant that the carbon content could be controlled much more precisely, making it possible to produce the very homogeneous steel necessary for thin flexible blades, as used in large saws.

The Vejby cog from Denmark, almost contemporary to the Bremen cog, was also built exclusively with sawn oak planks. But those planks were made from logs of excellent quality, far better than those of the Bremen find. The sawing technique, then, had become superior to splitting. The Vejby cog was built on the Polish coast, judging from the coins found in the mast step, and is, therefore, an example of one of the important resources which were to be found in the Baltic area: high-quality ship timbers. Because of those

supplies the shipbuilding industry in the region became one of the most important in Europe, building ships and exporting timber even to Mediterranean countries in the fifteenth and sixteenth centuries. However, local timber and older techniques were still in use in small-scale shipbuilding. A small, early fifteenth-century trading vessel found in the Danish town of Århus proved to be built of radially split planks from oaks grown in southern Scandinavia.

Axes and saws

Axes held a very important position in carpentry. They were used for rough work, for felling and preparing the wood for sawing, or converting it into timber. They were also necessary for more delicate tasks such as fitting timbers and planks together. Corresponding to the many tasks, axes had a number of different, specialised forms.[8] Three of those were clearly important to shipbuilding. The cutting axe was used for felling, cutting and cleaving trees. The broad axe was specially designed for hewing the sides of timbers or planks. The hand axe was for the smaller, delicate jobs. The three groups cannot be separated clearly, but their main characteristics can be distinguished. The cutting axe concentrated a heavy weight behind a narrow edge, making it possible to use the axe with a great deal of force without causing damage to the connection between head and shaft. As the construction of the shaft hole was improved by making it more tube-like, the width of the edge was allowed to increase, making the tool more flexible. The broad axe had a long, relatively straight edge ground from one side only. This made it effective for trimming hewn planks or timbers, but it was not a tool for removing large quantities of wood. This was done with the cutting axe. The main characteristic of the last type, the hand axe, was that it was a multipurpose one-handed axe, considerably lighter and meant to be used with less force than the cutting axe. Among the numerous axes found in wrecked medieval ships this is by far the most common. It was the ship carpenter's tool on board.

Although evidence is sparce, all the three types were undoubtedly in use in shipbuilding in Mediterranean Europe during the early and high Middle Ages, as they were in the Roman era. It is not the axes but the saw which is given the prominent position in the few depictions of shipbuilding that are left from the period before 1200. One of the panels from the eleventh-century Salerno Ivories does show a broad axe in use when illustrating the building of the Ark. The shape of the axe is quite sur-

Noah directing the building of the Ark, a scene from the eleventh-century Salerno Ivories. The panel shows a number of the tools used in Mediterranean shipbuilding: the framed plank-saw, the bow-drill and caulking hammer and iron. To the right, a carpenter is working with a broad axe of an unusual shape, perhaps a kind of double axe.

prising, but as the details of the picture in other respects are accurate, it must be regarded as trustworthy. A hammer-like protection of the butt was not unusual on Roman axes, and that might be what is seen here. It might also be an example of an adze axe or a double axe, a tool shown on a twelfth-century mosaic in Palermo.

From early and high medieval northern Europe there is no lack of axe illustrations. One specific type is shown in most shipbuilding scenes, including the Bayeux Tapestry. It is a broad axe, the slender T-shaped axe, which was already common as a tool in seventh-century England.[9] The T-shaped axe is in most cases shown in one specific situation in the iconographic material: in use for smoothing the side of a roughly hewn plank or piece of timber. This was without doubt its main function. The tool is mostly represented on pictures from northern Europe, but there are Mediterranean examples, such as the twelfth-century

5. W L Goodman, *History of Woodworking Tools*, p137.

6. Per Kohrtz Andersen, *Kollerupkoggen* (Thisted 1983), p29; J Bill, 'Gedesbyskibet. Middelalderlig skude-og faergefart fra Falster', *Nationalmuseets Arbejdsmark* (Copenhagen 1991), p191.

7. F van Tyghem, *Op en Om De Middeleeuwse Bouwwerf* (Brussels 1966), pp26ff.

8. F van Tyghem, *Op en Om De Middeleeuwse Bouwwerf*, pp3f.

9. D W Wilson, 'Anglo-Saxon Carpenters' Tools,' In M Claus, W Haarnagel and K Raddatz (eds), *Studien zur europäischen Vor-und Frühgerschichter* (Neumünste 1968), pp144f.

Above: A shipbuilding scene from the famous late eleventh-century Bayeux Tapestry. Trees are felled with cutting axes, while the T-shaped broad axe is used for shaping the planks. In the tapestry, the broad axe is used as a sign of the shipbuilder. In a preceding scene, it is shown in the hands of the person who is given the order by William to build the invasion fleet. Here it is in the hands of a man directing the work from inside one of the ships. In the upper vessel, a breast-auger is in use, while a hand axe and another tool are in use in the other one. (By courtesy of Basil Greenhill)

Below: Broad axes similar to those of modern days appear from the early sixteenth century onwards. Woodcut by H Sebald Beham.

depictions from Gerona, Spain. The general tendency is for pictures of the tool to originate from areas where oak was used for planking.

Over time, the axe changed its form. The curved top end of the blade disappeared and the blade grew broader, but shortly after 1400 the type seems to have disappeared (quite rapidly), being replaced by less T-shaped axe types with shorter edges. This happened at about the same time as the framed plank saw took over, supplanting splitting techniques and thereby reducing the amount of smoothing

work for the axe. The changed character of the work to be done with the broad axe continued to alter its design. As the work was now tougher, concentrated on square-hewing timbers, the tool grew heavier, the edge shorter and the shaft hole longer and more tube-like. In the fourteenth century the broad axe reached a distinct 'bearded' shape, well on its way to achieving the final design of the broad axe which was in use from the sixteenth century onwards.

Over time the saw replaced the axe in other

until the late fourteenth century that different types of saws become a common motif in the pictorial material. By that date it is the hand saw which dominates, and such saws were then larger, often intended for two-handed use. The explanation might be technological, reflecting metallurgical improvements. The advantage of larger hand saws was that they were more efficient: with them larger logs could be cut, the dimensions of the wood no longer being restricted by the size of the frame containing the saw blade.

Another saw type, the cross-cut two-man saw, was also dependent on the ability to make long blades strong enough to be used without a wooden frame. This saw appears as a carpenter's tool from the fourteenth century onwards.[13] It was probably based on the same developments in metallurgy that permitted the increasing size of the hand saw. The introduction of effective cutting saws for timbers of large dimensions meant savings in wood and time, as the saw produces little waste and also produces a regular finish immediately on the cutting surface. The savings were substantial in timber and plank production, but perhaps of less importance in the subsequent woodworking procedures in shipbuilding.

10. Large Viking Age saws are rare. The 24in (61cm) long hand saw from the late Viking Age Mästermyr find is the best example, but it may well have been used for other purposes such as cutting bone and antler. G Arwidsson, *The Mästermyr Find* (Stockholm 1983), p13.

11. Concerning the Scandinavian material, see O Crumlin-Pedersen, 'Wood Technology and Forest Resources in the light of Medieval Shipfinds', in C Villain-Gandossi *et al* (eds), *Medieval Ships and the Birth of Technological Societies*, Vol I (Malta 1989), p31. Non-Scandinavian vessels where tool marks have been recorded are the well-preserved tenth-century vessel found at Graveney, Kent, England, and the cog from about 1200 excavated at Kollerup in Denmark. Neither of those showed any trace of saws used during the construction. V Fenwick, *The Graveney Boat* (Oxford 1978), p101; Kohrtz Andersen, *Kollerupkoggen*, p29.

12. The oldest example found is an illustration of Noah in the thirteenth-century Oxford Psalter. The work is probably from the Low Countries. R W Unger, *The Art of Medieval Technology: Images of Noah the Shipbuilder* (New Brunswick, New Jersey 1991), p71 and Fig 20.

13. Tyghem, *Op en Om De Middeleeuwse Bouwwerf*, Fig 144; Goodman, *The History of Woodworking Tools*, Fig 146; Bill, 'Gedesbyskibet . . .', Fig 4.

fields as well. The small hand saw, with a straight blade and a tongue for the handle in one end, was used all over Europe as well as in Viking Age Scandinavia.[10] There are no traces that it was used in northern European shipbuilding,[11] and it was undoubtedly too small for such heavy tasks as cutting oak planks and timbers. The frame saw, which was not as dependent on the quality of the steel, was already in use in Roman times, just like the hand saw, and remained in use in the Mediterranean world. From the thirteenth century onwards the frame saw appears in depictions of shipbuilding from northern Europe,[12] but it is not

Finishing tools

Another tool used on planks and timbers was the adze. The adze is characterised by having a cutting edge at right angles to the handle, but it can have a number of different designs. Used with a long shaft, the tool is comparable to the broad axe as it is well suited to dressing the surfaces of planks and timbers. There are no signs of the adze being used for this purpose in northern European shipbuilding in the early medieval period, although the tool is known in several variations from Saxon, Scandinavian and east European finds. The situation was different in the Mediterranean world, where the adze was already used by Egyptian ship carpenters and where it remained in use in shipbuilding throughout history. The explanation may be functional. The adze has one important quality which the broad axe lacks: the tool can be used on massive timber structures, like house walls and ships' sides, in situations where it is difficult or impossible to use the broad axe. In shipbuilding the adze was connected with the carvel, or flush-skin, tradition. Typically, when the adze appears in northern European depictions of shipbuilding it is together with carvel-built ships, and in the triangular Medi-

Seventeenth-century boatbuilding. The vessel is built shell-first with use of both boatbuilders' clamps and the 'knaps', pieces of wood nailed to the planking to keep it in place. From A C Rålamb, Skeps Byggerij eller Adelig öfnings Tionde Tome *(1691).*

terranean variant, not in the north European T-shaped one. The tool became almost synonymous with shipbuilding and it is only in the easternmost regions of Europe that the long-shafted adze is still in use outside this trade today.

The plane was mostly for finer carpentry and never held any prominent position in medieval shipbuilding. The surface finish of planks and other elements was generally left as produced by the saw or broad axe. Planes were necessary for smoothing the edges of the planks in carvel-built ships, either to make them tight or to provide the correct, narrow notch for the subsequent caulking. In clinker-built ships the overlapping parts of the planking and grooves for caulking materials could be planed. Only pine planking seems to have been planed on the open surfaces.

While continental planes were successors to the Roman types, very much like those still used today, some of the planes from northern Scandinavia were of a completely different design. A cutting edge followed one of the long sides of the blade and the two tongues were at right angles to the surface. The steel was mounted in a wooden handle, which also acted as a sole. The tool was very useful when working fresh softwood, and what appear to be traces from a plane can be seen on the pine planking from the mid eleventh-century, probably Norwegian, large cargo vessel found at Skuldelev in Denmark.[14] The tool can be

used to clear surfaces of axe marks and irregularities, but it does not provide flatness as a true plane does. It was smoothness, rather than flatness, that was the desired quality of split planks.

Types of drill

The task of making holes was important in shipbuilding, and many different solutions to this were found. The drill bits themselves could have different shapes, mainly spoon-shaped or spiral, and force and pressure could be provided in different ways. The bow drill was used for small holes, while the auger was used for holes of any size. Both of these tools were known all over Europe throughout the Middle Ages. The breast auger, where the carpenter used his own weight to press the spoon-shaped tip into the wood, is generally considered a ship carpenter's innovation from the tenth or eleventh century. It eased the task of drilling holes in oak timbers and other hardwoods.[15] Although there is no evidence yet, the tool might have had a longer history in the North. In clinker-built ships large drilled holes are found where wooden treenails are used to

14. O Olsen and O Crumlin-Pedersen, 'The Skuldelev Ships (II)', *Acta Archaeologica* 38 (Copenhagen 1967), p161.

15. R W Unger, *Dutch Shipbuilding Before 1800* (Assen 1978), p61; Goodman, *The History of Woodworking Tools* p172.

Fifteenth-century Venetian oar-makers at work. Both small hand axes (left) and planes (right) are being used to finish the looms. This is a workshop trade sign and may have been hung outside the relevant department of the Arsenale.

fasten the ribs to the external planks. This technique of fastening the frames emerged at the latest in the seventh century in Anglo-Saxon and Scandinavian boatbuilding, in societies without a pictorial tradition which might show evidence of the tool.[16]

Another important development was the introduction of the brace in the early fifteenth century.[17] The tool improved efficiency as it could be rotated continuously without shifting hands. Its use was restricted to smaller holes, as the C-shaped crank-handle was not well suited to take large pressures. The invention must have proved important in clinker construction, where thousands of holes were made to take the rivets.

Trade-specific tools

Few tools are really specific to shipbuilding, but there were two that were essential to certain techniques of the trade. Furthermore, neither has left much evidence or is particularly striking, so both are seldom recognised for what they were and what they were used for, either archaeologically or in contemporary pictures.

Clinker building is connected with a 'shell-first' technique where the hull is modelled by very carefully controlling the angle of the over-

lapping parts of the planks. Internal timbers are inserted only after the shape of the ship has been created by the planking. Therefore, it was essential to be able to fix the planks firmly, but temporarily, to the growing shell to make measurements and corrections. This was done with a simple but ingenious tool: a pair of wooden tongs held together by a cross-piece and designed to grip over the broad planks used in shipbuilding. The tension pressing the planks together was achieved by a wedge hammered in between the two tongs. The oldest known illustration is from the late seventeenth century, but archaeological examples are known from medieval finds at Gdansk in Poland and Bergen in Norway.[18] The boatbuilder's clamp is still in use today in a slightly modernised form, but its importance declined with the general decline of clinker building.

The use of caulking irons and mallets is dependent on the presence of a substantial frame system and sturdy planking capable of absorbing the force of having the caulking hammered into the notches between the planks. Thus it is closely connected with the carvel technique, especially the skeleton-first variant which was used during the Middle Ages. In the clinker technique, any systematic attempt to caulk the ship after building by use of caulking irons would result in damage to the planking. Therefore, other techniques and tools were applied.

Probable caulking irons, predating the age of skeleton-built ships, have been found, for example at Pompeii and in the seventh-century

wreck at Yassi Ada.[19] The tool from Yassi Ada has a very thin blade compared with later caulking irons, but the massive hull construction of the vessel surely would be well suited to the use of a lighter caulking tool, which supports the interpretation of the use of the object. The change to the faster and cruder skeleton building technique must have increased the importance of caulking and promoted the development of tools for this purpose. In a thirteenth-century quatrefoil in Sainte Chapelle, Paris, the caulking process is shown in detail. The ship carpenter is hammering the twined caulking material into the notches between the heavily fastened planks.

While the shell-first technique in the North was originally used in clinker-built vessels, as well as in flush-planked cogs, another method to achieve the same flexibility was necessary. The tool developed was simple: a piece of wood, a 'knap' or clamp, was simply fitted and nailed to the outside of the planking, holding it together until the internal frames were in-

16. Ship finds with such wooden nails are Sutton Hoo and the Grestedbro wreck from southwestern Jutland. O Crumlin-Pedersen, 'The Grestedbro Ship', *Acta Archaelogica* 39 (Copenhagen 1968).

17. Goodman, *The History of Woodworking Tools*, p175; Tyghem, *Op en Om De Middeleeuwse Bouwwerf*, p34.

18. A C Rålamb, *Skeps Byggerij* (1691; facsimile report Stockholm 1943); Christensen, 'Boat Finds from Bryggen', p170ff.

19. G F Bass and F H van Doorninck, Jr, *Yassi Ada: A Seventh-century Byzantine Shipwreck*, Vol I (College Station, Texas 1982).

serted. Although the technology is well known from seventeenth-century Holland, it has also been found on the late fourteenth-century Vejby cog.[20]

Conclusions

Ship carpentry in the Middle Ages left a number of traditions and tools that have survived into modern times. Some of them are highly characteristic of shipbuilding, representing specific responses to constructional problems,

while others do not differ from what is found in other carpenters' trades. The strenuous conditions which ships were built to survive, combined with the high commercial risks of their employment, makes it likely that ship carpenters were quick to utilise technological progress in order to improve the quality of their work while making no concessions to safety. The sparse evidence for the tools and technology of the medieval shipwright seems to point to a close connection between tools used and wood species utilised. It is likely, therefore, that the scanty evidence which has survived illustrates the development very well. The use of oak in the North and softwoods in the South made the use of different tools and technologies necessary through most of the Middle

Ages. It was not until the fourteenth century, when metallurgy made it possible to produce saws capable of sawing hardwoods effectively, that those varieties could be used in the same way and to the same extent as softwoods. Those improvements broke down the border established by the limited width and thickness of radially split planks and made possible, over the longer term, the conversion from shell to skeleton construction in northern Europe.

Jan Bill

20. Unger, *Dutch Shipbuilding before 1800*, pp156f; concerning the Vejby cog, the information was kindly supplied by the archaeologist in charge of the excavation, O Crumlin-Pedersen of The Danish National Museum.

A selection of the tools carried by a late sixteenth-century ship's carpenter. These were recovered from Novaya Zemlya, and are remnants from Willem Barentsz's ill-fated expedition to find a northeast passage, 1596–97. (Rijksmuseum, by courtesy of Richard Unger)

11

Treatises on Shipbuilding Before 1650

THROUGHOUT the Middle Ages shipbuilding was a craft learned through apprenticeship, transmitted from one generation to the next orally and by example in the workplace. The master shipwright might, or might not, have been literate, but treatises on shipbuilding did not exist. Only in the fifteenth century did the principles of ship design and construction begin to be committed to paper. This is quite likely the result of a concatenation of influences in both the shipbuilding community and society at large.

For millennia shipwrights in the Mediterranean basin had built up their hulls by joining each plank to the next with strong mortise and tenon joints. Only as the hull grew were frames added to reinforce it. The lines of traditional hulls were created as the vessel took shape. By the end of the first millenium of the Christian era, through slow evolution, the practice of first erecting frames on the keel, then nailing on planks, arose.[1] The newer building techniques were, in some respects, cruder in manufacture, but they were more sophisticated in concept. They required the shipwright to visualise and predict accurately the lines of the hull before construction. It was no longer a simple matter to follow the lines by eye as the hull developed. This necessity to predict lines before construction is fundamental to the idea of design. Still, so long as the basic designs did not change, or changed only very slowly, they could be passed on by apprenticeship methods from one generation of shipwrights to another.

Beginning around 1300 with the introduction of the cog into the Mediterranean, a vigorous cross-fertilisation of the northern and southern shipbuilding traditions began to pro-duce rapid changes in ship design and a proliferation of types. At the same time more widespread literacy led to the habit of writing down details of technical subjects in works ranging from merchants' handbooks to architectural treatises. Therefore, it is not surprising that the art of shipbuilding came to be recorded in a growing number of notebooks, handbooks, and treatises.

Written sources before the treatise

For the student of maritime history, written treatises are invaluable. Cold northern waters have preserved several wrecks so that marine archaeology has provided much material for historians of the northern tradition. In the Mediterranean, the shipworm has left little trace of wooden vessels. Pottery amphorae that were for centuries the standard shipping container for a variety of goods overlaid and protected at least portions of ancient wrecks there but, as wooden barrels replaced amphorae, the cargo became as vulnerable as the hull. From

1. Richard Steffy, 'The Mediterranean Shell to Skeleton Transition: A Northwest European Parallel?' in *Carvel Construction Technique: Skeleton-first, Shell-first*, Fifth International Symposium on Boat and Ship Archaeology, Amsterdam 1988, edited by Reinder Reinders and Kees Paul (Oxford 1991), pp1–9.

A page from the mid fifteenth-century treatise by Zorzi da Modon, known as Timbotta, which includes a drawing of a Venetian great galley. Although not a properly scaled technical drawing as understood from the eighteenth century onwards, the basic proportions are credible. BL Cotton, Titus A XXVI, f48v. (British Library)

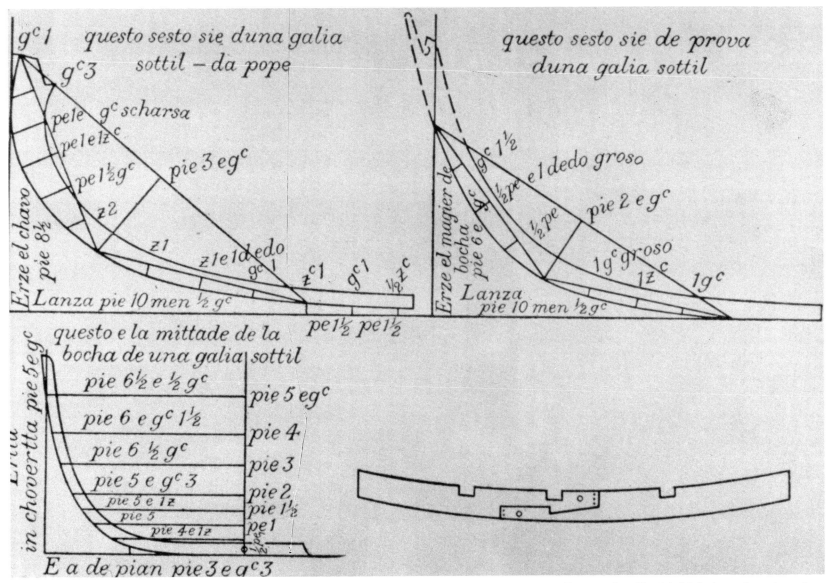

The figure carries the following inscriptions:

- *questo sesto siẹ duna galia sottil – da pope* (g^c 1, g^c 3, pele g^c scharsa, pele 1 z^c, pe 1½ g^c, pie 3 e g^c, z 2, Erze el chavo pie 8½, z 1, z 1 e 1 dedo g^c 1, z^c 1, g^c 1, ½ z^c, Lanza pie 10 men ½ g^c, pe 1½ pe 1½)
- *questo sesto sie de prova duna galia sottil* (g^c 1½, e 1 dedo groso, g^c 6, ½ pe, ½ pe, pie 2 e g^c, Erze el magier de bocha pie 6 e ½, 1 g^c groso, 1 z^c, 1 g^c, Lanza pie 10 men ½ g^c)
- *questo e la mittade de la bocha de una galia sottil* (Lrça in chovertta pie 5 e g^c, pie 6½ e ½ g^c, pie 5 e g^c, pie 6 e g^c 1½, pie 4, pie 6 ½ g^c, pie 3, pie 5 e g^c 3, pie 2, pie 5 e 1 z, pie 1½, pie 5, pie 1, pie 4 e 1 z, pe 1, E a de pian pie 3 e g^c 3)

Diagram from Zorzi da Modon's treatise, redrawn by Richard Unger, showing the method of forming the stern, stem and midships section of a galia sottil, or light galley. (By courtesy of Richard Unger)

roughly the tenth century onwards there are very few wrecks to supply information about the design and building techniques of southern shipwrights. Written works on marine design help to fill some of the gaps in knowledge of early ships. More importantly, written treatises reveal something of the conceptual foundations of design. For that reason they are valuable sources even where archaeological remains are available.

Fortunately written sources for the dimensions of medieval Mediterranean ships are not entirely lacking, at least not from about the thirteenth century; but these late medieval sources do not reveal much about ship design principles. They are transportation contracts or law codes that aim to ensure minimum carrying capacity or safety even though some charters specified hold dimensions and equipment for ships that were to be built for special purposes. From these laws and contracts it is often possible to arrive at the gross dimensions

of the ships – depth of hold, beam, length, number of masts, etc – but teasing out more detail is a very speculative business indeed.

Nonetheless, in these laws and contracts are the conceptual roots of the later treatises on shipbuilding. Mediterranean culture was, in general, more literate than that of the North. Still, the habit of relying on the written word came slowly even there. For example, the written contract was originally nothing more than an *aide mémoire* for witnesses in the event of litigation, but by the thirteenth century it was proof in itself of the existence of an agreement. The idea of relying on a contract to establish the interior dimensions of the hold of a ship not present, and in some cases not yet built, is an important step toward the notion of communicating design ideas by means of writing. The most famous contract of this type is the one negotiated in 1268 between the French king, Louis IX, and the city of Genoa, for ships to transport crusaders and their horses.[2] Regu-

lation of the dimensions of galleys at both Venice and Genoa in the fourteenth century was even more directly related to design since the laws were intended to preserve the lines of vessels that had proven successful as warships. In 1344 the Genoese 'Office of the Crimea' (*Officium Gazarie*) approved a change in the profile of the midship frame of light galleys after examining a prototype vessel. Literacy and the rapid evolution of ship design were combining to establish the habit of thinking of the dimensions of vessels in terms of written descriptions and dimensions.

Early shipbuilding treatises are often almost

2. See John E Dotson, 'Jal's *Nef X* and Genoese Naval Architecture in the 13th Century', *The Mariner's Mirror*, 59 (1973), pp161–70.

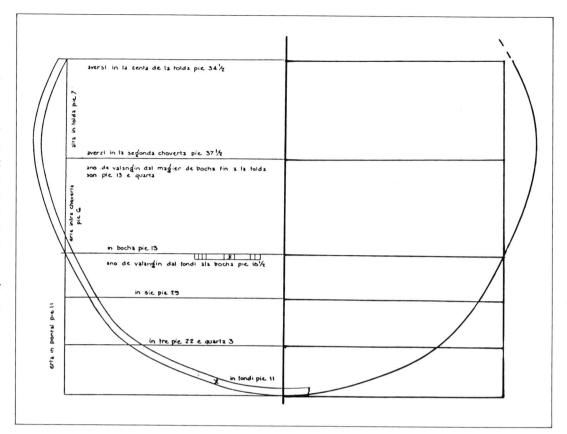

The formation of the midship bend of a large Venetian merchantman, from the mid sixteenth-century 'Instructione sul modo di fabricare galere', by Pre Theodoro de Nicolò, one of the master shipwrights of the Arsenale. After F C Lane 'Venetian Naval Architecture about 1550', The Mariner's Mirror 20 (1934).

as difficult to interpret as the contracts and law codes. In both cases the problem is the writer's assumption that the reader commands what was at the time, but no longer is, common knowledge. These treatises were not written to explain the process of ship design to novices, not even fifteenth-century novices. They were intended to communicate with other experienced shipbuilders, or to be a personal reference for the writer himself. They are often found as a part of more general collections of knowledge, sometimes even unrelated to the sea. Thus the mid fifteenth-century Venetian treatise by Zorzi da Modon contains material relating to a variety of subjects ranging from music to medicine as well as to shipbuilding.

Italian manuscript treatises

The first written treatises on shipbuilding and design were Venetian: Zorzi da Modon's treatise as well as the *Fabrica di galere*, the *Ragioni antique spettanti all'arte del mare et fabriche de vasselli*, and the *Arte di far vasselli*.[3] All of these date from the middle to the late fifteenth century and all appear to have some relation to a now vanished original. This suggests that there may have been an active network exchanging written information on maritime matters. These works, taken together, reveal a great deal about ship design in the fifteenth-century shipyards of Venice.

Surprisingly, some of the best builders of galleys at the Venetian Arsenal were Greeks. The most famous of these Greek masters was Theodoro Baxon (or Bassanus), who worked in the Arsenal in the late fourteenth and early fifteenth century and died around 1407. The success of his designs appears to have been a result of his ability to make galleys that were stronger than most, but just as fast – valuable characteristics in a warship. The Venetian Senate was so impressed by his galleys that they offered him lifetime employment at an extraordinary salary. So that his 'secrets' would not die with him, they ordered several specimens of his galleys to be preserved as models, and had their measurements taken to guide other builders. Alvise Chiggiato, a Venetian marine engineer who has written on historical maritime technology, suggests that this attempt to preserve Baxon's 'secrets' may mark the real beginnings

of the Venetian tradition of written treatises on shipbuilding.[4]

For a century and a half – since the publication of Auguste Jal's 'Mémoire No 5' in 1840 – scholars have been aware of the Venetian manuals and have been engaged in trying to understand them. These works describe a system of design that did not rely on plans, but on geometrical and proportional relationships based on a small number of fundamental measurements – building by *sesto e partixon* as the phrasing of the time had it.

In the *sesto e partixon* system, builders conceived of the hull as consisting of three parts: the largest, central part, and two smaller parts at each end where the line of the hull begins to

A diagram showing the working of the mezzaluna, *to produce properly faired 'narrowing lines'. From Furttenbach's* Architectura Navalis *of 1629, but the technique was in use from at least the fifteenth century.*

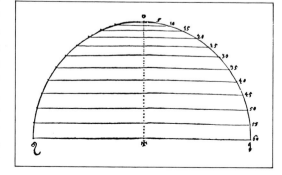

narrow rapidly to the stem and stern. The frames that marked the transitions between these 'blocks' were known as *chavi de sesto* ('heads of design') in the *Ragioni antique*. These frames, along with the midship frame, the keel, and the stem- and sternposts, provided the basic reference points for the development of the lines of the hull. One of the basic elements of this design system was known in Venice as 'partixon', literally 'a division'. There are many operations in shipbuilding that require smoothly diminishing measurements. The most obvious of these is the need to decrease the width of the frames toward the bow and stern. To produce a smooth curve reducing the floor of the vessel from the midship frame to the *chavi de sesto*, a semicircle (variously called a *mezzo tondo*, a *mezzo redondo*, or a *mezzaluna*) with a diameter equal to the breadth of the

3. Zorzi da Modon's treatise was published in large part by R C Anderson in *The Mariner's Mirror* 11 (1925), where Zorzi da Modon is identified as Giorgio Timbotta. The *Fabrica di galere* is in Florence, Biblioteca Nazionale Centrale, ms Magliabecchiano, XIX. 7. *Ragioni antique spettanti all'arte del mare et fabriche de vasselli* has been published by G Bonfiglio Dosio (ed) (Venice 1987). *Arte di far vasselli* is in Vienna, Oesterreiche Nationalbibliothek, Foscarini collection, no 477, Cod CCCXVIII.

4. Alvise Chiggiato, 'Le "Ragioni antique" dell'architettura navale', in Giorgetta Bonfiglio Dosio, *et al*, *Ragioni antique spettanti all'arte del mare et fabriche de vasselli* (Venice 1987), plxviii.

floor amidships was divided into equal parts along its arc; then lines parallel to the diameter joined opposite pairs of points along the arc. The lengths of these parallel lines diminished in the desired way. The semicircle that produced this curve for the floor was the *partixon de fondi*; a similar technique was used to reduce the breadth of the frames at deck level, and to develop the slight rise in the keel toward either end before the stem and stern were joined, as well as other smooth curves. Each of these had its own *partixon*, using a *mezzaluna* based on a different measurement. Using other proportional operations of this kind, the shipwright could extrapolate from a few basic measurements all the necessary lines to construct a hull.

From these measurements the lines of a galley could be realised with only a few simple devices such as curves and measuring sticks. This is consistent with medieval design principles in other areas, such as architecture. No one of the manuals provides the key to understanding the way the design of a ship progressed according to these principles, but by gleaning information from a number of them it is now possible to form a fairly clear idea of the system in use in the fifteenth century, and probably even earlier.

According to Chiggiato all that was required to define fully the lines of a vessel were the maximum dimensions and, at most, some twenty other measurements. From this brief, non-graphical description – there were no drawings or plans – the lines of the hull can be completely developed provided the reader knows the necessary proportional relations. In fact, Chiggiato maintains, the system was not only self-correcting – errors would produce impossible results – but more accurate than a modern 1:20 drawing.[5] He believes that the key to understanding these early treatises has been found in the *Ragioni antique*, which alone records the measurements of actual vessels. By using the measurements found in the *Ragioni antique* to produce profile plans of vessels, it is possible to check one's understanding of the process. In this way Chiggiato has produced very convincing lines of a galley whose dimensions were recorded in the *Ragioni antique*. Regarded in this light, the drawings found in several early treatises should not be considered primitive plans, but merely illustrative of the

The proportions of a large Venetian sailing ship of about 1550, reconstructed by F C Lane from the 'Instructione' of de Nicolò. The keel length was 100ft Venetian (34.7m), the maximum breadth 37½ft (13m). After F C Lane, 'Venetian Naval Architecture about 1550', The Mariner's Mirror 20 (1934).

operations required to produce lines from given measurements. When needed for actual construction of a galley, the lines would have been developed by direct measurement in the shipyard, without reference to drawings.

These early Venetian treatises were conservative in their aim. They preserved design techniques that had been used, conceivably, for generations, and, if Chiggiato is correct, they originally preserved the lines of certain existing vessels so that they could be reproduced. Nonetheless, by their nature they led in the direction of a more revolutionary way of thinking about the design of ships. Italian shipwrights were widely regarded as the most accomplished and knowledgeable in fifteenth-century Europe, and the ships they created were the most advanced types in use. When other government – or private – shipyards, especially outside Italy, wanted the best of the new designs built, the most efficient course was to hire expert Italian shipwrights. These men brought with them the idea, the habit even, of written treatises that recorded the detailed elements of ship design. Perhaps, since they would be directing foreign work-gangs more or less unfamiliar with the designs that were to be realised, written treatises were indispensable to the success of these ventures. If the Venetian Arsenal found it advisable to preserve the lines of successful vessels in written form within the very system, and among the workers who had built those vessels, then written reference works would have made the transfer of design to workers whose experience was in a different tradition much more efficient. This is not to

suggest that the sawyers, carpenters, riggers, sailmakers, and other specialist labourers who built the ships learned to do so by reading the Italian treatises. If they could have done so, it would not have been necessary to hire Italian master shipwrights. The treatises served as *aides mémoires*, and helped conceptual clarification for the masters themselves while their drawings may have facilitated communication of design ideas to the work force. Written treatises diffused through the shipyards of Europe, based upon the Italian example.

The idea of written treatises may have originated in the Venetian state's desire to preserve, and to propagate among its other masters, the lines of certain successful warships, but very soon the utility of the written treatise was applied to merchant vessels as well. The fifteenth century was a period of rapid development for sailing ships. The need to systematise the innovations of the period for ready reference was as pressing as the need to preserve the lines of successful galleys. Again, Venice was in the forefront of maritime development. Galleys had won the Serenissima a preponderant place in Mediterranean commerce, but relatively handy sailing ships able to carry large numbers of cannon could challenge the galley in many circumstances. The carrack, as this new vessel was commonly called, reached its highest level of development in Venetian shipyards. The mid fifteenth-century work of Zorzi da Modon gives dimensions for a variety of ships ranging

5. Alvise Chiggiato, 'Le "Ragioni antique" dell'architettura navale', plix.

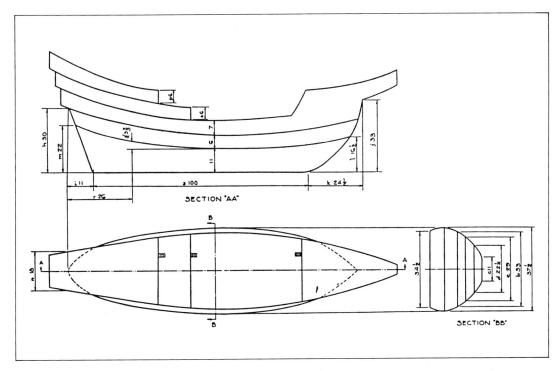

in capacity from 200 *botte* to 1000 *botte*.[6] The process for developing the lines of a sailing ship was essentially the same as that for a galley. Zorzi da Modon and other writers of early treatises refer to the use of the *mezza redondo* as well as other proportional instruments for developing the lines of ships. However, they provide even less detailed information than for galleys.[7] As well as for the hull, Zorzi da Modon gave directions on rigging and sailmaking. It is in the instructions on rigging that the importance of proportion based on the ship's beam is especially clear when he says, 'Note that nobody can rig any ship or lateener if first the man does not know the measurements of the ship, for a ship is better rigged by seeing the measurement of her beam.'[8] Again, it appears that the beam measurement, or the half-beam, is the foundation for the proportional system. In the sixteenth century the growing importance of oceanic trade and exploration, for which galleys were completely unsuited, made sailing ships increasingly the central subject of shipbuilding treatises.

Polemical and scholarly works

By the late sixteenth century the idea of written treatises was so widespread that they quickly developed from a master shipwright's private reference into an accepted method for publicising current practices. There is considerable difference in spirit between the manuscript Italian works on shipbuilding and the published works that began to appear at the end of the sixteenth century. The Italian manuscripts are notebooks, rough and often highly technical, while the published works are more erudite and, it seems, directed at a wider audience. The influence of humanistic scholarship is evident in these late sixteenth- and seventeenth-century printed works. In fact, the first printed books to deal with ship construction were antiquarian humanists' studies concerned with the ships of classical antiquity. Around 1450 Leon Battista Alberti wrote a work entitled *Navis*, which no longer exists, but which dealt with the art of design as applied to ships as his other works on sculpture, painting, and architecture did in those fields. At least one humanist, Vettor Fausto (died 1546), became actively engaged in the building of galleys in the Venetian Arsenal. He was responsible for the building of a quinquireme galley, rowed *alla sensile*, that was launched in 1529.[9] Successful in performance trials, the quinquireme *alla sensile* did not become a standard type. It did, however, establish Fausto's reputation as a designer of galleys. Though he claimed that his quinquireme was based on ancient models, it was a logical extension of the trireme light galley that had been the naval standard since the early fourteenth century. If he had a secret it was not in any revival of ancient designs but in his mathematical and mechanical training that allowed him to apply a theoretical understanding of levers to problems of rowing systems. He continued to work in the Arsenal into the 1540s. Unlike the usual *proti* (or foremen) of the Arsenal, Fausto seems to have worked as a naval architect: he designed galleys but did not work with his own hands to realise his designs. Unfortunately, he left no treatises, and only secondhand reports of his design activities survive. This separation between an educated, theoretically grounded architect and labourers who actually built the design did not immediately influence subsequent practice at Venice or elsewhere. Nonetheless, in 1593, seeking to gain more speed in the large *galeazze* rowed *a scaloccio* that were becoming a powerful element of the fleet, the Venetians turned to none other than Galileo Galilei for an analysis of the size of oars and their placement that would best suit these larger vessels. The theoretical and mathematical training of humanist education was beginning to make itself felt in naval architecture as in other fields of design. Before 1650 only a half-dozen or so works on shipbuilding of a practical nature were published. To a greater or lesser extent humanist influence is evident in all of them.

At the end of the sixteenth century, Baldissera Drachio Quinzio, who had served in the Venetian navy and Arsenal since mid century, wrote on the ideal galley. Drachio, in a

6. The *botta*, etymologically related to the English 'butt', was used to express the capacity of ships in the same way as the English 'ton', also originally a wine cask. The *Ragioni antique* explains that to find the capacity of any round ship in *botte*, one should multiply the depth in hold by the beam (both measurements in *pie*, or Venetian feet, approximately 34.8cm or 1.1 English feet) by the length of keel (given in *passi*, the Venetian pace of five feet, approximately 173.8cm or about 5.5 English feet) and divide the product by six. (*Ragioni*, p97.) When this formula is applied to the ships' dimensions given in the work of Zorzi da Modon, it yields larger estimates than he gives. The *Fabrica di galere* gives the formula keel × beam × depth divided by 30 (all measurements in Venetian feet) and yields the capacity of the ship in *botte*. A more detailed method of determining capacity was used by the Venetian government and is described in the *Capitolare dei Consoli dei Mercanti*. There are two copies of the *Capitolare*. One is in the Archivio di Stato di Venezia, Archivi dei Mercanti, busta 1, and probably dates from the beginning of the sixteenth century. The other is found in the Museo Civico Correr, Rep. Commissioni, 331, and dates from the end of that century. The method described involved using a measuring cord to determine the length of the ship and barrel hoops that were used to measure available space at several places in the hold. Essentially the barrel hoops were used to determine the number of *botte* that could be stacked in the hold at predetermined points and the length provided a multiplier to complete the estimate. See F C Lane, *Navires et constructeurs à Venise pendant la Renaissance* (Paris 1965), pp239ff for a more detailed discussion of this problem. It is especially evident from this last method

that the focus is on the actual carrying capacity of the ship in terms of the volume of its hold. Lane estimated the volume occupied by a *botta* to be around 25.5 to 29.4 cubic feet English, or 714 to 821 litres.

7. A Chiggiato has extended and revised his study based on the *Ragione antique* to examine many other sources. He shows how, with some minor modifications the same system was used to describe the lines of a wide variety of vessels. See: Alvise Chiggiato, 'Contenuti delle architetture navali antiche', *Rivista dell'Ateneo Veneto* (1991), pp141—211.

8. R C Anderson, 'Italian Naval Architecture about 1445', *The Mariner's Mirror* 11 (1925), p155.

9. Medieval galleys were rowed by oarsmen who, sitting several men to a bench, each pulled an individual oar. This system came to be known as rowing *alla sensile* ('by small [oars]'). From about 1300 to the middle of the sixteenth century the most common light galleys in use by the Italian maritime cities were triremes rowed by three men on each bench pulling three oars. Each of these galleys would have had twenty-five to thirty benches on a side. Each bench was angled with its inboard end toward the stern to allow room for the oars to be pulled through their stroke without fouling one another. Earlier, the usual galley had been a bireme with two men to a bench. Adding a third man to each bench had increased the available power by fifty per cent and had allowed the building of stronger, more seaworthy galleys that were just as fast as their predecessors. The problem of increasing power by adding rowers beyond a practical maximum of three was a difficult one. Each additional man added proportionately less power. Four men are only

twenty-five per cent more powerful than three, and so with diminishing returns for each additional man. But even more important were the problems of leverage and oar weight involved in using increasingly long oars. (See John Coates 'The Naval Architecture of European Oared Ships', Paper No 9 given at the meeting of The Royal Institution of Naval Architects held on 30 April 1993 forthcoming in the *Transactions of the Royal Institution of Naval Architects*, for an informed and detailed discussion of the problem of rowing galleys.) Fausto seems to have been able to solve that problem through his mathematical and theoretical understanding of levers, but his quinquireme galley, with five men to a bench, apparently had other problems. It was larger than the standard triremes, but more expensive to build and operate, and while it was as fast as the trireme, it was no faster. During its first operational cruise many of the crew sickened and died from exposure and overcrowding (Lane, *Navires et Constructeurs*, pp60–62). Ultimately the solution to building larger galleys that could carry heavier artillery was along different lines. Four or five, or even more, men could, it was discovered, pull at one large sweep instead of on individual oars. This had the further advantage that only the inboard man who set the rhythm needed to be a trained oarsman, the others merely provided muscle. The huge oar used was too large in diameter to be grasped directly so a ladder-shaped wooden piece was fastened to it to provide a grip for the rowers. The etymology is uncertain, but it was from that ladder-like grip, from the ranks of rowers on each oar, or from the step that the rowers used in the rising and falling stroke to pull the large oar that this style of rowing came to be known as *a scaloccio* (ladder, or rank, style).

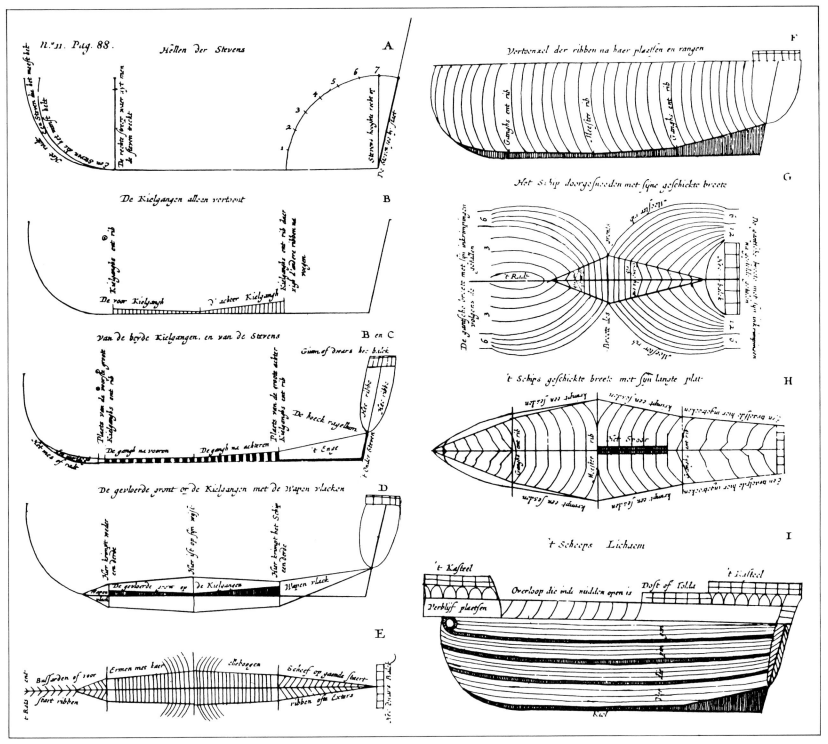

Diagrams by the Portuguese Fernando de Oliveira from his Livra da fábrica das Naos *of the mid sixteenth century, as published by Witsen in his* Scheepsbouw *of 1671. They reveal an early attempt to depict the shape of a hull by objective graphical means, so that an intending builder could obtain enough guidance to interpret the designer's wishes accurately.*

manuscript work known as the *Visione del Drachio*, told how in a dream on 21 December 1593 he found himself in the Arsenal. Francesco Bressan, the *proto* who had been his teacher, came to him and revealed the secrets of the ideal galley.[10] Bressan had been the rival of Vettor Fausto in the Arsenal, representing the more conservative craft traditions of building, suspicious of the educated humanist. Drachio, certainly no humanist, nonetheless appreciated the successes of learned design, even while regarding Fausto's theoretical grounding with a mixture of awe and superstition. He proposed that all galleys should be made to a single design determined by the *proto*, rather than allowing each master to build according to his own ideas. But that design would be decided by a kind of contest among the best masters, not by calculation and theory.[11]

Spain and the earliest printed works

If Italy was the seed bed in which the notion of shipbuilding treatises took root, then the Span-

10. *Visione del Drachio*, Archivio di Stato di Venezia, Archivio Proprio Contarini, busta 25.

11. Ennio Concina, *Navis: L'umanesimo sul mare (1470–1740)*, (Turin 1990), p155ff.

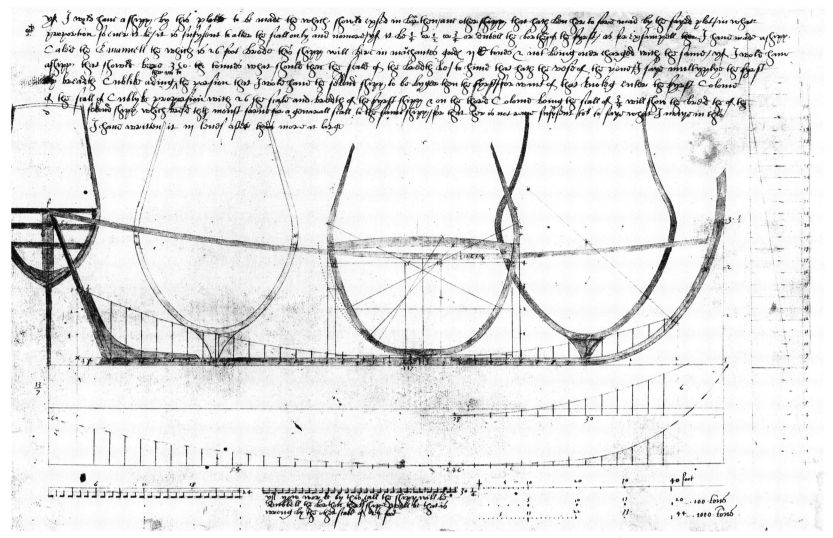

ish Empire is where it reached maturity. It is not surprising that Spain's vast Atlantic Empire, with its enormous demand for shipping of all kinds, both mercantile and naval, saw the first published treatises on ship construction. The first printed manual of shipbuilding techniques was published in Mexico City in 1587. This was Diego Garcia de Palacio's *Instrucción náutica para navegar*, a work that concentrates on the maritime requirements of the Spanish Empire in the Americas.[12] Garcia de Palacio has been identified as a member of King Philip II's Council of War and was familiar with circumstances in the New World. Among his other works is a report on conditions in what is now Guatemala, and, more closely related to the *Instrucción náutica*, a *Diálogos militares*. As in his earlier *Diálogos militares*, the naval work is written as a dialogue, a classical form favoured in humanistic writing. Publication implies an attempt to disseminate information, perhaps even to educate. Garcia de Palacio's works aimed to make known the conditions, requirements, and opportunities of Spain's burgeoning empire in Central America.

The *Instrucción náutica* is divided into four chapters, or books. The first three are devoted to the art of navigation, tides, prediction of the weather, astronomy and astrology, and chartmaking. Only the fourth is concerned with the building and rigging of ships. In a discussion which begins with the four elements – earth, air, fire and water – he explains the place of water and of ships in the cosmos and in human life. The basic ship which Garcia de Palacio discusses is the *nao* of four hundred *toneladas*. But, he explains, the size and proportions of ships must be suited to the waters in which they will see service. After giving dimensions for his basic *nao*, with drawings that detail how these dimensions are realised, there is another set of drawings for a *nauio menor*. He then explains that these basic dimensions may be varied 'with the good discretion of the master builder'. A much greater proportion of Garcia de Palacio's book is dedicated to sails and rigging than to hull design.

Garcia de Palacio's book marks the beginning of a different tradition of more formal published treatises aimed at a wide audience,

One of the diagrams from the late sixteenth-century shipbuilder's notebook known as the 'Fragments of Ancient English Shipwrightry'. It shows the stem-keel-sternpost structure and four frame sections; it is designed to show the design technique known as whole moulding. (Magdalene College, Cambridge)

but the creation of manuscript works intended for private reference or limited circulation did not end with the appearance of published books on shipbuilding. Drachio's *Visione* post-dates the *Instrucción náutica*, and several other manuscript works were produced in the late sixteenth and seventeenth centuries. These later works vary widely in character. Some of them, such as the Portuguese studies of Father Fernando de Oliveira, the *Livro da fábrica das Naos*, and the *Livro primeiro da architectura naval* of João Baptista Lavanha, were as fully developed and in accord with current influ-

12. This work has been published in a facsimile edition as Diego Garcia de Palacio, *Instruccion nautica para navegar (1587)* (Madrid 1944); more recently it has become available in an English translation by J M Bankston as *Nautical Instruction, 1587* (Bisbee, Arizona 1986).

ences as any published work.[13] At the other extreme is the manuscript of Matthew Baker, now usually known as *Fragments of ancient English shipwrightry*. This manuscript was continued into the early seventeenth century by another hand. Baker was a master shipbuilder for the English royal navy during the reign of Queen Elizabeth I, and therefore well-placed and extremely knowledgeable about the design techniques of his day. He appears to have been influential in English shipbuilding circles. His notebook consists largely of the drawings which have been frequently reproduced, but contains little analysis of the way in which the moulds of hulls were developed. While the draughts are spectacular and informative in the ways that draughts and plans can be, the lack of text limits Baker's usefulness.

Lavanha's *Livro* was a systematic treatise that treats naval architecture as a branch of the more general subject. In discussing the requirements of shipbuilding he begins with the very basic requirements of selecting the wood to be used. It is in his insistence on yet another basic requirement that Lavanha seems most modern: that the draughting of a plan on paper is the true beginning of design. Indeed, he begins his discussion of design with detailed instructions on how to make a drawing to scale. Beginning with the keel, stem and sternpost he gives precise geometric instructions so modern in spirit that anyone today, with a little work, could follow them. This is a very different approach from the Italian manuscript treatises of a century earlier that used drawings on paper only as an aid to visualising the way in which the measurements and geometric operators would produce full-scale curves in the mould loft. Because it remained unpublished until modern times, Lavanha's work must have had only limited influence. However, since Lavanha was sufficiently well-placed in Portugal and Spain to have been a member of a Spanish commission on shipbuilding, his ideas were certainly not without influence. Another Portuguese work, also unpublished, dates from about the same time as Lavanha's *Livro*, or perhaps even a little earlier. This is the *Livro de traças de carpintaria* by Manuel Fernandes, completed in 1616.[14] The numerous illustra-

tions in this work are much like others of the era in showing how to determine the curve of stem- and sternposts. Several show not only the midship frame but at least two other frames as well.

The second published work concerned with shipbuilding appeared in Italy. Bartolomeo Crescentio's *Nautica Mediterranea* was published, according to the title page, in Rome in 1607. However, the colophon carries a date of 1602, while the two dedications are dated 1601. The work contains six books and an appended portolan of the Mediterranean. Book One explains in considerable detail, and with many illustrations, the design and building of galleys, galleasses, and galleons. Crescentio was certain that the naval architect, and he uses the term *architetto*, should 'give form and design to the builder'.[15] Yet it seems that he did not completely understand the old methods, the *Ragioni antique*. He maintained that the frames that produced the sharper narrowing of the hull, from the *chavo de sesto* to the end of the vessel, 'had the eye of the Master for their model'. Chiggiato has shown that the shape of these frames was also determined by strict geometric proportion.[16] This may reflect a cultural gap between the theoretically trained architect and the craftsmen-builders, or it may

indicate that by 1600 the old methods were beginning to be lost. Though most of Crescentio's work is very practical, he could not resist the temptation to include a chapter on 'How to row a galley with twenty rowers'. The secret is an unlikely device that would allow one man to manipulate three oars at once with a crank and wheel attached to a cumbersome framework linking the three oars.

13. Lavanha's work, *Livro primeiro da architectura naval*, is so fully developed that one can only wonder that it did not appear in print. The work has now been published, with a lengthy introductory study: João G Pimentel Barata, *O 'livro primeiro da architectura naval' de João Baptista Lavanha*, in *Ethnos* 4 (1965), pp221–298; Instituto Português de Arquelogia História e Etnografia, Lisbon. The date of this work is uncertain: Pimentel Barata dates the ship specifications contained in it to around 1598 and the MS to the first quarter of the seventeenth century. I have been unable to obtain a copy of Pimental Barata's work in the original and so have used an unpublished translation into French by the Bureau des traductions, Division des services multilingues, Secrétariat d'État du Canada.

14. This work is now available in facsimile: Manuel Fernandes, *Livro de traças de carpintaria* (Lisbon 1989).

15. 'dare forma et disegno al fabro', Bartolomeo Crescentio, *Nautica Mediterranea* (Rome 1607), p10.

16. Crescentio, p18; Chiggiato, pplxxivff. Lavanha describes a method of using ribbands to establish these curves after a number of floor timbers had been fixed to the keel.

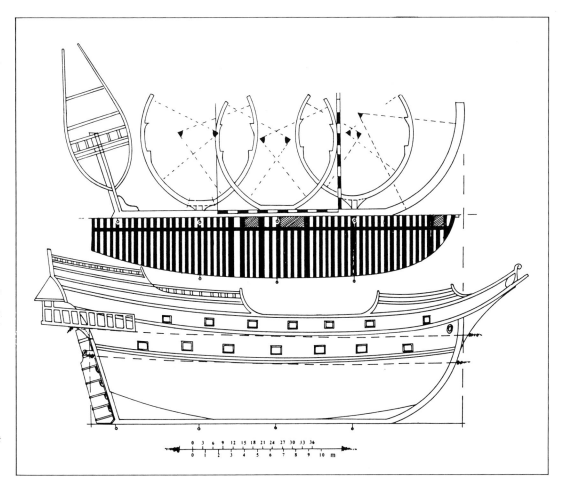

A small Portuguese galleon of 300 tons after Manuel Fernandes's Livro de traças de carpintaria *of 1616. There is a fairly crude elevation, or sheer draught, a plan view showing lower deck beams, and a keel profile with selected cross sections. Important developments include the fact that the drawing is to scale and that its three parts are aligned – as yet there is no body plan, but it is clearly a stage in the evolution of the classic three-view draught, representing the ship in all three planes.*

In 1608, at Seville, Thomé Cano completed the *Arte para fabricar y aparejar naos*, which was published in 1611. Again, the Spanish work is concerned with ocean-going sailing ships, unlike Crescentio's treatise that gives much more detail for the construction of galleys. Both Garcia de Palacio and Cano give considerable attention to the overall hull proportions – ratios of beam to keel to length – that would produce the best combination of seaworthiness and carrying capacity over the long voyage from Spain to the New World and back. The traditional proportions had been expressed as *as*, *dos*, *tres*, that is, taking the beam as one, the length of keel should be double, and the overall length treble. It is not likely that this was ever more than a very rough approximation; Garcia de Palacio suggests for his basic *nao* of 400 *toneladas* that the keel of 34 *codos* should have a beam of 16 *codos* 'which is almost half the keel'.[17] These proportions, which establish the basic dimensions of the ship, do not provide a system for establishing the curves of the hull as did the Venetian manuscript treatises. That seems to have been left to the master builders.

A few years after the appearance of Crescentio's work another small volume was published in Rome. This was Pantero Pantera's *L'armate navale* (Rome 1614). Containing no illustrations, this work is concerned mostly with naval tactics and organisation. Though often not as detailed in its consideration of ships as other works of the same period, *L'armate navale* nonetheless contains valuable information. Pantera's descriptions of the sails carried by large Venetian ships is an important indication of how rapidly the development of sails and rigging had progressed in the fifteenth century. Pantera also discussed the positioning of artillery on great galleys that were used as warships. Other considerations range from the sailing characteristics of galleons to sources of timber for shipbuilding.

These printed treatises were not directed to an audience of builders, but to educated amateurs. The Spanish works were intended to provide the bureaucrats of the new empire with a knowledge of navigation and of ships that would fit them to administer and communicate with their overseas possessions. Crescentio dedicated his volume to Cardinal Aldobrandino, whom he addressed as 'Generale dell'Armata'. Perhaps this is nowhere more clearly seen than in the *Architectura Navalis* of Joseph Furttenbach. Published in Ulm in 1629, the work is very much in the spirit of the baroque.

A perspective illustration of a large warship from Furttenbach's Architectura Navalis *of 1629.*

It is lavishly illustrated with many fold-out plates and diagrams in the text. In three parts the *Architectura Navalis* discusses galleys and similar vessels, sailing ships, and the Battle of Lepanto. Though written and published in Germany by a German, Furttenbach's work is thoroughly Italian in inspiration. All of the technical terms are in Italian and it plainly reflects Italian, probably more specifically Genoese, design philosophy. Written in the midst of the series of conflicts now known as the Thirty Years War, the *Architectura Navalis* is one of a series of works produced by Furttenbach on military topics.

The first treatises in English on naval architecture do not appear until the seventeenth century. The works of Henry Mainwaring, John Smith and Nathaniel Boteler, while very valuable in other respects, touch only incidentally on naval architecture. Mainwaring and Smith wrote glossaries of sea terms, while Boteler's work took the form of a dialogue between a veteran captain and a landlubber admiral. Robert Dudley's *Arcano del Mare*, three folio volumes published in Florence in 1645–46, is an unusual Anglo-Italian hybrid. In organisation and general approach these volumes bear more resemblance to Garcia de Palacio's book than to any English treatise of this period. Also, Dudley's three large volumes are more extensive and ambitious than the Spanish work. Book Four of the six books is devoted to shipbuilding.

In France, in 1643, works on naval architecture began to combine the detailed practicality of the early Italian notebooks with the learned theory of the published treatises to produce a new and more modern type. The *Hydrographie* of Georges Fournier is in many ways similar to Crescentio's *Nautica Mediterranea* in its wide concern with all aspects of maritime endeavour, ranging from shipbuilding through dockyard organisation to navigation and many other topics as well. The section on shipbuilding is exceptionally detailed, including an extensive discussion of the way to draw a ship's lines. This is the first of the treatises since the *Ragioni antique* to concern itself with a specific vessel, in this case the *Couronne* of 1638. The *Hydrographie* is the harbinger of numerous works of the late seventeenth and early eighteenth century that treat naval architecture in a way that is at the same time ordered, rational, and practical. Though they are outside the scope of this volume, works such as the Englishman Edmund Bushnell's *The Compleat Ship-Wright* (1664), a series of Dutch works beginning with Nicolaes Witsen's *Architectura Navalis et Regimen Nauticum* (1671), and Dassié's *Architecture Navale* (1677) mark the fusion of the practicality of the craftsman-shipwright with the rational and mathematically based theory of the humanist amateur. Finally the promise of Vettor Fausto began to bear fruit.

John E Dotson

17. Garcia de Palacio, *Instruccion nautica para navegar*, f90. The *codo real* was a measurement of length used in shipbuilding equal to 22 inches English or 56.5cm. Carla Rahn Phillips, *Six Galleons for the King of Spain* (Baltimore 1986), p228.

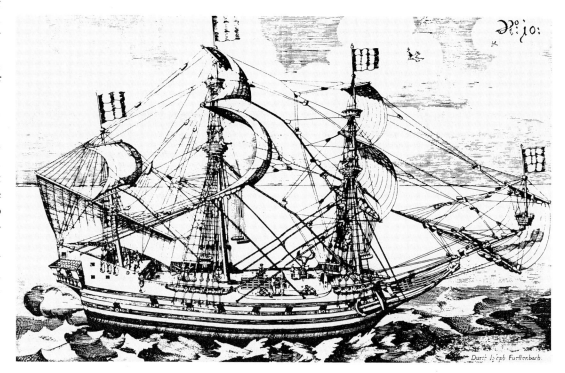

12

Illustrations of Ships: Iconography and Interpretation

MUCH OF the evidence for the appearance of medieval ships depends on a relatively small scattering of visual representations in a variety of artistic media – mosaics, paintings, sculptural bas-reliefs, manuscript illustrations, and so on. Very rarely was the artist primarily concerned to depict a ship in precise technical detail, and his aims usually lay elsewhere. Moreover, his work was probably circumscribed by the conventions or forms in which he operated, which could distort the image to the point where its face value would seem to be slight. An earlier generation of nautical historians was prone to dismiss as 'artistic licence' features which did not tally with current knowledge or seamanlike common sense. However, recent archaeological discoveries have often underlined the accuracy of depiction, even in works of overtly naive style, suggesting that the artist was imitating a real object even if he did not understand what it was (an example of this would be the dark triangles shown on the hulls of cogs in many miniatures and now identified as fairings for the ends of the through-beams). Nevertheless, to make the best use of visual sources in the study of the ship requires knowledge of the traditions and iconography of medieval and Renaissance art, which are the subjects of this chapter.

The use of symbolism in representations of ships in the early Middle Ages

There are representations of merchant ships going back as far as the second/third centuries BC, such as the mosaics at Ostia (Sullecthum

ships), and at Themetra and Althiburus in Tunisia. All of them are remarkable for their precision, and demonstrate advanced artistic skill. There are also pictures of ships in the very earliest examples of Christian art, but a comparison between these two historical sources reveals almost identical iconographical designs borrowed from pagan art, although technical content was by this time falling away. They illustrate how art had forsaken realism for symbolism, and also the fact that maritime activity itself was contracting. In fact, from a technical point of view, there was now a clear contrast between a much more elaborate form of symbolism in shipping archetypes on the one hand, and a striking decline in representational skills on the other. That conclusion is quite inescapable if we compare sources dating from the later centuries of Antiquity or the early Middle Ages with examples demonstrating the relative naturalism and credibility of the preceding period.

Few clichés of deeply felt experience have been more effective than that of the ship in a storm. There is indeed no episode in the lives of the saints that finds its way more regularly into miniatures than one incorporating a real or symbolic sea crossing. In the Middle Ages, the great source of symbols was nature, and in particular the sea. The sea symbolised a chang-

ing and unstable world, while the stormy sea represented the dangers and difficulties that we face here on earth. When human life was compared to a sea crossing, the perils of which may be seen to be the risks of existence itself, it became an archetype which medieval Christianity adopted with the greatest of ease. Christ it was who steered Christians through their lives, while the Church was symbolised by a ship – a vessel in which believers took their places with a view to overcoming their worldly problems and tempestuous passions. Ships also appeared in numerous representations of Biblical times; in the crossing of the Lake of Genesareth and the stories of the prophet Jonah and Noah's Ark, the ship became one of the richest of all symbols in the Biblical and Christian traditions.

A close look at the many and varied representations of ships shows some continuity in the Middle Ages of the ways of thinking and feeling not only from late Antiquity but also from the preceding era. It is true that representations depict Biblical events, scenes from the Old Testament and the Gospels though rarely from the lives of the Apostles. Despite the topics chosen, the astonishing vitality of Classical artistic culture, which had developed to an unparalleled degree by the beginning of the Hellenistic period, should not be underesti-

One of the earliest certain illustrations of the lateen rig is to be found in a late ninth-century Greek manuscript, now in the Bibliothèque Nationale (MS grec 510, f 3r). One vessel has the sail set and the other furled showing details of the rig in two situations. A noticeable feature is the hooked masthead, which was probably designed to allow the halliard to stand forward of the mast. (By courtesy of Christiane Villain-Gandossi)

The storm at sea, one of the commonest medieval themes is well represented by this miniature from the Codice Virgiliano *of about 1450 (Biblioteca Riccardiana, Florence). The Mediterranean ship types represented are both contemporary galleys and sailing ships, and the various winds to which they were subject are personified in each corner of the illustration.* (By courtesy of Christiane Villain-Gandossi)

mated. That culture still managed to maintain its prestige during succeeding centuries. The iconographical theme of ships, if later representations in collections put together by specialists are anything to go by, showed the long standing and persistent influence of Hellenistic traditions. It has to be said, however, that the illustrations progressively lost their reliability as far as technical considerations are concerned.

Iconographical evidence

The earliest representations of ships in pre eighth-century Christian art reflect the general trends that prevailed during that circumspect, reticent period. For the most part, Christian art went in for frescoes as a means of expression, opting by and large for simple, isolated, uncontextualised images in catacombs. As burial began to replace cremation from the second century onwards, there developed in tandem the new art form of sculptured sarcophagi. These became well established during the third and fourth centuries. Some of them provide us

with schematised details of rigging; they include the sarcophagi in the second- to fourth-century catacombs of Praetextatus, St Callixtus and Priscilla, and there are other examples in the Capitoline Museum and the Museo delle Terme in Rome. However, given the limitations of form and dimensions that sarcophagi placed on artists, most ships were presented as long, slender vessels without noticeable sheer. An illustration of this is to be found on the fourth-century Spoleto Sarcophagus in Rome; here, Christ is at the helm giving direction to his apostles, while the latter are depicted in a boat symbolising the Church.

In the fourth century, richly coloured mosaics began to replace painting, particularly in Syria, Asia and North Africa, and they flourished notably during the reign of the Emperor Constantine. However, instead of providing evidence of the deeply felt religious hopes of the faithful, these mosaics demonstrated the doctrine of power. In most parts of the region they initially represented mythological scenes; in areas close to the coast, by contrast, they tended to depict seascapes (the owners often had interests in maritime trade). Other themes included that of Noah's Ark in the fifth-century Church of Misis (Mopsuestia) in southeastern Turkey and that of the miracle of the loaves and fishes in the Church of Sant'Apollinare Nuovo, Ravenna.

Another medium of figurative art was graffiti. For those with the patience to disen-

tangle the intricate, and apparently disorderly, lines, graffiti are a priceless source of information on the history of ships. Graffiti representations were based on real life. Moreover, although they were often highly schematic in style and were the work of seafaring folk, they tended to be free of anachronisms and were particularly rich in technical detail, despite the fact that views were always in profile, rather like children's drawings.

From the eighth/ninth centuries onwards, the second phase of Christian art is associated with a new form of culture, that of the scholars. The main iconographical evidence that the scholars left behind is manuscripts. Carolingian and Byzantine miniatures were heavily influenced by earlier works of art, and they were to be the links in the historical chain that perpetuated traditional forms. It is for this reason that iconography from the latter period of Antiquity has survived.

Tracing the development of ship design through iconography

Since Antiquity, a prime source for studying the development of ship design has been representations on enamel objects, frescoes, stained glass, ivory objects, mosaics, sculptures, tapestries and, above all, miniatures. The images appearing on these varied iconographic sources include simple open boats, single-masted ships with square or lateen sails, vessels

Religious manuscript illuminations are usually more concerned to make theological points than to accurately reflect the realities of the outside world, but even so can often provide reliable details. This single-masted ship, for example, has a form of windlass that seems to be employed not only as a means of belaying the sheets, but also to adjust the backstay. From Gregorii Dialogi *(Koninklijke Bibliotheek, Brussels, Ms 9916, f 61r)*

with superstructures, multi-masted carracks, flat-bottomed boats, coastal and river vessels, galleys and other long ships, and idealised or imaginary boats. It must be borne in mind, however, that they were all depicted in such a stylised form that it is often difficult, and sometimes impossible, to identify them with any confidence. The task of interpreting the miniatures involves making a large number of comparisons with other iconographical evidence; that is the only way of finding out how the different parts of ships evolved.

On the other hand, even the oddest features, if consistently represented, probably reflect reality. For example, nearly all miniatures in ninth- to eleventh-century Greek manuscripts depict the most interesting detail of a very curved stempost and sternpost ending in three points. This trident, which appears in many drawings of Byzantine ships, is a very specific device that is not found anywhere else, and is probably associated with changes to the manner of shell-first construction, in which the number of tenons was reduced (see Chapter 4). It is likely that the trident enabled shipbuilders to secure sections of the centre of the hull to the sternpost and stempost during construction, probably by means of two longitudinal timbers running at deck level from stem to stern. Planking could then commence at both deck and keel levels. An example of this can be seen in the twelfth-century Pala d'Oro ship in San Marco, Venice.

The relationship between image and word

Research into the development of the three-masted ship from iconographical sources has established two facts. Firstly, fourteenth-century documents depict thirteenth-century

This three-masted ship in the 'Legend of St Anthony' (Alte Pinacothek, Munich) by the anonymous artist known as the 'Meister der Heilige Sippe' demonstrates the relative sophistication of ship representation reached by about 1500. The sail plan, with small fore and mizzen, and even smaller bonaventure mizzen, seems convincing, and suggests a genuine portrait, although some of the details of the rigging are doubtful. (By courtesy of Christiane Villain-Gandossi)

ships, while late fifteenth-century paintings (mainly those of the Italian masters) show greatly improved designs, because much less time had elapsed between the ships' earliest voyages and their appearances in paintings. Secondly, when we are fortunate enough to have at our disposal useful, and accurately dated, iconographical documents, we are able to observe that objects are represented in pictures several decades before they are referred to in writing. An example of this is steering gear.

Documents that list harbour dues seem to draw a distinction between the side rudder and the centreline, or sternpost, rudder.[1] At all events, the need to install a large tiller, and the difficulty of using it, made a much bigger impression on people at the time than any changes in the way the rudder was attached. This is reflected in texts which distinguish large ships from small ones, or at least cargo carriers from smaller, lighter craft, by reference to the type of rudder. An English regulation of 1263 relating to dues payable in the port of Lincoln states that boats equipped with a 'helmrother' (a rudder with a tiller) paid two pence, while boats equipped with a 'handrother' (a hand-held rudder) paid only one penny.[2] The regulations also provide evidence of the use of the sternpost rudder in the west in the mid thirteenth century.

This invention was to be found in figurative representations some seventy years before it was referred to in written texts. The earliest

The seal of Damme (1309), with its cog-like hull, depicts an early example of the centreline rudder. The ironwork of the rudder has obviously caught the artist's attention, since he depicts the gudgeons and pintles in a degree of detail lacking elsewhere. (By courtesy of Christian Villain-Gandossi)

illustrations were sculpted and appeared on the baptismal fonts of the Cathedrals of Winchester and Zedelgem; they are dated around 1180, and come from the same workshop in Tournai. A manuscript in the Bibliothèque Sainte Geneviève in Paris, dating from the middle of the twelfth century, also appears to include an example of this rare type of steering device. Artists were obviously very struck by the ways in which these rudders were attached to ships (with gudgeons and pintles), and took considerable pleasure in including them in their work. The rudder, which was very long and broad, and was studded with stylised ironwork, became a well-established iconographical theme.

When iconography produces evidence of an invention, or simply of the social acceptance of an object – such as the representation of the stern rudder – we need to be very careful about the way we interpret the development, as artists' enthusiasm for new objects can sometimes run away with them. In fact, the hinged centreline rudder was adopted over a long period of time. Indeed, it is clear from reading building contracts and inventories of shipping tackle that single side rudders survived for some time, and even coexisted with the sternpost rudder, particularly in the Mediterranean. Iconography in this field can be misleading since it provides little evidence of the side rudder during the thirteenth and fourteenth centuries. Initially, the reason was undoubtedly that seals and similar documents depicted more important ships, of the type that were specially equipped for war when the need arose; later on, it was because for artists the centreline rudder had become a motif in its own right. Like any other aspect of the history of ship design, it is important to examine documentary and iconographical evidence very systematically.

This is equally true of the date of the invention of the whipstaff, the vertical lever that allowed the helmsman to stand one deck above the tiller itself and to give himself a better view. The French words '*manivelle*' and '*manuelle*' for this device appeared in dictionaries in 1611 and 1641 respectively, but a rudimentary 'bar' known as a '*heaume*', '*barre de timon*' or '*barre*' had been in existence since the middle of the sixteenth century. It may be that the extension or rod at the end of the tiller that the helmsmen used to move the tiller back and forth at a distance – it can be seen on a few miniatures – was an early form of whipstaff. Evidence in the Bibliothèque Nationale in Paris supports this view.[3]

Comparison of reliable representations and of accurately dated documents provides the

historian specialising in ships with some excellent basic information. In this context, it should be said that the historian will have a natural preference for a reliable document that also includes a clear picture from the same period. Such documents are, alas, rare.

Art historians, too, find it useful to analyse representations of ships for several reasons. These, of course, include the artistic trends which a given artist may have been encouraged to follow by his temperament or personal tastes, or by a given school or movement. However, the art historian is also able to distinguish elements that are particular to given representations. Some of these elements are all to do with the normal conventions that were followed by medieval artists; others are more closely related to the theme itself – in this case, the ship in its natural surroundings.

The main characteristics of the miniature as an iconographical source

If we wish to extract any evidence from miniatures, there are several criteria that have to be understood. Miniatures are naive, stylised, and even systematically disproportionate, and they come nowhere near to providing reliable pictures. Just the same, we do have to make the best of what has been handed down to us. Miniatures produced by well informed artists are instantly recognisable. Other miniatures can nonetheless provide useful information which, if closely examined, can tell us how the artist exaggerated the details that made an impression on him, concealed those that displeased him – and simply curved the lines of the ship to suit his purpose. With very few exceptions, we cannot expect iconographical documents to provide exact dates of any details included, even when we know the date of the documents themselves. For example, a given detail relating to the hull or rigging may appear in a picture from a period when it had already disappeared, or only survived in a very small number of cases. Similarly, a long period of time can elapse between the introduction of a technical advance and an artist deciding to incorporate it into one of his works. There again, an accurately identified document may not be the earliest iconographical illustration of the object in question. All we can be sure of, when a dated picture provides us with clear evidence of a

1. For example, K Hoehlbaum, *Hansisches Urkundenbuch* (Halle 1876), p144.

2. See Birch's *Royal Charters of the City of Lincoln* quoted in *The Mariner's Mirror* XVII (1931), pp185–196.

3. See for example, *Ms fr 1454, f 1v*.

Illustrations can be useful in defining and dating specific developments in ship design. The origins of the whipstaff, for example, may be traced in the tiller extension visible in this miniature from the Bibliothèque Nationale in Paris. (By courtesy of Christiane Villain-Gandossi)

new technical device (or the absence of one previously in use), is that the practice was introduced before the date mentioned. That, after all, is better than nothing!

It is possible to deduce from a close study of miniatures certain characteristics that are peculiar to the subject matter that they depict. These characteristics are also valid for the vast majority of other forms of iconographic evidence.

The limitations of the art form

For the most part, ships are more crowded together in miniatures than they are in real life. Similarly, there is a tendency to exaggerate their height at the expense of their length. Sometimes, whether consciously or not, the artist is influenced by the events taking place in the composition. For example, pressure from the frame or the edge of the picture can interfere with motifs that should be some distance from the border. This often happens when the artist has chosen to produce a relatively long,

horizontal shape; then the boat takes on a long, slender form without much sheer, instead of being curved. On seals, by contrast, ships have to have a crescent-shaped silhouette so as to fit conveniently into the circular frame. At the opposite extreme, the Bayeux tapestry provides us with the clearest evidence of all. Here, the majority of the hull occupies a markedly horizontal space as a result of the area available for representation.

The quest for symmetry

For the most part, the impetus to symmetry is likely to be inspired by a more or less conscious desire for it, but it may also be little more than a case of individual assimilation brought about by natural laziness. If the artist has to reproduce the same motif several times, he may disregard the variations, choose just one of the

Nowhere is the distortion of image to fit the form more evident than in the three-masted ship on this bowl. Dated between the end of the fourteenth and the early fifteenth century, the bowl is thought to originate from Malaga in southern Spain and is now in London's Victoria and Albert Museum. Stylistically most features are islamic but the coat of arms – and presumably the ship – are Christian, but whatever its provenance it is one of the earliest detailed depictions of a three-masted ship. (By courtesy of Richard Unger)

motifs and repeat it. Depending on the sort of person the artist is, the motif he chooses may be the one he prefers for some reason, or else it may be the most ornamental, the simplest, or just the easiest one to reproduce. Once it has been selected, it will become his 'standard' motif which he will copy again and again, and be able to produce from memory. That is why miniatures depict so many double-ended vessels, with hawses at the bow and the stern, that can be rowed in either direction.

Dated 1548 this manuscript illustration from the Bibliothèque Nationale (Ms fr 25374, fo 28v) is a lively and detailed picture of a mid sixteenth-century warship. Although the perspective is distorted the main features of the ship and its rig are quite clear. The carrack forestage of the early part of the century has not yet been replaced by the galleon's low beakhead, while the stern seems to suggest three levels of after superstructure above main deck level. (By courtesy of Christiane Villain-Gandossi)

Schematism and stylisation

There is no need here to go over the various forms of didactic schematism. Schematism is a means of simplifying forms by expressing only the most characteristic lines; what is eventually depicted, therefore, is a side view of the ship in the water.

The multiplication of certain elements

There were features that particularly attracted the artist's eye, and which were reproduced on many occasions. They included the nails used in clinker hull construction, reef points which were used to cover the whole surface of the sail, systematically woolded masts, and innumerable hawses or scuppers. Other aspects that appealed to artists were ratlines on shrouds, the extremities of through-beams on cogs and the markings on the mast top.

Imprecise proportions and perspectives

This is an appropriate moment to return once again to the matter of incorrect dimensions, imprecise relationships between sails and hull, wrong perspectives, and sails often represented frontally on a ship otherwise depicted in profile. Some of the mistakes derive from deliberate alterations; alternatively, a copyist might include details borrowed from a number of different sources. It was not unusual in the fifteenth century to find combinations of vessels in which some were in profile while others were viewed from an oblique angle.

It was common for objects to become difficult to recognise as a result of successive stylisations and transcriptions. It can be instructive, in this context, to trace the links going back as far as the Early Christian period, as it was this era that gave inspiration to the medieval world, which then copied it and adapted it to its own needs.

Comparisons of iconographical sources

A comparison of all iconographic sources leaves miniatures at a disadvantage. Take, for example, Iacopo di Barbari's splendid engraving (1500) of ships, now in the Museo Navale, Venice, showing dozens of different types including carracks, busses, nefs and two-masted vessels with sail set from only a small section of the mast. Not for the first time, the scene and the client for whom the engraving was made must have been of the greatest importance. Another highly informative representation that is worthy of the closest examination is the side rudder on a bas-relief in the Church of Sant'Eustorgio in Milan.

Graffiti were schematised, and it is true that the dimensions were frequently wayward but, for the most part, they conformed to the models of the period. The artists were simple folk who had little talent for artistry, so while they expressed themselves in a simple manner, at least they portrayed exactly what they saw.

There was an element of stylisation on seals, but fewer liberties were taken on the whole, particularly on the seals of towns and sea ports. Artists generally contented themselves with highlighting the main events and the aspects of

seafaring which they considered to be the most interesting. At all events, the representational skills were always characterised by great accuracy. Good examples of seals are those of Nieuport (1237), Pamplona (1279), Damme (1309) and Fuenterrabía (1335).

By far the most useful information, however, has come from painters, and in particular Carpaccio and Botticelli. The latter's magnificent perspective view of a ship on the vault of the Sistine Chapel is a fine example. Much has been written about Carpaccio's series of paintings of the legend of Saint Ursula in the Academy, Venice. Sadly, less has been made of his 'St George and the dragon' in the Scuola di San Giorgio degli Schiavoni, Venice: this includes a rare picture of a ship under full sail. Details include square rigged main and fore masts, two mizzen masts, and a bowsprit with a spritsail, a fine portrait of a large ship of the end of the fifteenth century.

Christiane Villain-Gandossi

Bibliography

Compiled by Robert Gardiner with the assistance of the contributors

GENERAL AND INTRODUCTORY

There is no one book which gives an up-to-date overview of the present state of knowledge relating to medieval ship development. Of those listed in this section, Anderson represents the old-fashioned antiquarian's approach, while Landstrom's work is an artist's interpretation of actual ship appearance, drawn with considerable understanding of the subject, albeit from evidence which is often insufficient. With one foot in the academic tradition and the other in the world of practical shipwrightry, the collaboration between Greenhill and Manning is stimulating, but it only covers a few 'highlights' of medieval development. Of the purely academic studies, Unger's is the most ambitious, but, while good on the economic context, is too dependent on outmoded sources to be reliable regarding the technology of ships.

R and R C ANDERSON, *The Sailing Ship* (London 1926).
Once considered the standard introduction, it is still worth reading for the ideas contained on boat and ship development, though some are now very dated.

GEORGE BASS (ed), *History of Seafaring* (London 1972).
An exciting book in its time because of its overview of much that was most recent in the world of nautical archaeology. It helps to put fresh published work in context.

H EWE, *Schiffe auf Siegeln* (Rostock 1972).
An invaluable collection of ship images on medieval seals and essential reading if the development of the medieval ship from the Viking boat onwards is to be understood.

BASIL GREENHILL, *Archaeology of the Boat* (London 1976).
An excellent introduction to the various strands which exist in boat archaeology. Contains a comprehensive bibliography. A second edition is due soon.

BASIL GREENHILL and SAM MANNING, *Evolution of the Wooden Ship* (London 1988).
Comprehensively illustrated and discussed evolution of wooden boats into ships as understood by the authors, who combine the skills of a maritime historian and a practical shipwright. Only the first half is relevant to this bibliography but it will be found quite stimulating.

FRANK HOWARD, *Sailing Ships of War 1400–1860* (London 1979).
Only the first few pages consider the military aspects of the ships in the medieval period and show how techniques changed. It is based on a limited range of published documentary sources and is better for its illustrations than its text.

BJÖRN LANDSTRÖM, *The Ship* (London 1961).
Landstrom's collection of artistic reconstructions, based on the best available evidence, was an outstanding success and is still worth considering even though a few of his ideas have been overtaken by new information. For the period of this volume many of the original iconographical sources are also reproduced.

ARCHIBALD R LEWIS and TIMOTHY J RUNYAN, *European Naval and Maritime History 300–1500* (Bloomington, Indiana, 1985).
A general survey of navies in the Middle Ages, incorporating the evolution of important ship types, including the cog.

SEAN MCGRAIL, *Rafts, Boats and Ships: From Prehistoric Times to the Medieval Era* (London 1981).
Mostly concerned with prehistory, but contains a concise summary on the knowledge of the cog derived from underwater archaeology. In the National Maritime Museum's 'The Ship' series.

PETER THROCKMORTON (ed), *History from the Sea* (London 1987).
Published in New York as *The Sea Remembers*, this survey of underwater archaeology is a more modern version of Bass's *History of Seafaring*. It is put together by a fine collection of scholars and is excellently illustrated, but being written around underwater finds is somewhat thin on medieval coverage.

RICHARD W UNGER, *The Ship in the Medieval Economy* (Montreal 1980).
This is a pioneering attempt to place the ship in its rightful place within the medieval economy. Intending readers should be abreast of the latest thinking in maritime archaeology since some of its ideas relating to boat and ship development are misleading. No blame attaches to Unger since his sources are the cause of this problem.

DESCENDANTS OF THE VIKING BOATS

B and E ANDERSEN, *Rasejlit — Dragens Vinge* (Roskilde 1989).
Contains a vast quantity of technical information about the structure and rigging of Norse/Viking boats and their reconstruction.

C and G CRAINGE, 'The Pevensey Expedition: Brilliantly Executed Plan or Near Disaster?', *The Mariner's Mirror* 79/3 (1993), pp261–273.
A most interesting recent article which attempts to bring together the weather and tidal problems which beset William of Normandy's planning of his invasion of England.

OLE CRUMLIN-PEDERSEN, 'The Skuldelev Ships', *Acta Archaeologica* 38 (1967), pp73–174.
Much of what is written still about these boats is in fact taken from this article. It is a prime source and should be read in conjunction with the first book in this section of the bibliography. The author has published extensively in the major journals dealing with maritime archaeology.

B AND O FAEROYVIK (ed A E Christensen), *Inshore Craft of Norway* (London 1979).
A collection of drawings of nineteenth-century boats, with detailed commentary, which are worth studying since they show their old Norse origins.

K LLOYD GRUFFYDD, 'Wales' Maritime Trade in Wine during the Late Middle Ages', *Cymru a'r Mor/ Maritime Wales* 15 (1992).
This is a detailed paper which, besides dealing with the Welsh aspects of the wine trade, gives an insight into the busy maritime commercial scene surrounding that important product.

SEAN MCGRAIL, *Ancient Boats in Northwest Europe* (London 1987).
This is not a book to be opened half-heartedly: it contains a wealth of information in a most compact form but it repays the concentration required to assimilate it. However the approach is being made to maritime archaeology, this book is probably essential reading.

C A MARCHAJ, *Sailing Theory and Practice* (New York 1964).
——, *Aero-Hydrodynamics of Sailing* (London 1979).
It is necessary to have a nodding acquaintance with the knowledge contained in either or both of these books if the physical laws which control the behaviour of sailing ships are to be understood and applied to unravelling the developing stages of any ancient vessel.

E NYLEN, *Bildstenar* (Visby 1978).
This is a small book packed with information about the pre-Viking grave stones found in Gotland and on mainland Sweden. All the stones showing boats and their rigs are given plenty of attention.

N J G POUNDS, *An Economic History of Medieval Europe* (London 1974).
The importance of economics as a means of understanding historical events is made clear. There is a very useful chapter on maritime trade and trade routes.

J T TINNISWOOD, 'The English Galleys 1272–1377', *The Mariner's Mirror* 35 (1949), pp276–315.
This is the best of all the earlier attempts to understand the building accounts for some of the English galleys. It is comprehensive and easily understood but also leaves the door open for future interpreters. It should be read in conjunction with Ewe's book on seals quoted in the previous section.

W ZIMMERMANN, *Nef der Cinque Ports* (Munich 1982).
This book is intended for ship modellers but the intricacy and wealth of information examined, backed up by excellent interpretive drawings, make this an invaluable aid to understanding the development of boats and ships in medieval times.

THE COG

This section relates to both chapters on cogs since there is much overlap between their employment as cargo carrier and warship.

CARL O CEDERLUND, 'Explaining a 13th C cog wreck near Smäland, Sweden', in C VILLAIN-GANDOSSI, S BUSUTTIL, P ADAM (eds), *Medieval Ships and the Birth of Technological Societies, Vol I; Northern Europe* (Malta 1989), pp81–133.
A careful study of an early cog, with documentation.

OLE CRUMLIN-PEDERSEN, 'Cog-Kogge-Kaag, Træk af en frisisk skibstypes historie', *Handels-og Søfartsmuseet pa kronborg* (Helsingor 1966, pp81–144.
A careful study of the cog and its place in the evolution of the ship as of the publication date. The author challenges Heinsius' views on the cog.

——, 'Danish Cog Finds', in SEAN McGRAIL (ed.), *The Archaeology of Medieval Ships and Harbours in Northern Europe* (Greenwich 1979), pp17–34.
An important review and comment on the results of archaeological work. The author believes that a mix of influences contributed to the evolution of the sea-going ship.

DETLEV, ELLMERS, 'Frisian and Hanseatic Merchants Sailed the Cog', in ARNE BANG-ANDERSON, BASIL GREENHILL and EGIL HARALD GRUDE (eds), *The North Sea. A Highway of Economic and Cultural Exchange-Character-History* (Oslo 1985).
A fine study of the cog focusing on archaeological research. The Bremen cog is used as an example.

——, *Frühmittelalterliche Handelsschiffahrt in Mittel-und Nordeuropa* (Neuminster 1971).
This important work discusses the cog as a critical element in European shipping.

——, 'The Cog of Bremen and Related Boats', in SEAN McGRAIL (ed), *The Archaeology of Medieval Ships and Harbours in Northern Europe*, pp1–15.
A comparative look at the Bremen Cog and its place in late medieval shipping.

ANGELA EVANS, 'The Clinker-built Boats of the North Sea', in *The North Sea*, pp63–78.
A study of clinker vessels including Viking Ships with implications for development of the cog.

SIEGFRIED FLIEDNER, '*Kogge* and *Hulk*: Ein Beitrag zur Schiffstypengeschichte', *Die Bremer Hanse-Kogge, Fund, Konservierung, Forschung*, Monographien der Wittheit zu Bremen, No 8 (Bremen 1969), pp39–122.

——, *The Cog of Bremen* (Bremen 1972).
A good introduction to the cog found in 1962.

IAN FRIEL, 'Documentary Sources and the Medieval Ship: Some Aspects of the Evidence', *International Journal of Nautical Archaeology* 12 (1983), pp41–62.
A look at the sources of information on medieval ships useful to researchers.

PAUL HEINSIUS, *Das Schiff der Hansischen Frühzeit* (Weimer 1956).
An important early study of the Hanseatic trade. The author believed that the cog was a new type unrelated to the earlier ships and active about 1200 in the German North Sea and Baltic regions.

HERBERT J HEWITT, *The Organization of War Under Edward III, 1338–1362* (Manchester 1966).
A pioneer study of the preparations and support for waging war in fourteenth-century England.

J S KEPLER, 'The Effects of the Battle of Sluys on English Naval Impressment', *Speculum* 48 (January 1973), pp70–77.
An analysis of financial records and administration to examine how fleets were raised.

KLAUS-PETER KIEDEL and UWE SCHNALL (eds), *The Hanse Cog of 1380* (Bremerhaven 1985).
An excellent study of the Bremen cog by experts. The drawings and illustrations provide documentation from discovery to conservation.

WERNER LAHN, *Die Kogge von Bremen, Volume I: Bauteile und Bauablauf*, Deutsches Schiffahrts-museum publication, Vol 30 (Hamburg 1992).
With English translation and detailed bibliography on cog research up to 1992.

SIR NICHOLAS H NICOLAS, *History of the Royal Navy*, 2 vols (London 1847).
The first volumes of what was intended to be a full history of the Royal Navy, but was cut short by the author's death. Well researched for its day, covering the period down to 1422.

COLIN F RICHMOND, 'The War at Sea', in K FOWLER (ed), *The Hundred Years War* (London 1971), pp96–121.
A good summary of the naval side of the war based on primary sources.

TIMOTHY J RUNYAN, 'Merchantmen to Men-of-War in Medieval England', in C SYMONDS (ed), *New Aspects of Naval History* (Annapolis, Maryland 1981), pp33–40.
The impressment of mercantile vessels and their use for war, based on documents from the Public Record Office, London.

——, 'Naval Logistics in the Late Middle Ages', in J A LYNN (ed), *Feeding Mars: Logistics in Western Warfare* (Boulder, Colorado 1993).

——, 'The Organization of Royal Fleets in Medieval England', in T J RUNYON (ed), *Ships, Seafaring and Society: Essays in Maritime History* (Detroit 1987).
An examination of the composition of royal war fleets based on archival records. Examines the administrative structure and finances during the Hundred Years War.

——, 'Ships and Fleets in Anglo-French Warfare, 1337–1360', *The American Neptune* 46 (Spring 1986), pp91–99.
This study includes the results of a survey of 1300 ships to ascertain information on ships in the English navy.

BERTIL SANDAHL, *Middle English Sea Terms*, 3 vols (Uppsala 1954–1982).
An important reference work to understand the complex nautical terminology in medieval Latin, Norman French or early English.

JAMES W SHERBORNE, 'The Battle of La Rochelle and the War at Sea, 1372–75', *Bulletin of the Institute of Historical Research* 42 (May 1969), pp17–29.

——, 'The English Navy: Shipping and Manpower, 1369–1389', *Past and Present* 37 (July 1967), pp163–75.

RICHARD W UNGER, 'Warships and Cargo Ships in Medieval Europe', *Technology and Culture* 22 (1981), pp233–52.
Addresses the technological aspects of medieval ships.

THE MEDITERRANEAN ROUND SHIP

G F BASS and F H VAN DOORNINCK, JR, *Yassi Ada, Volume I: A Seventh Century Byzantine Shipwreck* (College Station, Texas 1982).
An important report by the excavators of the site.

L CASSON, 'The Origins of the Lateen', *The American Neptune* 31 (1971)
The earliest evidence for the lateen surveyed.

V CHRISTIDES, 'Two Parallel Naval Guides of the Tenth Century: Qudama's Document and Leo VI's *Naumachia*: A Study on Byzantine and Moslem Naval Preparedness', *Graeco-Arabica* 1 (1982).

——, *The Conquest of Crete by the Arabs (c824): A Turning Point in the Struggle between Byzantium and Islam* (Athens 1984).

L DIMMOCK, 'The Lateen Rig', *The Mariner's Mirror* 32 (1946).

JOHN E DOTSON, 'Jal's Nef X and Genoese Naval Architecture in the Thirteenth Century', *The Mariner's Mirror* 59 (1973), pp161–70.

BARBARA M KREUTZ, 'Ships, Shipping and the Implications of Change in the Early Medieval Mediterranean', *Viator* 7 (1976), pp79–109.

F C LANE, *Venice and History* (Baltimore 1966).
In particular, the chapter 'Diet and Wages of Seamen in the Early Fourteenth Century'.

——, *Venetian Ships and Shipbuilders of the Renaissance* (Baltimore 1934).
The great expert on maritime Venice discusses the development of ships in the Middle Ages and sixteenth century, with reference to both sailing ships and galleys.

L V MOTT, 'The Development of the Rudder, AD 100–160: A Technological Tale' (MA Thesis, Texas A & M University 1991).

R Bastard de Péré, 'Navires méditerranéans du temps de Saint Louis', *Revue d'Histoire Economique et Sociale* 50 (1972), pp327–56.

John H Pryor, 'The Naval Architecture of Crusader Transport Ships: A Reconstruction of Some Archetypes for Round-hulled Sailing Ships', *The Mariner's Mirror* 70 (1984), pp171–219, 275–92 and 368–86.
A detailed study based on the evidence of the building contracts. There is an appendix to this material in Vol 76 (1990), pp255–73.

——, *Geography, Technology and War: Studies in the Maritime History of the Mediterranean 649–1571* (Cambridge 1988)
A major academic survey of the evolution of the sea trade, naval warfare and maritime technology, and the factors that influenced them.

——, and S Bellabarba, 'The Medieval Muslim Ships of the Pisan *Bacini*', *The Mariner's Mirror* 76 (1990), pp99–113.
An analysis of the large three-masted Muslim ships depicted on early eleventh-century ceramic dishes.

J R Steffy, 'The Reconstruction of the Eleventh Century Serçe Liman Vessel: A Preliminary Report', *International Journal of Nautical Archaeology* 11 (1982), pp13–34.

F H Van Doorninck, Jr, 'The Fourth Century Wreck at Yassi Ada: An Interim Report on the Hull', *International Journal of Nautical Archaeology* 5 (1976), pp115–31.
Useful for comparison with hull construction techniques of later wreck finds.

The Carrack

R and R C Anderson, *The Sailing Ship. Six Thousand Years of History* (London 1926; reprinted many times).
Now very dated, but the starting point for much later research. The book contains a good deal of valuable information, and the notes on ship illustrations are useful.

F Braudel, *The Mediterranean and the Mediterranean World in the Age of Philip II*, 2 vols (2nd revised edition, London 1975).
A work of far wider historical and geographical scope than its title suggests, with much relevance to maritime history.

Ian Friel, 'England and the advent of the three-masted ship', *International Congress of Maritime Museums, 4th Conference Proceedings, Paris 1981* (Paris 1983).
Discusses English documentary evidence for ship construction and rig developments in the fifteenth century.

——, 'Henry V's Grace Dieu – a review of the documentary evidence', *International Journal of Nautical Archaeology*, 22 (1993).
Detailed discussion of the documentary evidence for the construction of medieval England's largest ship – probably a clinker-built carrack.

L Guilleux La Roerie, 'More about the ship of the Renaissance', *The Mariner's Mirror* 53 (1957), pp179–93.
Development of Morton Nance's work (see below).

F C Lane, 'Tonnages, Medieval and Modern', *Economic History Review*, Second Series XVII (1964), pp213–33.
Excellent study of the complexities of the history of tonnage measurement.

——, 'Progres technologiques et productivité dans les transports maritimes, de la fin du Moyen Age au debut des temps modernes', *Revue Historique* 510 (1974), pp277–302.
Valuable discussion of the economic factors that helped to promote the spread of changes in maritime technology.

L G Carr Laughton, 'Early Tudor Ship Guns', *The Mariner's Mirror* 46 (1960), pp242–85.
Thorough and still very useful study of the documentary evidence for English naval guns in the late fifteenth and early sixteenth centuries.

R Morton Nance, 'The Ship of the Renaissance', *The Mariner's Mirror* 41 (1955), pp180–92 and 261–95.
Significant analysis of the iconography of the carrack.

M M Oppenheim, *A History of the Administration of the Royal Navy 1509–1660* (London 1896).
A pioneering work in its day, but now very dated. However, it contains much useful information.

—— (ed), *Naval Accounts and Inventories of the Reign of Henry VII 1485–6 and 1495–7*, Navy Records Society Vol VIII (London 1896).
The accounts include inventories and maintenance records of the largest ships in Henry VII's fleet (in fifteenth-century English), and give a clear idea of the costs and complexity of equipping and arming large war carracks of the period. General historical conclusions should be viewed with caution.

S Rose (ed), *The Navy of the Lancastrian Kings. Accounts and Inventories of William Soper, Keeper of the King's Ships, 1422–1427*, Navy Records Society Vol 123 (London 1982).
This work is the main published source for the history of Henry V's ships and navy, and contains a transcript and translation of accounts of dealing with the upkeep of royal vessels.

M Rule, *The Mary Rose. The Excavation and Raising of Henry VIII's Flagship* (2nd Edition, London 1983).
To date, this is the most extensive publication of the *Mary Rose* evidence: updated information appears in successive Mary Rose Trust Guides.

G V Scammell, *The World Encompassed. The first European maritime empires c800–1650* (London and New York 1981).
A wide-ranging and important study, synthesising the technical, economic, political and other aspects of the maritime history of the period.

A W Sleeswyk, 'The engraver Willem A Cruce (WA) and the development of the chainwale', *The Mariner's Mirror* 76 (1990), pp345–61.
The paper makes a plausible case for identifying the Master WA as the Flemish goldsmith Willem A Cruce, and linking the *Kraeck* engraving with a Burgundian ducal marriage of 1468.

P van der Merwe, 'Towards a three-masted ship', in *International Congress of Maritime Museums, 4th Conference Proceedings, Paris 1981* (Paris 1983), pp121–29.
Important discussion of the etymology of the ship types *cocha* and carrack.

The Caravel

E A d'Albertis, *Le construzioni navali e l'arte della navigazione al tempo di Cristoforo Colombo* (Rome 1897).
An important publication that embodies the state of knowledge resulting from the research prompted by the 400th anniversary of the 1492 Columbus voyage, under the auspices of the various national Columbus Commissions of 1892. Covers caravels and other ship types.

Gago Coutinho, *A náutica dos descobrimentos* (Lisbon 1969).
The indispensable pendant to Quirono da Fonseca's *Caravela portuguêsa*. Covers the main points of contention in the acerbic debate between the two authorities, concerning various features of the Portuguese caravel and its handling characteristics.

L Denoix, 'Caractéristiques des navires de l'époque des Grandes Découvertes', *V Colloque international d'histoire maritime* (Paris 1966).

Clinton Edwards, 'Design and Construction of Fifteenth-Century Iberian Vessels', *The Mariner's Mirror* 78 (1992), pp419–432.

Martin Malcolm Elbl, 'The Portuguese Caravel and European Shipbuilding: Phases of Development and Diversity', *Revista da Universidade de Coimbra* 33 (1985), pp543–572.

Carlos Etayo Elizondo, *Naos y carabelas de los descubrimientos y las naves de Colón* (Pamplona 1971).
Valuable contribution to the debate about the form and characteristics of caravels, with many useful insights. The polemical nature of the book colours some of the conclusions.

Manuel Fernandes, *Livro de traças de carpintaria*, 1616 (Lisbon 1989).
An outstanding facsimile reproduction of the original manuscript from the Library of the Palace of Ajuda in Lisbon. Contains Fernandes's drawings of a caravel and specifications for two types of seventeenth-century caravels.

Quirino da Fonseca, *A caravela portuguêsa e a prioridade técnica das navegações Henriquinas* (Coimbra 1934; 2nd edition Lisbon, 1973).
One of the great essential works on the Portuguese caravel, containing a wealth of data, drawings, and some good illustrations. The book's perspective is distorted by the author's determination to prove the uniqueness and absolute technical perfection of Portuguese caravels. Fonseca clashed over many questions of interpretation with Gago Coutinho.

Alberto Iria, *As caravelas do Infante e os caiques do Algarve* (Lisbon 1963).
Presents interesting ideas about the origins of the caravel, summarises the arguments of Gago Coutinho and Quirino da Fonseca, and discusses very cautiously the evidence for the caravel's handling qualities. Looks for the origins of the later Portuguese *caique* in the late fifteenth- and early sixteenth-century caravel.

Henrique Lopes de Mendonça, *Estudos sobre navios portuguezes dos séculos XV e XVI* (Lisbon 1892).
The fundamental older work on Portuguese caravels and other ship types, such as the barque and the *caravo*, with insightful observations that have withstood the test of time rather well. Foreshadows Quirino da Fonseca's concept of the uniqueness of the Portuguese caravel. Contains important full transcriptions of building specifications from the anonymous *Livro Nautico* manuscript of c1570–1595.

JONATHAN NANCE, 'The Columbus Foundation's *Niña*: A Report on the Rigging and Sailing Characteristics of the *Santa Clara*', *International Journal of Nautical Archaeology* 21 (1992), pp295–308.

XAVIER PASTOR, *The Ships of Christopher Columbus* (London 1992).
Briefly describes the evidence available for the tentative reconstruction of Columbus' three ships. Offers descriptions and photographs of the earlier reconstructions and replica ships, as well as a number of drawings that cover the ships' hull lines, rigging, fittings, guns, and other features.

JACQUES PAVIOT and ERIC RIETH, 'Un compte de construction de caravelles portugaises à Bruxelles en 1438–1439', *O Arqueólogo Português*, Ser IV, 6/7 (1988–1989), pp307–331.

JOÃO DA GAMA LOBO PIMENTEL BARATA, 'A caravela. Breve estudo geral', *Studia* 46 (1987), pp157–192.
The most recent, posthumously published survey of the caravel's development, by the leading authority on Portuguese shipbuilding of the fifteenth to seventeenth centuries.

——, *O traçado das naus e galeões portugueses de 1550–80 a 1640* (Lisbon 1970).
Contains a wealth of useful observations and documentation about sixteenth- and seventeenth-century Portuguese shipbuilding and its methods.

THE GALLEON

KENNETH R ANDREWS, *Ships, Money and Politics: Seafaring and Naval Enterprise in the Reign of Charles I* (Cambridge 1991).
Primarily concerned with commercial and administrative matters, especially privateering, though shipbuilders and shipowners figure prominently in the story. Useful appendices of ships by tonnage, port, ordnance, and chartering fees.

GERVASIO ARTIÑANO Y DE GALDÁCANO, *La arquitectura naval española (en madera)* (Madrid 1920).
Analyses the changes in Spanish hull shapes over time, within the context of maritime history. Rich illustrations enhance a text that is still useful, despite its age.

SILEX (pub), *El buque en la armada española* (Madrid 1981).
Chapters organised chronologically, each by a Spanish expert in the field, trace the history of ships used by the Spanish navy. A fundamental reference work, lavishly illustrated in colour, though somewhat difficult to use because it lacks an index.

JOSÉ LUIS CASADO SOTO, *Los barcos españoles del siglo XVI y la Gran Armada de 1588* (Madrid 1988).
Based on archival research by himself and a team of Spanish scholars, the author's study of ship design is part of a distinguished series of volumes to commemorate the 1588 Armada sent against England. Fundamental for the study of sixteenth-century naval history.

PIERRE and HUGUETTE CHAUNU, *Séville et l'Atlantique*, 8 vols in 12 (Paris 1955–59).
Exhaustive examination of Spain's Atlantic fleets from about 1500 to 1650. Tables listing individual ships, with their types and tonnages, are particularly helpful for a study of the galleon.

KARL R H FRICK, *Vergessene Flotten: Flotten und*

Flottenbaupläne im Heiligen Römischen Reich deutscher Nation vom 15 Jahrhundert bis 1632 (Graz 1990).
Concentrates on political and administrative aspects of the Holy Roman Empire's fleet. Useful discussion of tonnage measures for ships in northern and eastern Europe.

Histoire de la marine française (Paris 1934).
Collection of illustrated essays, including several by Charles de la Roncière, dealing with the French ships and shipping within the broad context of French and European history.

AUGUSTE JAL, *Glossaire Nautique*, 3 vols (Paris 1848).
Classic maritime dictionary, particularly useful for French historical nautical terms, but also helpful for equivalents in other countries. Although now superseded by more recent scholarship, this work was vastly erudite and virtually invented the field of nautical research in its modern forms.

GEORGE S KEYES (ed), *Mirror of Empire: Dutch Marine Art of the Seventeenth Century* (Cambridge and New York 1990).
Excellent collection of depictions of ships in paintings, engravings, watercolours, and other media during the heyday of the Dutch empire. Includes the most famous Dutch artists specialising in this genre, many of them noteworthy for their careful attention to detail.

PETER KIRSCH, *The Galleon; The Great Ships of the Armada Era* (London and Annapolis, Maryland 1990).
Modern attempt to understand the galleon as a European-wide ship type. Nicely illustrated, knowledgeable about England, and cites sources from other areas in northern Europe. Demonstrates little knowledge about maritime history in southern Europe, however, which detracts from the general value of the work.

F C LANE, *Venice, A Maritime Republic* (Baltimore 1973).
Brilliant summation of the author's long career as an expert on Venice in its heyday. Although little concerned with galleons, Lane's analysis of shipbuilding and seaborne warfare is an indispensable reference point for anyone interested in the naval and maritime history of this period.

BRIAN LAVERY, *The Arming and Fitting of English Ships of War, 1600–1815* (London and Annapolis, Maryland 1987).
Beautifully illustrated and thoroughly researched examination of shipbuilding technology, including hull design and construction, cables and rigging, guns and carriages, ships' boats, and fittings and equipment of all kinds. Indispensable, although largely relating to periods outside the scope of this bibliography.

L M AKVELD, S HART and W J van HOBOKEN (eds), *Mariteme geschiedenis der Nederlanden* (Bussum, Netherlands 1977).
Essay collection by local specialists. A broad examination of the maritime dimension of Dutch history in its heyday, rather than a technical examination of naval matters. The chapter on ship types in Volume 2 is fairly detailed, but only six pages are devoted to shipbuilding.

COLIN MARTIN and GEOFFREY PARKER, *The Spanish Armada* (London 1988).
Careful scholarly examination of documentary and archeological evidence for the 1588 armada campaign. Lavishly illustrated, including photographs of ship fittings from armada wrecks.

TIMOTEO O'SCANLAN, *Diccionario marítimo español* (1831; reprinted in facsimile Madrid 1974).
Classic Spanish nautical dictionary. Extended descriptions of ship timbers and fittings, including how they are at-

tached and used, as well as definitions of ship types, rigging, and equipment.

W G PERRIN (ed), *The Autobiography of Phineas Pett*, Navy Records Society (London 1918).
Written by an eminent English shipbuilder of the mid seventeenth century, Pett's story is one of the very few such autobiographies in any language. Perrin's introduction and a set of documentary appendices establish the historical context.

CARLA RAHN PHILLIPS, *Six Galleons for the King of Spain. Imperial Defense in the Early Seventeenth Century* (Baltimore 1986).
Detailed examination of Spanish ship design and construction in the sixteenth and early seventeenth century, based on archival research and set into a broad context of European political and economic history.

M J RODRÍGUEZ-SALGADO and SIMON ADAMS (eds), *England, Spain and the Gran Armada 1585–1604. Essays from the Anglo-Spanish Conferences London and Madrid 1988* (Savage, Maryland 1991).
Collection of essays by experts in English and Spanish naval history, containing much new information and revised interpretations of the armada campaign of 1588.

ABBOTT PAYSON USHER, 'Spanish Ships and Shipping in the Sixteenth and Seventeenth Centuries', in *Facts and Factors in Economic History. For Edwin Francis Gay* (Cambridge, Massachusetts 1932; reprinted New York 1967).
Useful early survey, now out of date in many particulars, but still widely cited by authors who read only English.

THE FLUIT

JAN VAN BEYLEN, *Schepen van de Nederlanden Van de late middeleeuwen tot het einde van de 17e eeuw* (Amsterdam 1970).

J R BRUIJN, 'Dutch Privateering during the Second and Third Anglo-Dutch Wars', *Low Countries History Yearbook 1978 (Acta Historicae Neerlandicae XI)*, pp79–93.

AKSEL E CHRISTENSEN, *Dutch Trade to the Baltic About 1600 – Studies in the Sound Toll Register and Dutch Shipping Records* (The Hague 1941).

RALPH DAVIS, *The Rise of the English Shipping Industry in the Seventeenth and Eighteenth Centuries* (London 1962).

IRENE DE GROOT and ROBERT VORSTMAN, *Sailing Ships: Prints by the Dutch Masters from the Sixteenth to the Nineteenth Century* (Maarssen, Netherlands 1980).

A J HOVING, 'A 17th century Dutch 134-foot *pinas*', *International Journal of Nautical Archaeology* 17/3 and /4 (1988), pp211–222, 331–338.

JONATHAN I ISRAEL, *Dutch Primacy in World Trade 1585–1740* (Oxford 1989).

——, *The Dutch Republic and the Hispanic World 1606–1661* (Oxford 1982).

J KUYPER, 'Pieter Jansz Liorne en de Nederlandse Scheepsbouw', *West-Friesland Oud en Nieuw* 24, pp60–75.

ALAN McGOWAN, 'The Dutch Influence on British Shipbuilding', in DAVID PROCTOR and CHARLES WILSON (eds), *1688: The Seaborne Alliance and Diplomatic Revolution* (Greenwich 1989), pp89–98.

DOUGLASS NORTH, 'Sources of Productivity Change in Ocean Shipping, 1600–1850', *Journal of Political Economy* 76 (1968), pp953–70.

ROB OOSTING, 'Preliminary Results of the Research on the 17th-Century Merchantmen Found at Lot E81 in the Noordoostpolder', in REINDER REINDERS and KEES PAUL (eds), *Carvel Construction Technique: Skeleton-first, Shell-first* (Oxford 1991), pp72–7.

P C VAN ROYEN, 'The First Phase of the Dutch Straatvaart (1591–1605): Fact and Fiction', *International Journal of Maritime History* 2/1 (June 1990), pp69–102.

RICHARD W UNGER 'Dutch Design Specialization and Building Methods in the Seventeenth Century', in CARL OLOF CEDERLUND (ed), *Postmedieval Boat and Ship Archaeology* (Oxford 1985), pp153–64.

——, *Dutch Shipbuilding Before 1800: Ships and Guilds* (Assen, Netherlands 1978).

——, 'Selling Dutch Ships in the Sixteenth Century', *Maritime History* 3 (1973), pp155–66.

——, 'The Netherlands Herring Fishery in the Late Middle Ages: the False Legend of William Beukels of Biervliet', *Viator* 9 (1978), pp335–56.

THEODORUS VELIUS, *Chroniick van Hoorn . . .* (3rd ed Hoorn, Netherlands 1648).

GARY WALTON, 'Sources of Productivity Change in American Colonial Shipping, 1675–1775', *Economic History Review*, Second series, 20/1 (April 1967), pp67–78.

NICOLAES WITSEN, *Architectura Navalis et Regimen Nauticum ofte Aeloude en Hedendaagsche Scheeps-bouw en Bestier* (1st ed 1671; 2nd ed, Amsterdam 1690).

CORNELIS VAN YK, *De Nederlandsche Scheeps-bouw-konst open Gestelt* (Amsterdam 1697).

MEDITERRANEAN COASTAL SHIPPING

Many of the titles listed in the Mediterranean Round Ship section are also relevant to this, but those below are more general background books.

H AHRWEILER, *Byzance et la mer* (Paris 1966).

M BALARD, *La Romanie génoise (XIIe-début du XVe siècle)*, 2 vols (Genoa and Rome 1978).

C CARRERE, *Barcelone, centre économique à l'époque des difficultés 1380–1462*, 2 vols (Paris and The Hague 1967).

P CHAUNU, *L'expansion européenne du XIIIe au XVe siècle* (Paris 1969).

E CONCINA, *L'arsenale della Repubblica di Venezia. Tecnica e istituzioni dal Medioevo all'età moderna* (Milan 1984).

S GOITEIN, *A Mediterranean Society* (Princeton, New Jersey 1964–1967).

J GUIRAL-HADZIIOSSIF, *Valence, port méditerranéen* (Paris 1985).

J HEERS, *Gênes au XVe siècle. Activité économique et problèmes sociaux* (Paris 1961).

——, *La navigazione mediterranea nell'Alto Medioevo*, Settimane di Studie del Centro italiano sull'Alto Medioevo (Spoleto 1978).

J-C HOCQUET, *Le sel et la fortune de Venise, Volume 2: Voiliers et commerce en Méditerranée 1200–1650* (Lille 1979).

F C LANE, *Navires et constructeurs à Venise pendant la Renaissance* (Paris 1965).

——, *Le navi di Venezia* (Turin 1983).

A R LEWIS, *Power and Trade in the Mediterranean, AD 500–1100* (Princeton, New Jersey 1951).

F MELIS, 'Werner Sombart e i problemi della navigazione del Medioevo', in *I transporti e le communicazioni nel Medioevo* (Florence 1984).

M TANGHERONI, 'L'Italia e la navigazione mediterranea dopo la fine dell'Impero d'Occidente', in *Optima Hereditas* (Milan 1992).

A TENENTI and U TUCCI (eds), *Storia di Venezia, Volume XII: Il Mare* (Rome 1991).

F THIRIET, *La Romanie vénitienne au Moyen Age* (Rome 1958).

GUNS AND GUNNERY

JEAN BOUDRIOT, *The Seventy-four Gun Ship. Volume 2: Fitting Out the Hull* (East Rotherfield, Sussex 1986).
Devoted to eighteenth-century practice but useful for outlining some of the basic problems of shipboard artillery; beautifully illustrated.

CARLO CIPOLLA, *Guns, Sails and Empires: Technological Innovation and the Early Phases of European Expansion 1400–1700* (New York 1965).
An important book pointing out the significance of European technological advantages – especially the cannon and the full rigged ship – in the establishment of the early empires.

PHILIPPE CONTAMINE, *War in the Middle Ages* (Oxford and New York 1984).
A highly regarded recent study and a counter-weight to the old condescending view of medieval warfare as tactically primitive and organisationally chaotic. Good on the introduction of gunpowder artillery.

LUIS COLLADO, *Platica Manual de Artilleria* (Milan 1592; Italian ed, Venice 1586).

HOWARD DOUGLAS, *A Treatise on Naval Gunnery, 1855* (reprint of the 4th ed, London 1982).
Although relatively late in the history of black powder, this book summarises much of the lore of naval gunnery built up over centuries.

FRANK FOX, *Great Ships: The Battlefleet of King Charles II* (London 1980).
Early sections deal with the ships around which line of battle tactics were evolved.

ALFRED G A GREENHILL, 'Ballistics', *Encyclopaedia Britannica* (11th ed, 1911), Volume III, pp270–79.

JOHN F GUILMARTIN, JR, 'Ballistics in the Black Powder Era', in ROBERT D SMITH (ed), *British Naval Armaments, Royal Armouries Conference Proceedings* I (London 1989).

——, 'Early Modern Naval Ordnance and European Penetration of the Caribbean: the Operational Dimension', with Appendix, 'The Internal Ballistics of Black Powder', appendix to *International Journal of Nautical Archaeology* 17/1 (January 1988), pp47–53.

——, 'The early Provision of Artillery Armament on Mediterranean War Galleys', *The Mariner's Mirror* 50 (1973), pp257–80.

——, 'The guns of the *Santissimo Sacramento*', *Technology and Culture* 24/4 (October 1982), pp559–601.

——, *Gunpowder and Galleys: Changing Technology and Mediterranean Warfare at Sea in the Sixteenth Century* (Cambridge 1974).
An important, and now classic, work dealing with the effects of the introduction of gunpowder artillery on Mediterranean concepts of naval warfare.

L GWEN-DJEN, J NEEDHAM and P CHI-HSING, 'The Oldest Representation of a Bombard', *Technology and Culture* 29/3 (October 1988), pp594–605.

HM WAR OFFICE, *Treatise on Ammunition* (8th edition, London 1905).

HM WAR OFFICE, *Treatise on Service Explosives* (London 1895).

HENRY KAHANE and ANDREAS TIETZE, *The Lingua Franca in the Levant: Turkish Nautical Terms of Italian and Greek Origin* (Urbana, Illinois 1958).

BRIAN LAVERY, *The Arming and Fitting of English Ships of War, 1600–1800* (London 1987)
Mostly concerned with later centuries but some information on naval guns and gunnery as understood at the beginning of the seventeenth century.

COLIN MARTIN and GEOFFREY PARKER, *The Spanish Armada* (London 1988).
Based on recent archaeological work, the book's view of Armada artillery modifies the orthodoxy established by Michael Lewis's *Armada Guns* (1961).

J R PARTINGTON, *A History of Greek Fire and Gunpowder* (Cambridge 1960).
A standard academic history; now dated in details.

CLIFFORD J ROGERS, 'The Military Revolutions of the Hundred Years' War', *The Journal of Military History* 57/2 (April 1993), pp241–278.

JOE J SIMMONS, III, 'Wrought-iron Ordnance: Revealing Discoveries from the New World', *Interna-*

tional Journal of Nautical Archaeology 17/1 (January 1988), pp25–34.

ROBERT D SMITH, 'Port Pieces: The Use of Wrought-Iron Guns in the Sixteenth Century', *Journal of the Ordnance Society* 5 (1993), pp1–10.

NICCOLO TARTAGLIA, *Three books of colloquies concerning the arte of shooting in great and small pieces of artillerie, variable randges, measure and weight of leaden yron and marble stone pellets, minerall saltpeeter; gunpowder of divers sorts and the cause of why some sortes of gunpowder are corned and some sortes of gunpowder are not corned.* CYPRIAN LUCAR, translator and author of appendix (London 1588; original, Italian edition 1546).
The most useful of early gunnery manuals in English.

SHIP CONSTRUCTION: TOOLS AND TECHNIQUES

G ARWIDSSON, *The Mästermyr find. A Viking Age Tool Chest from Gotland*, Kungl Vitterhets Historie och Antikvitets Akademien (Stockholm 1983).

JAN BILL, 'Gedesbyskibet. Middelalderlig skude – og faergefart fra Falster', in *Nationalmuseets Arbejdsmark, 1991* (Copenhagen 1991), pp188–198.

A E CHRISTENSEN, 'Boat finds from Bryggen', in *The Bryggen Papers, Main Series* I (Oslo 1985), pp47–278.

OLE CRUMLIN-PEDERSEN, 'The Grestedbro Ship', *Acta Archaeologica* 39 (1968), pp262–267.

——, 'Wood Technology and Forest Resources in the Light of Medieval Shipfinds', in C VILLAIN-GANDOSSI *et al* (eds), *Medieval Ships and the Birth of Technological Societies*, Vol I, pp25–42 (Malta 1989).

VALERIE FENWICK, *The Graveney Boat: A Tenth-Century Find from Kent*, BAR British Series 53 (Oxford 1978).

W L GOODMAN *The History of Woodworking Tools* (London 1984).
The standard work on the tools of the carpentry trades; illustrated.

M GUÉROUT, *et al, Le Navire Génois de Villefranche – un naufrage de 1516?* (Paris 1990).

PER KOHRTZ ANDERSEN, *Kollerupkoggen* (Thisted, Denmark 1983).

O OLSEN and OLE CRUMLIN-PEDERSEN, 'The Skuldelev Ships (II): A Report of the Final Underwater Excavation in 1959 and the Salvaging Operation in 1962', *Acta Archaelogica* 38 (1967), pp73–174.

Å E RÅLAMB, *Skeps Byggerij eller Adelig öfnings Tionde Tom* (1691; facsimile edition Stockholm 1943).
Although a late seventeenth-century work, the text contains some far older shipbuilding practices.

FRIDA VAN TYGHEM, *Op en Om De Middeleeuwse Bouwwerf. De gereedschappen en toestellen gebruikt bij het bouwen van de vroege middeleeuwen tot omstreeks 1600. Studie gesteund op beeldende, geschreven en archeologische bronnen*, 2 vols (Brussels 1966).

D M WILSON, 'Anglo-Saxon Carpenters' Tools', in M CLAUS, W HAARNAGEL and K RADDATZ (eds) *Studien zur europäischen Vor- und Frühgeschichte* (Neumünster, Germany 1968), pp143–150.

TREATISES ON SHIPBUILDING BEFORE 1650

R C ANDERSON, 'Early Books on Shipbuilding and Rigging', *The Mariner's Mirror* 10 (1924), pp53–64.
A survey of printed works to the mid eighteenth century, all very briefly considered. This study often has more to say about the books than their content.

——, 'Italian Naval Architecture about 1445', *Mariner's Mirror* 11 (1925), pp135–163.
This article contains most of the matter on shipbuilding and design contained in the *Libro* of Zorzi da Modon.

——, 'Jal's Memoire N°5 and the Manuscript *Fabbrica di galere*', *The Mariner's Mirror* 31 (1945), pp160–67.
Anderson critically discusses Jal's seminal work, and indicates that he omitted some important sections of the *Fabbrica*.

GIORGETTA BONFIGLIO DOSIO (ed), *Ragioni antique spettanti all'arte del mare et fabriche de vasselli: manoscritto nautico del sec XV*, Comitato per la pubblicazione delle fonti relative alla storia di Venezia, *Fonti per la storia di Venezia, sez V: Fondi vari* (Venice 1987).
This scholarly edited text may be difficult for many since its fifteenth-century Venetian is not easy, even for those who know Italian. The introductory essays, in Italian and English, are valuable, especially the one by Alvise Chiaggiato.

ENNIO CONCINA, *Navis: L'umanesimo sul mare, 1470–1740* (Turin 1990).
Humanists considered marine architecture a part of the *arte del disegno*. Concina traces their interests from early controversy over the nature of the Greek *trieres* to influence on contemporary shipbuilding.

BARTOLOMEO CRESCENTIO, *Nautica Mediterranea* (Rome 1607).
This classic of maritime lore is valuable, but must be used with caution.

JOSEPH FURTTENBACH, *Architectura Navalis* (Ulm 1629; facsimile reprint, Hildesheim 1975).
Containing beautiful engraved plates, Furttenbach's book is more Italian than German, even though it is written in the latter language.

DIEGO GARCIA DE PALACIO, *Instrucción Náutica para Navegar* (Mexico City 1587; facsimile reprint, Madrid 1944).
As the title suggests, the real emphasis of this work is on navigation, but the chapters on ships and rigging are valuable. The first printed book on shipbuilding.

——, (translated by J M BANKSON), *Nautical Instruction, 1587* (Bisbee, Arizona 1986).
English translation of the above.

F C LANE, *Navires et constructeurs à Venise pendant la Renaissance* (Paris 1965).
Lane's study of Venetian shipbuilding in the Renaissance is a classic. This French translation of Lane's *Venetian Ships and Shipbuilders of the Renaissance* (Baltimore 1934) contains revisions. Though this is still a fundamental work, the present state of knowledge has rendered some of its details obsolete.

PANTERO PANTERA, *L'armata navale* (Rome 1614).
This work lacks the illustrations that make Crescentio's *Nautica mediterranea* so valuable, but contains much useful information on artillery carried on galleys and great galleys as well as other matters.

REINDER REINDERS and KEES PAUL (eds), *Carvel Construction Technique: Skeleton-first, Shell-first* (Oxford 1991).
This collection of thirty-one studies from the Fifth International Symposium on Boat and Ship Archaeology, Amsterdam 1988, ranges from the historical and archaeological to the anthropological.

JOÃO DA GAMA LOBO PIMENTEL BARATA, 'O livro primeiro da architectura naval de João Baptista Lavanha', *Ethnos* 4 (1965), pp221–298.
Published by the Instituto Portugês de Arquelogia História e Etnografia, Lisboa. The long introductory article explains and sets Lavanha's work in context.

ERIC RIETH, 'Un systeme de conception des carénes de la seconde moitié du XVI siècle', *Neptunia* 165/166 (1987) and 169 (1988).
This work includes drawings and text from Fernando de Oliveira, *Livro da fábrica das Naos*, as well as from Manuel Fernandes, *Livro das traças de carpintaria*.

MARITIME ICONOGRAPHY

RICHARD W UNGER, *The Art of Medieval Technology. Images of Noah the Shipbuilder* (New Brunswick, New Jersey 1991).

CHRISTIANE VILLAIN-GANDOSSI, 'Iconography of post-medieval ship', in C O CEDERLUND (ed), *Postmedieval Boat and Ship Archaeology*, BAR International Series 256 (Oxford 1985).
Deals with ships from the late fifteenth century.

Glossary of Terms and Abbreviations

Compiled by Robert Gardiner. As for other volumes in this series, the glossary assumes a basic knowledge of ships and omits the most basic terminology; it also avoids those words which occur only once and are defined in situ. For this period there are particular problems with ship type definitions: firstly, little is known about many of the vessels mentioned in contemporary sources; secondly, ship designations carried different – often radically different – meanings from place to place and over the course of time; thirdly, it is by no means clear that in many documents the writer was attempting a precise technical description – the plethora of words whose etymology suggests an original meaning little more specific than 'ship' reinforces this doubt. As a result, many of the following entries consciously avoid the dogmatic. For those wishing to analyse what known evidence there is, the best single source is still Augustin Jal, *Glossaire Nautique*, 3 vols (Paris 1848), and the ongoing project to revise this great work, *La Nouvelle Glossaire Nautique d'Augustin Jal* (Paris 1973– ; letters A to G published to date). However, to receive the full benefit of Jal's amazing scholarship the reader will need to master not only French but a range of European languages, live and dead, in which the original quotations are printed.

aftercastle. A structure at the stern end of a ship, derived from the free-standing tower-like additions on northern European vessels of the Viking tradition and the raised platforms employed on Mediterranean 'round' ships (and, indeed, galleys). Over time the structure became more integrated with the hull topsides, developing into the half-deck, quarterdeck and poop arrangements of carracks and galleons. *See also* forecastle.

al scalaccio. System of rowing in which oars were manned by more than one man. In Venice and other Mediterranean galley powers it replaced the older system of one man per oar called *alla sensile* (*qv*) in the mid sixteenth century, and eventually in the largest vessels six or seven men to an oar became possible, although four or five was more general.

alla sensile. System of rowing with each oar handled by one man, as opposed to the multi-manned *al scalaccio* (*qv*). Translating as 'in the simple fashion', *alla sensile* was the usual system throughout the Middle Ages, until superseded in the Italian maritime republics in the mid sixteenth century. The arrangement of the oars themselves, however, could be far from simple.

aplustria. The stern ornament of ancient ships, usually in the shape of a fan or a plume;

survived on Mediterranean craft into the Middle Ages.

arêch. Ancient Arab measurement of length, 1 arêch equalling about 0.4m or 1ft 4in.

arbalest. A crossbow. Known in various forms since ancient times; besides the familiar man-portable weapon, there were also larger versions for fixed applications, like fortifications and ships.

arsenal. Armoury where weapons were manufactured, maintained and stockpiled. The term obtained Europe-wide currency due to the fame of the Venetian Arsenale, the republic's great naval base and the seat of her maritime power. The word and the concept comes, via the Turkish *tersana*, from the Arabic *dar-sina-'a*.

astrolabe. A name applied to a range of complex astronomer's instruments, but in a maritime context the seaman's version was a relatively simple navigational device employed to measure the altitude of heavenly bodies. It consisted of a graduated metal ring (usually brass) which was suspended vertically when in use, with a sighting rule that pivoted from the centre of the ring, allowing it to be lined up with the target and its elevation read off the scale. There is a reference to astrolabes in use by the pilots of Majorca as early as 1295.

balener, baleinier, (and other variant spellings). Etymologically connected with the English balinger (*qv*), in medieval French and southern European usage, it was a light, shallow draught vessel suitable for privateering and used by naval forces for scouting. It may well have been rowed as well as sailed, and in fifteenth century lists it is classed as larger than galiotes, barques and caravels but smaller than nefs. Later the term was applied to whalers, but it is unlikely that there was any design continuity between these vessels and the previous employers of the name.

balinger. English late medieval craft possibly derived from the clinker-built double-ended craft descended from Viking boats known in the Middle Ages as galleys – *ie* capable of being rowed as well as sailed, as distinct from the sail-only cogs. In the fifteenth century they seem to have been the light scouting and raiding forces of the English navy. *See also* balener.

barca. Often a non-specific term for a ship, but in some contexts synonymous with the French barque (*qv*); also applied to the largest boat of a medieval Mediterranean 'round' ship (*qv*).

barinel, or varinel. Portuguese craft of the late Middle Ages, which was light, manoeuvr-

able and of shallow draught. Propelled by both sail and oar, the type was a predecessor of the caravel (*qv*) in its employment for voyages of exploration. Some sources suggest that it was effectively the same as the Atlantic balener (*qv*) and that it developed from a two-masted rig of two square sails to a square main and lateen mizzen, and from the 1430s to a three-masted rig.

barque. As understood in the nineteenth century a barque was a vessel with three or more masts, square rigged on all but the fore-and-aft mizzen, but earlier usage was more complex. The term was applied to a two-masted coastal trader of Italian provenance in the late Middle Ages, and the term was used in the North from the fifteenth century for a fast craft suitable for both naval and privateering employment. Mediterranean barques of the 1400s seem to have carried three lateen rigged masts, and the type was a predecessor of the caravel in Portuguese voyages of exploration.

barza. A large three-masted ship adopted in Venice in the late fifteenth century from an Iberian prototype; possibly a step towards the galleon, one recorded example of this period reached 1200 tons.

base. A small breech-loading cannon with separate chambers, firing a shot of about ½lb. In late sixteenth- and early seventeenth-century lists the term seems to apply to the smallest of the conventional muzzle-loading guns, and some examples were mounted as shipboard swivel guns.

basilisk. A large cannon of relatively great length in relation to bore; late sixteenth-century English examples fired a shot of about 15lbs weight.

beak, beakhead. The protrusion beyond the stem proper underneath the bowsprit that characterised galleons and their successors. Probably developed from the overhanging bow of the galley, the beakhead served as a platform from which to handle the headsails and the site of the crew's latrines.

beam ends. In some medieval ship types, like the cog, the transverse beams passed through the hull planking, the beam ends being visible outside the hull (and clearly depicted in many of the ship portraits on town seals). By rebating the strakes into the beams, the hull achieved a degree of transverse rigidity that shell-first (*qv*) construction otherwise lacked.

berços. Portuguese swivel guns; the word is the same as the English base (*qv*).

bergantin, bergantino. Variant of brigantin (*qv*).

bertone. An Italian description, common in the sixteenth and early seventeenth centuries, of a specific type of vessel hailing from England or, more properly, from the British Isles. It was high-sided and capacious but not long, and may have derived its description by analogy from the Turkish *bortun*, with which the Italians would have been familiar. However, since very little is known about the *bortun*, and the type cannot be identified with any English term, this is not very helpful. Some scholars feel the etymology of the word may originally denote 'Breton'.

bireme. A galley with two tiers of oars; sometimes also used of vessels rowed *alla sensile* (*qv*), with pairs of oars per bench.

black powder. Gunpowder. In its earliest form it was a mixture of saltpetre, charcoal and sulphur in approximately equal measure by weight, but later the percentages 75/15/10 were preferred. Serpentine powder, the earliest type, was ground to a fine powder while dry and mixed together, but the more powerful corned powder was developed by mixing the ingedients with wine or urine and grinding the ensuing liquid slurry; this was then dried, broken into grains and processed to give uniform sizes.

Blockkahn. A logboat-derived small boat found on some North German lakes; the bow and stern were formed of solid blocks which gave the vessel its name. It is thought to be the distant ancestor of the cog (*qv*). *See also* Kanebloke.

bocca. Italian term for midship section or, strictly, the point of maximum breadth. Important in the early geometry-based design systems.

bombard.
Early large-calibre cannon, usually made of wrought iron staves arranged around a cylindrical former over which heated hoops were passed; on cooling these shrank on to the staves, binding them together. The earliest versions had separate chambers and were thus breech-loading. Also called lombards in some early sources.

bonaventure mizzen. A fourth mast, an auxiliary mizzen, carried aft of the mizzen proper, and like the latter carrying a lateen sail (and even a lateen topsail in some cases). Also called the counter mizzen, it was generally confined to very large ships of the sixteenth century, and died out in the early decades of the 1600s.

borderers. Medieval ship carpenters.

botte (plural botti). Measurement of carrying capacity, widely used in medieval Mediterranean shipping. Occurring as early as the thirteenth-century Statutes of Marseilles, the word originally referred to a barrel, like the English 'butt', so means much the same as 'ton', itself derived from 'tun', a wine cask. Note that both the *botte* and the ton originally denoted volume (and still does for gross tonnage) rather than weight.

boyer. Sprit rigged Dutch coastal trader; by the mid sixteenth century the usual sail plan was a triangular jib, sprit main with two square sails, and a mizzen lateen. Boyers averaged about 100 tons.

braces. Rigging that pivots the yards; to brace up was to swing them to as sharp (*ie* small) an angle with the keel as feasible; bracing in was the reverse.

brails. Rigging leading to the edges of a sail, used to gather it in prior to furling.

Bratspill. The windlass of a cog; turned by removeable handspikes, it was used to raise the anchor and possibly other heavy shipboard lifting.

Bremen cog. The name generally applied to the Hanseatic cog discovered in the river Weser near Bremen in October 1962. The ship, which was washed away during a storm before completion, is now in the Deutsches Schiffarhtsmuseum, Bremerhaven where it has been conserved and re-assembled.

brigantin (and many variant spellings in many languages). A light, fast galley, smaller than a galiote (*qv*) in size, decked and rigged with a single mast and sail. The name does not occur before the fourteenth century, but later the type was widely used as a corsair by both Christian and Muslim powers in the Mediterranean. A Venetian example from around 1500 was nearly 17m long by 3m broad (55ft x 10ft), with fourteen pairs of oars; originally the oars were single-manned but later two men per oar was common, and eventually brigantins with twenty-eight oars per side were recorded.

bucius. A type of galley referred to in twelfth-century Italian sources. Unfortunately virtually nothing more is known about the type, although there is a Genoese bucius that seems to be a smaller version of the lateen nef. Reference is also made in legal documents of the same period to the buccius-navis or buss-nef, which suggests a hybrid between a galley and a 'round' ship, although one mention of 1250 gives the vessel a crew of 33, which is surely too small for a type that regularly proceeded under oars.

buntlines. Rigging from the foot of a square sail passing over the forward surface to the yard; used to spill the wind from the sail when necessary.

burchio, burchi. Venetian local craft, known from at least the thirteenth century. Originally a long, low rowing craft, which could also set a single square sail from a mast near the bow, the hull had upturned ends and short decks fore and aft; they are sometimes depicted with a barrel-shaped canopy over the open hold. A principal employment was as water carriers, but the type later grew into a far larger, barge-like vessel with very little sheer, sometimes called the *burchio da Verona*.

buss. From the fifteenth century a sea-going fishing vessel with bluff bows, a square stern and a relatively long hull; they were usually rigged with three masts, each with a single square sail, all except one of which were struck when fishing; the one remaining sail gave the vessel enough way to keep the nets taut. There are also early references to *buzi* or *buze* (Venetian 1191 and 1255), *burchia*, *bussa*, *bucca*, *bucea* and *butz*, which may be connected etymologically with buss but almost certainly have no other relation.

bussola. Compass

buyscarveel. A development of the fishing buss (*qv*) at the end of the fifteenth century into a cargo carrier; seen as a step towards the evolution of the fluit (*qv*).

calphatours. Medieval caulkers (French *calfateur*).

calzensis (plural **calzenses**). Single piece block masts, with integral masthead blocks; a common feature of the lateen rig.

cannon. Generic term for gunpowder artillery piece larger than a hand-held weapon; more specifically, it came to define the species of larger calibres of medium length, the English categories in decending order of size being: cannon royal, double cannon, cannon of eight, cannon serpentine, whole-cannon, cannon of seven, bastard cannon and demi-cannon. The exact weight of shot fired by these varied over time, but in seventeenth century naval employment, a cannon of seven fired a 47lb ball and a demi-cannon a 27lb shot.

caramoussal. A Turkish craft of the sixteenth century. Strongly associated with corsair activities, they were low, lateen rigged vessels, rather like a galley or xebec in hull form.

caravel, carabela, caravela, caravelle. Relatively fine-lined Portuguese craft of the fifteenth and sixteenth century, originally a fishing craft or coastal trader, but most famously associated with the great voyages of exploration. They were originally lateen rigged on two or more masts, and were known for their weatherly qualities, but later variants adopted square canvas for better performance before the wind. *See also* aravela da armada and caravela redonda.

caravela da armada. A sixteenth century development of the caravel (*qv*), designed for more capacity and superior naval characteristics while retaining some of the better sailing qualities of the original type. They usually carried a forward-raked fore mast with square sails and three other lateen rigged masts.

caravela redonda. A caravel with square canvas on at least the fore mast. There is an example as early as 1438–39 built by Portuguese shipwrights for Philip the Good of Burgundy and at this time the ships seem to have carried a square main and lateen mizzen. Later three-masted versions became common, with square fore and main canvas and lateen mizzen; most famous of the latter configuration was Columbus' rerigged *Nina*.

caravelões. Small caravels, used for fishing and coastal trading from the late fifteenth century.

caravo, carabo. Portuguese term for a craft much used by the Moorish states of North Africa. One reference of 1342 suggests that craft of this type transported fifty or sixty horses from Africa to Spain, but no real detail of their form or rig is known.

carrack. The derivation of the word is uncertain: there were small Arab *karaques* in the thirteenth century, and the term may have been passed to the West via Muslim influence in Iberia, but the ship type seems to owe nothing to the Arab craft. The carrack was a development of the northern European cog – called variously *cocas*, *coggones* or *coche* in the Mediterranean - combined with some features of the local skeleton-first (*qv*) and multi-masted traditions. There are Venetian references to such vessels from 1302–1312, and a 'coche baonesche', or Biscayan cog, was built at Genoa before 1350; the main features were a square sail and centreline rudder. In English documents the words carrack or tarit occur from 1350, applied to vessels of this type and usually Genoese in origin. The carrack seems to have acquired more sail from quite early, a Catalan contract of 1353 specifying main and mizzen, and the English captured a number of two-masters from the Genoese early in the fifteenth century (one was actually renamed *Le Carake*). By the middle of the 1400s three-masted examples were known and the multi-decked forestage and aftercastle were becoming more marked. Carracks tended to be very large for their day, and with the application of the hull-mounted gunport, carracks became the capital ships of sixteenth century navies, until superseded in the latter half of the century by the galleon.

carvel. A method of construction in which the strakes of planking butt at the edges, creating a flush hull surface – as opposed to clinker (*qv*) in which the strakes overlap and are clenched through this overlap. Carvel as a method of construction implies the initial setting up of a frame to which the strakes are fastened, which in turn means that some form of preconceived design is necessary in order for a properly faired shape to result. The term is closely associated with caravel (*qv*) and the technique was probably imported into northern Europe from the Mediterranean, where in late Antiquity frame-first carvel had replaced the earlier shell-first structure where mortise and tenon joints formed the connections between strakes.

cerbatanas. Early breech-loading guns of relatively small calibre.

chavo de sesto. In the earliest naval architectural treatises dealing with the Renaissance galley, this term was applied to the 'heads of design', the endmost full frames in the hull before the fining of the bow and stern lines radically altered the shape.

chiatta, chiatte. Italian small cargo and ferry boat, possibly flat-bottomed. Later usage suggests a transliteration of the French *chatte* (cat), but the earlier vessel seems to have been a different type.

Cinque Ports. An association of English Channel port towns that played a large part in the naval defence of medieval England. As its name suggests, there were originally five towns – Dover, Hastings, Romney, Hythe and Sandwich – but Rye and Winchelsea were added later. In return for commercial and legal privileges, the towns agreed to provide ships as required by the crown, so Cinque Port vessels formed the core of any naval armament up to the establishment of a permanent royal navy by Henry VII and VIII. The oldest surviving charter dates from 1278 but the exact date of its foundation is unknown; it still has a ceremonial function and the Lord Warden is currently the Queen Mother.

clenchatores. A term in medieval clinker (*qv*) shipbuilding for the artisan who 'clenched', or hammered down over roves, the nails that fastened together the overlapped edges of the planking strakes. Variations on the word included clencheres, cleyncherers and clyngkeres; they were also called repurcussores.

clencheres. *See* clenchatores.

cleyncheres. *See* clenchatores.

clinker. Method of construction in which overlapping strakes are fastened along the edges (usually with nails 'clenched' over roves, from which the term derives). It is a shell-first technique, without the benefit of a pre-erected frame, although strengthening timbers are sometimes added later.

clyngkeres. *See* clenchatores.

cocas, cocha, coche. Italian, and specifically Genoese, ship type. A reference of 1232 clearly points to a 'round' ship rather than a galley, but other characteristics are vague. May be an Italian version of 'cog' (*qv*), via the French *coque*, and later applications of the word suggest a proto carrack (*qv*).

codos. Spanish measure of length, varying according to source: early references work out at 574–575mm and 557–559mm, but in 1618 it was 560mm. Cubic codos were used for tonnage, being divided by eight to produce Spanish *toneladas*.

cog. The classic sailing ship of northern Europe in the high Middle Ages, the cog was developed on the Frisian coast from whence its usage spread to down the North Sea coasts and into the Baltic before reaching the Mediterranean. Its capacious flat-bottomed form, with straight raked stem- and sternposts, is believed to derive from the technology of expanded logboats, but by the thirteenth century the type had evolved into a sea-going vessel of several hundred tons in its largest form. It acquired a stern rudder on the centreline to replace the steering oars and was powered by a single square sail.

coggones. Mediterranean term for cogs (*qv*) or cog-derived vessels. *See also* cocas.

cokingi. Coast defence troops of the Carolingian empire, possibly suggesting that cogs (*qv*) were an important part of the forces.

collaturi. Tie tackles used to raise the long yards of the lateen rig. Also called jonchi.

contado. The agricultural hinterland supporting Italian city states.

Contarina ship. The remains of a vessel of about AD 1300 discovered in the Po delta in Italy in 1898. Its remains have disappeared but there is a model of the structure in the Museo Storico Navale, Venice.

corridoria. Gangway, usually along the sides of the ship.

corsia. The central fore-and-aft gangway of a galley, running between the port and starboard rowing benches.

counter mizzen. *See* bonaventure mizzen.

crane. In the specific context of English carracks, a winch for hauling ammunition into the topcastle; associated gear included cranelines and crane bags.

culverin. Species of cannon characterised by medium calibre and a very long barrel in relation to bore diameter. In English service a whole culverin fired a shot of about 17lbs and the demi-culverin of about 9lbs. The term became extinct around 1700 when guns became designated by their weight of shot.

dar accina'ah. Alternative transliteration of Arabic *dar-sina-'a*, a workshop. *See* arsenal.

Das Grosse Kraweel. 'The Great Carvel'; *See* Peter of La Rochelle.

demi-cannon. Species of large calibre gun. *See* cannon.

dromon. The characteristic warship of the Byzantine Empire. The term first appears at the end of the fifth century in the letters of the Emperor Theodoric as a one-masted, single-banked light galley. By the ninth and tenth century the dromon could have more than one lateen rigged mast and two banks of oars. The principal weapon was not a ram as in ancient times but Greek Fire, a primitive form of napalm projected by bellows from a syphon or syphons in the hull of the ship. During the Crusades chroniclers like William of Tyre describe dromons as capacious vessels capable of transporting men and cargo, but it may be that 'dromon' was so closely associated with the Byzantines that it was used to describe any Imperial vessel, in much the same way that later centuries made any Spanish ship a 'galleon'.

East Indiamen. Ships (not men) trading with the East Indies, which included not only the Indian subcontinent but modern Malaysia, Indonesia and Southeast Asia.

ell. A traditional unit of length, varying considerably from time to time and place to place. In Scandinavia on metrification, it was equated with 0.647m (25.5in), but in Viking times it seems to have been only about 3/4 of that.

Eltang boat. A Danish boat find dating from the twelfth century.

esloria. Spanish length between stem- and sternposts at the height of the deck.

esperas. Small cannon, usually about 3pdr calibre.

falcon. Small gun of the culverin type (*qv*) firing a shot of 1½–3lbs.

firrer. Type of steering oar used on kahns (*qv*) and sail-powered logboats. The rig was balanced in such a way that immersing the firrer to a greater or lesser extent altered the fore and aft centre of gravity, causing the boat to turn into or off the wind. The firrer differed from normal steering oars in that its blade did not need to be turned itself in order to manouevre the boat.

fisherman's anchor. The most familiar type of ground tackle with iron shank and arms and a stock (usually wooden) set in a plane at right angles to the arms.

flaill. An unidentified piece of equipment issued to English carracks of the early fifteenth century. It was associated with the windlass and one of its duties was to help raise the heavy yards; one suggestion is that it was some kind of pawl.

fluit, fluyt, flute, etc. Characteristically Dutch merchantman, ship rigged and of large carrying capacity, with extreme tumblehome and a narrow 'fluit' stern. They were usually austere in decoration, with a plain stemhead, few if any guns, and a small crew relative to tonnage; there were, however, more conventional versions, with more powerful armament, for trading in dangerous waters. They were essentially a product of the late sixteenth century, but dominated the Dutch carrying trade in the seventeenth. Known as 'flyboats' to the English.

footropes. Ropes suspended beneath the yards of square rigged ships for the crew to stand on when furling or reefing sail; also known as horses.

forecastle. A structure at the bow of a ship, derived from the free-standing tower-like additions on northern European vessels of the Viking tradition and the raised platforms employed on Mediterranean 'round' ships (and, indeed, galleys). Over time the design became more integrated with the hull topsides, developing into the multi-decked defensible structures of carracks and galleons. See also aftercastle.

forloke or **forelok.** A T-shaped wooden chock used in early breech-loading guns to fix in position the breech block or 'hall'.

fowler. A small breech-loading anti-personnel weapon; probably from 'fowling piece', derived from the kind of gun used for shooting wildfowl.

frame-first. A term used by modern historians for ship- and boatbuilding in which the hull strakes are fastened to a pre-erected framework, as opposed to shell-first construction like clinker. In many contexts it is synonymous with carvel (*qv*), but is preferred as being a more precise definition than the old dichotomy between carvel and clinker, since there are other methods of building hulls shell-first than clinker.

fusta, fustes. A small galley. In the thirteenth century, at the time of Alfonso the Wise, it came immediately after galleys in a list of ships in descending order of size; by the fifteenth century it formed a specific sub-group within the galleys category, but seems to have ranged in size almost up to whole galleys and down to brigantins (*qv*). Little detail is known about them, but they had around 12–15 rowing benches originally and were probably single-manned, but by the beginning of the sixteenth century they had two or three oars a side per bench.

futtock. Portion of a ship's frame, between the lowest (floor) and highest (top-) timbers. By the seventeenth century there were four or five futtocks in overlapping pairs contributing to a 'framed bend', or rib.

gad. English term for a long iron dart thrown from the fighting tops of warships in late medieval naval battles.

galea grossa. The great galley, the largest form of oared ship known in the Mediterranean of the late Middle Ages. In Venice, which claimed the invention of the type, they were employed initially as merchant ships in high-value trades; as early as 1320 such vessels could carry 150 tons and later galleys were even larger.

galeazza (plural **galeazze**). Large Genoese galley, but slightly smaller than a regular galley with a smaller crew. However, in Venetian usage they seem to have been as big as the *galea grossa* (*qv*).

galeones. Term used for unspecified type of craft from at least the thirteenth century on the south and east coasts of the Iberian peninsula.

galleotta, galiote, galliota, etc. Late medieval small bireme galley, having between 16 and 22 rowing benches, two masts and two side rudders.

galizabras. A small galleon of the sixteenth century; one reference of 1568 relates to a vessel of 200 *toneladas*.

galleaza, galleazza. Variant forms of galeazza (*qv*).

galleon. Sea-going full rigged ship of the sixteenth century and later, characterised by a relatively high length-to-breadth ratio, a long beak under the bowsprit and a crescent profile rising somewhat higher at the stern than at the forecastle. Compared with carracks (*qv*), the lines of the galleon were finer, the superstructures lower, and under sail both speed and handling were superior. Galleons were usually heavily armed, although they were not necessarily specialist warships. The term came to be closely associated with the Iberian powers, and in particular Spain, so that by the seventeenth century almost any large Spanish ship could be described as a galleon.

gallioni. Small galleys or galiotes used by the Venetians in the fifteenth century for river and coastal patrol; the word may be the origin of 'galleon' (*qv*).

garboard. The strake of planking nearest to the keel, into which it is usually fitted by means of a 'rabbet' (rebate). It is thought to be derived, via Dutch, from 'gathering board' - presumably because it was where loose water would fetch up before being funnelled to the pumps.

gaskets. A securing for a furled sail, made from rope or canvas.

Gokstad ship. A Viking vessel found in a burial mound at Gokstad in southern Norway in 1880. Dating from about AD 850, the craft was large (79ft, 24m long) and relatively high-sided with shuttered tholes for the oars; that the craft was seaworthy was proved by the sailing of a replica across the Atlantic in 1893. The original was carefully reassembled and is now in Oslo's Viking Ship Museum.

gonnes. Medieval English spelling of 'guns'.

great ship. In general terms, more or less synonymous with the later 'capital ship', and used as such as early as the first decades of the fifteenth century. At the beginning of the seventeenth century it applied specifically to the large galleon-derived pure warships of the English navy. In the Stuart period there were a few even larger 'ships royal', and in the reorganisation of the 1650s the great ships were rerated as Second Rates.

grip, grippo, grippi. A common designation in the Mediterranean during the Middle Ages for a small coastal cargo carrier; little is known about them for certain but they may have been sail-and-oar hybrids. The word occurs frequently in Venetian sources.

gudgeon. The part of the rudder hinge that was attached to the ship, containing a ring into which the pintle (*qv*) of the rudder itself fitted.

the Hanse. A trading confederation originally based on north German towns but coming to dominate the trade of most of northern Europe and the Baltic. The Hanseatic League dates its foundation to Lübeck in 1159 and by the first half of the thirteenth century it included Hamburg, but eventually it was to unite the merchants of over thirty German towns into 'hansas' or chambers of commerce; it also set up outstations in important foreign entrepots like Bristol and London, Bergen in Norway, Visby in Sweden, and Novgorod in Russia. The Hanse aimed at commercial monopolies, and was particularly powerful in shipping and fishing, the characteristic ship-type being the cog (*qv*), a very cost-effective carrier in its day. The League declined in importance from the late fifteenth century, as trade patterns changed, new methods of business organisation were introduced, and a more competitive spirit was fostered.

hekboot. Dutch merchant ship, sometimes called a hagboat in other northern European languages. A three-masted full rigged ship, the hekboot had a more conventional hull with less tumblehome than the fluit (*qv*).

helderes. See holders.

herikochum. A term occurring in an early medieval German source denoting a fast warship, possibly a variant of the cog (*qv*).

holders. In clinker construction the assistants who 'held up' (*ie* pressed a hammer against the head of each nail as it was clenched). There were other versions of the term, such as helderers and tenenties contra.

hulk. Rather mysterious ship type of North Sea origins whose working career paralled, and eventually outlasted, that of the cog. What small iconographical evidence there is suggests a banana-shaped hull of very rounded form. A Dorestad coin of AD 800 may show one, and documents of the period indicate that the hulk was a very important carrier in trade between Britain and continental Europe. As a regular type-name the word declined in the fifteenth century, and eventually changed its meaning to indicate a dismasted vessel or one laid up and unfit for sea; if there is any connection between the two usages scholars have been unable to make a convincing case for it.

Humber keels. Barge-like riverine craft of the English east coast powered by a single square sail. This may be a survivor, in usage if not in form, of the medieval ship type the keel (*qv*).

jekta. Norwegian coastal vessels with a single square sail that represent a survival of Viking boat design and construction down to the early twentieth century when the last of the type were still in use.

jonchi. *See* collaturi.

Kahn. Primitive fishing boat from North German lakes thought to be the ancestor of the sea-going cog. *See also* Blockkahn.

Kalmar wrecks. Excavations in the medieval harbour of Kalmar in southeastern Sweden during the 1930s revealed eighteen partially complete wrecks and fragments of a further six. Best preserved is a small coastal trader of the thirteenth century (probably the oldest of the ship finds).

kanebloke. Term used in a Hamburg document of 1260 denoting a Blockkahn (*qv*).

karaque. Muslim ship designation, although there is little firm evidence about its characteristics. The word may be the origin of 'carrack', coming into European usage through the Muslim influence in the Iberian peninsula.

katschip. A Dutch merchant ship; in effect a smaller and simpler version of the fluit (*qv*), with pole masts, no topsails and a gaff mizzen.

keel. (i) The principle longitudinal element in the construction of a ship, in effect the 'backbone' of the vessel to which the 'ribs' or transverse frames are attached. (ii) A ship type designation, in early medieval English usage denoting a low, clinker vessel of Viking derivation; also called nefs at this time, although the latter were usually specifically warships.

keelson, or kelson. A longitudinal framing timber fitted on top of the keel (*qv*) proper, usually serving to fix the transverse framing timbers in place.

khitti. Arab craft of the early Middle Ages; characteristics unknown.

knaar. The sea-going cargo carrier of the Viking age, famous from many references in the sagas and other Scandinavian literature. Compared with longships, the knaar was shorter, deeper and more capacious, and probably not intended for regular beaching; relatively seaworthy, the knaar was the most probable vehicle of the Viking exploration of the North Atlantic.

Kollerup. Danish site where the wreck of a cog-like vessel was discovered in 1978. The ship had no keelson but a substantial transverse frame, positioned relatively far forward, incorporated the mast step; there were also signs of a transverse bulkhead let into the frame and some form of planked decking in the hold.

kongebuss. High medieval variant of the knaar (*qv*); connections with the later buss (*qv*) may be little more than etymological.

kugghamn. Literally 'cog harbour', as at Birka.

Ladby boat. A tenth-century craft found in a chieftain's burial mound on the Danish island of Funen in 1935. Only the impression remained of a vessel some 67ft long.

lap-strake. Another term for clinker (*qv*).

lateen. Sail or rig characterised by triangular canvas set from a long yard attached to the mast at an angle of about 45 degrees from the horizontal, the forward end being the lower. It was a fore-and-rig rig dating from at least late Antiquity and was the usual form of sail for most types of medieval Mediterranean craft, including galleys. In the late Middle Ages it was also added to square rigged vessels, usually as a small after sail to help balance the rig and aid going about, and retained this role with the development of the three-masted ship rig.

lembus (plural lembi). There are frequent references in medieval sources to Mediterranean small craft by this name , but it is not at all clear whether the various types have anything in common. One document of 1391 mentions a fore and main mast, the fore being larger, with two lateen and one square sail; the vessel was regarded as fast, and was large enough to have an eight-oared boat, but did not seem to have any oars of its own. However, a source of 1398 mentions a craft with thirteen benches (twenty-six oars) so may have been of the small brigantin type (*qv*); there was also a smaller version called a *lembutus* described in a reference of 1474 as having six benches.

leny. A general Mediterranean term for a ship, derived ultimately from the word *lignum* (*qv*). Some references suggest a craft larger than a barque (*qv*) but smaller than a nao (*qv*).

lignum, ligne, line, etc. Ultimately derived from the Latin for a wooden vessel, the term had widespread medieval currency in the Mediterranean world in many linguistic variations. It was often unspecific and even where a particular type was meant it is now virtually impossible to judge what was intended. A fourteenth-century source, for example, suggests a rowing craft below the galley in size, but other references imply a large vessel.

lignum (plural ligna) de bandis. There are numerous Genoese references to these craft, which were variants of the above but with high freeboard, achieved by raised gunwales. A document of 1361 about a *lembum de bandis* gives a crew of only four plus the captain so they may not have been rowing craft.

lignum (plural ligna) de orlo. A lignum (*qv*) with a topside bulwark or a screen of weather cloths.

lignum de teriis. A lignum (*qv*) which closely resembled contemporary galleys.

linh. See lignum.

long ships. Used with two separate meanings according to context: (i) a loose description of a Viking warship, as opposed to the knaar (*qv*), or (ii) in the Mediterranean, a galley, in contrast to the 'round' ship, which was propelled by sail.

lombard. See bombard.

marano (plural marani). An Italian vessel of unknown characteristics. The earliest occurence is a chronicle of 1079, and there is a reference as late as 1345. An apparently different type was developed in the early fourteenth century to carry stone from Istria, and its employment spread to other trades; by 1469 there was a fleet of *marani* that averaged 700 *botti*.

markab. An unspecified ship type that makes frequent appearances in early Arabic texts.

marciliana, marsiliane. A Venetian local ship type used for trading in the Adriatic which had a capacious flat-bottomed hull capable of both riverine and sea-going employment carrying about 70–80 tons of cargo. By the seventeenth century the largest had four masts but early types seem to have been three-masters.

martelogio tables. Trigonometrical tables of fourteenth-century origin used in navigation to account for the divergence between the Pole Star and the celestial pole.

Mataro model. Votive ship model, probably made in the latter half of the fifteenth century, originally from the Catalan monastery of San Simon de Mataro; now in the Prins Hendrik Museum, Rotterdam. Because so much of its detail is convincing, even if the proportions are crude, the model has come to be regarded as important evidence for the appearance of ships of that period – most reconstructions of Columbus' *Santa Maria*, for example, draw heavily on the model for inspiration.

mesan. In the Middle Ages the term, following its Greek derivation, applied to the centre sail of a galley. The name seems to have been retained when the sail was moved (perhaps replaced by a larger 'main' sail); in most maritime countries the move was aft, becoming a *mezana* or *mesana* in southern European languages and mizzen in English. In France, on the other hand, it must have been shifted forward, since *misaine* denotes the fore mast or sail in that country.

mexeriqueiras. The very smallest version of the caravel (*qv*), averaging about 16–20 tons, and generally employed as a dispatch boat.

mortise and tenon. Woodworking joint in which slots (mortises) are cut in one piece, into which tongues (tenons) are inserted in order to fasten it to another. The tenon can be integral with one of the pieces, or can be separate, mortises being then cut in both parts to be joined together. The technique was widely employed in shipbuilding in Antiquity, shell-first (*qv*) hulls being laboriously constructed by fixing flush strakes of timber together using this joint. Such a hull was light and strong, but required a high level of skill and was labour-intensive; it also made the pre-planning of hull shape difficult.

mude. Venetian system of state-organised galley voyages. By the fifteenth century the mercantile great galleys (*qv*) were built in the Arsenale (*qv*) to a standard state-approved design, and chartered to merchants under terms of competitive auction. They sailed in convoys on set routes to a predetermined timetable, the galleys being named after the route on which they operated - the Galley of Flanders, or the Galley of Romania, for example.

nao. One of many terms ultimately derived from *navis*, the Latin for 'ship'; for most of the Middle Ages in the Mediterranean it was applied to the most common form of sail-powered merchant ship, only relatively new or unusual types being distinguished by individual names like *cocha* or caravel. Therefore its characteristics varied, and it was used of both carracks and smaller craft in some contexts: in fifteenth-century Catalonia, for example, nao implied a vessel of one or two deck ranging in size from 300 to 700 *botti*. Columbus's famous *Santa Maria* is usually described as a nao of this type.

nau. Variant of nao (*qv*).

nauio menor. Literally 'smaller ship', in old Spanish.

nave. See navis.

naveta. Portuguese small craft.

navíos. In Spanish its literal meaning is little more than 'ship', but it was usually reserved for large vessels and by the seventeenth century in a naval context it meant a ship of the line, in much the same way as *vaisseau* in French.

navis. Latin for 'ship'. Because of the continuing employment of vulgar Latin as the language of western European bureaucracy, the term occurs widely in medieval sources. Often its use is entirely non-specific, but in the Mediterranean it tended to carry connotations of 'round' (*ie* sailing) ships of burden, and in the later centuries replaced *cocha* as the usual term for such craft, particularly as such ships began to develop carrack-like characteristics and the three-masted rig.

nef. Another ship-type designation that could mean little more than 'ship', but which had more precise meanings in certain situations. In early medieval England, for example, it was used of warships that were not cogs but belonged to the older Viking design tradition. In the Mediterranean, on the other hand, it was virtually synonymous with 'round ship' (*qv*), but in later usage it came to be reserved for the largest vessels: the famous Venetian *Roccaforte* of 1264 was so described; by 1354 both two- and three-decked nefs are documented; and by 1441 there is mention of a Genoese nef of 1500 tons.

Noortsvaerder. Dutch term for a vessel in the Norway timber trade; they were usually fitted with special timber loading ports in the bow which were sealed before sailing.

Nydam boat. A heavy clinker-built rowing boat discovered in a peat bog at Nydam in what is now Schleswig-Holstein in 1859; it is dated to about AD 350–400 and is now displayed at Schloss Gottorp near Hedeby. The boat is about 80ft (24m) long and was rowed by thirty oarsmen and steered by a single oar lashed to the quarter. It is regarded as the type of vessel likely to have been used in the Dark Age migrations, such as the Anglo-Saxon invasions of Britain.

Oostervaerder. Dutch term for vessel trading with the 'East' (*ie* the Baltic).

orcha. A late medieval Venetian adaptation of a ship type from the Hanse towns, possibly a hulk. The word is probably connected with the Spanish *urca* (*qv*).

ordo. A regulation; also used specifically of an arrangement of oars.

Oseberg ship. A Viking vessel found in a burial mound at Oseberg in southern Norway in 1904. Dated to about AD 800, the craft was of lower freeboard than the Gokstad ship (*qv*), and like that vessel can now be seen in reassembled form in the Viking Ship Museum, Oslo.

pamphylos. Greek ship of burden widely employed in the western Mediterranean in Antiquity; the ancestor of the panfile (*qv*).

panfile. Believed to be decended from the ancient pamphylos (*qv*), but its precise evolution and characteristics are unknown. During the thirteenth to fifteenth centuries references suggest a rowing craft similar to a galley, with two (probably lateen rigged) masts; it was generally undecked, but covered versions are known by the fifteenth century.

paroma. A strap for the halyards of a lateen yard.

parral or **parrel.** An assemblage of beads called trucks and wooden dividers called ribs strung onto a series of horizontal ropes. Forming a collar between the yards and their masts, and designed to allow the yards to be hoisted and lowered easily, it vaguely resembled a flexible abacus, although the beads were intended to revolve to reduce friction while the ribs stopped them moving from side to side.

passavolantes. Species of early artillery of relatively small calibre (approximately 6pdr).

patache. Small pinnace-like vessel (usually less than 100 tons); three-masted and square rigged, they were used on duties where speed and manoeuvrability were at a premium.

pedreros. Stone-firing guns; they had thinner and shorter barrels than cannon designed for iron shot, and so were lighter. Also called perriers (*qv*).

perriers. Short-barrelled lightweight guns firing stone shot. The larger calibres were considered obsolete by 1650 (although the Turks fired stone shot at Duckworth's squadron when it penetrated the Dardanelles in 1807), but some smaller sizes survived as anti-personnel weapons; in France the term continued to be used of swivel guns.

Peter of La Rochelle. The name of a large French-built carrack abandoned in Danzig in 1462 as a result of the owner's financial problems. A skeleton-first three-master, the ship is generally credited with introducing carvel construction to Hanseatic shipyards, who repaired and fitted the vessel in 1470 for the war with England. She was then renamed *Peter von Danzig*, although also known as *Das Grosse Kraweel* ('The Great Carvel'), and was armed with 19 guns in the superstructure.

Peter von Danzig. *See* Peter of La Rochelle.

pinas. *See* pinnas.

pinnace. In the sixteenth century, an English version of the Dutch *pinnas* (*qv*) but confined to smaller vessels; they were usually fast warships, used for scouting and dispatch duties - what a later age would call a frigate.

pinnas or **pinas** (plural **pinnassen**). A Dutch fine-lined, galleon-type vessel of the sixteenth and seventeenth centuries, usually employed as a warship.

pintle. The part of the rudder hinge fixed to the rudder itself, consisting of a downward-facing pin engaging the gudgeon (*qv*) on the sternpost.

pole masts. In conventional sailing ships the masts were usually set up in sections – lower mast, topmast, topgallant, etc – but pole-masted vessels (usually small craft) had single-piece masts without the extra weight of doublings, crosstrees, and so forth associated with fidded masts.

pontal. Spanish measure of 'depth in hold'.

portulan. An early form of chart found in the Mediterranean from the thirteenth century, possibly originating in the Italian maritime republics and improved in Catalonia. The principle feature of such charts was the network of rhumb lines emanating from compass roses to indicate directions. Coastlines were sketched in together with principal ports and landmarks.

qārib. Arab craft of unknown characteristics, but as used in Muslim Spain probably lateen rigged. It may be the same type as the caravo (*qv*).

quadrant. A quarter of the circumference of a compass when marked in degrees. Also a navigational instrument based on a quarter circle, used to measure the altitude of a heavenly body, to establish latitude. The earliest form was employed by Portuguese explorers in the fifteenth century.

quinquireme. A galley with five oars to a unit, or 'room', not in five separate banks as was once thought.

qunbar. Arab craft of unspecified characteristics, although the term seems to have been used in the Muslim world for sea-going cargo ships of the Western 'round' ship type.

repurcussores. *See* clenchatores.

retourschepen. Ships of the Dutch East India Company, designed to make the long round trip to the Far East, bringing back the rare, and consequently very valuable, goods that made the trade so profitable. As a result, the ships were large, well armed for self-defence, and costly to both build and operate; they were regularly employed as auxiliary warships in wartime.

rhumb lines. On medieval charts the extensions from the radial lines of a compass rose, along which mariners steered a constant course. Only on a plane surface would it represent the shortest distance between two points, but for relatively short distances the effect of the earth's curvature can be considered negligible. Charts usually employed a Mercator's projection so that rhumb lines could be drawn as straight lines, thus facilitating rhumb-line navigation.

Roccaforte. The name of a large Venetian nef (*qv*) that took part in a famous convoy defence in 1264. The ship measured 125ft x 46ft x 30ft height amidships, for 550 tons, and carried 500 men.

round ships. In the Mediterranean of the Middle Ages the generic term for sailing ships, as opposed to long ships or galleys.

rumos. Portuguese measure of length (approximately 1.5m).

saete; also occurs as **sagette.** Fast Genoese oar-and-sail craft, rigged with a single lateen mast and ranging in size from 14 oars to 80 oars.

saetta. Long, light Mediterranean vessel of 50–100 tons, rigged with three lateen masts.

saeta-polacra. A full rigged version of the saetta (*qv*).

sandalion. Byzantine craft; originally a small dromon (*qv*), but later applied to large fishing craft and a 200-ton grain carrier. *See also* xandalum.

schirazzi. Small fast Ottoman craft.

schotbussen. Early firearms; small guns firing over the gunwales of fifteenth-century Hanseatic vessels.

selvagens. Large guns of 16–20pdr calibre; there is a Portuguese reference of 1513 to their unsuitability for employment in small ships.

Serçe Liman wreck. An eleventh-century merchantman which probably sank in

1024/1025 discovered near Marmaris in Turkey in 1973; the wreck was excavated in 1977–79.

sheerstrake. The uppermost strake of planking of the hull proper, below the gunwale.

shell-first. A term used by modern historians for ship- and boatbuilding in which the hull strakes are fastened together to form the hull shape without the benefit of a pre-erected framework (although strengthening frames may be added later). Overlapping clinker (*qv*) and the ancient Mediterranean method of securing strakes with internal mortise and tenon joints are examples.

side rudder. Steering oar, usually fitted to one or both quarters. Probably the most ancient steering device, surviving well into the Middle Ages in the Mediterranean; cumbersome and inefficient for large vessels, it had some advantages for smaller craft, where it might act as a leeboard to make the boat more weatherly.

siropes. Unidentified piece of equipment associated with the windlass and flaill (*qv*) on English carracks.

Skuldelev wrecks. A fleet of five vessels discovered in Roskilde fjord on the Danish island of Sjaelland and excavated in an operation that began in 1962. The craft had been deliberately scuttled to block the navigable channel some time in the eleventh century, and were of different types: Wreck 1 was a large merchant ship, identified as a knaar (*qv*); Wreck 2 was a very large longship; Wreck 3 was a small coastal carrier; Wreck 5 was a smaller longship; and Wreck 6 was a small open boat. They were all old when sunk and represent a cross-section of designs from the late Viking era. The remains are now displayed in a purpose-built museum at Roskilde.

sottili. Of a galley, light, fine-lined (and consequently fast); in the sixteenth century it referred specifically to a galley with three men to an oar. The English king Henry VIII had a Mediterranean galley in his fleet called the *Galley Subtile*, clearly a name derived from this term.

springald. Type of catapult.

square sails. Canvas set from yards that at rest were carried at right angles to the centreline of the ship; as opposed to fore-and-aft canvas set from stays or yards on the centreline, or nearly so.

Straetsvaerder. Dutch term for ship trading through the 'Straits' (of Gibraltar) into the Mediterranean. They tended to be more strongly built and much more heavily armed than fluits (*qv*), and were more galleon-like in appearance, with a full head and quarter galleries.

tarida, tarit, tarrita. Muslim craft mentioned from the twelfth century; usually associated with large size, the earliest references suggesting a form of great galley. They were capacious transports, one document of 1281 claiming that they could carry 30 horses and 30 men-at-arms. Usage of the term spread to other Mediterranean powers, and in later centuries seemed to imply a large carrack-like sailing vessel.

tenenties contra. *See* holders.

tonelada. Spanish measure of tonnage. *See* codo.

topcastle. Fighting top at the head of a mast; could be a lookout position in peacetime, but in war was used as a position from which to rain down missiles on the decks of enemy ships.

treenails, trenails, trennels, etc. Wooden dowels used as fastenings in shipbuilding; preferable in some situations to nails or bolts since they do not corrode.

trireme. Galley with three oars to a unit or 'room'; in ancient times they were at different levels, but did not constitute three separate banks as once thought.

troccia. Truss or parrel (*qv*) for a lateen yard.

trunnions. Short cylindrical extensions at right angles to the barrel of a gun, used to retain it to its carriage with a strip of metal called a capsquare; the trunnions formed the axis on which the gun was elevated and depressed.

urca. Spanish term for a large ship of burden, occurring from the fifteenth century onwards; later used to differentiate between transports, which were so described, and warships.

vachete, vachette. Small craft of the eastern Mediterranean, often associated with the Genoese.

varinel. *See* barinel.

Vejby cog. A Polish-built cog lost about 1370 on the north coast of the Danish island of Sjaelland; the ship was carrying fine textiles and household utensils.

verlangers. Dutch term of the second half of the sixteenth century for lengthened ships; they often reached a length-to-breadth ratio of 5:1 or 6:1.

verso. *See* berços and base.

votive ship. Usually a model dedicated to a church or saint as a thank offering or a mark of piety by seafarers.

wegges. Wedges; an unidentified piece of equipment associated with the windlass-powered sail-raising gear of English carracks. *See also* flaill.

whipstaff. A vertical lever attached to the end of the tiller to allow the helmsman at least one deck higher and possibly in sight of the sails.

Wippe. German term for a kind of 'see-saw' derrick; used from the thirteenth century onwards and one of the earliest forms of harbour cranes.

xandalum. From the sandalion (*qv*) of late Antiquity; in post Byzantine times the name was applied to a wide range of vessels, probably with little more than etymology to link it to the earlier type.

Yassi Ada wreck. A seventh-century coastal trader of about 60 tons discovered in Turkish waters in 1958 and excavated in 1960–64. It is important as an example of the transition from classical mortise-and-tenon shell-first construction to the less labour-intensive skeleton-first techniques of later centuries.

Index